Designs for Learning Environments of the Future

Michael J. Jacobson · Peter Reimann

Editors

Designs for Learning Environments of the Future

International Perspectives
from the Learning Sciences

 Springer

Editors
Michael J. Jacobson
Centre for Research on Computer-supported
Learning and Cognition (CoCo)
Faculty of Education and Social Work
The University of Sydney
Sydney NSW Australia
michael.jacobson@sydney.edu.au

Peter Reimann
Centre for Research on Computer-supported
Learning and Cognition (CoCo)
Faculty of Education and Social Work
The University of Sydney
Sydney NSW Australia
peter.reimann@sydney.edu.au

ISBN 978-0-387-88278-9   e-ISBN 978-0-387-88279-6
DOI 10.1007/978-0-387-88279-6
Springer New York Dordrecht Heidelberg London

Library of Congress Control Number: 2009942989

Printed on acid-free paper

Springer is part of Springer Science+Business Media (www.springer.com)

Preface

This volume began with a request to consider a follow-up to the *Innovations in Science and Mathematics Education: Advanced Designs for Technologies of Learning* book co-edited by Michael Jacobson with Robert Kozma nearly a decade ago. All of the chapters in that volume represented the work of US-based researchers, many of whom had been funded by the US National Science Foundation in the middle to late 1990s. In the intervening years, however, increasingly we see research into the design and use of technology-based learning innovations conducted by international teams of researchers, many of whom are now identified with the emerging field of the *learning sciences.*[1] Consequently, in planning for this new book, it was decided to request chapters from selected contributors to the earlier Jacobson and Kozma volume to illustrate more recent developments and research findings of relatively mature programs of research into innovative technology-enhanced learning environments, as well as to solicit chapters reflecting newer research activities in the field that also include international researchers.

It is important to realize, however, that the societal context in which research such as this is conducted has changed dramatically over the last decade. Whereas in the late 1990s, relatively few schools in countries such as the United States or in Europe (where computer scientists and engineers had developed the Internet and technologies associated with the World Wide Web) even had access to this globally distributed network infrastructure, let alone with significant numbers of computers with high resolution displays and processing capabilities. Today, countries such as South Korea have high speed Internet connectivity to all schools in the nation and nearly all developed countries have national plans for educational advancement that prominently feature discussions of using ICT ("information and communication technologies" that are essentially Internet connect multimedia computers) to help stimulate educational innovations. Further, there is increasing access in businesses, government, and homes to a variety of network-based information resources and Web-based tools, as well as sophisticated digital media such as networked 3D computer games and virtual worlds used daily by millions around the world.

---

[1] For an excellent collection of papers dealing with theory and research in the learning sciences with background information about the field, the *Cambridge Handbook of the Learning Sciences* edited by Keith Sawyer is highly recommended.

Approaching the second decade of the twenty-first century, it may be safely said that many of the "advanced technologies for learning" of the 1990s are now accessible in various forms by relatively large groups of teachers and students. It is less clear that many of the learner-centered pedagogical innovations such technologies may enable are as widely implemented as unfortunately didactic teaching approaches are still predominately used in the major educational systems around the world. A challenge we now face is not just developing interesting technologies for learning but also more systemically developing the pedagogical and situated contexts in which these learning experiences may occur, hence the major theme of this volume: *designing learning environments of the future*.

We recognize, of course, that one of the few certainties in life in the present century is rapid technological change. Still, we have solicited chapters to provide a representative (but not comprehensive) survey of a wide range of types of learning technologies that are currently being explored by leading research groups around the world, such as virtual worlds and environments, 2D and 3D modeling systems, intelligent pedagogical agents, and collaboration tools for synchronous and asynchronous learner interactions. More important, we believe, are that these various research projects explore important learning challenges, consider theoretical framings for their designs and learning research, and (in most chapters) discuss iterations on their respective designs for innovative learning environments. We hope these considerations of how research findings in these various projects may inform thinking about new designs for learning might serve as models for other researchers, learning designers, teachers, and policy makers who certainly will have to grapple with dynamic changes in the contexts of learning over the next few decades.

The chapter authors are all internationally recognized for their research into innovative approaches for designing and using technologies that support learner-centered pedagogies. This collection will be of interest to researchers and graduate students in the learning and cognitive sciences, educators in the physical and social sciences, as well as to learning technologists and educational software developers, educational policymakers, and curriculum designers. In addition, this volume will be of value to parents and the general public who are interested in the education of their children and of a citizenry in the twenty-first century by providing a glimpse into how learning environments of the present and future might be designed to enhance and motivate learning in a variety of important areas of science and mathematics.

Contents

1   **Invention and Innovation in Designing Future Learning Environments** 1
Michael J. Jacobson and Peter Reimann

2   **MaterialSim: A Constructionist Agent-Based Modeling Approach to Engineering Education** 17
Paulo Blikstein and Uri Wilensky

3   **Learning Genetics from Dragons: From Computer-Based Manipulatives to Hypermodels** 61
Paul Horwitz, Janice D. Gobert, Barbara C. Buckley, and Laura M. O'Dwyer

4   **The Development of *River City*, a Multi-User Virtual Environment-Based Scientific Inquiry Curriculum: Historical and Design Evolutions** 89
Diane Jass Ketelhut, Jody Clarke, and Brian Carl Nelson

5   **Design Perspectives for Learning in Virtual Worlds** 111
Michael J. Jacobson, Beaumie Kim, Chunyan Miao, Zhiqi Shen, and Mark Chavez

6   **Learning to Learn and Work in Net-Based Teams: Supporting Emergent Collaboration with Visualization Tools** 143
Peter Reimann and Judy Kay

7   **Learning Mathematics Through Inquiry: A Large-Scale Evaluation** 189
Ton de Jong, Petra Hendrikse, and Hans van der Meij

8   **Scaffolding Knowledge Communities in the Classroom: New Opportunities in the Web 2.0 Era** 205
Vanessa L. Peters and James D. Slotta

9 From New Technological Infrastructures to Curricular Activity Systems: Advanced Designs for Teaching and Learning 233
Jeremy Roschelle, Jennifer Knudsen, and Stephen Hegedus

10 Toward a Theory of Personalized Learning Communities 263
Eric Hamilton and Martine Jago

11 Afterword: Opportunities for Transformational Learning 283
Peter Reimann and Michael J. Jacobson

Index 287

Contributors

Paulo Blikstein
School of Education and (by courtesy) Department of Computer Science, Stanford University, 520 Galvez Mall, Stanford, CA 94305, USA
paulob@stanford.edu

Barbara Buckley
WestEd, 400 Seaport Court, Suite 222, Redwood City, CA, USA
bbuckle@wested.org

Brian Carl Nelson
Mary Lou Fulton Institute and Graduate School of Education, Arizona State University, PO Box 870611, Tempe, AZ 85287-0611, USA
brian.nelson@asu.edu

Mark Chavez
School of Art, Design and Media, Nanyang Technological University, Singapore
mchavez@ntu.edu.sg

Jody Clarke
Harvard Graduate School of Education, 14 Appian Way, 711 Larsen Hall, Cambridge, MA 02138, USA
jody_clarke@mail.harvard.edu

Janice Gobert
Department of Social Science and Policy Studies, Worcester Polytechnic Institute, 100 Institute Road, Worcester, MA, USA
jgobert@wpi.edu

Eric Hamilton
Pepperdine University, 24255 Pacific Coast Highway, Malibu, CA 90263, USA
hamilton@peperdire.edu

Stephen Hegedus
University of Massachusetts, Dartmouth, 200 Mill Road, Fairhaven, MA 02719, USA
shegedus@UMassd.Edu

Petra Hendrikse
University of Twente, Enschede, The Netherlands
H.P.Hendrikse@gw.utwente.nl

Paul Horwitz
Concord Consortium, 25 Love Lane, Concord, MA 01742, USA
paul@concord.org

Michael J. Jacobson
Centre for Research on Computer-supported Learning and Cognition (CoCo),
The University of Sydney, Sydney, NSW 2006, Australia
michael.jacobson@sydney.edu.au

Martine Jago
Pepperdine University, 24255 Pacific Coast Highway, Malibu, CA 90263, USA

Ton de Jong
Faculty of Behavioural Sciences, Department of Instructional Technology,
Cubicus Building, Room B 335, P.O. Box 217, 7500 AE Enschede, The Netherlands
a.j.m.dejong@utwente.nl

Judy Kay
School of Information Technologies, the University of Sydney,
Sydney, NSW 2006, Australia
judy@it.usyd.edu.au

Diane Jass Ketelhut
Temple University College of Education, 1301 Cecil B. Moore Ave,
Ritter Hall 450, Philadelphia, PA 19107, USA
djk@temple.edu

Beaumie Kim
Learning Sciences Laboratory, National Institute of Education,
Nanyang Technological University, Singapore
beaumie.kim@nie.edu.sg

Jennifer Knudsen
SRI International, 333 Ravenswood Ave, Menlo Park, CA 94306, USA
Jennifer.Knudsen@sri.com

Hans van der Meij
Faculty of Behavioural Sciences, Department of Instructional Technology,
Cubicus Building, room B 316, P.O. Box 217, 7500 AE Enschede
The Netherlands
H.vanderMeij@gw.utwente.nl

Chunyan Miao
School of Computer Engineering , Nanyang Technological University, Singapore
ascymiao@ntu.edu.sg

Laura M. O'Dwyer
Department of Educational Research, Measurement and Evaluation,
Lynch School of Education, Boston College, MA, USA
laura.odwyer.1@bc.edu

Vanessa Peters
Ontario Institute for Studies in Education, University of Toronto,
252 Bloor Street West Toronto, Ontario M5S 1 V6, Canada
vlpeters@gmail.com

Peter Reimann
Centre for Research on Computer-supported Learning and Cognition (CoCo),
The University of Sydney, Sydney, NSW 2006, Australia
peter.reimann@sydney.edu.au

Jeremy Roschelle
SRI International, 333 Ravenswood Ave, Menlo Park, CA 94306, USA
Jeremy.Roschelle@sri.com

Zhiqi Shen
School of Electrical and Electronic Engineering, Nanyang Technological
University, Singapore
zqshen@ntu.edu.sg

James D. Slotta
Ontario Institute for Studies in Education, University of Toronto,
252 Bloor Street West Toronto, Ontario M5S 1 V6 Canada
jslotta@oise.utoronto.ca, jslotta@gmail.com

Uri Wilensky
Center for Connected Learning and Computer-Based Modelling,
Department of Learning Sciences, School of Education and Social Policy,
and Department of Computer Science, McCormick School of Engineering,
Northwestern Institute on Complex Systems, Northwestern University
uri@northwestern.edu

Chapter 1
Invention and Innovation in Designing Future Learning Environments

Michael J. Jacobson and Peter Reimann

The best way to predict the future is to design it.

As a central theme of this volume is the *future*, above we suggest a corollary to the famous Alan Kay observation that the best way to predict the future is to invent it, while also acknowledging his seminal technology contributions and his passionate vision for new ways of learning such resources enable. This theme of the future is endlessly fascinating and nearly always – as Kurt Vonnegut observed about life in *Slaughter House Five* – something that happens while making other plans.

A second theme – *design* – is one in "vogue" in the field of the learning sciences as there is design-based research, learner-centered design, learning by design, and so on. "Design" has connotations of someone creating an artifact that is generally new or innovative, which suggests a question: What is the relationship of design to innovation? John Seely Brown (1997), for example, wrote that in corporate research at Xerox Palo Alto Research Center (PARC), a view emerged that *innovations are inventions implemented*. A distinction is thus made between "inventions," that is, novel and initially unique artifacts and practices, and "innovations" that become more widely disseminated or appropriated by commercial environments – which, by extension, we suggest may also include communities of practice or social environments more generally. However, inventions are not "pushed" fully formed into an environment, as was Athena from the head of Zeus with armor, shield, and spear in hand. Rather, they are introduced into an environment and often foster changes in it that lead to iterative changes and developments of the original invention itself and the environment. Put another way, the transformation of inventions to innovations reflects *coevolutionary* processes of iterative changes of artifacts, practices, and the environment. J. S. Brown also notes that in the corporate world, it was often the case that considerably more resources were required for efforts involving innovations versus those necessary to create inventions initially.

M.J. Jacobson (✉) and P. Reimann
Centre for Research on Computer-supported Learning and Cognition (CoCo),
The University of Sydney, Sydney, NSW 2006, Australia
e-mail: michael.jacobson@sydney.edu.au

M.J. Jacobson and P. Reimann (eds.), *Designs for Learning Environments of the Future:*
International Perspectives from the Learning Sciences, DOI 10.1007/978-0-387-88279-6_1,
© Springer Science+Business Media, LLC 2010

By extension, we suggest that considerations of future learning environments may distinguish between the *design of "inventions"* (i.e., designing new pedagogies) and new types of learning environments, and the *design of "innovations"* (i.e., designing *implementations* of pedagogical and learning environment inventions). From this perspective, learning and technology research may focus on pedagogies and learning environments from the *invention* or the *innovation* perspective, or as a coevolutionary (and thus inherently longer term) trajectory from invention to innovation. For example, the history of the *SimCalc* Project exemplifies this last scenario. The initial design goals for *SimCalc* from the middle 1990s may be viewed as an advanced learning technology-based *invention* to help students learn core ideas about the mathematics of change and variation (i.e., calculus; see Roschelle, Kaput, & Stroup (2000)), whereas the research reported in this volume details research into *SimCalc* as it has been iteratively evolved and designed as an *innovation* being more widely utilized to help students understand challenging conceptual dimensions of algebra (see Roschelle, Knudsen, & Hegedus, this volume).

Whereas the notion of a learning environment has frequently been used to depict technical aspects, such as specific learning software, it has become accepted over the last decade that there is much more to the "environment" than the technology employed. The chapters in this book clearly incorporate this more holistic view that includes – in addition to the technology – tasks, assessment forms, and social (including organizational) aspects of educational settings such as classrooms. This widening of scope has resulted partly from research that has identified teaching practices and school leadership as two critical factors affecting the breadth and depth of uptake of learning technologies in schools, once issues of access to technology and teachers' basic technology skills have been addressed (Kozma, 2003; Law, Pelgrum, & Plomp, 2008). Teaching and leadership practices are, in turn, strongly affected by assessment regimens and accountability systems, and their objectives and rationales as expressed in educational policies.

Since the earlier volume was published (Jacobson & Kozma, 2000), a variety of learning technologies – often referred to as *information and communication technologies* (ICT) – have become ubiquitous in many educational sectors, at least in economically developed countries. As Kaput argued for in mathematics education, technology has become "infrastructural" (Kaput & Hegedus, 2007). In many classrooms, more or less advanced learning technologies are increasingly essential to the accomplishment of teaching and learning. However, as is the case for any infrastructure (such as roads or electricity), positive effects are neither immediate nor guaranteed; results depend on how the infrastructure is used. In the classroom, the key infrastructure users are the teachers because they not only use learning technologies themselves, but also they orchestrate the use for *other* users, the students. With respect to the technologies and pedagogical concepts included in this book, they all are infrastructural in the sense that they do not address a specific curricular area or focus on teaching a small set of skills, but they all create a space of possible designs. Some of them do so with a focus on representational designs, others are primarily concerned with designs for participation and ways of learning.

1 Invention and Innovation in Designing Future Learning Environments

As we approach the second decade of the twenty-first century, many of the "advanced technologies for learning inventions" that were a focus of research in the 1990s – such as artificial intelligence, virtual reality, globally distributed hypermedia, network mediated communication, and so on – have now safely achieved the status of "invention." Thus a major challenge we now face is to engage in the even more challenging research concerned with the coevolution of *innovations* of learning environments and infrastructures and how these might enhance or even transfer learning in significant ways.

We make no pretenses for "predicting" how future environments for learning might look or be used. Rather, we have selected chapters for this volume that are representative of international learning sciences oriented research that are exploring a range of *designs for invention* and *designs for innovation*. We next provide an overview of the chapters, followed by a consideration of a set of thematic strands that emerged as we look across these chapters.

Chapter Overviews

In Chap. 2, Blikstein and Wilensky discuss the *MaterialSim* project in which engineering students program their own scientific models using the NetLogo agent-based modeling tool to generate microlevel visual representations of the atomic structure in various materials being studied. NetLogo also provides a multiagent modeling language to program rules defining the behaviors of agents in a system, which in the case of this research, consisted of the interactions of individual atoms. Of central importance in this chapter is the dramatic distinction between NetLogo-enabled visual and algorithmic representations versus the more typically used equation-based representations of the materials studied in these types of engineering courses, which based on classroom observations of a university level engineering materials science course consisted of 2.5 equations per minute in a typical lecture! An important argument advanced in this chapter is that the isomorphic visual and algorithmic representations of the relatively simple microlevel interactions of particular phenomena a computer-modeling tool like NetLogo affords may lead to dramatically enhanced learning compared to the highly abstracted mathematical representations typically used in traditional engineering education. Put another way, this research argues that *representations profoundly matter for learning*. Further, providing tools for learners to construct and shape these representations as part of modeling activities perhaps might matter even more.

The third chapter by Horwitz, Gobert, Buckley, and O'Dwyer presents research on "hypermodels," which builds on earlier work involving *GenScope* (Horwitz & Christie, 2000). *GenScope* was a "computer-based manipulative" representing genetics at different levels from microlevels of DNA and genes to macrolevel phenotypic and population expressions of organism traits. Learners may manipulate settings at the DNA and gene level in *GenScope* and then view how different traits would look on an organism. As is discussed in this chapter, however, just providing learners with a representationally rich, interactive, and open-ended (i.e., unstructured) environment such as *GenScope* did not necessarily lead to enhanced learning of genetics in many classrooms. In response to earlier mixed empirical findings, this research team worked on new ways to support or scaffold learners using an open-ended model or simulation tool using *hypermodels*. Briefly, a hypermodel provides a "pedagogical wrapper" around the core model or simulation engine that specifies particular sequences of learning activities involving the model or simulation engine for students as well as scaffolds for learning important conceptual aspects of the domain being represented. A centrally important aspect of this new research involves *model-based reasoning* (MBR), in which learners form, test, reinforce, revise, or reject mental models about the phenomena related to their interaction with hypermodels and other representations. This chapter reports on research involving the *BioLogica* hypermodel environment and its use to scaffold or structure genetics learning activities in classroom settings.

Ketelhut, Clarke, and Nelson, in Chap. 4, describe the main elements of three design cycles for the *River City* multiuser virtual environment (MUVE) that took place over 8 years. Conducted in the form of a design-based research project involving almost 6,000 students, the development of *River City* was driven by comparisons between "experimental" classes that used *River City* and conventional classes, all taught the same curriculum. One of pivotal design intentions was to let students themselves identify "factors" that might be causing diseases simulated in *River City* as part of science inquiry activities. The *River City* research team was able to explore important questions concerning the value of "immersive" science inquiry learning given their opportunity to experiment with thousands of students over a number of years. For instance, regarding the possible novelty affect of having students use a new approach such as a virtual world to learn, it was found that most students extended their engagement with the activities in *River City* beyond the first hours of using the system. It was also found that students who were academically low achieving profited from this kind of learning compared to traditional classroom instruction. In the last design cycle (2006–2008), a potential issue from the previous cycle – that of higher achieving students benefitting less compared to low-achievers – was addressed by incorporating a learning progression into the design of the environment in which some content was only accessible after certain prerequisite objectives had been achieved. Interestingly, the content then made available at this stage is not a higher "game level," as would be the case for a typical entertainment game, but rather was made available in a "reading room." This design approach thus raises interesting questions about the relation to – and possible synergies with – conventional text content and related learning activities and those activities with which students are engaged "in" a virtual world for learning.

In Chap. 5 – by Jacobson, Kim, Miao, Shen, and Chavez – discusses a number of design dimensions and research issues for learning in virtual worlds as part of the *Virtual Singapura* (VS) project. VS provides a virtual experience for students to engage in science inquiry skills, similar to *River City*, but the scenario is based on historical research into disease epidemics and cultural contexts in nineteenth century Singapore, rather than the fictional contexts of *River City* or *Quest Atlantis* (Barab, Thomas, Dodge, Carteaux, & Tuzun, 2005). In addition, the synthetic characters in VS are based on the diverse cultural groups in Singapore during that period. Intelligent agent technology is used so the synthetic characters may adaptively respond to interactions with the avatars of the students, providing different information about the scenario based on changing class activities in VS on different days and on the behaviors of the students in the virtual world. Research findings from two studies are reported, with the first study discussing the initial pilot testing of VS and the second study exploring the issue of learning in a virtual world for transfer to new problem and learning settings. A discussion is provided at the end of the chapter about ways to enhance learning in virtual worlds through different pedagogical trajectories for unstructured and structured virtual learning experiences and through nonvirtual activities.

In Chap. 6, Reimann and Kay address the question of how net-based team collaborations can be augmented beyond the provision of basic communication and document management facilities so that the students are provided with information that helps them to coordinate with each other and to learn more over time. This work involves undergraduate computer scientists who are conducting their capstone project in programming teams, and with graduate students who are working in teams that engage in prototypical research activities (e.g., building a model, writing a report). Teams in these projects use a variety of communication and documentation technologies such as wikis and file repository systems. Reimann and Kay describe a number of approaches that all build on providing mirroring and/or visualization feedback information about aspects of the teams' work in a visual format back to the teams. The rationale for this approach is provided in terms of an analysis of research on teaching team skills in general and team writing in particular. One type of visualization focuses on participation in terms of students' contributions to the *Trac* collaboration that combines a wiki, a ticketing system, and a file repository system. The authors describe how various aspects of participation in a programming team can be visualized with a combination of time lines (i.e., Wattle Trees), social network diagrams, and a visualization type based on Erikson and Kellog's (2000) social translucence theory. An exploratory study is discussed that showed this type of information was effective and largely acceptable to students, in particular to those students who had a leadership role in their team. Reimann and Kay report further on developing visualizations for the overall structure of a wiki site, taking the form of a kind of hypertext network overlaid with participation information (WikiNavMap). They also describe visualizations that are not based on participation data or the linking of wiki pages, but make use of the information contained in the text as it develops over time in the form of multiple versions of individual wiki pages. Their chapter closes with a discussion of techniques that provide textual and graphical feedback on the content of wiki pages (and other online document formats such as Google Docs) and how formative feedback to learners and teams might be connected to new ways to provide summative feedback such as grades.

In Chap. 7, De Jong, Hendrikse, and van der Meij describe a study that deployed mathematical simulations developed with the *SimQuest* authoring tool in 20 classes from 11 Dutch schools. The simulations were closely linked to chapters on functions in the mathematics textbook used in these classes, which were covered over a 12-week period. Despite the fact that the *SimQuest* simulations plus the support materials were carefully studied in trials with more than 70 students of the same age group as targeted in the study in conjunction with teachers, the take-up in the schools was subject to many variations, some productive and some not. De Jong and colleagues discuss two main obstacles for the use of *SimQuest* inquiry tasks in the participating Dutch classrooms. First, there were severe time constraints in classrooms that led teachers to skip specified activities that relied on technologies if there were technical difficulties. Second, the textbook used in the classes was not optimally aligned to the *SimQuest* inquiry activities. Interestingly, the time devoted to design the curriculum and the classroom alignment (what Roschelle et al., this volume, call activity design) was of the scale of months, whereas the development of the *SimQuest* software took years of a calendar time (and many more person years).

Chapter 8, by Peters and Slotta, describes opportunities that the Web 2.0 (a combination of technologies and ways of using these technologies) offers for educators. In addition to the affordances of immersive environments such as Second Life, they identify collaborative writing with media such as wikis and blogs as particularly relevant for knowledge construction purposes. To be useful for learning and knowledge construction in a school context, Web 2.0 technologies need to be carefully structured and related to tasks, activities, and content. Peters and Slotta propose their Knowledge Community and Inquiry (KCI) model as a pedagogical framework. KCI combines elements of collaborative knowledge construction with scripted inquiry activities that target-specific learning objectives. Of particular consequence in KCI pedagogy is sequencing, which begins with a (comparatively) unstructured phase during which students collaboratively generate a shared knowledge base in the form of a set of wiki pages, for instance, followed by a phase with guided inquiry activities. In the first study that Peters and Slotta describe, students generated a number of wiki pages concerning human diseases without any "seed" knowledge provided to them and without intervention from the teacher. Only after this student-generated knowledge base was generated did the students engage in more structured inquiry tasks, building on and using the student-generated content, in addition to normative curriculum materials. The first study they report showed that this approach led to deeper domain knowledge (assessed in terms of students' examination scores) compared to a group with conventional teaching regarded by teachers involved in the intervention as yielding good learning and classroom practices. Interestingly, students asked for more guidance concerning the open phase because they felt that a graded task should be accompanied by more structure. To accommodate this need and to potentially deepen the engagement of students even further, a second study is reported where the open phase was more structured, not in terms of steps, but in terms of the structure of the collaboration product (a document), which led to good learning results. However, challenges are discussed regarding the time required of the co-design process, and the productive use of data logs as a means for student assessment.

The challenge of large-scale integration of innovative learning technologies into schools is the focus of the research reported in Chap. 9 by Roschelle, Knudsen, and Hegedus. They suggest that any "advanced" technology design needs to include the means "...for bridging the gap between new technological affordances and what most teachers need and can use." An advanced design in this sense focuses on one or more of three levels (building on Kaput & Hegedus, 2007): (a) representational and communicative infrastructure, (b) curricular activity system, and (c) classroom practices and routines. The chapter focuses on long-term research in the *SimCalc* project regarding the question of how the *MathWorlds* software (the "infrastructure") can be connected to a curricular activity system. To develop an activity system, the first step is to identify a *rich task* that is pivotal to the curriculum and that brings together a number of concepts relevant to the curriculum. At the same time, the task should allow for a learning progression over a clearly specified amount of time that fits into the usually tight school agenda. In addition to taking into account the demands of the curriculum, a rich task should contribute to the long-term development of students' engagement with a body of knowledge. Roschelle and associates discuss two examples of such rich mathematics and learning tasks. The second step in activity design involves developing *support materials* for teachers and students. In the model put forward in this chapter, this comprises the development of teacher guides, student workbooks, and workshops for teacher development. Finally, the chapter contains examples of how to design such materials and measures, and describes experiences with the method from a number of *SimCalc* studies.

In Chap. 10, Hamilton and Jago discuss learning environments that provide customization and interpersonal connections as *personalized learning communities* (PLCs). They propose a set of design principles for PLCs, explain the rationale for each principle, and then illustrate how the PLC design principles are being used as part of the ongoing ALASKA project (Agent and Library Augmented Shared Knowledge Areas). ALASKA is designed to be a PLC in which students learn mathematics – currently precalculus – using a tablet computer that accepts pen or touch input. Intelligent agents interact with the learners via simple dialogs and can answer a set of domain-specific questions. Additional features of ALASKA include a library of applets and tools and a communication system that provides thumbnail and full-size views of student screens and the ability to arrange peer tutoring between students to teachers. This system is presently under development, so the "Miriam Scenario" is described to illustrate a hypothetical situation in which the ALASKA system is used as an instantiation of the PLC design principles and representative interactions.

The final chapter is an Afterword by Reimann and Jacobson that considers issues related to how research into the design of learning environments as discussed in the chapters of this volume might inform perspectives on the transformation of learning more generally. Fostering transformation of learning will require, at least, attention to assessment methods and teaching practices. Future learning environments, it is argued, should enable formative assessments that provide dynamic feedback about both individual learning and the learning of groups. These environments should also augment the pedagogical palette that teachers have available for enabling new ways of teaching and learning. Although technology-based innovations may be necessary for certain types of future learning environments, they are unlikely to be sufficient, and therefore must be aligned with pedagogical approaches, content, and assessments. Affecting learning transformations of educational systems may result from large-scale "top down" policy initiatives. An alternative, one perhaps more likely, is in a manner similar to how fads and "hits happen," from the accumulation of many small examples of transformational learning that stimulates future interest in and adaption of such approaches that may be amplified and propagated across entire educational systems.

Thematic Strands

The chapters in this volume each focus on different research issues and types of learning. While they are diverse, they share perspectives and thematic strands that link them together within a community of research practice. At a general level, these chapters reflect different aspects of research in the field of the learning sciences in terms of various theoretical frames and methodologies employed in these research projects. In addition, as discussed in the first section of this chapter, there is a shared interest in design, although some focus on *designs for invention* and others on *designs for innovation*. Three chapters discuss work that involves certain inventions – such as the use of intelligent agent technology in the *Virtual Singapura* project in Chap. 5, the deployment of data mining technologies outlined in Reimann's and Kay's Chap. 6, and the pedagogical agents and set of design principles for personalized learning communities described by Hamilton and Jago in Chap. 10. The majority of the chapters in this volume are best regarded as designs for innovation, which we believe provide opportunities to do research that contributes both to theory as well as to use-inspired issues – the so-called Pasteur's Quadrant (Stokes, 1997).

We have identified three other thematic strands across these chapters: *advanced representational affordances*, *advanced designs for interaction and participation*, and *advanced educational designs*. Whereas there may important be elements of all three of these themes in all of the chapters, we next discuss the chapters that seem most closely aligned with each of these themes.

Advanced Representational Affordances

The range of technologies used in chapters in this volume range from globally distributed multimedia web pages (i.e., with text, digital video, images, and animations and computer modeling, simulation, and visualization tools) to relatively newer technologies such as virtual reality worlds, intelligent agents, and data mining systems.

Collectively, these technologies greatly expand the *representational affordances* (Kozma, 2000) that are available to designers of learning environments compared to traditional instructional modalities. We view the notion of "affordances" in a way similar to the perspective of Norman (1988) as *possibilities for action that are readily perceivable by individuals* using artifacts, which provides a cognitive nuance to Gibson's (1979) ecological articulation of this term as *opportunities for action*. Multiple, often dynamic, and interlinked representations provide *possibilities for learning* that different design approaches may leverage for various types of learning environments. Further, multiple and often linked representations are not just cosmetic and felicitous, but rather, *foundational* given views that expertise in many areas requires not just abstract conceptual knowledge but also *representational flexibility*, which is the ability and facility to use various representations and to link across them as part of discipline-oriented activities (Kozma, Chin, Russell, & Marx, 2000).

Whereas the use of advanced representational affordances of various learning technologies is reflected in all the research discussed in this volume, the *MaterialSim* project nicely illustrates this thematic strand. For example, multiple representations using NetLogo consist of the visualization of the behavior of atoms in the materials being modeled, graphical and quantitative output of the model runs with different parameter settings (i.e., designed affordances), and the computational rules in the NetLogo programming environment. These representations may then be linked to the relevant abstract mathematical models, which in traditional instruction are the *primary* representation provided to the learner, despite their nonisomorphic relationship to the microlevel behavior of atoms in materials studied in engineering courses such as this. A deep understanding of the physics of materials science requires learners not just to memorize complex formulas, but also to be able to link various representations across micro- and macrolevels of phenomena and different types of symbolic coding and representational forms in conjunction with constructing appropriate mental models about the behavior of the atoms that interact to form various materials and structures. The chapter discusses important research toward achieving such transformative learning gains.

The Horwitz, Gobert, Buckley, and O'Dwyer research involving *Hypermodels* also exemplifies advanced representational affordances, in particular, those that are *readily perceivable by individuals*. Not only does *BioLogica* provide representations of microlevels of genotypic representations (e.g., DNA, genes), but these are also linked to macrolevel phenotypic trait expressions of organisms. These representations and affordances for learning were also available in the earlier *GenScope* system (Horwitz & Christie, 2000), but in an open-ended and unstructured way that the researchers believed resulted in mixed learning findings in earlier studies. Hence their chapter here details design decisions that were intended to constrain the affordances options for learners so that more salient representations for particular learning activities were likely to be selected, which their research suggests resulted in enhanced learning outcomes. Other chapters in this volume provide interesting perspectives about the theme of advanced representational affordances and learning, such as the *River City, Virtual Singapura,* and *SimQuest* projects.

Advanced Designs for Interaction and Participation

A second theme in this volume pertains to interaction, participation, and collaboration. Reimann and Kay's chapter deals with this issue in a general form, while Ketelhut et al. and Jacobson et al. come to it from the perspective of how to foster science inquiry in schools. The chapter by Roschelle and associates contributes to this theme by researching classroom activities that extend mathematical operations into students' interaction with networked handheld devices.

Computers may promote science learning by engaging large numbers of students in scientific inquiry without the logistical difficulties and dangers associated with experiments involving real materials in real laboratories. The "virtual laboratory" is a frequently used metaphor in educational simulation designs, which are exemplified in the chapters on the *SimQuest* (De Jong et al., this volume) and *BioLogica* (Horwitz et al., this volume) projects. Whereas these chapters focus on teaching scientific thinking in general (e.g., variable control, hypothesis testing), and on the interaction with domain-specific representations such as the Punnett Square in *BioLogica*, also represented in this volume is the genre of *inquiry environments*, such as *River City* and *Virtual Singapura*. These inquiry environments are not only three-dimensional, but also inherently "social" as they build on the metaphor of an *inhabited* virtual world, with the population being made up of the students themselves (represented through *avatars*), plus *nonplayer or synthetic characters*. It is the participatory nature of virtual inquiry worlds that distinguishes them from simulation environments that may well employ 3D technologies as well, but are designed for supporting individuals' interactions with the simulated entities and processes.

Virtual worlds specifically designed for education (for another example, see *Quest Atlantis* (Barab et al., 2005)) are different from the more general case of open virtual worlds (such as *Second Life*) in that they incorporate specific scenarios, such as the presence (or absence) of a sewage cleaning system in the world, and that they have their own dynamics, such as things developing over time in the virtual world with or without user interventions. In addition, inquiry-oriented virtual worlds typically include specific research tools, such as virtual microscopes, which learners may use as part of the inquiry activities they are engaged in.

Virtual worlds provide for representational richness (if well-designed) and make it easy for learners to interact and communicate with each other. The research reported in the chapters on virtual worlds in this volume suggests that learners are engaged, including students who do not relate well to textual resources, as in the *River City* research (Ketlehut and associates, this volume). All this should lead to better learning and improved learning outcomes, and there is increasing evidence – part of which is provided by chapters in this book – that this potential materializes. However, there are substantial costs involved in producing high quality virtual worlds for learning, which may be offset by relatively low costs for dissemination of these learning environments if appropriate computers and infrastructures are available. Certainly policy decisions about implementing future learning environments will be informed by cost–benefit analyses of development and deployment expenses of new types of environments such as virtual worlds with alternatives such as traditional classrooms. We note even traditional classrooms such as those for science also may have significant costs associated with specialized laboratory equipment (and sometimes hazards), and thus hope these analyses also consider *benefits* such as the potential for enhanced learning gains, motivation, and engagement, as well as the safety and flexibility of laptop and mobile technologies.

Another aspect of designs for interaction and participation is to bring digital content into the physical world – *augmentation* – rather than to attempt to simulate the physical world in a digital form – *virtualization*. Augmentation may be seen in the *SimCalc* project, where students engaged with mathematical content that is "in" their classroom rather than "in" a virtual space. There are many situations where virtualization is advantageous, for instance, in situations where the objects of learning are difficult to experience, such as *MaterialSim* and *BioLogica*, or dangerous. We expect that designs for augmentation and virtualization will be important approaches for types of future learning environments in areas such as science, history, and geography.

In addition, even with the important interest in visual representations now possible with virtual worlds and computer visualizations, we should not dismiss textual formats. It is important to remember that in the rhetoric about multimodality, the "multi" includes textual notation formats, which are, of course, powerful representational forms at the core of knowledge creation and communication for over three millennia. For instance, Ketelhut, Clarke, and Nelson began to address this issue by equipping *River City* with a "level" that targets those who quickly progress through the game-like elements. As noted above, the new content that is then made available is *not* virtual, but rather is text available in a "reading room." This raises the interesting question of the relation between conventional text content (and related learning activities) and experiences in interactive and immersive 3D environments. Furthermore, Reimann and Kay demonstrate that text written by students does not have to be treated as a static product, but rather that the processes of creating text can be dynamic when provided with sources of continuous feedback.

Advanced Educational Design

The theme of *advanced educational design* weaves several perspectives about learning environments reflected in different chapters in this volume. The distinction proposed by Roschelle, Knudsen and Hegedus (Chap. 9) for three levels of learning technology design that has influenced their research – (a) representational and communicative infrastructure, (b) curricular activity system, and (c) classroom practices and routines – may be applied to other chapters in this book. For example, all chapters contribute to (a) by necessity, and many make direct or indirect contributions to (b). However, there are relatively few contributions to (c). In particular, the attention given to curricular activity systems, and hence to addressing the gap between what technology can do and what teachers and students see as its affordances, is significant. This is a central theme in the chapters by Roschelle and colleagues and by Peters and Slotta, and figures prominently also in the chapters by Ketelhut, Horwitz, and De Jong, and their respective coauthors.

With most technology innovations, initially there is a relatively large gap between the *affordances perceived by the users* of a new technology-enabled learning environment and the *affordances the designer intended.*[1] As discussed above, we suggest that from the perspective of designing educational environments, affordances may be viewed as *possibilities for learning* that encompass pedagogical and assessment decisions that directly influence learning activities. Since teachers will likely perceive innovative learning environments and pedagogies through the lens of their current classroom practices and routine activities, the perceived affordances of learning innovations will likely be a way to enhance aspects of these established practices rather than to initially try out new learning and teaching opportunities that probably were intended by designers. The chapter by De Jong and associates illustrates this tendency as they found teachers did not use the *SimQuest* system in ways intended by the researchers due in part to the perception of a lack of alignment with the textbook that was being used. Unfortunately, this "possibilities perception gap" for affordances is frequently not recognized nor addressed by learning environment designers and developers. On a positive note, when this gap is recognized, as we believe it was in the Roschelle and associates chapter, the research suggests that appropriately designed and implemented infrastructure changes can, in fact, change classroom practices and transform learning.

We see other examples of the third design level – classroom practices – in this volume exemplified in the chapters by Ketelhut and Jacobson with their respective colleagues. Both groups are involved in designing not only for content and activities, but also for the enactment of these activities where students interact with content, each other, and synthetic characters in virtual learning environments with distinctive affordances relative to conventional classrooms. Since the relevant parameters of these virtual worlds are designed in advance, and can be better controlled at "run time" than is the case for real classrooms (and other learning settings, such as museums or laboratories), these research projects illustrate perhaps the greatest design opportunities for learning environments that implement innovative practices such as multiuser interactions and collaborations, varying pedagogical approaches, different degrees of structure and openness in learning activities, monitoring profiles of behavior and accomplishments of learners in the virtual worlds, and providing formative and summative assessments to individual as well as collaborative groups and teachers.

Another aspect of the theme of *advanced educational design* concerns design decisions related to the nature and sequencing of *structure* provided to the learner. For example, in the research reported involving the virtual worlds of *River City* and *Virtual Singapura*, guided inquiry approaches were used in which there was initially high structure provided in terms of scaffolds and constrained learning tasks, whereas over time, the scaffolding was reduced for more open-ended

---

[1] As noted above, this conceptualization of affordances is influenced by the work of Norman and Draper (1986) on user-centered design, but here we generalize from just the design of the computer interface to the design of overall environments for learning.

activities (i.e., less structure was provided). As Jacobson and associates discuss in Chap. 5, guided inquiry may be regarded as a "high-to-low structure" sequence. Jacobson and his colleagues note that most research to date involving learning in virtual worlds has employed guided inquiry or high-to-low structure sequences of learning activities. They speculate that future work with these types of environments should also investigate virtual learning in which low-to-high pedagogical trajectories are employed, such as is suggested in research involving "productive failure" (Jacobson, Kim, Pathak, & Zhang, 2009; Kapur, 2008).

In reflecting on advanced educational designs, we suggest that there is emerging a 10-year (±2) rule for successful designs of educational learning environments. As reflected in chapters in this volume, many of the learning tools and environments considered a success in terms of research and implementation have been iteratively developed for over a decade. For example, KCI research that built on the earlier environment Slotta helped develop, WISE (*Web-based Inquiry Science Environment*), *BioLogica* and the earlier *GenScope* systems of Horwitz and associates, the *SimCalc* project of Rochelle and colleagues, and the *River City* project that Ketlehut and associates discuss, with another important technology-based environment not reflected in this volume, *Knowledge Forum* (Scardamalia & Bereiter, 2006), having evolved its design over almost two decades. It is perhaps not surprising that developing sophisticated technology-enabled learning environments would require a decade-long time frame to evolve from "learning inventions" of promise initially researched in a few classrooms to innovations that in turn are iteratively revised and implemented in larger numbers of classrooms and diverse educational settings as part of extended (and costly) research initiatives. Indeed this decade range timeframe is comparable to innovation processes in other fields (Shavinina, 2003).

In light of the substantial effort over a significant period of time that is necessary to design high quality, theoretically grounded, and empirically validated learning environments, it would clearly be advantageous if these efforts were accompanied by the articulation of a *design methodology* that could inform designers of future learning environments. In the learning sciences, *design-based research* (Barab, 2006; Collins, Joseph, & Bielaczyc, 2004; Kelly, Lesh, & Baek, 2008; The Design-Based Research Collective, 2003) has been advanced to inform empirical research in real world contexts, but not necessarily the design of artifacts and environments themselves. In contrast, a *design methodology* for environments that help learners construct deep and flexible understandings of important knowledge and skills would, we propose, articulate a *language for design and representations of design* that are theoretically principled and empirically informed. Such a design methodology of "research-based" or "best practices" would allow a broader range of professionals to contribute to the development and implementation of innovative pedagogies and learning environments beyond the relatively small circle of influence of typical academic research projects in this area. The design methodology we envision is not dogmatic, but rather seeks ways to document different design processes and high-level design decisions. For instance, a design methodology might build on the work on educational patterns and pattern languages (Goodyear, 2005; Linn & Eylon, 2006; McAndrew, Goodyear, & Dalziel, 2006; Quintana et al., 2004) in terms of ways to document and communicate design ideas about different types of learning environments. Such a reification of design elements and approaches would, we believe, stimulate the coevolutionary iterations of design innovations for future learning environments.

Conclusion

The chapters in this volume are representative of international research efforts that are exploring ways in which environments for learning may help students achieve goals of importance in twenty-first century education. The centrality of *design* in its iterative and coevolutionary manifestations is of importance in several of the research programs discussed in this volume, in particular, those of longer duration. In addition, we hope that the thematic aspects of these programs of research – such as designing learning environments with rich representations and opportunities for interaction and partici-pation, as well as pragmatic educational designs more broadly that encompass curricular activity systems and classroom practices and routines – may help provide perspectives from which to view not only the research in this volume but other work in the field as well. These chapters report on significant accomplishments for advancing our understanding of learning and teaching, as well as many lessons learned. In closing, our hope is that collectively these accomplishments inspire and the lessons challenge researchers and educators for *today*. After all, enhancing learning environments of the future is "simply" about how our students might better learn tomorrow.

References

Barab S, Thomas M, Dodge T, Carteaux R, Tuzun H (2005) Making learning fun: Quest Atlantis, a game without guns. Educational Technology, Research, and Development 53(1):86–107
Barab SA (2006) Design-based research. In: Sawyer RK (ed) The Cambridge handbook of the learning sciences. Cambridge University Press, New York, pp 153–169
Brown JS (1997) Introduction: Rethinking innovation in a changing world. In: Brown JS (ed) Seeing differently: Insights on innovation. Harvard Business Review, Boston, MA, pp ix–xxviii
Collins A, Joseph D, Bielaczyc K (2004) Design research: theoretical and methodological issues. The Journal of the Learning Sciences 13(1):15–42
Erikson T, Kellog WA (2000) Social translucence: An approach to designing systems that mesh with social processes. ACM Transactions on Computer-Human Interaction 7(1):59–83
Gibson JJ (1979) The ecological approach to visual perception. Berkeley Publications Group, New York
Goodyear P (2005) Educational design and networked learning: Patterns, pattern languages and design practice. Australasian Journal of Education Technology 21(2):82–101
Horwitz P, Christie MA (2000) Computer-based manipulatives for teaching scientific reasoning: An example. In: Jacobson MJ, Kozma RB (eds) Innovations in science and mathematics edu-cation: Advanced designs for technologies of learning. Lawrence Erlbaum Associates, Mahwah, NJ, pp 163–191
Jacobson MJ, Kim B, Pathak SA, Zhang B (2009) *Learning the physics of electricity with agent-based models: Fail first and structure later?* Paper presented at the 2009 Annual Meeting of the American Educational Research Association. San Diego, CA

Jacobson MJ, Kozma RB (eds) (2000) Innovations in science and mathematics education: Advanced designs for technologies of learning. Lawrence Erlbaum Associates, Mahwah, NJ
Kapur M (2008) Productive failure. Cognition and Instruction 26(3):379–424
Kaput J, Hegedus S (2007) Technology becoming infrastructural in mathematics education. In: Lesh RA, Hamilton E, Kaput J (eds) Foundations for the future in mathematics education. Lawrence Erlbaum Associates, Mahwah, NJ, pp 173–192
Kelly AE, Lesh RA, Baek JY (eds) (2008) Handbook of design research methods in education. Routledge, New York
Kozma RB (2000) The use of multiple representations and the social construction of understanding in chemistry. In: Jacobson MJ, Kozma RB (eds) Innovations in science and mathematics education: Advanced designs for technologies of learning. Lawrence Erlbaum Associates, Mahwah, NJ, pp 1–46
Kozma RB (ed) (2003) Technology, innovation, and educational change: A global perspective. ISTE, Eugene, OR
Kozma RB, Chin E, Russell J, Marx N (2000) The role of representations and tools in the chemistry laboratory and their implications for chemistry learning. The Journal of the Learning Sciences 9(3):105–144
Law N, Pelgrum WJ, Plomp T (2008) Pedagogy in ICT use ("Sites 2006"). Springer, Berlin
Linn MC, Eylon BS (2006) Science education: Integrating views of learning and instruction. In: Alexander PA, Winne PH (eds) Handbook of educational psychology, 2nd edn. Lawrence Erlbaum Associates, Mahwah, NJ, pp 511–544
McAndrew P, Goodyear P, Dalziel J (2006) Patterns, designs and activities: unifying descriptions of learning structures. International Journal of Learning Technology 2:216–242
Norman DA (1988) The design of everyday things. Addison-Wesley, Reading, MA
Norman DA, Draper SW (eds) (1986) User centered system design: New perspectives on human-computer interaction. Lawrence Erlbaum Associates, Hillsdale, NJ
Quintana C, Reiser BJ, Davis EA, Krajcik J, Fretz E, Duncan RG, Kyza E, Edelson D, Soloway E (2004) A scaffolding design framework for software to support science inquiry. The Journal of the Learning Sciences 13(3):337–386
Roschelle J, Kaput JJ, Stroup W (2000) SimCalc: Accelerating students' engagement with the mathematics of change. In: Jacobson MJ, Kozma RB (eds) Innovations in science and mathematics education: Advanced designs for technologies of learning. Lawrence Erlbaum Associates, Mahwah, NJ
Scardamalia M, Bereiter C (2006) Knowledge building. In: Sawyer RK (ed) Cambridge handbook of the learning sciences. Cambridge University Press, Cambridge, UK, pp 97–115
Shavinina LV (2003) Understanding innovation: Introduction to some important issues. In: Shavinina LV (ed) The international handbook on innovation. Elsevier Science, London, pp 3–14
Stokes DE (1997) Pasteur's quadrant: Basic science and technological innovation. Brookings Institution Press, Washington, D.C
The Design-Based Research Collective (2003) Design-based research: an emerging paradigm for educational enquiry. Educational Researcher 32(1):5–8

Chapter 2
MaterialSim: A Constructionist Agent-Based Modeling Approach to Engineering Education

Paulo Blikstein and Uri Wilensky

Introduction

For the past two decades, the engineering education community has started to come to terms with an unfortunate paradox: despite a view of engineering as the ultimate design profession, very little actual experience in design is incorporated into undergraduate engineering curricula. Recently, pressured by decreasing enrollment, unmotivated students, and an avalanche of new demands from the job market, several engineering schools have started to roll out ambitious reform programs, trying to infuse engineering design into the undergraduate curriculum. A common element in those programs is to introduce courses in which students design products and solutions for real-world problems, engaging in actual engineering projects. These initiatives have met with some success and are proliferating into many engineering schools. Despite their success, they have not addressed one key issue in transforming engineering education: extending the pedagogical and motivational advantages of design-based courses to theory-based engineering courses, which constitute the majority of the coursework in a typical engineering degree, and in which traditional pedagogical approaches are still predominant.

   In this chapter, we describe and analyze a series of studies designed to address this exact issue, in which we investigate undergraduate students' learning of

P. Blikstein (✉)
Learning Sciences and Technology Design Program, School of Education and
(by courtesy) Department of Computer Science, School of Engineering,
Stanford University, Stanford, CA, USA
e-mail: paulob@stanford.edu

U. Wilensky
Center for Connected Learning and Computer-Based Modeling, Department of Learning
Sciences, School of Education and Social Policy and Department of Computer Science,
McCormick School of Engineering, Northwestern Institute on Complex Systems,
Northwestern University, Evanston, IL, USA

This chapter is based on Blikstein and Wilensky (2009).

M.J. Jacobson and P. Reimann (eds.), *Designs for Learning Environments of the Future:*
International Perspectives from the Learning Sciences, DOI 10.1007/978-0-387-88279-6_2,
© Springer Science+Business Media, LLC 2010

theoretical content in materials science through designing (i.e., programming) their own computer models of scientific phenomena. Our research design emerged from extensive classroom observations followed by a literature review of engineering and materials science education, as well as analysis of class materials, and interviews with students. Our observations (consistent with the literature review) indicated that students' understanding of the subject matter was problematic, and that the teaching was not up to the challenge of the sophistication of the content. Based on this diagnosis, we have iteratively designed constructionist (Papert, 1980) model-based activities for materials science - *MaterialSim* (Blikstein & Wilensky, 2004a; 2004b, 2005a; 2005b; 2006a; 2008) - a suite of computer models, learning activities, and supporting materials designed within the approach of the complexity sciences and agent-based modeling. The activities were built within the NetLogo (Wilensky, 1999b) modeling platform, enabling students to build models, and investigate common college-level topics such as crystallization, solidification, crystal growth, and annealing.

The studies consist of both design research and empirical evaluation. Over 3 years, we conducted an empirical investigation of an undergraduate engineering course using MaterialSim, in which we investigated: (a) The *learning outcomes* of students engaging in scientific inquiry through interacting with MaterialSim; (b) The *effects of students programming their own models* as opposed to only interacting with preprogrammed ones; (c) The *characteristics, advantages, and trajectories of scientific content knowledge* that is articulated in epistemic forms and representational infrastructures unique to complexity sciences; and (d) The *design principles* for MaterialSim: what principles govern the design of agent-based learning environments in general and for materials science in particular? Twenty-one undergraduates enrolled in a sophomore-level materials science course participated in three studies in 2004, 2005, and 2006, each comprised of a survey, preinterview, interaction with the prebuilt computer models, students' construction of new models, and a postinterview.

2.5 Min per Equation

Our classroom observations suggested that the ever-growing sophistication and extent of college-level content in engineering (and, in particular, materials science) pose a difficult challenge to current teaching approaches. One reason is that the important equations and mathematical models taught in undergraduate materials science courses are not only complex, but are connected in nontrivial ways to multiple sets of other theories, concepts, and equations. Teachers end up resorting to multiple equations and models to derive and explain a single canonical phenomenon, and those equations and formulas are oftentimes located in a different areas of mathematical modeling (statistical mechanics and geometrical modeling, for example). What is more, many "engineering theories" are combinations of empirical models or approximations, and not pristine, rigorous, and easy-to-describe theories.

As a result, what takes place in a typical engineering theory course lecture is not a linear progression of equations, from simple to complex. Conversely, when a new phenomenon is taught to students, a very large number of new connections with previously learned topics will likely arise on multiple levels, generating even more specialized equations to account for those connections. The sheer number of equations generated makes a comprehensive exploration infeasible in the classroom. Our classroom observations revealed that, in a typical 30-minute period, students would be exposed to as many as 12 unique equations with 65 variables in total (not counting intermediate steps in a derivation) – or approximately 2.5 minutes for each equation and 45 seconds for each variable!

This overloading with equations and variables seems a likely candidate for explaining the students' difficulties described above. We decided to investigate this hypothesis and investigate: what kind of understanding did this multiplicity of explanation levels and the "overloading" of equations foster in students? In addition to understanding the consequences of the traditional pedagogical approaches, we wanted to explore possibilities of an alternate approach, and examine the consequences of using agent-based models (Collier & Sallach, 2001; Wilensky, 1999a; Wilensky & Resnick, 1999) enacted as microworlds (Edwards, 1995; Papert, 1980) for students' understanding of materials science content since our previous research suggested that using such a modeling approach might be a better match of content to student cognition.

The agent-based modeling approach, as we will explain in detail, enables modelers to employ simple individual-level rules to generate complex collective behaviors. These simple rules capture fundamental causality structures underlying complex behaviors within a domain. Wilensky, Resnick, and colleagues (Wilensky, 1999a; Wilensky & Reisman, 2006; Wilensky & Resnick, 1999) have pointed out that such rules could be more accessible to students than many of the equations describing the overall, macroscopic behaviors of a system. The agent-based approach is also a better fit with the constructionist pedagogical framework (Papert, 1991). The history of constructionist pedagogy has included three principal modes of learner activity: (a) designing and programming computational artifacts (programming-based constructionist activities – PBC); (b) exploring computer-based microworlds (microworlds-based constructionist activities – MBC); and (c) engaging in the first two modes with computationally augmented physical structures (tangible-based constructionist activities – TBC). Agent-based modeling can be used in any of these three modes. In the second mode, models can function as constructionist microworlds, as agent-based models can represent the underlying logic of a system, enabling students to investigate and modify features of that structure and explore the consequences of those changes, and through that exploration and investigation come to understand the domain. In the first mode, students design and program their own agent-based models and gain a deep sense of the design space of domain models. In the third mode, students can connect physical sensors and motors to agent-based models and let the models take input from real world data and drive real world action (*bifocal modeling*, Blikstein & Wilensky, 2007). In the MaterialSim project, we have designed artifacts and activities to engage students in each of these three modes. In this chapter, we will explore the first two modes, i.e., microworlds-based (MBC) and programming-based constructionist activities (PBC).

The conjecture that using agent-based modeling (ABM) would be a better cognitive match for students is based on research that suggests that this approach fosters more generative and extensible understanding of the relevant scientific phenomena. In the case of materials science, instead of multiple models or numerous equations, this framework focuses on a small number of elementary behaviors that can be applied to a variety of phenomena. Instead of a *many-to-one* approach (many equations to explain one phenomenon), we attempt here a *one-to-many* approach (one set of local rules to explain many phenomena), through which students would see diverse materials science phenomena not as disconnected one from the other, but rather as closely related emergent properties of the same set of simple atomic or molecular rules. A second major focus of our study was to determine: What kind of understanding do students develop of the materials science content when they study it from this agent-based, *one-to-many* perspective?

In addition to those two driving questions, we wish to explore one further dimension of this pedagogical approach. There have been several recent studies of students using ABM to learn science; in many of these studies the approach taken was to design sequences of models and microworlds for students to explore (e.g., Levy, Kim, & Wilensky, 2004; Stieff & Wilensky, 2003). We extend this approach to the domain of materials science but mainly we wish to find out what the effect will be from *moving beyond microworlds and enabling students to choose phenomena of interest to them and construct their own models* in the domain of material science (for another such approach, see Wilensky & Reisman, 2006).

In this chapter we are focusing on the interviews and laboratory studies prior to the classroom implementation (subsequent design experiments on classroom implementations are reported in Blikstein, 2009). We report on a particular pedagogical design and present evidence in the form of excerpts and samples of students' work, which demonstrates that the experience with MaterialSim enabled students to identify and more deeply understand unifying scientific principles in materials science, and use those principles to effectively construct new models.

Materials science is one of the oldest forms of engineering, having its origins in ceramics and metallurgy. In the nineteenth century, the field made a major advance when Gibbs found that the physical properties of a material are related to its thermodynamic properties. In the early twentieth century, the field of materials science concentrated on metals and university departments were often called "metallurgical engineering departments." The field has since broadened to include polymers, magnetic materials, semiconductors, and biological materials and since the 1960s has been called materials science. Today, with the explosion of research in nanotechnology, alternative energy, and new materials, it has gained a very significant role in the realm of technological innovation. However, the teaching of materials science has not kept up with the rapid advances in the field. Therefore, before diving in to the study, we step back and contextualize the teaching of materials science within the landscape of engineering education, its recent critique, and calls for reform.

A New Scenario in Engineering Education

In 2007, approximately 400,000 students took college-level engineering courses in the United States alone (American Society for Engineering Education, 2007). As early as the 1960s, education researchers (Brown, 1961; Committee on the Education and Utilization of the Engineering, 1985; Jerath, 1983; MIT Center for Policy Alternatives, 1975; Panel on Undergraduate Engineering Education, 1986) have pointed out that engineering education lags behind in its adoption of newer approaches to teaching and learning. In recent years, there have been numerous calls for reform from the engineering education community and several schools have implemented reform initiatives (Einstein, 2002; Haghighi, 2005; Russell & Stouffer, 2005). The driving force behind engineering education reform programs were both new societal needs (Dym, Agogino, Eris, Frey, & Leifer, 2005; Committee on the Education and Utilization of the Engineering, 1985; Katehi et al., 2004; Tryggvason & Apelian, 2006) and technical advances. As basic science and engineering become increasingly intertwined in fields such as nanotechnology, molecular electronics, and microbiological synthesis (Roco, 2002), students and professionals have to deal with time scales from the nanosecond to hundreds of years, and sizes from the atomic scale to thousands of kilometers (Kulov & Slin'ko, 2004). This wide range of subjects and problems makes it prudent not to try to cover all the relevant knowledge so that students master the knowledge in each domain, but instead to help students develop adaptive expertise (Bransford & Schwartz, 1999; Hatano & Oura, 2003) that they can apply to new problems and situations.

However, most engineering curricula remain in coverage mode – curricula are still so overloaded with transient or excessively detailed knowledge that there is no time for fostering students' fundamental understanding of content matter (Hurst, 1995). This phenomenon of curricular overloading is not exclusive to higher education. Tyack and Cuban (1995) identified the "course adding" phenomenon in most of twentieth century reform initiatives across all levels of education – new courses are regularly added to the curriculum to satisfy new societal needs. However, the situation becomes more problematic as we envision engineering schools in two or three decades from now. At some point the limit is reached and if courses need to be added, others must be removed – but can we afford to exclude anything from the curriculum? A major challenge is in how to go about deciding what courses can be dispensed with (and what knowledge).

A common approach in many universities has been to add hands-on engineering design courses to the curriculum. Design-based courses represented one attempted solution to the overcrowding of courses as they enable multiple content domains to be taught together. Design courses have been highly successful (Colgate, McKenna, & Ankenman, 2004; Dym, 1999; Dym et al., 2005; Lamley, 1996; Martin, 1996; Newstetter & McCracken, 2000), but they are not the universal answer for all problems afflicting engineering education. First, a significant part of engineering education consists of basic science (physics, chemistry), engineering science (fluid mechanics, thermodynamics), and mathematics (calculus, linear algebra). It is challenging for design-based courses to focus on the core conceptual elements of these highly theoretical knowledge domains as the physicality of students' projects can be an obstacle for learning invisible or microscopic phenomena such as chemical reactions, pure mathematics, or quantum physics. Secondly, the technological tools used in those reform initiatives (such as modeling and design software) are the same employed by professional engineers in their everyday practice and not especially designed for learning. Using professional-based tools might be tempting as they enable students to achieve more rapidly the desired engineering design. In the specific case of materials science, however, this might not be the best choice. Most software tools used in engineering courses do not afford insight into the computation underlying their design and functioning. For engineering practice, indeed, a tool has to yield reliable and fast results – understanding what's "under the hood" is not necessarily useful. However, in materials science, this could be disadvantageous for learners. The computational procedures might embody an essential, perhaps crucial, aspect of the subject matter – *how* the conventional formulas and representations capture the phenomena they purport to model. Manifestly, no computer-modeling environment can uncover all of its computational procedures – it would be impractical example, to have students wire thousands of transistors to understand the underlying logic of the modeling environment. Nevertheless, we believe that most of these environments could be made profitably more transparent to students. However, the epistemological issues regarding the tools and knowledge representations in traditional engineering teaching run deeper.

First, in materials science, many of the traditional formulas *themselves* are opaque – they embody so many layers of accumulated scientific knowledge into such a complex and concise set of symbols that they do not afford common-sense insight and grounding of the causal mechanisms underlying the phenomena they purport to capture. Different from the basic sciences, engineering knowledge is a complex matrix of empirical "engineering laws," theories derived from fundamental mathematical or physical models, approximations, and rules of thumb. Making sense of this complex matrix is challenging for novices. Although using formulas and conventional engineering representations is perhaps conducive to successful *doing* (designing a new alloy, for example) it does not necessarily lead to principled understanding (knowing how each of the chemical elements interact and alter the properties of the alloy.[1]) Particularly, we are interested in *"extensible" understanding* – learning principles from one phenomenon that could be applied to other related phenomena.

Secondly, there is an important distinction to be made in how representations relate to the phenomena they purport to describe. We are not arguing that aggregate equational representations are intrinsically ill suited for learning engineering or science as there are many cases in which equational representations are fruitful for

---

[1] For more on design for learning versus design for use see, for example, Soloway, Guzdial, & Hay, 1994.

learning. Sherin (2001), for example, showed how the symbolic manipulation of formulas could lead to a gain in conceptual understanding in physics.

We are arguing that in some cases aggregate equations can hide important information needed for learning. In some areas of science, equations are directly postulated at the macro level, i.e., they are not necessarily an aggregation of simpler, local behaviors, or the microscopic behaviors are not relevant to the phenomenon under scrutiny. For example, in simple Newtonian motion, we are interested in predicting the motion of bodies, but looking at the individual atoms of the body might not offer additional insight into the phenomenon – the macroscopic and microscopic behaviors could be analogous, i.e., the body and its atoms would be moving in the same fashion. In such areas, aggregate equations reveal most of the needed information. In other domains, however, the opposite is true: equations are an aggregation of microscopic behaviors, and those offer fundamental insights into the phenomenon, and are not analogous to the aggregate equations (for example, statistical mechanics, or diffusion). Therefore, for the latter categories of phenomena, aggregate equational representations might generate an *epistemological gap* (Blikstein, 2009) – the mathematical machinery needed to derive macro behaviors from microbehaviors is intricate, and rigorous mathematical frameworks to guide such work are still being developed (see, for example, Parunak, Savit, & Riolo, 1998; Yamins, 2005; Wilkerson-Jerde & Wilensky, 2009). This *epistemological gap* makes it difficult to keep track of how micro- and macro-level parameters are related and influence each other, or to understand how intuitive, simple microbehaviors are represented in aggregate analytical forms. Our research, indeed, suggests that an exclusive use of equational representations for those types of phenomena can constitute an obstacle for students in acquiring conceptual understanding in domains of engineering in which the interaction of microscopic entities is at the core of the content matter. For those phenomena, in which equational representations show an aggregation of microbehaviors, it seems to be especially beneficial to unpack and deconstruct the traditional aggregate representations, restructuring domains of knowledge around the study of local, individual, "nonaggregated" phenomena (Wilensky et al., 2005; Wilensky & Papert, in preparation; diSessa, 2000).

For the most part, however, professional engineering tools whose main goal is arriving at results rather than uncovering processes emphasize aggregate-level simulation to predict macroscopic variables (Wilensky, 1999a; 2003). However, the focus on microbehaviors could make such content intrinsically more learnable and accessible. For example, *temperature* is a macroscopic, aggregate description of a microscopic state of individual molecules (their speed or energy), just as *pressure* is an aggregation of the number of collisions between gas molecules and the walls of the container. At an *aggregate* level, those variables are dependent on a number of different events and phenomena, and thus numerous equations and models have to be employed to predict them, oftentimes "mixing-and-matching" different levels of explanation and mathematical modeling approaches. On the other hand, at the microscopic level, the number of events and phenomena influencing a local interaction is dramatically lower than at an aggregate level, because many of the variables observed macroscopically are emergent properties of the local behaviors.

In this chapter, we describe a learning design framework that benefits from this fact, focusing on simple agent-level behaviors (i.e., atomic- and molecular-level interactions) from which complex macroscopic behaviors emerge. We believe that this framework is especially useful in a scenario of increasing technological complexity and specialization. Materials science has transformed itself considerably over the last decade, with the advent of nano- and biomaterials, as well as the explosion of computational materials science as a core research strand. The number of materials, alloying elements, fabrications techniques, and industrial applications has grown so quickly and vastly that "covering" all the knowledge by simply adding new information to the curriculum would be infeasible. Additionally, the high level of abstraction that the new advances in materials science are bringing makes it increasingly difficult to give students any real world "feel" for the ideas learned in the classroom, as well as clear connections with their previous knowledge. While many archetypal problems in introductory physics would involve one falling body or two colliding objects, typical undergraduate problems in materials science involve simultaneous interactions of billions of atoms. Those interactions generate cascading effects that are hard to predict or understand with conventional mathematical equations, or any real-world intuitions. We posit that the microbehaviors are easier to understand and model, and could be connected to previous knowledge and intuitions about how individual people or physical bodies behave (Wilensky, 1999a). Thus, unifying, behaviors embedded in agent-based models are helpful for acquiring solid understanding of these principles, which bridge the micro- and macrolevels (Wilensky & Resnick, 1999). Consequently, we argue that the new computational tools should not be simple add-ons to the present curriculum, but part of their backbone – eventually restructuring the encoding of the content matter itself. In this, we follow the framework of Wilensky and Papert and their coinage of the word "restructuration," (Wilensky et al., 2005; Wilensky, 2006; Wilensky & Papert, in preparation) to refer to the reencoding of knowledge in an alternate representational system.

Our approach is one attempt in this direction. It builds up from previous research on the use of multiagent simulation tools in schools to investigate a wide range of phenomena. Wilensky and Resnick (1999) first noted the need to pay attention to "levels" and possible "slippages" between them, and highlighted the importance of the understanding of emergent behaviors for learning science. Wilensky, Papert, and colleagues have argued that computational representations have reached a point of development where we can embark on a program of radical "restructuration" of the science curriculum using these representations (Wilensky et al., 2005; Wilensky & Papert, in preparation). Goldstone and Wilensky (2008) have called for such a restructuration of science curricula using common transdisciplinary "patterns" such as energy minimization, positive feedback, and simulated annealing. In terms of implementation in school and universities, over the past decade and a half, educators have successfully employed agent-based modeling in undergraduate chemistry (Stieff & Wilensky, 2003), high-school chemistry (Levy et al., 2004; Levy, Novak, & Wilensky, 2006), probability, and statistics (Abrahamson & Wilensky, 2005; Wilensky, 1995), robotics

(Berland & Wilensky, 2004, 2005), physics (Sengupta & Wilensky, 2008; Wilensky, 1993; 1999a; 2003), evolution, population dynamics, and mathematics (Centola, Wilensky, & McKenzie, 2000; Wilensky, Hazzard, & Longenecker, 2000; Wolfram, 2002). Ironically, despite the widespread use of agent-based modeling in materials science, we have not found significant research investigating the use of such models for learning and teaching materials science.

We will present and discuss a series of three laboratory studies of a computer-based learning environment which addresses the aforementioned challenges by offering students opportunities to build their knowledge by designing computer models based on simple computational behaviors. The user studies were comprised of classroom observations, pre/post interviews, pre/post surveys, and data analysis from individual sessions with students using the designed materials.

Before diving into the study, some background information on materials science content and teaching is necessary to illustrate the differences between traditional and the agent-based representations. As the divergences in representation are at the core of this study, the next section will be dedicated to describing these two representations and how they differ. This will prepare the way for the description of our design and data analysis.

Equational vs. Agent-Based Methods in Materials Science

Grain Growth: A Central Phenomenon in Materials Science

Most materials are composed of microscopic "crystals." Even though we commonly associate the term "crystal" with the material used in glassware manufacturing, its scientific use is different. A crystal is an orderly arrangement of atoms, a regular tridimensional grid in which each site is occupied by an atom. In materials science, scientists use the term "grain" to refer to such an arrangement. Most materials are composed of millions of these microscopic grains, and their average size is one of the most important characteristics of a material, contributing to, among other properties, strength, toughness, and corrosion resistance. For example, a car built with steel with a wrong grain size could just break apart during normal use, or be destroyed even in a minor accident. However, grain size can change, too – high temperature is the main driving force. This phenomenon, known as *grain growth*, is exhaustively studied in materials science: small grains disappear while bigger ones grow (the overall volume is maintained). Airplanes turbines, for instance, can reach very high temperatures in flight – an incorrectly designed material could undergo grain growth and simply break apart. The photographs in Fig. 2.1 (magnified 850×) show typical results after 20 h under 900°C.

Because grain growth is such a central phenomenon in materials science, and since it is an excellent example of how the same phenomena can have two different – and correct – representations, in what follows we will describe in detail these two representations.

Equational Representation of Grain Growth

In this section we describe the classical approach to modeling grain growth in materials science. This approach primarily employs mathematical equations. For those who want to skip over the mathematical details, it is sufficient to note that the classical approach makes use of several non-trivial equations to describe the phenomenon.

Burke (1949) was one of the first to introduce a law to calculate grain growth and proposed that the growth rate would be inversely proportional to the average curvature radius of the grains:

$$R = kt^n$$

where R is the mean grain size of the grains at a given time, t is time, k is a constant that varies with temperature, and n depends on the purity and composition of the material, as well as other initial conditions.[2]

In other words, Burke's law states that large grains (lower curvature radius) grow faster, while small grains (high curvature) have slower growth, or shrink. The mathematical formulation of Burke's law also reveals that, as grains grow, the growth rate decreases. A system composed of numerous small grains (see Fig. 2.1, left) would have a very fast growth rate, while a system with just a few grains (see Fig. 2.1, right) would change very slowly. One of Burke's approximations was to consider grains as spheres with just one parameter to describe their size (the radius). For most practical engineering purposes, this approximation yields acceptable results – however, as we previously discussed, its practical efficacy does not necessarily mean that this approach is the best way to understand the phenomenon. Due to the applied and integrative aspect of engineering research and practice, oftentimes explanations are drawn from a variety of sources: empirical equations, geometrical proof, thermodynamics, algebraic deductions, or statistical mechanics.

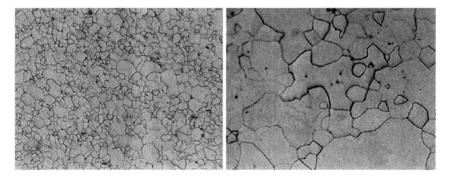

Fig. 2.1 Metallic sample before and after grain growth (Blikstein & Tschiptschin, 1999)

---

[2] Its theoretical value is 0.5 for pure materials under ideal conditions.

Our classroom observations revealed that, for example, when explaining grain growth and deriving Burke's law, at least three sources were employed during the classes covering the phenomenon:

- The *Laplace–Young equation for pressure*, which is commonly used in fluid dynamics to calculate surface tension in liquid–gas interfaces.
- *The flux equation*, based on statistical mechanics, which calculates the probability of atoms to move around the material.
- Geometrical approximations, which makes it possible to assume that grains or impurities in the materials are perfect spheres.

A detailed account of these equations is given elsewhere (Blikstein, 2009). We refer to this pedagogical approach as "many-to-one": many models and equations to describe one phenomenon. Our research suggests that although the many-to-one modeling approach in useful in the hands of experienced engineers in real-world situations, or very skilled researchers with high mathematical skills, this multitude of models can be an obstacle to student understanding. The mathematical machinery needed to weave together the geometrical approximations, the Laplace–Young equation, and the flux equation is very elaborate, and to achieve the simplicity and elegance of Burke's law, many assumptions and simplifications were made by the instructor. What is more, the resulting derivations and equations are specific to canonical cases, and the introduction of additional variables (for example, impurities, or temperature gradients) requires an even greater mathematical sophistication.

Agent-Based Representation of Grain Growth

Apart from equational models, heuristics (engineering "rules of thumb") are also important instruments for engineering practice. For example, when explaining grain growth, teachers commonly resort to a classic rule of thumb: large grains grow and small grains shrink. However, despite the usefulness of such heuristics to help students gain intuition into particular topics, they are not very generalizable, do not have a formal representation, and are usually domain-specific. The "large grains grow, small grains shrink" rule of thumb, for example, was shown to be particularly inaccurate when, in the early eighties, scientists started to use computer simulation as a research tools in materials science. Anderson, Srolovitz, Grest, & Sahni (1984) proposed the widely known theory for computer modeling of grain growth using a multiagent-based approach (then referred to as the "Monte Carlo method"). This kind of simulation not only made predictions faster and more accurate, but also allowed for a completely new range of applications. Researchers were no longer constrained by approximations or general equations, but could make use of actual atomic behaviors and realistic geometries. As stated by Srolovitz, Anderson, Sahni, and Grest (1984):

> While it is generally observed that large grains grow and small grains shrink, instances where the opposite is true can be found. [...] The results indicate the validity of a random walk description of grain growth kinetics for large grains, and curvature driven kinetics for small grains. (p. 796)

    In other words, Srolovitz *et al.* state that the classic rule of thumb for grain growth
("large grains grow, small grains shrink") is not always valid, and that randomness
plays an important role. Given the microscopic dimensions and small time scale of
the phenomenon, practically the only way to visualize this new finding is through
computer simulation. In contrast, the *traditional* methods for investigating grain size
and growth reflect the tools (and visualization techniques) that were available in the
1950s: mathematical abstractions, geometrical modeling, approximations, and
empirical data. These traditional methods and techniques, having become the methods
of choice to explain the phenomena, made their way to textbooks and classrooms,
and thus were established as the mainstream path to study grain growth.

    Agent-based simulation of grain growth offers a different perspective. Its principle
is the thermodynamics of atomic interactions, which is a simple and powerful model
with explanatory power covering a wide range of phenomena. The first step is to
represent the material as a 2D matrix, in which each site corresponds to an atom
and contains a numerical value representing its crystallographic orientation (the
angle of orientation of the atomic planes in one particular grain compared to an
arbitrary fixed plane). Contiguous regions (with the same orientation) represent the
grains. The grain boundaries are fictitious surfaces that separate volumes with
different orientations. The stability of each atom is the matrix depends on the
number of different neighbors around it. The more different neighbors one atom
has, the more unstable it is, and more likely to migrate to a different location.
The algorithm is comprised of the following steps:

- Each atom of the matrix has its energy[3] calculated based on its present
  crystallographic orientation (2) and the crystallographic orientation of its
  neighborhood – the more neighbors of differing orientation, the higher the
  atom's energy. Figure 2.2 (left side) shows the central atom with four different
  neighbors, hence the value of its *initial energy* is **4**.

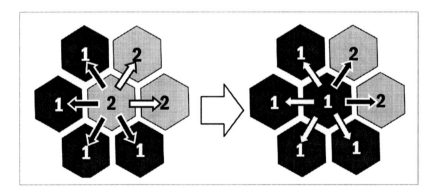

Fig. 2.2 Initial and final free-energy calculations. *Black* and *white arrows* denote different or
equal neighbors

---

[3] Although the technical term would be "free energy," for simplicity we will use "energy."

- One new random crystallographic orientation is chosen for that atom among the orientations of its neighbors. In this case, as observable in Fig. 2.2, the current value of the central atom is **2**, and the attempted new value is **1**.
- The atom's energy is calculated again, with the new proposed crystallographic orientation (**1**). Fig. 2.2 (right side) shows that there are only two different neighbors in the new scenario, thus the *final energy* decreases to **2**.
- The two states are compared. The value that minimizes the energy is chosen. In this case, the initial energy was **4** and the new energy is **2**, so the latter value is lower and constitutes a state of greater stability. Therefore, the more different neighbors one has, the less stable one is, and thus more inclined to switching to a different orientation.

The agent-based approach captures the intricacy of the phenomenon with a single parsimonious model. In addition to the elegant simplicity of this model, it embodies the one-to-many modeling framework as it may also be used generatively to understand other phenomena as well, such as diffusion or recrystallization. The agent-based model of grain growth has been extensively tested and verified, and shown to achieve the same results as its aggregate, equational counterpart (Anderson et al., 1984; Srolovitz et al., 1984).

Unfortunately, even though new computational research tools are enabling researchers in materials science to accelerate scientific discovery and explore uncharted territory, computational methods have not yet reached mainstream engineering classrooms. Thornton and Asta (2005) conducted a comprehensive survey about the state of computational materials science in undergraduate and graduate courses at the 20 leading programs in the United States. Whereas many universities are creating or planning to initiate computational materials science courses, the prevailing mindset is that students should learn modeling *after* learning the "science." In other words, computer modeling is regarded as "icing in the cake" to take place after the "real" scientific understanding is achieved. Our work, in contrast, evaluates the usefulness of a different approach: learning the science *by* modeling.

Grain growth is a prototypical example. In the previous sections, we described how it is common practice to teach students to consider grains as spheres (which they are not), grain boundaries as real entities (whereas they are just imaginary lines between grains), and to make use of numerous metaphors and rules of thumb (e.g., "big grains swallow small grains," "particles hold boundaries," etc.) to describe and predict changes in the material.

Both traditional methods and computer-based methods of investigating grain growth rely on *modeling*. The scientific enterprise is the process of creating useful approximations to help us understand critical or interesting properties of reality (see, for example, Pagels, 1988). Models from each historical period reflect the tools available at that time. The example of grain growth is illustrative of a common practice in many fields of academic research, in particular engineering. The availability of certain technologies for research shapes how researchers approach a certain problem, and the subsequent "encoding" of the knowledge is heavily influenced by those technologies. As the initially empirical or exploratory hypothesis gradually transitions to becoming a full-blown theory, they transmit much of those influences to the theories themselves, and consequently to the curricula. In this chapter, we argue that the current "encoding" of the knowledge about grain growth, and materials science in general, is a function of the available research technology, and the state of the field, and not an intrinsically superior way of encoding knowledge. In the following section, we describe the software infrastructure used in the project, and the design of the MaterialSim models.

Software Design: NetLogo and MaterialSim

NetLogo

NetLogo (Wilensky, 1999b) is a direct descendant of the Logo language (Papert, 1980). It is a freely available, integrated multiagent modeling environment, designed and developed by the second author at Northwestern University's Center for Connected Learning and Computer-Based Modeling. It includes a graphical user interface for exploring, experimenting with, and visualizing models, as well as a multiagent modeling language (MAML) used for authoring models (see Fig. 2.3). Such languages enable users to easily create and manipulate numerous computational entities ("agents") and define simple rules that govern their behavior. For example, to create 100 agents (or "turtles," in NetLogo's lingo) on the computer screen, the user has to simply type:

```
create-turtles 100
```

To make all of those 100 turtles move 10 units forward, users would type:

```
ask turtles [forward 10]
```

Users can also define simple rules that govern the behavior of the agents. NetLogo agents can perform simple rule-based behaviors, such as to seek being surrounded by agents with similar properties, or to avoid areas already occupied by other agents. For example, to ask all turtles to check for neighbors (within a one-patch[4] radius) and move backwards 10 units in case there are at least four neighbors around, we would use the following command:

```
ask turtles [if (count neighbors in-radius 1) > 4 [back 10]]
```

Such simple agent rules, however, may give rise to complex emergent *aggregate* phenomena, many of which are congruent with their traditional macroscopic formula-based descriptions. In addition to the modeling language itself, NetLogo includes a graphical user interface with advanced visualization features, such as multiple topologies and 3D representations. It also includes some specialized tools such as BehaviorSpace (Wilensky & Shargel, 2002), which enables users to explore

---

[4] The NetLogo world (or screen) is divided into a grid of square cells called patches. The size of the patches can be defined by the user.

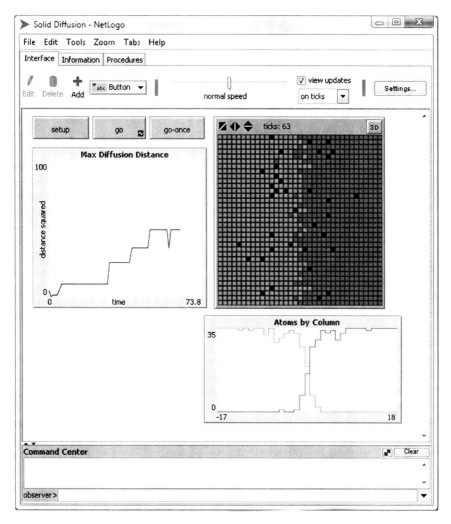

Fig. 2.3   The NetLogo modeling environment, with a "Solid Diffusion" model

a wide parameter space by running multiple experiments, and automatically logging the data. NetLogo comes with a large library of sample models as well as model-based curricula.

MaterialSim

We chose the NetLogo modeling-and-simulation environment as a platform as it is well adapted to the activities of the studies, in particular, NetLogo's "low-threshold, no-ceiling" (Papert, 1980; Tisue & Wilensky, 2004; Wilensky & Rand,

2009) design enables learners to achieve sophisticated results within a relatively short period of time, and its built-in visualization tools allow dynamic, flexible, and customizable views. MaterialSim is a set of models and activities built by the authors within the NetLogo environment, for investigating materials science phenomena such as crystallization, solidification, casting, grain growth, and annealing. MaterialSim's design is different from many other curriculum projects where instructional designers often prepare a series of models for students. MaterialSim, instead, focuses on students *programming* models. This design choice was based on previous research and on the learning goals of the project. For example, previous studies on students programming their own agent-based models report that participants were able to infer behaviors based on incomplete or sparse information, as well as gain deep understanding of how changes in microbehaviors can alter a given system (e.g. Berland & Wilensky, 2004; Centola et al., 2000). In contrast, scripted curricula (e.g., Gobert et al., 2004; Horwitz, Gobert, Wilensky, & Dede, 2003) start out with well-defined content coverage. Whereas studies of the scripted curricula report positive learning results, they do not necessarily afford insights into areas outside of their target phenomena in their more "convergent" approaches, nor allot sufficient time for a deeper examination of elementary "under-the-hood" behaviors. Since these curricula do not make use of programming or modeling, it is understandable that students' familiarity with the behaviors and rules may not be as well-developed as in PBC modeling activities. In addition, since one key goal of MaterialSim is to train students to see commonalities across materials science phenomena, having a *strong programming and modeling component* was a key design principle.

Creating models is not foreign to undergraduate engineering – it is common for engineering students to have modeling assignments and learn several programming languages while obtaining their degree. However, traditional model-based activities in engineering oftentimes do not afford understanding of microscopic behaviors or elementary physical/chemical principles. Therefore, another key design principle is to *build activities which foreground these microbehaviors*, and in which students develop a high level of familiarity with the language and the ABM paradigm. In this study, the design foci are:

- *Programming exemplars* (solidification and grain growth) as to present students with the important algorithms and coding examples which could be useful in the process of building other models.
- *Support materials* to help students in learning how to program in NetLogo.
- *Easily transportable code examples*, which students could easily reuse across models.
- *Readily-available validation tools*, as to enable students to verify the validity of their models.
- A *persistent library* of student-generated models from previous years, from which students can reuse code and get inspiration for their models.

MaterialSim's grain growth model, the main exemplar model of the suite (Fig. 2.4), was conceived to enable four kinds of activities:

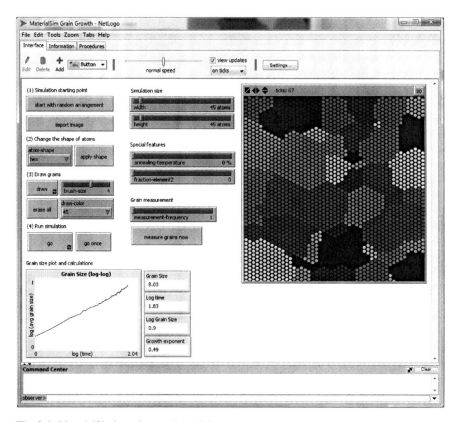

Fig. 2.4 MaterialSim's grain growth model

- *One-dimensional exploration*: Users can change variables, draw microstructures using the cursor, and observe their behavior over time.
- *Multidimensional exploration*: Students can run experiments sweeping entire parameter spaces, to determine critical points, system rules, mathematical relationships, and patterns.
- *Bifocal exploration* (Blikstein & Wilensky, 2006b): Students can connect real-world and virtual experiments, importing digital pictures from real experiments, and observing their "virtual" evolution. "Bifocal" refers to the simultaneous focus on the model and on the physical phenomenon.
- *Model building*: Students can change, create, or extend the system by coding their own procedures, modifying existing ones, or creating whole new models from scratch, by using the NetLogo modeling language.

In addition, the grain growth model offers a number of learning-oriented features, summarized in Table 2.1

Table 2.1 Summary of the learning-oriented features of the grain growth model

Simulation setup	Atoms' shape	Drawing tools	Additional parameters
(1) Simulation starting point	(2) Change the shape of atoms	(3) Draw grains	Special features
(4) Run simulation			
Users can start either from a random arrangement of atoms or from a preset stage, which can be drawn by the user using the mouse or converted from a digital photo. This enables easy exploration of "what-if" scenarios and the comparison with real-world data	The appearance of the atoms can be changed for better visualization of particular aspects of the phenomenon. The "lines" mode, for example, was useful to understand the differences in crystallographic orientations	To investigate particular scenarios, users can draw their own microstructures and observe their behaviors, or retouch existing microstructures	The "annealing-temperature" slider enables experiments with different levels of thermal activity. The "fraction-element2" slider introduces a percentage of dispersed particles of a different material in the sample. Therefore, users can change the temperature and the type of material in order to study their effects on grain growth

Research Design and Methods

The research took place during three spring quarters at the materials science department of a midwestern research university, with sophomore students enrolled in the "Microstructural Dynamics" undergraduate course. In the first year (2004), six undergraduate students (volunteers) participated in the study. In the second year (2005), 11 students volunteered to participate, and 4 students participated in the third year (2006), with 21 participants over 3 years. The average class size was 15 students. Each student participated in two individual sessions. The first, 75-minute long, was comprised of the following parts:

- Short Likert-scale/open-ended presurvey to assess students' familiarity with computers and their attitudes about the course.
- Preinterview about grain growth and related phenomena, in which students were asked the content questions during a semistructured interview. These questions were based on exams and assignments used in the course (for example, "What is a grain?" "What is grain growth?" "What is the driving force for grain growth?" "What is the effect on grain growth of dispersed precipitates?")
- General presentation of the NetLogo programming environment.
- Demonstration of five canonical agent-based models from the NetLogo models library (fire spread, virus contamination, racial segregation, gas molecules in a container, and a chemical reaction).
- Hands-on interaction with one MaterialSim model: grain growth (with simultaneous interview). This included running the model with different values for matrix size, temperature, composition, as well as recording and plotting experiments sweeping the whole parameter space of one variable.

As homework, participants were asked to choose a challenging and/or interesting topic from the course and think of a model to build, which would be implemented during the next session. Students also had the option of extending the functionality of the existing grain growth model.

The second session (150 minutes) was dedicated to:

- Introduction to the basic commands of the NetLogo modeling language.
- Implementation (i.e., coding) of the new model. Participants were always in front of the computer and in control of the task. The first author would help students as needed with language commands and general programming issues.
- Final interview.

We scheduled the sessions approximately one week after students' exposure to the topic of grain growth in their regular classes. All sessions were video-taped, and students' computer interactions were recorded using real-time continuous screen-capture software. Approximately 65 hours of video were captured, which were selectively transcribed and analyzed. Experiments conducted by students, as well as the models they built, were saved and analyzed. The first author attended the Microstructural Dynamics course 2004, 2005, and 2006, and analyzed the class materials and related literature. The classroom observations also generated data about the number of equations, variables, drawings, and plots explained during the class periods (and time spent in each item). Finally, participants were asked to fill up an anonymous web-based postsurvey, as to assess their (self-reported) interest and motivation doing the study, as well as usefulness of computer simulation for understanding certain topics in Microstructural Dynamics.

Data Analysis

Preinterview Explanations

The preinterviews were semistructured, following the questions listed in the Research Design section. At times the interviewer would ask additional questions to further explore one aspect of the responses. Students could also draw pictures to illustrate their explanations, which were all scanned. It was an open-book interview so that students could use any class materials, books, or websites to answer the questions. For the analysis, we randomly selected six students from the first two studies (2004 and 2005). The goal of the preinterviews was to evaluate students' explanations of core content in materials science, to which they were exposed during their regular classes one or two weeks before the interview. For the analysis, we compared explanations for the same phenomenon across different students, and also parsed and coded each explanation as to understand in detail the materials science concepts present in each, as well as how they were connected. In what follows, we will summarize results which were more comprehensively analyzed elsewhere (see Blikstein, 2009, and Blikstein and Wilensky, 2009).

The data shows that even for basic topics, such as describing what a grain is, students explanations were surprisingly dissimilar. Students resorted to a variety of metaphors and models for characterizing a grain: Betty,[5] for example, based her explanation on the visual appearance of a grain seen under the microscope. Liz tried to base her explanation on the appearance of a grain of rice. Ken tried to explain grains using another topic in the course, dislocation theory, which deals with the atomic structure of a material. As the interview progressed and questions started to deal with more complex and dynamic phenomena, the diversity of explanations just increased.

---

[5] All names were changed for anonymity.

When explaining what grain growth was, Bob used the metaphor of free will ("molecules come into the grain and line up"), and employed ideas about diffusion and impurities in contradictory ways. He did not resort to the Laplace–Young equation to explain the process of decreasing free energy by simply increasing the curvature radius. He incorrectly associates excess free energy to impurities or imperfections in the crystal structure, taking purity as a synonym for low energy, and grain growth as a cleansing mechanism by which grain boundaries would "sweep" impurities out. However, the Laplace–Young equation (studied in class) states a very different idea. Namely, the driving force is the curvature or pressure difference – impurities are not eliminated by grain growth, and growth can exist in pure materials. Betty, when trying to answer the question, mistakes grain growth for another phenomenon, recrystallization, which was taught in a previous section of the course. In recrystallization, similarly, crystals grow, but the mechanism and the kinetics are quite different. Ken, departing from yet another idea (rules of thumb about curvature), stated that "curvature is not good, so they will want to shrink."

When asked about the effect of impurities on grain growth, again, students tried to employ a variety of micromodels: a *force-feedback* model, where impurities particles pull boundaries away, slowing grain growth; a *classical mechanics* model, in which grain boundaries can "hit" a particle and slow down, models based on atomic movement inside the material, or purely *geometrical* models, in which the shapes of grain would change with no impact on the behavior of the material. As an example of a prototypical response, let us observe an excerpt of Ken's interview:

> **Interviewer:** What is the effect of dispersed particles?
>
> **Ken:** if you have two precipitations and if you have a dislocation line, you need to exert a force Tau on it, to move the dislocation line, but once it gets to the precipitation, it has to bow out and that will cost more energy, so if you have precipitations it will strengthen the material and that depends on the density of precipitations.
>
> **Interviewer:** So grain growth slows down or not?
>
> **Ken:** That I am not very sure.

Ken knew how to recite back pieces of the theory (even mentioning the name of a variable, "a force Tau"), but could not articulate its physical significance, and failed to identify the overall effect of impurities in grain growth. Indeed, our classroom observations showed that instructors overloaded students with a multitude of equations and models without necessarily making a clear distinction between the atomic behaviors themselves and the mathematical descriptions of those microbehaviors. In the interview, the consequences of the myriad of fragmented pieces of information and models to which students were exposed during class were apparent. Students' explanations, sewn together on-the-fly, employed incomplete fragments of variety of models, erroneously blended different topics (recrystallization, dislocations, grain growth), and often mistakenly used the standard vocabulary and rules of thumb of the field. What is more,

none of the students (even considering the entire group of 21 students participating in the study) even tried to use the standard mathematical equations to
explain the phenomena. The data suggests, therefore, that the "many-to-one"
approach used in class had detrimental consequences for student learning, i.e.,
the representational infrastructure of aggregate equations was not a good match
to the content.

First Session of the User Study: Introduction and Model Exploration

The first session was dedicated to the exploration of the grain growth model.
The first activity was simple: observe and reflect on curvature as a driving force for
grain growth. Most of the students knew, from their previous classroom instruction,
that large grains "consume" small ones, growing toward their center of curvature,
and high-curvature boundaries tend to disappear. However, those concepts appeared
to be isolated ideas, separate phenomena, and hardly connected to the Laplace–Young
equation, which was supposed to be the mathematical evidence for the aforementioned phenomenon.

The goal of this activity was twofold. First, assess students' preexisting understanding of the phenomenon. Secondly, we carefully observed the cognitive
shift as the simulation progressed (Siegler & Crowley, 1991). This activity
consisted in drawing two grains divided by a curved surface and observing their
behavior. The pictures below are snapshots of the dynamic simulation that students
observed (Fig. 2.5).

Before the simulation, most students were unsure of what would happen.
Approximately half thought that the larger grain would grow at the expense of
the smaller, regardless of the curvature of the boundary separating them, while
the other half considered concavity, rather than size, as the main criterion.
As they started the simulation, and saw grains growing toward their centers of
curvature, they observed that the movement was not smooth or unidirectional,
but that there was intense activity on both grains with random flipping of atoms.

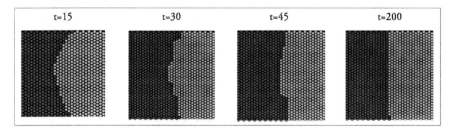

Fig. 2.5 The evolution of a curved grain boundary

The following excerpt suggests that visualizing this progression sparked some changes in Liz's understanding:

Interviewer: Can you describe what you see?

Liz: Just because one grain has a concave side and the other has a convex side, so it comes in towards the concave, because... [pause] does line tension applies in this situation?

Interviewer: Line tension?

Liz: That might be from dislocations... I might be mixing them up. Just because... when you have something... part of the grain is like, curving in, mostly likely other parts of the grain are curving in, so the tension of the grain boundary lines, so the force outside is greater than the force inside, so it will like shrink, it looks like that probably be like straight in the middle, rather than entirely red... just because if the red part also has some concave thing that is off the screen it will just like go together.

Liz is apparently mentioning ideas derived from the Laplace–Young equation, which relates surface tension and curvature. However, she cannot yet think at the "micro" level: To visualize what is happening on the computer screen, she has to imagine a large circle going off-screen, which is probably a consequence of what she remembers from class, where grains were always approximated as spheres. She does not yet construe the local interactions along the curved interface as a driving force, but only the "macro," aggregate-level effect of curvature.

The next activity was to draw a microstructure with many grains, but with one of them a lot smaller than the others, as we can see in Fig. 2.6.

Watching the evolution of this new microstructure was a crucial experience for Liz. She started to transition from memorized rules of thumb and topic-specific models to micro-level reasoning, which would lead her to generate hypothesis about the grain growth law by herself. This excerpt took place when she was observing a triple point – a region where three grains meet and the probability of an atom to flip to

Fig. 2.6 Four large grains surround a small grain (*left*), and a zoomed-in view of the structure showing a triple point (*right*)

any of the surrounding grains is the same, as there are *two* atoms of each grain around the central element (see Fig. 2.6.) While observing this phenomenon, Liz was told to zoom in and out the simulation, to also see what was happening at the microlevel (following a single atom).

Liz: Right here there is an equal position for red, yellow, and blue, but it just happens to be that blue won, it keeps winning.

Interviewer: How would you explain that?

Liz: Because... if you look at one of those points, either of the three colors, they all have the same number of other colors around it, so it is not favorable to choose one or the other...

Interviewer: What angle is here?

Liz: Oh, so this is the 120-degree angle between the... [pause]

Interviewer: Did you talk about it in class?

Liz: Briefly. He [the professor] said that when you reach a triple junction, it will become 120 degrees.

Interviewer: So are you saying that there is an equal probability?

Liz: Well, I just don't understand why blue is doing so much better, in general. Eventually just one has to become bigger, because this is the most energetically favorable thing, so maybe... blue was bigger, but now yellow is coming back, so maybe next time blue gets bigger again, and they will just keep going. Maybe it will just be like that for a long time.

Interviewer: So what happens to growth speed?

Liz: Eventually they will get like... two big ones... and then it will take forever.

Interviewer: So what could be the law?

Liz: It will eventually taper off... to some point... because if you have a lot or grains then you will... the rate of increase will be faster, but when average grain size increases it gets harder and harder to increase the rest of them, so it just goes...

Interviewer: Why is it harder and harder?

Liz: Just because there isn't a distinct... [pause] being in this orientation is more favorable than this other one so you have to pick and choose... the grains are doing that, but it is not happening quickly just because you know, either one can happen.

In this very short time watching the model, Liz was able to understand and generate hypotheses about two essential ideas: triple points and logarithmic laws (the literature refers to these ideas as particularly hard to understand (e.g., Krause & Tasooji, 2007)). Rather than trying to assemble statements pulled from regular instruction, Liz departed from what she knew about other phenomena and what she was actually seeing in the computer model. Even without formally mathematizing the time dependency of grain growth, she understood the reason for the triple point to be considered a "low-mobility" point in a microstructure. The central atom has two atoms (out of six) of each of the surrounding grains as neighbors, so the switch probability is the same (1/3), and there is no preferred growth direction. She also realized that the time law would not be linear: growth speed decreases over time and eventually "tapers off." Rather than *being told*, Liz arrived at this conclusion *on her own*, by drawing microstructures, changing variables, and observing the dynamics of the simulation. Particularly, when asked about the fundamental reason for the "tapering off" of grain growth, she affirmed that "[…] because there isn't a distinct orientation [which] is more favorable" – in other words, she got at the core of the explanation, the fundamental atomistic principle. This same idea could be useful to explain other phenomena in materials science, and we will see how students applied such generative ideas to other phenomena in the next section.

Similarly, Peter and Elise, notwithstanding their initial difficulties in explaining grain growth during the preinterviews, understood the logarithmic nature of the grain growth law:

Interviewer: What could be the rule for grain growth speed?

Peter: As the grains get bigger, each grain is increasingly hard to take away from because it's bigger, so the interfaces start to be between two large grains, instead of small grains, so an interface between a large grain and a large grain is less likely to have a lot of movement because both grains are large and they are already in a state where they don't want to shrink.

Interviewer: What will happen to this surface [between two grains]?

Elise: [It'll] shift up to be vertical. [Looking at the computer model.] Yes, it's just getting flatter.

Interviewer: Why do you think it wants to get flat?

Elise: It's like the nearest-neighbor thing, these want the most nearest green neighbors, the red ones want the most red ones.

Interviewer: [some minutes later, she is looking a triple point] What's happening here?

Elise: It has the same number around each other, so, the red, the angles are all at equilibrium, they are all a stable formation.

Interviewer: And what's that angle there?

Elise: It's a hexagon, I guess it's 360 divided by three, 120.

Generally, most students knew that the small red grain in Fig. 2.6 was going to disappear. From their reactions while observing the simulation, they seemed to be expecting a unidirectional "animation" of the grain being "eaten" by the surrounding ones, and eventually disappearing. This was consistent both with the heuristics and the types of results of aggregate tools, animations, and equations commonly seen in class, which are processes that happen unidirectionally and deterministically. However, what students observed was different: behaviors emerging from local interactions, which take place with some degree of randomness. At times, the small grain would grow, but most of the times it would shrink. Some of the students wanted to slow down the simulation and use the "zoom" tool to see the process in more detail, which meant they could only see the microlevel phenomenon (atoms flipping to different orientations). By zooming out again, they could observe the *emergent* behavior: curved surfaces disappearing as the Laplace–Young equation would predict. Thus, there is a qualitative difference between traditional learning tools and agent-based modeling: not only are students observing an expected outcome, but also *they are able to see the process unfolding* at various levels. The simulation was visually similar to the phenomenon, but, most importantly, its algorithm loyally emulates the micro-level processes underlying it. This is different from purely numeric simulations in which students are able to compare only outputs, and not the processes as they unfold. In addition, words commonly used in the classroom, such as "shrink," "consume," and "growth" acquired a new meaning. Those metaphorical terms, as our preinterview data suggested, can mislead students to interpret literally their meaning – working with MaterialSim, students realized that grains were not actually being "consumed" or shrinking: atoms were just switching places, and the metaphors were just describing the net, aggregate effect of such behavior. This was a central element of the whole experience and, as we will observe, deepened as students progressed in the study.

The last activity of the first day was to run automated experiments using NetLogo's "BehaviorSpace" module. This NetLogo feature enables users to automatically run hundreds of simulations, each under different parameter settings, sweeping entire parameter spaces. Students ran at least one set of experiments, plotted the data, and came up with theories to describe the phenomenon. Most students chose to model the influence of dispersed impurities on grain growth. The textbook explanation of this phenomenon takes approximately four pages. It begins with an account of how a force P appears when a grain boundary attempts to go through a particle, and then calculates the drag force by means of geometrical approximations (see Fig. 2.7).

Departing from those geometrical approximations (for example, all particles are considered to be perfect spheres), the formula is obtained with a series of

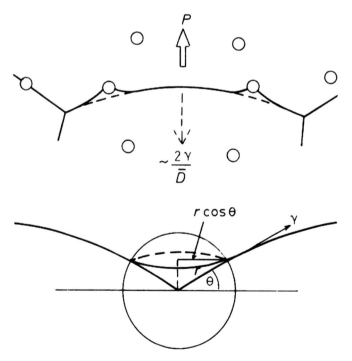

Fig. 2.7 The textbook picture explaining how dispersed particles affect boundary migration (Porter & Easterling, 1992, pp. 141)

derivations (Porter & Easterling, 1992, pp. 141), which relates the fraction of dispersed particles (f), the mean radius of the particles (r), and the maximum particle size after grain growth (D_{max}):

$$P = \frac{3f}{2\pi r^2} \cdot \pi r \gamma = \frac{3f\gamma}{2r} \Rightarrow \frac{2\gamma}{\bar{D}} = \frac{3f\gamma}{2r} \Rightarrow \bar{D}_{max} = \frac{4r}{3f}$$

However, the NetLogo algorithm is not based on this formula, or its geometrical approximations. Before running his experiments, Bob was asked if the model could actually match the "official" equation, since they departed from very different ideas, and he was skeptical. Thus he programmed NetLogo to run a series of simulations with percentages of particles varying from 0 to 8% (see screenshots and individual plots of grain growth speed in Fig. 2.8). He also constructed a plot to aggregate the results across all experiments, and subsequently tried to compare their own curve with the theoretical data (dotted line in Fig. 2.8's lower plot). To his surprise, the two curves had a very reasonable match. Other students, with slight variations, undertook the same project, or selected different aspects of the phenomenon. By exploring entire parameter spaces, and having not only the dynamic visualization but also actual numerical data to base their explanations on, these students were able to further generate original hypotheses and find meaningful correlations.

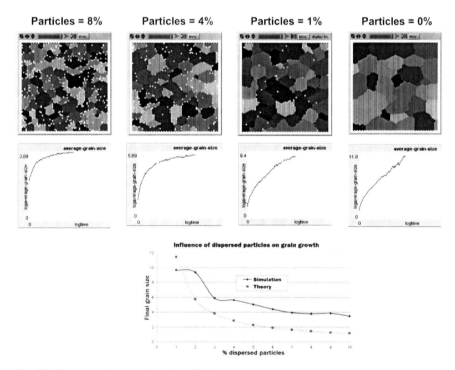

Fig. 2.8 Sequence of screenshots from Bob's experiment

Second Session: Building Their Own Models

The second session was the model construction part of the study. Students had 2½ hours to learn the basics of the NetLogo language and program a new model of a materials science phenomenon. For this session, which took place 2–3 days after the first session, students were asked to bring one idea of their own for a new model. They pursued questions of their interest or problems that they did not understand during regular instruction. By authoring new models or new features for the existing models, they could elaborate on answers to their research questions. Student achievement was impressive. A comparison between the preinterview data, when students relied on ready-made statements about the phenomena, and their performance on the last day of the study, when they built their own models relying just on fundamental atomic behaviors, suggests that student contact with an agent-based environment effected conceptual gain. Even more than exploring the existing models, constructing their own models was a transformative experience for most. In this section we will narrate and analyze some of those learning trajectories. The models chosen for this analysis represent typical student work, and the particular choice of which students to include in the data analysis attempted to provide representative examples of the various affordances of ABM employed by students.

Betty's Model

Betty built a model to investigate grain growth with a new and important feature: taking into consideration the misalignment between grains (see Fig. 2.9). In her innovative model, the more misalignment across the boundary of two grains, the harder it would be for an atom to jump from one grain to another. The construction of this model presented Betty with many challenges. The first was to convert the grain orientation's angle, which could lie in any of the four quadrants, to a normalized quadrant-independent measure that would be easier to compute. Betty's solution,

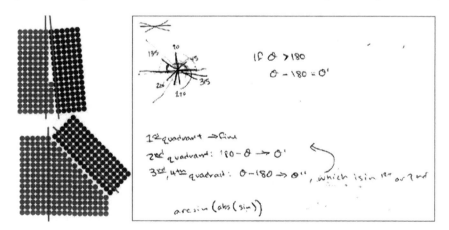

Fig. 2.9 Betty's sketches about angles, sine and arcsine

after much thinking, sketching, and trying out different trigonometric functions, was to use the *arcsine* function. The following picture shows some of her reasoning. From her drawing, we can observe that she was using geometrical analysis from a "micro" level, examining individual atoms, and trying to design an algorithm to account for the trigonometric issues in calculating their misorientation.

She considered that the probability for an atom to jump to the next grain should be dependent not only on the number of different atoms around it, but also on the average misorientation between the two grains. Low misorientation would promote easier migration, thus she needed a function to calculate the misorientation, and then to add a misorientation factor to the previous grain growth algorithm. Apart from the initial difficulty in figuring out the best trigonometric function for the angle comparison, Betty knew what she needed to do, without resorting to any of the textbook formulas. For her, at the microlevel, adding the misorientation effect was quite easy.[6] Therefore, she simply added one command to the original grain growth model to implement her change. Previously, in the traditional aggregate equation-based approach, making such a change would require long and mathematically demanding derivations. The resulting code of her misorientation calculating function was:

```
;;calculates the absolute value of the arcsin[7]
to-report misorientation [angle]
  report asin (abs (sin (angle)))
end
;;calculates the absolute value of the sum of the two
arcsins
to-report calculate-misorientation [angle1 angle2]
  report abs (misorientation (angle1) + misorientation
(angle2))
end
;;reports the average misorientation for a given atom
to-report compare-misorientation

let i 0

ask neighbors6
    [
    ;;calculates the misorientation between the current
    atom and each of its 6 neighbors
    set total-misorientation (total-misorientation +
    calculate-misorientation heading (heading-        of
    neighbors6))
    set i i + 1 ;update counter
    ]
```

---

[6] On a more advanced level, similar research was undertook and published by researchers, such as Ono, Kimura and Watanabe (1999)

[7] In the Netlogo programming language, semicolons mark the start of a comment line. Programmers use comments to clarify and annotate their code.

```
;;returns the average misorientation
report (total-misorientation / i)
```

end

Then, having her reporter agents calculate how much each given atom would differ from its neighbors angle-wise, she changed the original grain growth procedure, adding one extra simple "if" statement:

```
;;OLD PROCEDURE
  if future-free-energy <= present-free-energy
     [set heading (future-heading)]
```

```
;;BETTY'S NEW PROCEDURE
  if future-free-energy <= present-free-energy
     [
        if (present-heading - ([heading] of one-of
          neighbors6) < misorientation)
              [set heading (future-heading)]
     ]
```

Yet, aggregate and macroscopic models do not afford such insights as well. The agent-based approach, conversely, provided a "low-threshold" entry point for Betty to implement her ideas by constructing models. Her model was very consistent with known theory, even though she was not cognizant of this theory prior to the interventional study. Betty's model illustrates one of the main affordances of the agent-based representation: at the micro level, *the mathematical machinery required to add new phenomena or parameters to an existing algorithm is much simpler* than in traditional representations. Instead of employing numerous equations to add her misorientation effect, just a few lines of code, at the microlevel, were sufficient.

Jim's Model: Polymer Chains

Jim was taking a polymer science course at the time, and in previous classes he had learned about polymer chains and how they moved. Polymer chains can move and expand, but in most cases not if that process ends up breaking the chain itself. When he was choosing the idea for his authored model, he very quickly realized that the neighborhood based grain growth algorithm could be a good start for a polymer model. Very quickly Jim computationally modeled atoms for his polymer chains in this way:

Atoms are:

Moving randomly in all four directions (0, 90, 180, and 270 degrees)
But
Not breaking the chain
Not crossing the chain

His NetLogo implementation followed these three simple steps.

```
to move
  ;; choose a heading, and before moving the atom
  (monomer),
  ;; checks if the move would break or cross the chain
  set heading 90 * random 4
  if not breaking-chain? and not crossing-chain?
      [forward 1]
end
```

To check if the monomer movement would break the chain, he wrote a procedure that searched atoms at the four orthogonal directions. In case there were any
atoms there, the procedure returned "false" and that atom did not move. A similar
reporter was done for crossing chain, but with a different set of neighborhood
points. The model's interface (and typical initial setup) can be seen in Fig. 2.10.

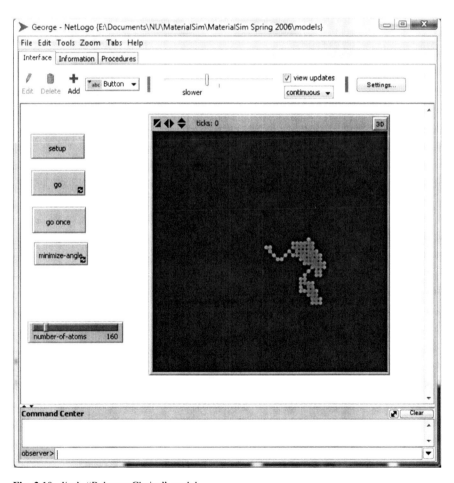

Fig. 2.10 Jim's "Polymer Chains" model

But the model worked only in a very limited way, because if there were too many atoms "clumped" together, they would never get a chance to move, since any movement would either break or cross the chain. One reason for this problem is that it failed to incorporate the attractive and repulsive forces between atoms. Therefore, even though some atoms could move, the chain would not greatly expand because most atoms were within a "one" radius of each other. Jim needed a spring-like repulsive force activated at particular time steps to relax the system, and an attractive force to keep the atoms close to each other. His answer was to create the one extra procedure with just a single line of code using NetLogo's *layout-spring* command, which applies to spring-like force to the links between the agents:

```
;; makes links act as springs (the number after the com-
mands are parameters of the spring)
layout-spring atoms links .4 1 0.1
```

By blending two algorithms, Jim got his model to work exactly as the animation shown in class by the professor – but in a short program of about 15 lines of code. In Fig. 2.11 we have a typical evolution of a polymeric chain. On the last frame (bottom, right), the atomic "movement" procedure was turned off, so just the spring-like forces were in place, generating a smoother chain.

Jim's model is another example of two important affordances of ABM: the easy *blending of algorithms* (in this case, he was able to easily "blend" two typical ABM

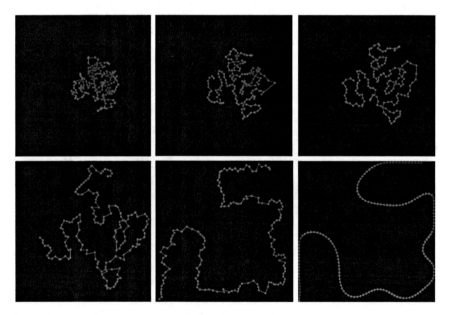

Fig. 2.11 The evolution of a polymer chain in Jim's model

algorithms, spring-behavior and restricted movement), and the *one-to-many generativity* (again, similarly to grain growth, a neighborhood-checking mechanism was at the core of the model). After understanding in detail the principles and algorithm behind the grain growth model, he was able to identify other opportunities to employ the same principles to model and understand other seemingly unrelated phenomena.

Peter's Model

Peter's model was another example of the one-to-many, transferable affordance of the agent-based representation. In the pre-survey, he identified diffusion and interface-controlled reactions as some of the hardest topics in the course. In the second session, he chose these topics for building a model. In materials science, it is particularly important to distinguish transformations that are interface-controlled (i.e., the slowest phase happens at the interface of the two materials) from diffusion-controlled (the slowest part is for atoms to "travel" to the interface, where the actual reaction is fast). Knowing the slowest phase of a given process, engineers can greatly optimize it. Peter's purpose was to build a model to investigate this phenomenon. Its textbook explanation is a five-page narrative with five different equations, which are put together to show that the driving force (referred to as $\Delta\mu_B^i$) is proportional to the temperature and the difference in concentration:

$$\Delta\mu_B^i = RT \ln \frac{X_i}{X_e} \cong \frac{RT}{X_e}\left(X_i - X_e\right)$$

Where X_i and X_e are the chemical compositions of the two materials, T is the temperature, and R is the gas constant (Porter & Easterling, 1992, pp. 177).

Peter ignored the existence of this long sequence of equations. He started his model from scratch, and his first step was to identify the basic atomic behaviors needed for implementing his idea. In his model, there were two types of materials in liquid form, and one type of solid material. Therefore, he needed one mechanism for atoms in the liquid to move, and one mechanism for liquid atoms to become solid. He concentrated in the microrules concerning the phenomenon, and realized that the rules he needed were not very different from the rules present in other models. After all, liquid atoms were just moving randomly and "bumping" into a solid, sticking to it according to a certain probability. The Solid Diffusion model, present in NetLogo's models library, had an efficient algorithm for making atoms move around in a material. The Grain Growth model provided Peter with the idea for the liquid-to-solid transformation. Even though those two models (Solid Diffusion and Grain Growth) had significant differences compared to the model Peter wanted to build, he managed to identify the common useful microrules, copy the code from one model to the other and, very importantly, make the necessary adaptations.

Peter's algorithm was straightforward: if the atoms are in the liquid, and they bump into a solid, they become solid (with a certain probability, dependent on their chemical properties), hence:

```
if ((breed = element1-liquid) and ;;if you are an atom
in the liquid
    (neighbor-breed = solid) and ;; and one neighbor of
yours is in the solid
      (element1-probability > random-float 100)) ;; and
depending on your diffusion speed
        [
            set color neighbor-color ;; switch the atom's
            color
            set breed neighbor-breed ;; switch the atom's
            breed
        ]
```

If the atom is in the liquid (breed different than solid, or "!=solid" in NetLogo language), and it meets an atom different than itself, the atoms switch places – in other words, diffusion is taking place:

```
if ((breed != solid) and ;;if you are in the liquid
    (neighbor-breed != solid) and  ;;and one neighbor
    of yours is also in the liquid
    (diffusion-speed > random-float 100)) ;; and depending
    on your diffusion speed
      [
        set [color] of random-neighbor color ;;switch
          the neighbor's color
        set [breed] of random-neighbor breed ;;switch
          the neighbor's breeds
        set color neighbor-color ;; switch the atom's
          color
        set breed neighbor-breed ;; switch the atom's
          breed
      ]
```

Note that the idea of asking atoms to check their near neighborhood came from the Grain Growth model, whereas the idea of atoms switching places as a way to diffuse through a material came from the Solid Diffusion model. In two dozen lines of code, and less than 2 hours, Peter was able to model both diffusion and solidification, manipulating exclusively local rules, and had a model the complexity of which was far beyond what is expected from the Microstructural Dynamics course, considering the classroom observations and analysis of class materials. Nevertheless, just as other students, he was concerned with the correctness of his work. He generated a series of plots and screenshots to match his data with the textbook plots, part of which are shown in Fig. 2.12.

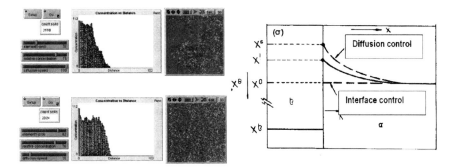

Fig. 2.12 Results of Peter's model with diffusion control (*top*, with diffusion speed = 100), interface control (*bottom*, with diffusion speed = 20), and the chart from the textbook, where we can identify a similar same shape for the two concentration curves. (Note that this last chart was rotated for clarity)

At the end of the session, the first author asked Peter about the next steps in his model's implementation, had he more time to work on it. Again, he demonstrated a solid understanding of how to easily manipulate those basic rules to generate new models, for example, how to invert a process by simply changing the probability of its microevents:

Peter: I did a liquid to solid model, now I want to be able to invert it, do a solid to liquid algorithm.

Interviewer: And how would you implement it?

Peter: It's simple: I'll just invert the probability. It's just the opposite probability. I don't have to change much.

[...]

Interviewer: And how would you implement, for example, dispersed particles in a grain growth model?

Peter: I would put in molecules that have zero probability to change to anything else, and zero probability of another molecule to change into them.

Peter's response demonstrated a deep understanding of the process and was in great contrast with his preinterview data, in which although he correctly identified and explained some phenomena, he failed to see how those principles and knowledge could be put to use to further his own knowledge about a particular topic or other phenomena.

Discussion

Computer modeling is posing a serious challenge to extant knowledge encoding schemes in engineering and materials science. Researchers have already detected this trend – computer modeling in materials science has more than doubled in the last 10 years (Thornton & Asta, 2005). However, materials science students are still obliged to master hundreds of equations and isolated facts. Even if students were to somehow try to connect those equations into a coherent corpus, the mathematical machinery required to accomplish that would be too demanding for most to succeed.

The examples of students' model building we have described were implemented in less than 3 hours, *including* the time dedicated to learning the basics of the NetLogo language. The relative ease with which students developed their own models, even within such a short timeframe, shows that model building is an approachable task for undergraduate students and supports one of our main claims: agent-based modeling, for some fields of engineering, offers a more principled understanding of the natural phenomena, which, in turn, grants more autonomy for students in learning new content or deriving new theories on their own. Participant students had previous knowledge of the phenomenon from their class work. Nevertheless, during the preinterview, they demonstrated difficulty in explaining related phenomena in a coherent fashion, resorting to a range of fragmented models and metaphors. The implementation of their own model within an agent-based modeling environment provided students with fewer, simpler rules that were closely related to the physical phenomenon, thus enabling them to better understand and extend the model by adding new proximal rules for the agents.

We compiled evidence suggesting that the agent-based encoding is a good fit to content in materials science. First, the undergraduate courses are overloaded with highly specialized information. Secondly, students demonstrated difficulty in explaining even the most basic concepts in the field, with frequent "slippage" between levels. Thirdly, throughout the classrooms observations and the interviews, one striking revelation was that the agent-based approach was not a total unknown for textbook authors, teachers, and students. The textbook oftentimes makes use of microbehaviors, simple rules, and agent-based heuristics. When explaining grain growth, the textbook authors use an agent-based approach:

> [...] A similar effect occurs in metal grains. In this case the atoms in the shrinking grain detach themselves from the lattice on the high pressure side of the boundary and relocate themselves on a lattice site on the growing grain. (Porter & Easterling, 1992)

However, the agent-based representation was in this context a mere illustration of the "real" content that would come after, encoded as equations. Arguably, even though the agent-based representations could be easier for students to understand, there was no technological infrastructure to "run" those models – the activities and software that we developed could provide this infrastructure. The availability of an expressive tool and an empowering learning environment were crucial elements. As a computational tool, NetLogo and its agent-based approach was a good fit for capturing students' intuitions and ideas at the appropriate level. In addition, the constructionist nature of students' interaction with the tool enabled them to build fluency with this new tool, and perceive themselves as scientists in their own right, transforming seemingly simple ideas and local rules into powerful kernels for scientific modeling. To further understand the cognitive model which

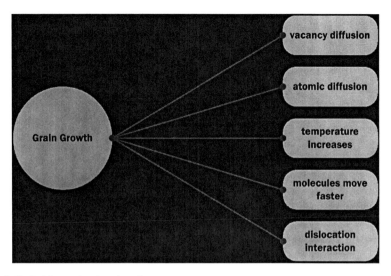

Fig. 2.13 Bob's one-level explanation

the ABM perspective might foster, let us consider again, for example, Bob's explanation of grain growth:

> **Bob:** Well, grains grow through diffusion, through **vacancy diffusion**, and **atomic diffusion**, for one, it is all over the place, **temperature increases, molecules move around** faster […].

His statement reveals a one-level description of the phenomena, which is compatible with our analysis of the current sparse and linear encoding of knowledge in materials science. Ideas such as "vacancy diffusion" and "increase of temperature" are connected to "grain growth" without a clear hierarchy (Fig. 2.13).

During the work with MaterialSim, students developed an extra "organizing" layer which grouped some of the surface manifestations on the phenomena under one unifying principle[8] (Fig. 2.14). Let us observe Liz's statement:

> **Liz:** It is because, it wants to be more **energetically stable**, or have **less energy** in the crystal, so it will grow, just to form one big grain, because that's the least energy configuration […]

Liz identified one unifying principle, "lowering free energy," from which many of those external manifestations derive. An agent-based modeling environment offers low-threshold tools to code and formalize this principle algorithmically, enabling her to "mobilize" this idea that was previously just a vague mental model. Finally, after the model building, students were able to mobilize these generalizable principles, encoded as computer code, to explain other phenomena that shared the same mechanism (Fig. 2.15).

---

[8] For elaboration on the idea of organizing layers, see "Papert's principle" in Minsky's Society of Mind (1996).

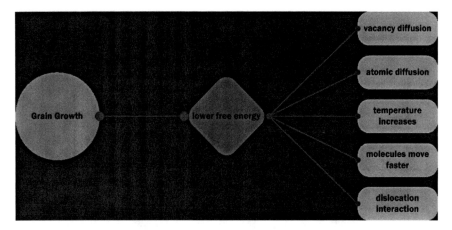

Fig. 2.14 Liz's two-level structure

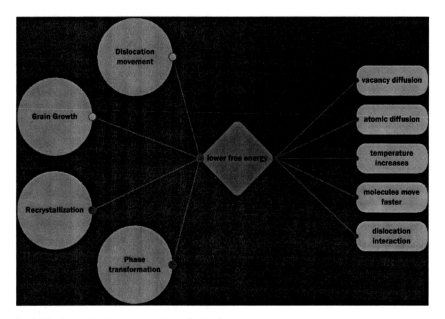

Fig. 2.15 A two-level structure with multiple phenomena

Conclusion

Design courses have become fashionable in many engineering schools. Robotics and engineering design competitions are common in various universities and even high schools. One question explored in this study was: can we extend the powerful ideas about engineering design, constructionism, and project-based approaches to theoretical engineering courses in fields such as materials science, in which students' projects would be quite different from robots?

Rich, motivating learning is often achieved through an approach of *learning-by-doing*. In areas such as mechanical engineering, *doing* and *understanding* could be tightly connected. When students are building a gearing system, all the components are clearly visible. In areas such as chemistry, atmospheric science, biology, and materials science, this is not usually the case. Learners might observe overall effects while having little understanding of the underlying causality or the fundamental components of the system, since the actual phenomenon it too removed from human size or time scale. Moreover, teaching tools in those disciplines often have relied on "aggregate," formulaic descriptions. This study suggests that the fragmentation and opaqueness of such descriptions could constitute an obstacle to learning. First, the traditional aggregate equational descriptions are more phenomenon and context-specific, and do not enable students to make broader inferences about phenomena with similar micromechanisms. The mathematical machinery required to manipulate and combine aggregate equations is highly complex and constitutes an obstacle for many students. Second, these descriptions often lead to heuristics that generate overgeneralizations – students often had memorized ideas about phenomena in materials science about which they had no deep understanding. Third, the traditional descriptions are formally detached from representations of the actual physical phenomena, i.e., the aggregate formulaic descriptions don't inform students, at first glance, much about the atomistic mechanism of the phenomenon under scrutiny.

On the other hand, agent-based modeling seems to provide phenomenally isomorphic representations that can lead to deep conceptual insights about the content areas discussed in this chapter, for three reasons:

1. Students' experience interacting with the MaterialSim models, and building their own models, foregrounded the fundamental physical processes taking place in the material, namely atomic movement and free-energy minimization. Not only were most of the algorithms exclusively based on those processes, but also the design of the visualization schemes enabled students to *see* them unfolding in real-time. Students observed both favorable and unfavorable atomic jumps, grains growing and shrinking, expected and unexpected results.
2. A core feature of this design is that students can apply a small number of kernel models to capture fundamental causal structures underlying behaviors in apparently disparate phenomena within a domain. For example, a free-energy minimization algorithm could enable students to understand not only grain growth, but also annealing, interfacial energy, recrystallization, diffusion, and phase transformations, which are traditionally taught as *separate* topics with their own models and equations. Most students were able to create their own models by transferring some "kernel" algorithms from one model to another, making the needed adaptations.
3. One of the pillars of constructionist theory is the importance of students conducting personally meaningful projects. Even though students had significant insights about the phenomena by interacting with predesigned models, our data

suggest that coding their *own* models was a particularly valuable learning experience. It was during the model-building process – writing code, testing and debugging their theories, and reconciling them with previous knowledge – that students had a deeper and more intense exposure to the tools and methods of agent-based modeling, being able to develop enough fluency with the computational representations. In addition, we have shown that learning a low threshold programming language such as NetLogo and coding a model can be done in short enough time to be feasible in actual university classrooms.

In conclusion, the research reported here suggests that *less is more*. Specifically, our findings suggest that agent-based approaches to representing knowledge offer a radically different avenue for students to engage in scientific inquiry. Exploring and learning about just a few simple underlying rules of natural phenomena, given the availability of a computational medium to manipulate, represent, combine, and analyze them, appears to be more generative for students than the current teaching approaches in materials science and engineering that employ numerous aggregate, equation-based representations. We hope these findings inform future research and development in STEM education in so far as extending to theoretical science and engineering courses the principles of student-centered, constructionist pedagogies – in particular, using the tools and approaches derived from the complexity sciences and agent-based modeling.

Acknowledgments We thank Professor Tschiptschin (Engineering School of the University of São Paulo, Brazil) for his inspiration and support, Professor Srolovitz (Yeshiva University), and the members of the Center for Connected Learning and Computer-Based Modeling at Northwestern University. We also thank Ann McKenna from the McCormick School of Engineering at Northwestern University. Special thanks for Spiro Maroulis and Michelle Wilkerson-Jerde (Northwestern University) and Professor Dor Abrahamson (UC Berkeley) for invaluable comments on earlier drafts of this chapter. This work was funded under the umbrella of three NSF grants: REC-0126227, HCC-0713619, and NSF EEC-0648316.

References

Abrahamson, D., & Wilensky, U. (2005). *ProbLab goes to school: Design, teaching, and learning of probability with multi-agent interactive computer models.* Paper presented at the Fourth Conference of the European Society for Research in Mathematics Education, San Feliu de Guixols, Spain
American Society for Engineering Education. (2007). ASEE profiles of engineering and engineering technology colleges. Retrieved from http://www.asee.org/publications/profiles/upload/2007 ProfileEng.pdf
Anderson, M. P., Srolovitz, D. J., Grest, G. S., & Sahni, P. S. (1984). Computer simulation of grain growth: I. Kinetics. *Acta Metallurgica, 32*, 783–792.
Berland, M., & Wilensky, U. (2004, April 12–16). *Virtual robotics in a collaborative constructionist learning environment.* Paper presented at the Annual Meeting of the American Educationalt Research Association, San Diego, CA
Berland, M., & Wilensky, U. (2005, April 11–15). *Complex play systems -- Results from a classroom implementation of VBOT.* In W. Stroup, U. Wilensky (Chairs), & C. D. Lee (Discussant),

Patterns in group learning with next-generation network technology. Paper presented at the Annual Meeting of the American Educational Research Association, Montreal, Canada

Blikstein, P. (2009). *An atom is known by the company it keeps: Content, representation and pedagogy within the epistemic revolution of the complexity sciences.* Unpublished doctoral dissertation, Northwestern University, Evanston, IL

Blikstein, P., & Tschiptschin, A. P. (1999). Monte Carlo simulation of grain growth. *Materials Research, 2*(3), 133–137.

Blikstein, P., & Wilensky, U. (2004a). *MaterialSim: an agent-based simulation toolkit for learning materials science.* In M. Hoit & T. Anderson (Eds.), *Proceedings of the International Conference on Engineering Education, Gainesville, Florida, USA*

Blikstein, P., & Wilensky, U. (2005a). Less is more: Agent-based simulation as a powerful learning tool in materials science. *Proceedings of the IV International Joint Conference on Autonomous Agents and Multi-agent Systems (AAMAS 2005), Utrecht, Holland.*

Blikstein, P., & Wilensky, U. (2006a). *From inert to generative modeling: two case studies of multiagent-based simulation in undergraduate engineering education.* Paper presented at the Annual Meeting of the American Educational Research Association, San Francisco, CA

Blikstein, P., & Wilensky, U. (2006b). 'Hybrid modeling': Advanced scientific investigation linking computer models and real-world sensing. *Proceedings of the Seventh International Conference of the Learning Sciences, Bloomington, USA.*

Blikstein, P. & Wilensky, U. (2007). *Bifocal modeling: a framework for combining computer modeling, robotics and real-world sensing.* Paper presented at the annual meeting of the American Educational Research Association (AERA 2007), Chicago, USA.

Blikstein, P., & Wilensky, U. (2008). *Implementing multi-agent modeling in the classroom: Lessons from empirical studies in undergraduate engineering education.* In M. Jacobson (Chair) & R. Noss (Discussant), Complex systems & learning: Empirical research, issues & "seeing" scientific knowledge with new eyes." In G. Kanselaar, J. van Merri'nboer, P. Kirschner, & T. de Jong (Eds.), *Proceedings of the International Conference of the Learning Sciences (ICLS)* (Vol. 3, pp. 266-267). Utrecht, The Netherlands

Blikstein, P. & Wilensky, U. (2009). An atom is known by the company it keeps: A constructionist learning environment for materials science using multi-agent modeling. *International Journal of Computers for Mathematical Learning, 14*(2), 81–119.

Blikstein, P. (2009). An atom is known by the company it keeps: Content, representation and pedagogy within the epistemic revolution of the complexity sciences. Unpublished Doctoral Dissertation, Northwestern University, Evanston, IL.

Bransford, J. D., & Schwartz, D. L. (1999). Rethinking transfer: A simple proposal with multiple implications. *Review of Research in Education, 24*, 61–100.

Brown, G. S. (1961). Today's dilemma in engineering education. *IRE Transactions on Education, E4*(2), 48.

Burke, J. E. (1949). Some factors affecting the rate of grain growth in metals. *Transactions of the American Institute of Mining Engineers* (180), 73–91.

Centola, D., Wilensky, U., & McKenzie, E. (2000, June 14–17). A hands-on modeling approach to evolution: Learning about the evolution of cooperation and altruism through multi-agent modeling – The EACH Project. *Proceedings of the Fourth Annual International Conference of the Learning Sciences, Ann Arbor, MI.*

Colgate, J. E., McKenna, A., & Ankenman, B. (2004). IDEA: Implementing Blikstein & Wilensky design throughout the curriculum at northwestern. *International Journal of Engineering Education, 20*(3), 405–411.

Collier, N., & Sallach, D. (2001). *Repast.* Chicago: University of Chicago. Retrieved from http://repast.sourceforge.net.

Committee on the Education and Utilization of the Engineering. (1985). *Engineering education and practice in the United States: Foundations of our techno-economic future.* Washington, DC: National Research Council.

diSessa, A. A. (2000). *Changing minds: Computers, learning, and literacy.* Cambridge: MIT Press.

Dym, C. L. (1999). Learning engineering: Design, languages, and experiences. *Journal of Engineering Education, 88,* 145–148.

Dym, C. L., Agogino, A. M., Eris, O., Frey, D. D., & Leifer, L. J. (2005). Engineering design thinking, teaching, and learning. *Journal of Engineering Education, 94*(1), 103–120.

Edwards, L. (1995). Microworlds as representations. *Proceedings of the 2nd International NATO Symposium on Advanced Technology and Education.*

Einstein, H. H. (2002). Engineering change at MIT. *Civil Engineering, 72*(10), 62–69.

Gobert, J., Horwitz, P., Tinker, B., Buckley, B., Wilensky, U., Levy, S., et al. (2004, July 31–August 2). *Modeling across the curriculum: Scaling up modeling using technology.* Paper presented at the Proceedings of the Twenty-fifth Annual Meeting of the Cognitive Science Society, Boston, MA.

Goldstone, R. L., & Wilensky, U. (2008). Promoting transfer through complex systems principles. *Journal of the Learning Sciences, 15,* 35–43.

Haghighi, K. (2005). Systematic and sustainable reform in engineering education. *Journal of Environmental Engineering-ASCE, 131*(4), 501–502.

Hatano, G., & Oura, Y. (2003). Commentary: Reconceptualizing school learning using insight from expertise research. *Educational Researcher, 32*(8), 26–29.

Horwitz, P., Gobert, J., Wilensky, U., & Dede, C. (2003). *MAC: A longitudinal study of modeling technology in science classrooms.* Paper presented at the National Educational Computing Conference (NECC), Seattle, WA

Hurst, K. D. (1995). *A new paradigm for engineering education.* Paper presented at the 25th Annual ASEE/IEEE Conference: Frontiers in Education '95, Atlanta, GA

Jerath, S. (1983). Engineering-education in perspective. *Mechanical Engineering, 105*(2), 92–93.

Katehi, L., Banks, K., Diefes-Dux, H., Follman, D., Gaunt, J., Haghighi, K., et al. (2004). *A New Framework for Academic Reform in Engineering Education.* Paper presented at the 2004 American Society for Engineering Education Conference, Salt Lake City, UT.

Krause, S. J., & Tasooji, A. (2007). *Diagnosing students' misconceptions on solubility and saturation for understanding of phase diagrams.* Paper presented at the American Society for Engineering Education Annual Conference, Portland, USA

Kulov, N. N., & Slin'ko, M. G. (2004). The state of the art in chemical engineering science and education. *Theoretical Foundations of Chemical Engineering, 38*(2), 105–111.

Lamley, R. A. (1996). A model for an engineering education. *Marine Technology and Sname News, 33*(2), 119–121.

Levy, S. T., Kim, H., & Wilensky, U. (2004, April 12–16). *Connected chemistry - A study of secondary students using agent-based models to learn chemistry.* Paper presented at the Annual meeting of the American Educational Research Association, San Diego, CA

Levy, S. T., Novak, M., & Wilensky, U. (2006). *Students' foraging through the complexities of the particulate world: Scaffolding for independent inquiry in the connected chemistry (MAC) curriculum.* Paper presented at the Annual Meeting of the American Educational Research Association, San Francisco, CA

Martin, F. (1996). Ideal and real systems: A study of notions of control in undergraduates who design robots. In Y. Kafai & M. Resnick (Eds.), *Constructionism in practice* (pp. 297–332). Mahwah, NJ: Lawrence Erlbaum Associates Inc.

MIT Center for Policy Alternatives. (1975). Future directions in engineering-education - system response to a changing world - report by center for policy alternatives for MIT School of Engineering. *Engineering Education, 65*(5), 382–382.

Minsky, M. (1986). The Society of Mind. New York: Simon & Schuster.

Newstetter, W. C., & McCracken, M. (2000). *Design learning as conceptual change: A framework for developing a science of design learning. Conference of the American Society of Engineering Education.* St. Louis, MO: ASEE.

Ono, N., Kimura, K., & Watanabe, T. (1999). Monte Carlo simulation of grain growth with the full spectra of grain orientation and grain boundary energy. Acta Materialia, *47*(3), 1007–1017.

Pagels, H. R. (1988). *The dreams of reason: The computer and the rise of the sciences of complexity.* New York: Simon & Schuster.

Panel on Undergraduate Engineering Education. (1986). *Engineering undergraduate education.* Washington, DC: National Research Council.

Papert, S. (1980). *Mindstorms: children, computers, and powerful ideas.* New York: Basic Books.

Papert, S. (1991). Situating constructionism. In S. Papert & I. Harel (Eds.), *Constructionism.* Cambridge, MA: MIT Press.

Parunak, H. V. D., Savit, R., & Riolo, R. L. (1998). Agent-based modeling vs equation-based modeling: A case study and users' guide. *Lecture Notes in Computer Science, 1534*, 10–25.

Porter, D. A., & Easterling, K. E. (1992). *Phase transformations in metals and alloys* (2nd ed.). London; New York: Chapman & Hall

Roco, M. C. (2002). Nanotechnology - A frontier for engineering education. *International Journal of Engineering Education, 18*(5), 488–497.

Russell, J. S., & Stouffer, W. B. (2005). Survey of the national civil engineering curriculum. *Journal of Professional Issues in Engineering Education and Practice, 131*(2), 118–128.

Sengupta, P. & Wilensky, U. (2008). *On the learnability of electricity as a complex system.* In M. Jacobson (Chair) & R. Noss (Discussant), Complex systems & learning: Empirical research, issues & "'seeing" scientific knowledge with new eyes. In G. Kanselaar, J. van Merri'nboer, P. Kirschner, & T. de Jong (Eds.), *Proceedings of the International Conference of the Learning Sciences (ICLS)* (Vol. 3, pp. 267-268). Utrecht, The Netherlands

Sherin, B. L. (2001). A comparison of programming languages and algebraic notation as expressive languages for physics. *International Journal of Computers for Mathematical Learning, 6*(1), 1–61.

Siegler, R. S., & Crowley, K. (1991). The microgenetic method: A direct means for studying cognitive development. *American Psychologist, 46*(6), 606–620.

Soloway, E., Guzdial, M., & Hay, K. E. (1994). Learner-centered design: the challenge for HCI in the 21st century. *Interactions, 1*(2), 36–48.

Srolovitz, D. J., Anderson, M. P., Grest, G. S., & Sahni, P. S. (1984). Computer simulation of grain growth - II. Grain size distribution, topology and local dynamics. *Acta Metallurgica, 32*, 793–801.

Stieff, M., & Wilensky, U. (2003). Connected chemistry: Incorporating interactive simulations into the chemistry classroom. *Journal of Science Education and Technology, 12*(3), 285–302.

Thornton, K., & Asta, M. (2005). Current status and outlook of computational materials science education in the US. *Modelling and Simulation in Materials Science and Engineering, 13*(2), R53.

Tisue, S., & Wilensky, U. (2004, May 16–21). NetLogo: A simple environment for modeling complexity. *Paper presented at the International Conference on Complex Systems (ICCS 2004), Boston, MA*

Tryggvason, G., & Apelian, D. (2006). Re-engineering engineering education for the challenges of the 21 st century. *JOM, 58*(10), 14–17.

Tyack, D. B., & Cuban, L. (1995). *Tinkering toward utopia: A century of public school reform.* Cambridge, MA: Harvard University Press.

Wilensky, U. (1993). *Connected mathematics: Building concrete relationships with mathematical knowledge.* Unpublished doctoral dissertation, MIT, Cambridge, MA

Wilensky, U. (1995). Paradox, programming and learning probability. *Journal of Mathematical Behavior, 14*(2), 231–280.

Wilensky, U. (1999a). GasLab-an extensible modeling toolkit for exploring micro-and-macro-views of gases. In N. Roberts, W. Feurzeig & B. Hunter (Eds.), *Computer modeling and simulation in science education.* Berlin: Springer Verlag.

Wilensky, U. (2003). Statistical mechanics for secondary school: The GasLab modeling toolkit. *International Journal of Computers for Mathematical Learning, 8*(1), 1–41. Special issue on agent-based modeling.

Wilensky, U. (2006). *Complex systems and restructuration of scientific disciplines: Implications for learning, analysis of social systems, and educational policy.* In J. Kolodner (Chair), C. Bereiter (Discussant), & J.D. Bransford (Discussant), Complex systems, learning, and education: Conceptual principles, methodologies, and implications for educational research. Paper presented at the Annual Meeting of the American Educational Research Association, San Francisco, CA

Wilensky, U., Hazzard, E., & Longenecker, S. (2000, October 11–13). *A bale of turtles: A case study of a middle school science class studying complexity using StarLogoT.* Paper presented at the meeting of the Spencer Foundation, New York

Wilensky, U., & Papert, S. (in preparation). Restructurations: Reformulations of knowledge disciplines through new representational forms. Working Paper. Evanston, IL. Center for Connected Learning and Computer-Based Modeling, Northwestern University.

Wilensky, U., Papert, S., Sherin, B., diSessa, A., Kay, A., & Turkle, S. (2005). *Center for Learning and Computation-Based Knowledge (CLiCK). Proposal to the National Science Foundation Science of Learning Centers.*

Wilensky, U., & Rand, W. (2009). *An introduction to agent-based modeling: Modeling natural, social and engineered complex systems with NetLogo.* Cambridge, MA: MIT Press.

Wilensky, U., & Reisman, K. (2006). Thinking like a wolf, a sheep or a firefly: Learning biology through constructing and testing computational theories. *Cognition & Instruction, 24*(2), 171–209.

Wilensky, U., & Resnick, M. (1999). Thinking in levels: A dynamic systems approach to making sense of the world. *Journal of Science Education and Technology, 8*(1), 3–19.

Wilkerson-Jerde, M., & Wilensky, U. (2009). *Complementarity in equational and agent-based models: A pedagogical perspective.* Paper presented at the Annual Meeting of the American Research Education Association, San Diego, CA

Wilensky, U. (2006). Complex systems and reformulating scientific disciplines: Implications for learning, analysis of social systems, and educational policy. Paper presented at the American Educational Research Association, San Francisco, CA.

Wolfram, S. (2002). *A new kind of science.* Champaign, IL: Wolfram Media.

Yamins, D. (2005). *Towards a theory of "local to global" in distributed multi-agent systems (I).* Proceedings of the Fourth International Joint Conference on Autonomous Agents and Multiagent Systems, Utrecht, The Netherlands.

Software and Model References

Blikstein, P. & Wilensky, U. (2005b). NetLogo MaterialSim Grain Growth model. Evanston, IL: Center for Connected Learning and Computer-Based Modeling, Northwestern University. http://ccl.northwestern.edu/netlogo/models/MaterialSimGrainGrowth.

Wilensky, U. (1999b). NetLogo [Computer software]. Evanston, IL: Center for Connected Learning and Computer-Based Modeling. http://ccl.northwestern.edu/netlogo.

Wilensky, U., & Shargel, B. (2002). *Behavior Space [Computer Software].* Evanston, IL: Center for Connected Learning and Computer Based Modeling, Northwestern University.

Blikstein, P., & Wilensky, U. (2004b). MaterialSim curriculum. Center for Connected Learning and Computer Based Modeling, Northwestern University, Evanston, IL. Retrieved from http://ccl.northwestern.edu/curriculum/materialsim.

Chapter 3
Learning Genetics from Dragons: From Computer-Based Manipulatives to Hypermodels

Paul Horwitz, Janice D. Gobert, Barbara C. Buckley, and Laura M. O'Dwyer

This chapter continues a theme explored in earlier research (Horwitz & Christie, 2000) related to the use of a *computer-based manipulative* called "GenScope" for teaching high school genetics. The major finding from that work was that although GenScope proved immensely popular among both students and teachers,[1] the learning results associated with its use were initially disappointing and only improved after the software was accompanied by a customized curriculum and extensive professional development (Hickey, Kindfield, Horwitz, & Christie, 2003; Hickey, Kruger, & Zuiker, 2003). In the present chapter we focus on the changes that were made to GenScope in response to these findings, and describe research and development efforts toward and with a "new and improved" version of the software called BioLogica. One of the main thrusts of the research we report on here has been the addition to GenScope of logging tools that enable us to: (1) monitor students' actions, including but not limited to their answers to embedded assessment questions, and (2) analyze them to make inferences concerning their content knowledge and model-based reasoning. The results of these fine-grained analyses were mainly used to inform our research, but in future could form the basis for timely, insightful reports on student learning, targeted for teachers and students, respectively.

P. Horwitz (✉)
Concord Consortium, 25 Love Lane, Concord, MA 01742, USA
e-mail: paul@concord.org

J.D. Gobert
Department of Social Science and Policy Studies, Worcester Polytechnic Institute,
100 Institute Road, Worcester, MA, USA

B.C. Buckley
WestEd, 400 Seaport Court, Suite 222, Redwood City, CA, USA

L.M. O'Dwyer
Department of Educational Research, Measurement and Evaluation, Lynch School of Education,
Boston College, Chestnut Hill, MA, USA

[1] GenScope remains popular today, but its use is limited to pre-OS X Macintosh computers.

M.J. Jacobson and P. Reimann (eds.), *Designs for Learning Environments of the Future:*
International Perspectives from the Learning Sciences, DOI 10.1007/978-0-387-88279-6_3,
© Springer Science+Business Media, LLC 2010

The GenScope Project (Horwitz, Neumann, & Schwartz, 1996; Horwitz, Schwartz, & Neumann, 1998; Hickey, Kindfield, Horwitz, & Christie, 1999; Horwitz & Christie, 2000; Hickey, Kindfield et al., 2003) developed a computer-based model of inheritance genetics consisting of six interacting levels representing, respectively, DNA, chromosomes, cells, organisms, pedigrees, and populations.[2] The levels are linked so that changes made at any one of them will affect the others as dictated by the underlying genetic model. Thus, a change at the DNA level (i.e., a mutation) will usually[3] create a new allele that, alone or in combination with a similar allele on the homologous chromosome, may give rise to a new phenotype, thus affecting not only the chromosome and cell levels, but the organism level as well. The new phenotype, in turn, will be inherited in a stochastic but deterministic way that can be studied at the pedigree level, and the new allele may or may not prove adaptive in a given environment, which will govern its subsequent increase or decrease in frequency at the population level.

GenScope provides a powerful and extensible model of genetics,[4] but it lacks explicit pedagogical guidance. For example, one study tested it using three high school classes: a traditionally taught class that served as the control group, and two GenScope classes, one in which the students exclusively used GenScope, and one in which the students used GenScope less intensively, but added a set of pencil-and-paper activities to the treatment (for a review of this study see Hickey, Kindfield et al. (1999)). Both GenScope classes outperformed the traditional class on the posttest, but the GenScope class that also did the paper-and-pencil instructional activities outperformed the GenScope-only class. These and other findings highlighted the need for a system that would include instructional activities with the software, guiding students' interactions with the genetics model, posing questions, and making explicit the connections between the behavior of the computer model and corresponding real-world processes.

In addition, our experience with GenScope led us to believe that the software might be designed to interpret and react to students' actions using context-sensitive algorithms, thereby providing individualized instruction. With this as a starting point, we were able to formalize the components and characteristics that would be needed in a more adaptive program. Two key features of such a system are:

- *Student feedback.* The students should receive context-sensitive assistance from the software, so that they need not rely entirely on the teacher, either to help them use the software effectively or to guide them to draw appropriate conclusions from their investigations.

---

[2] The population level was not used in the research described in Horwitz and Christie (2000).

[3] So-called silent mutations, which do not alter the encoded sequence of amino acids, have no effect in GenScope or in the real world.

[4] The model includes recombinant processes – such as crossing over between homologous chromosomes during meiosis – as well as interspecific interactions such as predator–prey and competitive relationships.

• *Teacher feedback.* The teacher should receive feedback about the students' use of the software in order to identify who is "getting it" and who is "stuck." This is important because it is difficult even for an exceptionally well-prepared teacher to determine what each student in the class is doing during online learning activities and to react accordingly.

Addressing these issues required us to depart from the open-ended discovery approach underlying GenScope in favor of explicitly scaffolding students' learning activities (more on this later). In order to accomplish this goal, we created an infrastructure that monitored students' actions and reacted to them in real time. By logging and subsequently analyzing these actions, we were able to create reports from the formative and summative interactive assessments for use by the researchers. Only limited reports, consisting primarily of students' answers to embedded assessment questions, were available to teachers. The technology required to do both the scaffolding and the assessment is what we have come to call a "hypermodel."

Hypermodels

Hypermodels (Horwitz et al., 1996) occupy a position in the educational technology spectrum somewhere between the highly linear, explicitly didactic approach characterized by the term "computer-assisted instruction" or CAI (Suppes, 1969; Steinberg, 1977; Kinzie, Sullivan, & Berdel, 1988), and the more open-ended, student-centered technologies often termed "constructivist" (Magoon, 1977; Papert, 1980; Driver & Oldham, 1986; Blais, 1988). The development of hypermodels was motivated by perceived drawbacks at the two extremes. CAI technologies, though they have been demonstrated to be effective in enhancing procedural skills, are less successful at teaching higher-order thinking and eliciting students' mental models (White & Frederiksen, 1998). On the other hand, the research literature has shown that students who use open-ended constructivist tools with little or no structure may become proficient in using the tool, but they often fail to convert that success into deep understanding of the subject domain (Horwitz 1999; Horwitz & Christie, 2000; Hickey, Kindfield et al., 2003; Hickey, Kruger & Zuiker, 2003; Kirschner, Sweller, & Clark, 2006).

Hypermodels are intended to respond to the demands placed on teachers when they use open-ended inquiry tools like GenScope. These demands often present significant barriers to the successful implementation of such technologies in real classroom settings. Although open-ended applications such as GenScope often "demo well," the practical difficulties of using them in the classroom may overwhelm the teacher, who must keep track of what students are doing, guide them through difficulties, encourage and praise them when they succeed, and help them reflect on the broader significance of what they are doing (Aulls, 2002).

As previously stated, hypermodels are designed to alleviate these problems by combining the best aspects of the CAI and constructivist approaches. Properly used, they give students the freedom to engage in open-ended investigations, while monitoring their actions and reacting to them in contextually meaningful ways – offering suggestions, asking questions, and using text or multimedia materials to link the computer activities to real-world analogs. Hypermodels integrate text, audio, animations, or video materials with a manipulable model of the subject domain, using each medium as a tool for navigating the other. The association with "hypertext" is intentional: just as clicking on a word, phrase, or graphic serves to navigate through a website, students' manipulation of a computer-based model can be used to navigate in an interactive model-based inquiry environment – triggering the presentation of a video clip, for instance, or bringing up a relevant question. In turn, students' answers to questions or choices of multimedia presentations can affect the configuration of the model.

Hypermodels are *scriptable* by curriculum developers and researchers, and thus provide a flexible tool for the creation of a wide variety of activities that can challenge students to solve problems, and then monitor and react to their actions. The activities structure students' investigations of a domain and offer metacognitive prompts as well as links to real-world science at appropriate "teachable moments."

Since hypermodels monitor students' interactions with the learning environment, they can also log them. The raw data produced by this process is too fine-grained to be of immediate practical use, but it can be analyzed and summarized so as to produce insightful progress reports for teachers, researchers, and the students themselves. We use these data to assess students' understanding of the subject matter, as well as to provide indices of their model-based inquiry within a domain. Logging students' data in this way provides researchers with a "bird's eye view into the black box" (Gobert, 2005), permitting a different lens on human learning than think alouds (Ericsson & Simon, 1980), which are often used to "get at" real-time learning processes. Logging students' interactions in this way provides us a trace of what students are doing without the face validity problems that can be encountered when using think aloud protocols (Nisbett & DeCamp Wilson, 1977). Additionally, logging complements think aloud protocols in that the two sources of data can be triangulated; in fact, early in the design phase of BioLogica, think aloud protocols were collected as indices of what the students were thinking as they proceeded through the activities. Think aloud data provided us some critical information about what scaffolding would be needed for students.

The first hypermodel we produced, and the one to be described in this paper, was *BioLogica,* a scriptable version of GenScope written in Java so as to run on the Windows, Macintosh, and Linux operating systems. In contrast to GenScope, BioLogica was designed as a more tightly scaffolded sequence of activities designed to teach students about Mendelian genetics through their interactions with the software. This scaffolding was intended to not only improve the students' model-based learning (Gobert & Buckley, 2000), but also to strengthen their inquiry skills in the context of their exploration of the underlying genetics model. Next we describe in more detail the theoretical framework underlying our activities and scaffolding.

Theoretical Framework: Model-Based Learning

The theoretical framework that guided the development of BioLogica activities and the scaffolding implemented in the Modeling Across the Curriculum (MAC) project stems from a synthesis of research in cognitive psychology and science education. As shown in Fig. 3.1, model-based learning (MBL) is a dynamic, recursive process of learning by constructing mental models (Gobert & Buckley, 2000). In the MAC project, it occurs through the interaction with the hypermodels of each domain. Model-based reasoning (MBR) involves the formation, testing, and reinforcement, revision, or rejection of mental models during interaction with hypermodels and other representations. MBL requires modeling skills and reasoning during which mental models are used to create and/or understand representations, generate predictions and explanations, transform knowledge from one representation to another, analyze data, and solve problems. It is analogous to the hypothesis development and testing observed among scientists (Clement, 1989).

In the classroom many factors influence the learner's mental models including characteristics of students and teachers such as their understanding of the nature of scientific models (Justi & Gilbert, 2002; Lederman, 2006; Gobert, O'Dwyer, Horwitz, Buckley, Levy, & Wilensky, revisions submitted). We now discuss evidence that students' use of hypermodels such as BioLogica can provide important information about both classroom usage and student learning.

Using a progressive model-building approach (White & Frederiksen, 1998), we developed 12 BioLogica activities that guide students through interaction with basic models of meiosis and fertilization and progress through increasingly elaborate models of inheritance.

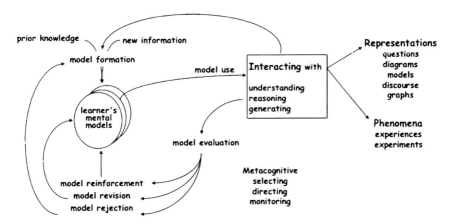

Fig. 3.1 Model-based learning framework

Scaffolding Model-Based Learning

In the MAC project we formalized the scaffolding that guides feedback to students. General scaffolds are based on a large research base in educational psychology and include: (a) advance organizers to evoke prior knowledge and provide students with a structure to fill in the concepts, (b) orienting tasks to give the student a cognitive goal for the task, (c) post organizers to encourage students to reflect on and concretize what they have just learned, and (d) a glossary of terms.

We implemented five model-based scaffolding elements to support the knowledge acquisition and reasoning required for progressive model-building (Gobert, Buckley, & Clarke, 2004).

- *Representational assistance* to guide students' understanding of representations or domain-specific conventions.
- *Model pieces acquisition* to focus students' attention on the perceptual components of the representations and to support their learning of one or more aspects (spatial, causal, functional, temporal) of the phenomenon or process under study.
- *Model pieces integration* to help students combine model components in order to come to a deeper understanding of how they work together as a causal system.
- *Model-based reasoning* to guide students' reasoning with their models.
- *Reconstruct, Reify, and Reflect* to encourage students to refer back to what they have learned, reinforce it, and then reflect to move to a deeper level of understanding.

Scaffolding of each type was implemented in the form of questions, assigned tasks, or explanations that focused on a phase of model-based learning, followed by feedback. The nature of the feedback varied according to the pedagogical purpose of the scaffolding. For example, we sometimes taught learners how to check their own answers, and we also used students' actions or answers to tailor the feedback that they received.

Activity Description

In all, we developed 12 BioLogica activities. Here we present a detailed description of the introductory activity. The remaining activities are described briefly in the appendix to this chapter.

The first activity in the BioLogica sequence is intended to introduce students to the idea that observed differences among organisms may be due to their genes. As we did with GenScope, we illustrate this and other concepts using dragons as a fictitious species.[5] The introductory activity starts off with a blank screen and just two buttons: one for creating male dragons, the other for creating females. Once the students have created their first dragon, they are asked to describe it, and then to make enough additional dragons to fill up the screen. BioLogica's dragons can differ in several ways: presence or absence of horns or wings, shape of tail, number of legs, color, and ability to breathe fire among others. These physical traits (which represent the dragon's *phenotype*) are randomly chosen each time a dragon is created, so the dragons on the computer screen tend to look quite different from one another. The students are asked to describe these differences. They are then introduced to some vocabulary, following which they are requested to "Click a dragon to see that dragon's genotype." (See Fig. 3.2.)

The students are then shown representations of chromosomes as box-like objects with lines drawn across them to represent the locations of genes. This depiction of chromosomes is common in biology textbooks and is intended to represent the linear nature of the DNA molecule that is at the core of the chromosome. BioLogica's chromosomes differ from the ones in the textbook, however, as they are "active": that is, one can alter the form of their genes and immediately observe the effect of the change, if any, on the organism. Most of the genes in the fictional dragon genome are actually modeled on those Mendel investigated in his famous pea experiments. They come in only two variants, or "alleles," and these combine according to Mendel's First Law.[6] The students are not told this, however. Rather, they are led to uncover this pattern, as well as the more complicated patterns of the other genes, by direct experimentation.[7] Once the students have made a certain number of changes in their dragons, BioLogica takes them back to the screen where they made the original eight dragons. It requests that they click on a dragon of the opposite sex, monitors to make sure they have done so, then puts up a new screen in which the students can compare the chromosomes of the two genders of dragon, and discover for themselves the differences between them.

After some questions and simple tasks, this introductory BioLogica activity eventually challenges the students to match their manipulable dragons to a "target" dragon of fixed phenotype. We explicitly chose not to mention that this can only be done with one of the dragons (because male and female dragons are different colors), but instead allow the students to uncover this fact independently.

All data collected by a BioLogica activity (which, in addition to students' answers to questions, can include the number of times they change a gene from one allele to another, or whether or not they examine the chromosomes of a particular organism using the "chromosome tool") is stored and made available for research. It is very easy, for example, to administer pre- and posttests in this way and to collect and score the data automatically. Indeed, from a software point of view, the assessments that were administered to the students were simply BioLogica activi-

---

[5] We use dragons for two reasons: (a) since everyone knows that they are imaginary, we can simplify their genetics without doing violence to the complexity of real organisms, and (b) by avoiding even a vague reference to real organisms (e.g., humans), we are able to postpone discussions of ethical and legal issues until the students have learned the science underlying them.

[6] One of the alleles is "dominant," the other "recessive." If an organism inherits one or two copies of the dominant allele it will exhibit the dominant trait; if it has two copies of the recessive allele it will exhibit the recessive trait.

[7] Note that this kind of computer activity is not a "simulation"; that is, even if one could alter an organism's genes, one would not expect the organism itself to react to the change.

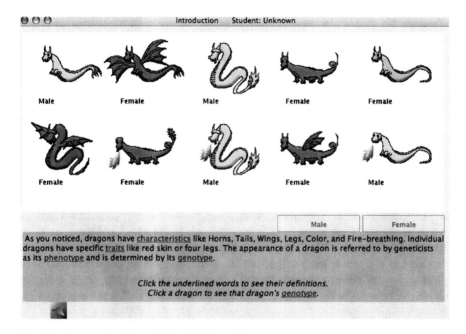

Fig. 3.2 A screen shot from the Introduction activity

ties consisting entirely of questions, which were made to look just like traditional paper-and-pencil items. It is important to note that for all BioLogica activities, answers to open-response questions are not parsed or analyzed in any way by the computer. The reason for including such questions, therefore, is not to influence future actions on the part of the computer, but to give students a chance to explain their state of knowledge, and to encourage them to reflect on what they have learned. All freestyle answers to essay questions are recorded by BioLogica, however, and made available to the teacher (as well as to researchers). This enables the answers to be evaluated and used as a component of the student's grade.[8]

Throughout all the BioLogica activities, we scaffolded students' interactions with the hypermodels as they worked their way through increasingly complex tasks. Within each activity we faded the scaffolding as they progressed. In the following section we describe the technological infrastructure underlying BioLogica, which permits fine-grained monitoring and logging of students' interactions within the activities.

Technological Details

To understand how a hypermodel works, it is helpful to take a look at the structure of the software itself. Hypermodels consist of three separate software layers embedded in an architecture designed to separate functions relating to domain content from more general ones relating to pedagogy (see Fig. 3.3).

At the lowest level of the hypermodel architecture is the *domain content engine.* This consists of a set of loosely coupled components, or *views,* which may be combined and integrated in a variety of ways. For instance, in the BioLogica hypermodel described above, the chromosome view and the organism view share a common database that contains, among other things, the genotype of every organism created so far. One of these views uses this information to display alleles on chromosomes, whereas the other, operating with a set of built-in rules, determines and displays the phenotype of each organism. Manipulations performed in the chromosome view that change a gene, say from a dominant to a recessive form, will be reflected, as appropriate, as changes in an organism's phenotype, represented in the organism view by, for example, the presence or absence of horns on a graphic of a dragon. Each view in BioLogica is implemented as a Java class, and each is capable of saving its state using the XML markup language. BioLogica's views are purposely kept quite simple. They are incapable of operating independently, but must be placed on the screen and configured by the next level up in the hierarchy, *Pedagogica.*

Pedagogica, as the name suggests, handles all things pedagogical. It is responsible for all interface details, including the placement of text boxes, buttons, and domain engine views in various locations on the screen. Pedagogica also controls the flow of an activity by shifting from one set of views to another in response to student

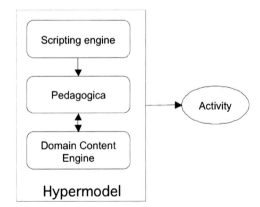

Fig. 3.3 Architecture of a hypermodel

---

[8] Without such formal accountability, we have found, students tend to ignore both the question and the answer.

actions. Pedagogica can set up "listeners," which are software agents that monitor views and other objects, and report at runtime on changes in their contents or properties. This enables the software, for instance, to react whenever a new organism is created, or when the student selects a gamete for fertilization. Since Pedagogica can communicate with the student through graphics and text, curriculum developers can use it to pose multiple-choice, survey, and open-response questions. It also controls the collection and storage of data, maintains and controls access to student records, and manages the registration and login functions.

Pedagogica is itself controlled by the third software layer, the *scripting layer*, which has the job of interpreting short scripts written in the Javascript language. These scripts implement the activities that the students actually see and interact with. They introduce the subject matter and configure the domain content engine appropriately (for instance, presenting two "parent" organisms with particular genotypes). They then monitor the students' actions, reacting to them as appropriate, and communicating occasionally with the students as they proceed with their investigations.

Processing Log Files to Support Research

The BioLogica hypermodels enabled not only just-in-time feedback to students as they worked through instructional activities, but also multilevel, longitudinal classroom-based research of student learning. The log files generated when students used BioLogica activities provided evidence about how BioLogica was used in classrooms as well as about students' developing knowledge and inquiry skills.

In order to do this, we first had to be sure that the data from which we were generating inferences and conclusions were accurate representations of what students were doing as they used BioLogica. This was accomplished by a series of verification and reduction steps, beginning with the comparison of log files with video of the computer screen recorded as students used the learning activities (Buckley et al., 2004). After we were certain that the log files accurately captured student actions and answers, we began the process of reducing them to forms and formats that were useful for reporting data to teachers and for importing data into a statistical package.

By creating activities with objects that automatically logged the same types of data each time they were used, we were able to structure the log files to support the data reduction algorithms used to make them useful for teachers and researchers. Each session generated hundreds of pages of raw log files, which would have been intractable were it not for the XML tags used to structure the output. Fig. 3.4 provides an excerpt depicting the data from a student crossing two dragons while looking at the wings pedigree.

As can be seen, data in this form are difficult to read, but can be used to verify accuracy. To provide a more accessible format, we processed the raw logs to produce a chronological report of the student's actions and answers. The example

```
Characteristic being observed: Trait: Wings
  </message>
  </action>
  <date> 2005.02.15.13.23.10 02/15/05 | 13:23:10 </date>
  <message>
    Genotype of mother: Hh,SS,ww,Ll,Tt,pp,Ff,Aa,BB
  </message>
  </action>
  <date> 2005.02.15.13.23.10 02/15/05 | 13:23:10 </date>
  <message>
    Genotype of father: Hh,SS,WW,Ll,Tt,p,F,a,B
  </message>
  </action>
  <date> 2005.02.15.13.23.10 02/15/05 | 13:23:10 </date>
  <message>
    Generation of mother: 0
  </message>
  </action>
  <date> 2005.02.15.13.23.10 02/15/05 | 13:23:10 </date>
  <message>
    Generation of father: 0
  </message>
  </action>
  <date> 2005.02.15.13.23.10 02/15/05 | 13:23:10 </date>
  <message>
    number of offspring: 40
  </message>
  </action>
```

Fig. 3.4 Example from raw log file depicting data from one cross

shown in Fig. 3.5 is the same cross shown in the raw log. This format is much easier to read and compare to student actions.

The report provides information in a useful form concerning a single student working on a single activity. In order to compare student performances on the same activity, we integrated chronological reports across students to produce a summary report like the one shown in Fig. 3.6 in which each student's use of an activity is reported in a single row in a table. The excerpt shown includes data about one task (T4) during which the student successfully completed the task by performing three crosses in 11.3 min. The excerpt also shows the autoscoring of student performance (T4cat) and the student's use of the various tools available for completing the task.

We also generated statistical reports that contained similar information about each student's interaction with each learning activity, but aggregated all of a student's sessions with one activity into one record. Statistical reports concatenated all answers and applied the autoscoring algorithms to the aggregated actions.

All of these various data reductions and report formats were useful in developing the algorithms for autoscoring and summarizing student actions, and for verifying the accuracy of the statistical records. As shown in Fig. 3.7, each raw XML file was

Elapsed Time	Interval (sec)	Action	Trait / node / question ID	Mother's genotype/ Student response	Generation/ score	Father's genotype/ Student response	Generation/ score	# offspring
13:23:10		Cross	wings	Hh,SS,ww,Ll,Tt,pp,Ff,Aa,BB	0	Hh,SS,WW,Ll,Tt,p,F,a,B	0	40

Fig. 3.5 Excerpt from Chronological Report depictingv the same cross shown earlier

Student ID	Class ID	Date	Total duration (min)	T4 Time	Success	Q42A	Tries	Crosses	T4 cat	F1 Crosses	cross	chromo 1	Snip 1	Snip Fam	read genome chart	Genome chart time (s)	Punnett Square	Task Desc
15021	5174	Tue Feb 15 12:52:32 CST 2005	34.2	11.3	1	I		3	WWxWw, wwxWw, wwxWW	B	1	4	11	12	2	1	4	0	95

Fig. 3.6 Excerpt from Summary Report summarizing student performance on Task 4

parsed to produce a concise report (the chronological file of student actions and answers). After carefully analyzing 6–12 concise reports, we created specifications for generating summary records from the raw XML files. To verify that the summary records were accurate, we compared the summary records of a different set of 6–12 logs to their corresponding concise reports. We found that students often took unpredictable actions that our original specifications did not adequately address. At this point, we corrected any errors in the specifications and in the summary report generator. We then analyzed the summary reports for students who had used an activity more than once, in order to develop specifications for how to aggregate their records to reflect the nature and extent of their interaction with a given activity. Pretests and posttests were treated as special cases because their purpose was to measure the students' knowledge and understanding at a given point in time, rather than to document their learning process.

We also created an implementation report generator that calculated for each student the gap (in days) between their last activity use and when they took the posttest[9] as well as what percentage of the core activities they had used. We used this report to calculate each student's BioLogica "dose." We averaged these by class as needed for statistical analysis. For a more complete description of the decisions that went into the development of summary and statistical records, please see (Buckley et al., 2004; Buckley, Gobert et al. (in press)).

---

[9] Early in the implementation we found that some teachers delayed administering the posttest until they were reminded that they would not receive their stipend for the year until we had their data.

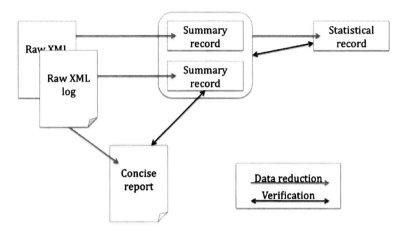

Fig. 3.7 Log file reductions and verification

Analyses Enabled by Logging Infrastructure

With the data available through the logging infrastructure, we conducted analyses that ranged from how many schools, classrooms and students were using our activities on any given day to what, for example, Student 32653 did when working on Task 2 in Monohybrid.

In the Modeling Across the Curriculum (MAC) project over the course of 3 years and three domains we collected log files generated by the work of 8,342 students in 411 classrooms in 61 schools taught by 146 teachers worldwide. For BioLogica alone we analyzed data from over 1,200 students in 54 classrooms. Due to the popularity of GenScope, we collected data from schools outside the group of recruited and supported member schools. Seventeen classrooms, comprising 573 students, were classified as Contributing Classrooms, which were classrooms whose teachers downloaded the software from the website, installed and used it with only minimal support from project staff. This very clearly demonstrated the scalability of the Modeling Across the Curriculum project.

We also implemented data quality criteria against which to judge the data included in our final analyses. For example, we excluded classrooms in which fewer than 50% of the class took both the pretest and posttest, reasoning that the data collected in such classrooms were unlikely to be sufficiently representative of the class as a whole. We also excluded logs that were less than 5 min in duration, on the basis that such a short time does not constitute a learning activity.

Learning Gains Versus Implementation Variables

We confined our exploration of student learning gains as a function of implementation variables to evidence that could be obtained by sifting through the massive amounts of log file data available. We considered time on task, but found that criterion to be a reliable indicator only in carefully controlled situations. For example, there are instances in which the student walks away from the computer without quitting the application and the log file isn't closed until the next time the computer is used (possibly as long as over the weekend). There are also the usual variations due to students' reading skills or stopping while a teacher talks; these are factors that we cannot tease out of our data.

Many iterations regarding how to conceptualize implementation variables in this context resulted in our adopting the following variables:

- The percentage of the core (nonoptional) activities used by a student for at least 5 min (referred to as *%Core*).
- Length of the intervention (referred to as *LOI*); calculated by subtracting the pretest date from the posttest date.
- Number of calendar days that elapsed between the last instructional activity used and the posttest date (referred to as PostTestGap).
- Time spent with instructional activities (referred to as *netLOI*); calculated by subtracting the PostTestGap from the LOI.

These variables were computed for each student, and their means and standard deviations were computed for each class. Subsequent analyses were done using these as predictor variables in order to better understand learning gains. Note that as the predictor variables are related to each other and therefore not independent, they were entered in the regression models individually.

In Table 3.1, we display the averages for the classes in which students achieved significant gains and those classes in which students did not.

From this table, it appears that successful classes used more activities over a longer period of time. Since students were clustered within classrooms, a traditional OLS regression approach would likely underestimate the standard errors associated with the regression coefficients and therefore increase the Type I error rate (Raudenbush & Bryk, 2002). We estimated this clustering effect by calculating the intraclass correlation coefficient (ICC) and found that approximately 50% of the variability in the posttest scores existed between classes. To account for this effect we constructed hierarchical linear models using data from 684 students clustered within 37 classes and including a random class effect.

Although some teachers taught more than one class, we had insufficient statistical power to estimate the variability between classrooms within teachers. Out of the 16 teachers who had their students interact with the hypermodels, four taught one class, six taught two classes, three taught three classes, and three taught four classes. Although there is a chance that the confounding of the variability among classes within teacher could contribute to biased estimates of the standard errors for the regression coefficients, we expect this effect to be negligible.

Table 3.1 BioLogica implementation data clustered by significant vs. nonsignificant gains

| BioLogica | #Classes | #Students | Yield | Implementation variables | | | | Learning measures | | | | |
				%Core	LOI	PostTestGap	Net LOI	Pretest	Posttest	Gain	Hake	Effect size
Overall	37	708	0.86	62	28	11	17	14.8	19.2	4.4	0.23	0.65
Significant gains	28	532	0.85	68	35	14	21	15.3	21.0	5.6	0.31	0.84
Nonsignificant gains	9	176	0.89	42	10	3	7	13.2	13.5	0.4	-0.02	0.05

Upon running multiple regressions, we found that the pretest scores accounted for 28.22% of the variance in the posttest scores. Holding pretest constant, *%core* activities accounted for an additional 10.83% of the variance in the posttest scores (see Table 3.2). Neither *PostTest Gap*, *LOI*, nor *net LOI* were significant predictors of posttest performance, nor did they account for any more of the variance in the posttest scores after holding the pretest scores constant.

Since all of our data is collected automatically and online, we are able to conduct large-scale research involving potentially tens of thousands of students.[10] The only issue limiting the scale of the research is the necessity for assuring adequate fidelity of implementation across multiple sites that are geographically remote from one another. The data reported so far pertains to such fidelity and involves classroom-grained variables. However, as we will see in the following section, hypermodels also support research at a very small grain size, but still involving very large numbers of students.

Performance Assessments: Information Inferred from Actions

We illustrate this type of research by describing one task in Monohybrid, a core activity that is crucial to understanding monohybrid inheritance and Mendelian genetics. Monohybrid Task 2 is an embedded, formative assessment that enables us to determine whether students:

1. Hold the naïve view of genetics that "like begets like,"
2. Can complete a Punnett square,
3. Know the allele combination that produces dragons with two legs, and
4. Can use the Punnett square to estimate the number of two-legged offspring that result from breeding a pair of two-legged parents.

In Task 2 (see beginning screen in Fig. 3.8), we present students with a pair of two-legged dragons represented by the half-filled square and circle at the top of the window. Note that the cross tool is grayed out, indicating that it is inactive. We ask students to predict how many legs their offspring will have when they use the cross tool (represented by an X) to breed the two parent dragons. As they have previously learned, they can use the cross to breed dragons: selecting it and dragging from one dragon to another of the opposite sex. This opens up a "family tree" representation with a predetermined number of offspring generated by the content engine according to the rules of inheritance. When students have made a prediction they are required to fill out a Punnett square[11] correctly, accessing a tutorial if

---

[10]The MAC Project ultimately involved over 8,000 students, spanning three different science disciplines.

[11]A Punnett square is a representation of a cross between two organisms. In its simplest form it consists of a two-by-two matrix representing all possible combinatorial outcomes involving the transmission of a single gene with two alleles from parents to offspring.

Table 3.2 Regression on implementation variables for BioLogica

	Model 1		Model 2		Model 3		Model 4		Model 5	
	Coeff. (s.e.)	Sig.	Coeff. (s.e.)	Sig.	Coeff. (s.e.)	Sig.	Coeff. (s.e.)	Sig.	Coeff. (s.e.)	Sig.
Intercept	12.53 (0.91)	<0.001	8.36 (1.09)	<0.001	12.83 (1.11)	<0.001	12.77 (0.94)	<0.001	12.35 (0.96)	<0.001
Pretest scores	0.45 (0.04)	<0.001	0.43 (0.04)	<0.001	0.45 (0.04)	<0.001	0.45 (0.04)	<0.001	0.45 (0.04)	<0.001
% Core			0.07 (0.01)	<0.001						
LOI					-0.01 (0.02)	0.651				
PostTestGap							-0.02 (0.02)	0.349		
Net LOI									0.00 (0.00)	0.553
R^2 (%)	28.22		39.05		28.22		28.22		28.22	

Dependent variable: posttest scores on BioLogica assessment
Coeff. coefficient, *Sig.* significance, *s.e.* standard error

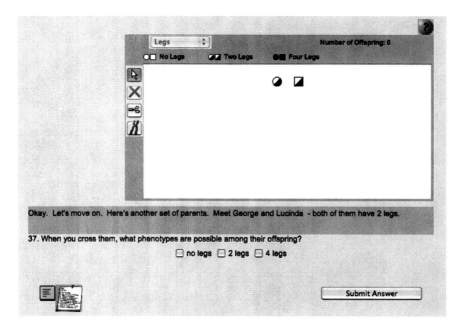

Fig. 3.8 Task 2 opening screen. The half-filled circle and square represent, respectively, a two-legged female and a two-legged male dragon. The icons along the *left side* represent, from *top to bottom*, the selection tool, the cross tool, the snip tool (used to delete unwanted organisms), and the chromosome-observing tool

needed. Students are then asked to identify which cells of the completed Punnett square correspond to offspring with two legs and to use that information to estimate the number of two-legged offspring resulting from the crossing of two-legged parents. At that point the cross tool is enabled and students are directed to use it to check their predictions against model-generated "experimental" data.

As students proceed through this task the hypermodel logs their prediction (multiple selections are possible), how many times they fill in the Punnett square and the alleles they enter for each attempt, how many times they try to select the correct alleles in the Punnett square and the alleles in the cells they select, their estimate of the offspring that will be produced, and whether they thought their prediction was borne out by the data generated when they crossed the dragons. This gives us considerable data regarding the nature of their initial predictions and their procedural knowledge for various inquiry skills, including interpreting their data.

In principle, these data enable us to provide information to teachers about their students' performances on this task. However, since the data analysis was not complete at the time of implementation, such reports were not actually produced in real time, though they were eventually made available to researchers. Table 3.3 provides an example of how the top level of such a report might appear. It shows the distribution of students by response or number of tries. Note that in the prediction column both the naïve and correct responses are marked. What this table tells the researchers is

Table 3.3 Report designed for teachers and researchers

Time range (min)	Prediction Q37R	#Students	%Students	Punnett square completion Tries	#Students	Punnett square selection Tries	#Students	Estimate offspring Q38R	#Students
2.1–6.5	A	3	1%	1	205	1	193	A	10
	B[a]	64	25%	2	9	2	5	B	14
	C	10	4%	3	3	3	29	C[b]	197
	CA	1	0%	>3	25	4	3	D	14
	CB	13	5%			5	6	E	6
	CBA[b]	127	50%			>5	11		
	BA	34	13%						
	Total answers	252			242		247		241
	Item difficulty		0.50		0.85		0.78		0.82

[a] Naïve conception
[b] Correct answer

that the prediction question has a difficulty level of 0.50 since 50% of the students got it right, but that 25% of them still hold the naïve conception that "like begets like." The remainder of the task shows us that a high percentage of the students have mastered the procedural skills necessary for the tasks that follow this one. A teacher given such a report on the web could double-click on the responses or number of tries indicating students having difficulty and get a list of those students for follow-up intervention.

For teachers' grading and our statistical analyses, student performances were also autoscored according to a rubric that allotted points for correct answers and completing the Punnett squares tasks with few attempts. We examined the relationship between performance on Task 2 (*Predict*) as represented by the Task 2 score and performance on the other Monohybrid tasks (3 and 4) and on the posttest (holding the pretest constant). Task 3 (*Produce*) asks "what parental genotypes would result in all the offspring having two legs?", requiring students to reason from effect to cause. Students must set the genotypes of the parents, breed them, and check the result. Task 4 (*Skip*) is an unscaffolded transfer task that asks the students to demonstrate the genetic mechanism that causes traits to appear to skip a generation, requiring that students reason over three generations.

Based on data from students who used the Monohybrid activity in 2005–2006 (including those who took both the pre- and posttests), we conducted correlations and found that all three tasks were weakly but significantly correlated with total pretest scores; additionally, Task 2 scores were significantly correlated with both Task 3 and Task 4 scores (Table 3.4). Further analyses are underway to examine the relationships between these three tasks (Buckley et al., in press).

Table 3.4 Correlations among total pretest scores and task scores

	Total score pretest	Task 2 – predict	Task 3 – produce	Task 4 – skip
Total score pretest	1.00	–	–	–
Task 2 – predict	0.29[a]	1.00	–	–
Task 3 – produce	0.29[a]	0.56[a]	1.00	–
Task 4 – skip	0.24[a]	0.34[a]	0.31[a]	1.00

[a] Correlation is significant at the 0.01 level (two-tailed)

As shown in the above analyses, students' interactions with hypermodels provide fine-grained data that can be analyzed so that researchers can examine the inquiry performances of individual students in a sophisticated way, as well as do this on a large scale. Additionally, teacher reports can both summarize and describe the performances of their students, and data can be aggregated to provide large-scale measures for administrators and policy makers.

Limitations of This Work

One of the goals of the MAC project was to provide reports on students' progress to the teachers in real time. We succeeded in doing this for the embedded question-and-answer assessments, however, the analyses and autoscoring of students' performance data was not complete in time for us to provide performance assessment data to teachers. For example, we were not able to point out to them, the students who consistently filled out Punnett Squares incorrectly, or made aimless crosses in the Invisible Dragons task. This was unfortunate because, as we have seen, performance data from specific tasks such as these turned out to be predictive of students' posttest learning. There remains an empirical question as to the level of teacher professional development that would have been necessary in order for teachers to benefit from these performance reports. Some potential barriers and/or difficulties here are: implementing inquiry-based activities into instruction (de Jong et al., 2005), and tailoring instruction for individual students (Fadel et al., 2007). Providing teachers with inquiry tasks that are scaffolded for student use, as we did with BioLogica, could potentially alleviate implementation difficulties – in fact, these were designed for this purpose. Simply providing performance assessment reports about students' learning is likely not enough support for teachers to tailor instruction for individual students, rather, these provide a necessary but not sufficient condition for teachers to determine what individual students need. Below we describe some recent work that may address these difficulties.

One of the most frustrating limitations of the BioLogica software initially was that the computer did not store and recall from one session to the next where the student was in an activity. Thus, at the end of a class period students who had not completed an activity would not be able to save it, and would be forced to start it at the beginning the next time they logged on. During the course of the MAC Project we were able to provide a partial solution to this problem by breaking the activities up into short, semantically meaningful chunks and enabling students to navigate directly between these. But the inability to "save state" was nevertheless a constant source of annoyance to students and teachers alike. We continue to work on this issue in our current research.

Finally, there is the issue of scalability. As a standalone application, BioLogica is relatively easy to install,[12] though it does require the prior installation of Java 1.4 or higher in order to run. However, in this mode the user receives few of the benefits of the data logging that have occupied so much of the foregoing discussion. True, the versions of BioLogica activities that we have put up on the server do create reports automatically whenever the user quits them, but these reports must be separately saved and retrieved, and their results are difficult to aggregate across multiple students or multiple activities. One reason for this is that when it runs as a standalone activity, BioLogica cannot take advantage of a server to use as a central repository for data.

Another, more fundamental, problem arises from the fact that in order to produce aggregated data across students, BioLogica must have access to those students' identities. If we are to produce a report that summarizes how an entire Biology class is doing, for instance, the students in that class must be recognizable entities to the software that produces and analyzes the data. This implies that each student must have a unique account that is accessible to the software. If the reports are to be used to give the students a grade, then they must be continually backed up and protected against vandalism and fraud. The difficulty of supporting such a complex data storage and retrieval process exceeds the resources of all but the most technologically advanced schools.

Next Steps

One of the major goals of our future work will be to "close the loop" by giving teachers the kind of detailed and insightful information that the MAC research team was only able to glean after months of careful analysis. Researchers at the Concord Consortium have started work on a 5-year project, funded by the National Science Foundation, called "Logging Opportunities in Online Programs for Science,"[13] which is creating timely, valid, and actionable reports to teachers based on logs of student actions generated in the course of using online curriculum materials. These reports will enable teachers to make data-informed decisions about alternative teaching strategies. An important goal of future research is to observe how teachers integrate such reports into their practice.

---

[12] Versions for Windows and MAC OS computers are available for free download at http://mac.concord.org/downloads/.

[13] NSF Project # 0733299.

One of the unavoidable consequences of moving from an open-ended, constructivist technology, as typified by GenScope, to the more tightly structured and scaffolded BioLogica activities is that, in their present form at least, the latter cannot easily adapt to individual students. Some students demand more structure than others, some are intimidated by a challenge that requires them to explore new territory, while others become bored when told step by step what to do. One solution to this problem would be to create several alternative versions of each activity and to leave it up to the teacher and/or the student to decide on which one to choose, or to modify the activity in real time as new performance is acquired. Such an approach might ultimately result in the creation of a technology capable of dynamically customizing itself to suit students' individual needs and desires. For instance, one can imagine an adaptive activity that starts out highly structured and then strips off its scaffolding progressively in response to student actions indicating increased understanding and self-confidence. The Science ASSISTments projects are developing assessments for science inquiry that both instruct and assess[14] (Gobert, Heffernan, Ruiz, & Kim, 2007; Gobert, Heffernan, Koedinger, & Beck, 2008). The assessment modules will examine students' log files to detect such "buggy" inquiry behavior as repeating trials or moving further from the target goal. The system is being designed to provide teachers with feedback as to their students' inquiry skills, as aligned to the NSES inquiry standards (National Research Council, 1996), as well as to intervene and tutor students on inquiry skills in real time.

Before such advances can be practical in educational terms, however, the process of creating sound educational activities must be simplified. It will never be trivial to design educationally effective curriculum materials, regardless of their technological basis, but the development of hypermodels such as those we have described requires a knowledge of programming far exceeding that of most teachers or curriculum developers. This severely limits the pool of potential designers of hypermodel-based curriculum. With this limitation in mind, the Concord Consortium has been experimenting with several alternative authoring environments that we expect will someday replace the cumbersome and obsolete Activity Construction Editor that forms part of Pedagogica. For example, the Technology Enhanced Learning in Science (TELS) Center, a joint project between Concord Consortium and the University of California at Berkeley, has worked on a Scalable Architecture for Interactive Learning (SAIL) a software environment that, when fully implemented, will support reuse and adaptation of interoperable components, making it possible to implement interactive curriculum and assessments by working at a very high level (Slotta, 2010).

The Concord Consortium's Molecular Workbench (MW) tool (http://mw.concord.org) is an example of an easily authorable environment. MW models can be embedded in a browser-like environment that links them to other interface objects like text boxes and buttons. A simple but increasingly powerful scripting language

---

[14] The terms "Assistments" was coined by Ken Koedinger for the Math Assistments program that was developed by him and Neil Heffernan.

enables an activity author to configure various aspects of the MW model, and offers a modest degree of runtime control. Another authoring environment produced by Concord Consortium, called DIY (for "Do It Yourself"), generalizes similar capabilities to other educational affordances, such as probeware and third-party interactive applets. We anticipate that all these different technologies will be integrated within a few years, making it possible for nonprogrammers to create complex and engaging curriculum activities and interactive assessments.

Lastly, none of the technologies discussed in this paper provide direct support to students for collaborative work. It would have been very helpful in the MAC Project, for instance, if students could have shared their activities as they were working on them. This would have enabled them to show their work to each other and to ask each other for help when needed. It would also have been useful if the teacher could have called up an individual student's work, either to go over it with that student or to show it to the class as a whole. We have been working on ways to make all the models and other objects that we use "serializable" – that is, to translate them into a set of instructions that will enable a computer to recreate them in their current state. Once that goal is accomplished, a student who wishes to share any of these objects, either with another student, with the teacher, or with the entire class, will be able to do so simply by transmitting instructions that will enable the recipient's computer to recreate the originator's model.

This brings up the intriguing possibility that students could be prompted by the computer to ask for help as they progress through an activity. A classroom server would keep track of each student's or group's progress and could link up students, either automatically or under control of the teacher, in pedagogically productive ways. Any communication or object sharing initiated by students using this technology would itself be monitored and could be used either by the teacher or as input to a research project concerned with the effects of technology-mediated collaboration.

The lack of technological infrastructure in most schools, as exemplified in the limitations section above, poses the major obstacle to using the hypermodel approach to instruction and assessment and in particular, scaling up technologies such as ours and others mentioned here. The difficulties in scaling up should come as no surprise; it is as though we have built a high performance automobile and demonstrated that it can go 80 miles/h but there are as yet very few paved roads on which to drive it. The situation is by no means hopeless, but the solution may take a while – recall that the interstate highway system was not launched until nearly 50 years after the introduction of the first mass-produced cars. We can only hope that the significant potential impact of computers in education will be achieved in less time than that!

Appendix: Description of the BioLogica Activities

1. *Introduction.* The *Introduction* activity, described in detail above, enables the students to develop a familiarity with the software as well as with the basic concepts of genetics. It provides an initial guiding question: What do dragons look like and why?

2. *Rules*. The *Rules* activity introduces students to dominance relationships among alleles while helping them learn the rules of inheritance in dragons in order to understand how genes affect appearance. The activity is in three parts: *Dominant and Recessive Relationships Among Alleles* focuses on which alleles are dominant and therefore mask the presence of other alleles for a gene. The students identify all possible combinations of alleles that produce a particular trait in an organism. *Some Traits are X-Linked* focuses on genes that are located on the X chromosome. Students investigate the impact of different allele combinations for X-linked genes. *Color and Fatal Combinations* examines polygenicity and the affect of lethal alleles using the two Color genes of BioLogica's dragons. Students explore what happens when more than one gene contributes to a single characteristic and learn about an allelic combination that is lethal.

3. *Meiosis*. This activity builds on *Introduction and Rules* and requires students to use what they learned about dragon genotypes and phenotypes to complete a series of challenges in order to address why members of a family do not always look alike. The first subactivity, *Introduction to Meiosis,* focuses on learning to use the meiosis model of BioLogica, understanding how chromosomes and alleles participate in meiosis, and linking the meiosis model's representations of gametes and chromosomes with the representations of those objects in the chromosome model, introduced previously. The meiosis model simulates the process of meiosis in a fashion similar to the diagrams of the phases of meiosis found in textbooks. The second subactivity, called *Designer Dragons,* challenges the students to create specific offspring bvy examining the chromosomes in the gametes of each parent and selecting those that will produce the desired phenotype in the offspring.

4. *Horns Dilemma*. This optional activity may be used as an enrichment experience for students who are looking for a challenge or as an assessment of students' models of meiosis and fertilization. It focuses on the inheritance of recessive traits, posing the question, "Can two horned parents have a hornless baby?" and challenging students to produce a hornless dragon from two parents that have horns, using knowledge gained in the previous activities.

5. *Monohybrid*. This activity is at the core of the BioLogica curriculum. It is here that students encounter for the first time the intergenerational consequences of the genetic processes they have been studying. The activity is in four parts. *Introduction to Pedigrees* teaches students how to use BioLogica's pedigree level to create and analyze pedigrees. *Pedigrees and Punnett Squares, Oh My!* makes connections between independent assortment in meiosis, random selection in fertilization, predictions made with Punnett squares, and breeding experiments that use the pedigree level tools. *Studying Patterns of Inheritance Using Pedigrees and Punnett Squares* guides students' reasoning as they determine probabilities for the inheritance of particular traits. Part four of the activity, *An Inheritance Puzzle,* challenges

students to put everything they have learned in the previous three parts together in order to solve a puzzle.

6. *X-linkage*. This is another core activity in the sequence. It includes three sections designed to address the central question: "What difference does it make if a gene is located on the X Chromosome?" *Introduction to Genes that are part of the X Chromosome* reviews how a gene is inherited when it is part of the X-chromosome. *X-Linked Traits* uses the fire-breathing gene in dragons to demonstrate the inheritance patterns of sex-linked traits from one generation to the next. *Determining if a Characteristic is X-linked* focuses on pedigree analysis as a tool for discriminating between autosomal and X-linked inheritance.

7. *Mutations*. The driving question for this activity is: "What happens when you change the DNA?" Students are introduced to mutations through the appearance of a novel trait in a pedigree. They then explore the role of DNA in mutations, modifying the base pair sequences of particular dragon alleles and examining the impact of these newly created alleles on the appearance of a dragon.

8. *Mutations 2*. This optional activity poses the question: "How are mutations inherited?" It builds on Mutations and Monohybrid by enabling students to investigate how a novel allele is inherited by offspring and its affect on the inheritance of the associated phenotype. It also gives the students more practice in using Punnett squares to determine the probability of inheriting a mutated trait.

9. *Dihybrid Cross*. This activity asks the question: "What is the likelihood that two traits will be inherited together?" It focuses on the inheritance patterns for two traits at a time, and examines the differences that occur when the genes for those traits are parts of the same chromosome or parts of different chromosomes.

10. *Scales*. This is another optional activity that challenges students to investigate the mode of inheritance of a new trait, posing a series of challenges designed to teach students to reason like geneticists.

11. *Plates*. This optional activity introduces another novel trait: scaly plates on the back of the dragons' neck. Students are challenged to determine the inheritance pattern of this new trait (which is X-linked and incompletely dominant) and the location of its gene by a process that approximates the reasoning of professional geneticists.

12. *Invisible Dragons*. Invisible Dragons presents a difficult problem for the students to solve using all the techniques they have learned throughout this series of activities. They must figure out the genetic make-up of two invisible dragons, one male and one female. They may cross the parent dragons, including making backcrosses (crosses between an offspring and parent), and view any of the resulting offspring. Their challenge is to deduce the parental genotypes by observation of the phenotypes of the offspring, using as few crosses as possible.

References

Aulls, M. W. (2002). The contributions of co-occurring forms of classroom discourse and academic activities to curriculum events and instruction. *Journal of Educational Psychology, 94*(3), 520–538.

Blais, D. M. (1988). Constructivism: A theoretical revolution in teaching. *Journal of Developmental Education, 11*(3), 2–7.

Buckley, B., Gobert, J., Horwitz, P. & O'Dwyer, L. (in press). Looking inside the black box: Assessing model-based learning and inquiry in biologica. *International Journal of Learning Technologies.*

Buckley, B. C., Gobert, J. D., Kindfield, A., Horwitz, P., Tinker, R., Gerlits, B., et al. (2004). Model-based teaching and learning with BioLogica™: What do they learn? How do they learn? How do we know? *Journal of Science Education and Technology, 13*(1), 23–41.

Clement, J. (1989). Learning via model construction and criticism: Protocol evidence on sources of creativity in science. In J. Glover, R. Ronning & C. Reynolds (Eds.), *Handbook of creativity: Assessment, theory and research.* NY: Plenum.

de Jong, T., Beishuizenm, J., Hulshof, C., Prins, F., van Rijn, H., van Someren, M., et al. (2005). Determinants of discovery learning in a complex simulation learning environment. In P. Gardenfors & P. Johansson (Eds.), *Cognition, education, and communication technology.* Mawah, NJ: Erlbaum.

Driver, R., & Oldham, V. (1986). A constructivist approach to curriculum development in science. *Studies in Science Education, 13,* 105–122.

Ericsson, K. A., & Simon, H. (1980). Verbal reports as data. *Psychological Review, 87,* 215–251.

Fadel, C., Honey, M., & Pasnick, S. (2007). Assessment in the age of innovation. *Education Week, 26*(38), 34–40.

Gobert, J. (2005). Leveraging technology and cognitive theory on visualization to promote students' science learning and literacy. In J. Gilbert (Ed.), *Visualization in science education* (pp. 73–90). Dordrecht, The Netherlands: Springer-Verlag.

Gobert, J., Heffernan, N., Ruiz, C, & Kim, R. (2007). *AMI: ASSISTments Meets Inquiry.* Proposal NSF-DRL# 0733286 funded by the National Science Foundation.

Gobert, J., Heffernan, N., Koedinger, K., & Beck, J. (2008). ASSISTments Meets Science Learning (AMSL). Proposal (R305A090170) funded March 1, 2010 by the US Department of Education.

Gobert, J. D., & Buckley, B. C. (2000). Introduction to model-based teaching and learning in science education. *International Journal of Science Education, 22*(9), 891–894.

Gobert, J., Buckley, B., & Clarke, J. E. (2004). *Scaffolding model-based reasoning: Representations, cognitive affordances, and learning outcomes.* Paper presented at the American Educational Research Association, San Diego, CA.

Gobert, J., O'Dwyer, L., Horwitz, P., Buckley, B., Levy, S.T. & Wilensky, U. (revisions submitted). *Examining the relationship between students' epistemologies of models and conceptual learning in three science domains: Biology, Physics, & Chemistry.* International Journal of Science Education.

Hickey, D. T., Kindfield, A. C. H., Horwitz, P., & Christie, M. A. T. (1999). Advancing educational theory by enhancing practice in a technology-supported genetics learning environment. *Journal of Education, 181*(2), 25–55.

Hickey, D. T., Kindfield, A. C. H., Horwitz, P., & Christie, M. A. T. (2003). Integrating curriculum, instruction, assessment, and evaluation in a technology-supported genetics learning environment. *American Educational Research Journal, 40*(2), 495–538.

Hickey, D. T., Kruger, A.C., & Zuiker, S. (2003). *Design experimentation with multiple perspectives: The GenScope assessment project.* Presented at the Annual Meeting of the American Educational Research Association, Chicago, IL.

Horwitz, P. (1999). Designing Computer Models that Teach. In N. Roberts & W. Feurzeig (Eds.), *Computer Modeling and Simulation in Pre-College Science Education* (pp. 179–196): Springer Verlag.

Horwitz, P., & Christie, M. (2000). Computer-based manipulatives for teaching scientific reasoning: An example. In M. J. Jacobson & R. B. Kozma (Eds.), *Innovations in science and mathematics education: Advanced designs for technologies of learning*. Hillsdale, NJ: Lawrence Erlbaum & Associates.

Horwitz, P., Neumann, E., & Schwartz, J. (1996). Teaching science at multiple levels: The GenScope program. *Communications of the ACM, 39*(8), 179–196.

Horwitz, P., Schwartz, J., & Neumann, E. (1998). *Implementation and evaluation of the GenScope™ learning environment: Issues, solutions, and results*. Paper presented at the Third Annual International Conference of the Learning Sciences. Charlottesville, VA: Association for the Advancement of Computers in Education.

Justi, R. S., & Gilbert, J. K. (2002). Science teachers' knowledge about and attitudes towards the use of models and modeling in learning science. *International Journal of Science Education, 24*(12), 1273–1292.

Kinzie, M. B., Sullivan, H. J., & Berdel, R. L. (1988). Learner control and achievement in science computer assisted instruction. *Journal of Educational Psychology, 80*(3), 299–303.

Kirschner, P. A., Sweller, J., & Clark, R. E. (2006). Why minimal guidance during instruction dose not work: An analysis of the failure of constructivist, discovery, problem-based, experiential, and inquiry-based teaching. *Educational Psychologist, 41*(2), 75–86.

Lederman, N. G. (2006). Syntax of nature of science within inquiry and science instruction. In L. B. Flick & N. G. Lederman (Eds.), *Scientific inquiry and nature of science: Implications for teaching, learning, and teacher education*. Dordrecht, Netherlands: Springer.

Magoon, A. J. (1977). Constructivist approaches in educational research. *Review of Educational Research, 47*(4), 651–693.

National Research Council. (1996). *Inquiry and the national science education standards*. Washington, DC: National Academy Press.

Nisbett, R., & DeCamp Wilson, T. (1977). Telling more than we can know: Verbal reports on mental processes. *Psychological Review, 84*(3), 231–259.

Papert, S. (1980). *Mindstorms: Children computers and powerful ideas*. New York: Basic Books.

Raudenbush, S. W., & Bryk, A. S. (2002). *Hierarchical linear models: Applications and data analysis methods* (2nd ed.). Newbury Park, CA: Sage.

Slotta, J.D. (2010). Evolving the classroom of the future: The interplay between pedagogy, technology and community. In Mäkitalo-Siegl, K., Zottmann, J., Kaplan, F., & Fischer, F. (Eds.). *Classroom of the Future: Orchestrating collaborative spaces*. Rotterdam, the Netherlands: Sense.

Steinberg, E. R. (1977). Review of student control in computer-assisted instruction. *Journal of Computer-Based Instruction, 3*, 84–90.

Suppes, P. (1969). Computer-assisted instruction: An overview of operations and problems. Information processing. In A. J. H. Morrell (Ed.), *Information processing proceedings of IFIP congress*. Amsterdam: North-Holland.

White, B. Y., & Frederiksen, J. R. (1998). Inquiry, modeling, and metacognition: Making science accessible to all students. *Cognition and Instruction, 16*(1), 3–118.

Chapter 4
The Development of *River City*, a Multi-User Virtual Environment-Based Scientific Inquiry Curriculum: Historical and Design Evolutions

Diane Jass Ketelhut, Jody Clarke, and Brian Carl Nelson

Introduction

Science has been an integral strand in K-12 public education for the last 150 years (DeBoer, 1991). During that time, debates have raged about what should be the goals of K-12 science education and what constitutes scientific literacy. One constant goal for science education throughout the years has been that of enabling learners to experience and understand scientific inquiry. Contemporarily, organizations such as the National Research Council (NRC), the American Association for the Advancement of Science (AAAS), and the National Science Teachers Association (NSTA) have published reports and support materials that attempt to define what it means to be scientifically literate and how to foster inquiry learning in the science classroom. Yet, despite this, many teachers in the United States are still unclear about how to implement inquiry in the classroom, thinking that when their students conduct a textbook-based "cookbook" experiment they are experiencing scientific inquiry (Wallace & Louden, 2002). Further, numerous studies have documented the difficulty of implementing authentic inquiry in the classroom (Windschitl, 2004; Chinn & Hmelo-Silver, 2002; Roehrig & Luft, 2004; Marshall & Dorward, 2000; NRC, 2005).

In order to address this difficulty and provide teachers with a platform for implementing active, authentic science inquiry experiences, we developed an interactive

D.J. Ketelhut (✉)
Temple University College of Education, 1301 Cecil B. Moore Ave, Ritter Hall 450,
Philadelphia, PA 19107, USA
e-mail: djk@temple.edu

J. Clarke
Harvard Graduate School of Education, 14 Appian Way, 711 Larsen Hall,
Cambridge, MA 02138, USA

B.C. Nelson
Mary Lou Fulton Institute and Graduate School of Education, Arizona State University,
PO Box 870611, Tempe, AZ 85287-0611, USA

M.J. Jacobson and P. Reimann (eds.), *Designs for Learning Environments of the Future:*   89
International Perspectives from the Learning Sciences, DOI 10.1007/978-0-387-88279-6_4,
© Springer Science+Business Media, LLC 2010

computer-based simulation, *River City*, centered on skills of hypothesis formation and experimental design that is delivered via a Multi-User Virtual Environment (MUVE). Educational MUVEs are a rapidly evolving technology that has recently gained widespread attention from educational researchers and instructional designers (Nelson & Ketelhut, 2007). MUVEs lend themselves to active inquiry learning because they enable multiple participants to enter and explore complex virtual worlds simultaneously, use interactive inquiry tools (such as microscope simulations), gather data from embedded visual objects modeled on real-world counterparts (such as photographs and digital books), communicate with other participants and with computer-based agents, and take part in collaborative learning activities of various types (Dede, Nelson, Ketelhut, Clarke, & Bowman, 2004; Nelson, Ketelhut, Clarke, Bowman, & Dede, 2005).

Our work centers around how these collaborative inquiry environments can be used in middle school science classrooms to simulate real-world experimentation and provide teachers with a model of how to deliver inquiry-based learning in a way that is engaging and meaningful to students. In particular, we are researching the efficacy of these environments for engaging students who do not perform well under traditional instruction and have been labeled as "at-risk" or "under-performing." We are studying whether MUVEs that are designed around deep content and challenging activities can engage students in and promote the learning of science.

This chapter details the 8-year development of *River City* from the initial design through its current large-scale version. Throughout the *River City* project's history, we have employed a design-based research (DBR) approach (Brown, 1992; Collins, 1992) to the iterative, formative development of the MUVE-based inquiry curriculum, with a current focus on resolving scalability issues involved in moving to large-scale implementations. In our discussion here, we reflect on the evolution of our design-based methodology over time and discuss what we have learned about designing for inquiry using DBR through several cycles of implementations. We will also present an overview of the affective and learning outcomes of the nearly 15,000 students and 100 teachers that have used *River City*. By reflecting explicitly on the evolution of our design strategy, we hope to provide a guide to others interested in design-based research for the use of MUVEs to facilitate scientific inquiry in the K-12 classroom.

Scientific Inquiry

As mentioned above, the call to include inquiry in the science classroom has appeared, surprisingly to some, in curricular and policy documents for the last 150 years (DeBoer, 1991). For example, Herbert Spencer in 1860 wrote: "Children should be led to make their own investigations and to draw their own inferences" (Spencer, 1860/1896). This is not too different from the National Science Education Standards that call for "students learning science by actively engaging in inquiries that are interesting and important to them" (National Research Council, 1996, p. 13). Whereas there are differences between Spencer's ideas and our current conceptions, not least of which is the emphasis on discovery learning, it is clear that scientists and science educators recognize the importance of integrating inquiry into the science classroom. Aspects of scientific inquiry can be conducted outside of the laboratory; however, for this chapter, we use scientific inquiry in a more narrow sense to refer to investigations that involve hypothesizing and testing, collecting and analyzing data, and making inferences.

Classroom Issues in Implementing Scientific Inquiry

Unfortunately, the goal of integrating scientific inquiry with science content in the classroom has not progressed as smoothly or as far as its long history would suggest it should have. Current obstacles to this integration range from teachers' failure to adopt inquiry curricula due to poor preparation, lack of resources, and the impact of high stakes testing (Nelson & Ketelhut, 2007).

Issues with integrating scientific inquiry into the science classroom began as far back as the beginning of the twentieth century. At that time, the issues revolved around the structure of schools as well as the preparation of teachers:

> The authorities of the school…are apt to (assign) classes in chemistry to teachers who have had almost no preparation in the subject, instead of delaying its introduction until they can afford to obtain a properly prepared instructor. They are prone to load four or five sciences on one teacher, regardless of the utter impossibility of organizing good laboratory instruction under such circumstances, even if the preparation of the teacher should, *by a miracle*, be not unequal to the task. (Smith & Hall, 1902, p. 26; emphasis added by authors)

As the school population grew exponentially in the early 1900s, a new problem arose that continues unabated today: the need for specialized resources conducting inquiry-based laboratories. The issue was perceived as being so problematic that alternatives to laboratories were debated. The National Society for the Study of Education in 1932 suggested that demonstrations might take the place of student-centered laboratories: "in the interests of economy both of time and of money, it seems desirable to perform more laboratory exercises by the demonstration than by the individual method" (National Society for the Study of Education, 1932, p. 106 as cited in DeBoer, 1991). The issue of resources still persists, particularly in urban schools where money for science experimentation is typically under budgeted (National Research Council, 2005).

Virtual Inquiry

The historical struggle over how to best implement inquiry in the classroom and the role of experimentation has led researchers to search for alternate methods for teaching inquiry. For example, the advancement of technology has led researchers to explore the option of moving scientific inquiry into the virtual realm. However, empirical research that directly compares physical to virtual experimentation using computer technologies is thin (Crosier, Cobb, & Wilson, 2002; Klahr, Triona, & Williams, 2007;

Rotbain, Marbach-Ad, & Stavy, 2008; Trindade, Fiolhais, & Almeida, 2002; Triona & Klahr, 2003; Yang & Heh, 2007; Zacharia, 2007). Moreover, this research covers a wide range of age groups and educational settings; from studying elementary students through preservice teachers, and from 2-h interventions to semester-long curricula. The outcomes of these studies are both broad and uneven, indicating that sometimes groups participating in virtual inquiry show:

- No significant differences in learning (Klahr et al., 2007; Triona & Klahr, 2003); or
- Fewer scientific misconceptions (Zacharia, 2007); or
- Increased process skills (Rotbain et al., 2008; Yang & Heh, 2007); or
- Increased positive attitudes (Rotbain et al., 2008; Yang & Heh, 2007).

The methodology in these studies varied widely as indicated above and therefore, the results cannot be easily synthesized. Further, none of these studies used immersive technologies to help simulate the laboratory experience, a potentially crucial aspect of inquiry learning that is possible due to advances in virtual environments.

Virtual Environments

Picture the following, a:

> …virtual environment accessed via the Internet by multiple users from remote locations. Each user enters and explores…by taking on a persona or character. The computer generated personalities have the ability to walk around, interact with others, move into various rooms, solve puzzles, and even create their own rules and structures. (Herzog, 1998)

This quote is actually from the late 1970s and is describing MUDs (multi-user domains/dungeons/dimensions) and MOOs (multi-user domains, object-oriented). These network-based virtual environments were very similar to the environments used for the *River City* project with one notable exception: their worlds, objects, characters, and storylines were all text-based. Initially designed as fantasy-based adventure games, MUDs and MOOs were also explored for their potential as learning environments (e.g., Fanderclai, 1995; Bowers, 1987; Falsetti, 1995).

As we describe elsewhere in an extensive review of the history of collaborative virtual environments for inquiry (Nelson & Ketelhut, 2007), numerous studies have explored the design, functionality, and potential impact of multi-learner virtual environments as vehicles for collaborative inquiry from situated learning and/or socio-constructivist perspectives (e.g., Bruckman, 1996; Corbit, 2002; Simons & Clark, 2004). One project called MOOSE Crossing offers an early example of an inquiry-based MOO. In MOOSE Crossing, students navigated a text-based virtual world and interacted with its objects and inhabitants through typed commands (Bruckman, 2000). Bruckman (1996, 2000) investigated how children created and shared (text-based) virtual artifacts while learning programming in MOOSE Crossing. When Bruckman investigated the effectiveness of the environment for learning, she found uneven results. In one study, she found that a subset of students actively participated in the curriculum and earned high marks on a programming skill measure. However, while students who actively participated in the curriculum embedded in MOOSE Crossing improved their programming skills, a large minority of the students demonstrated very little engagement. In fact, 40% of the sample group never wrote a single programming script (Bruckman, 2000). Bruckman cited this low level of engagement as a key reason for uneven results in her study.

A more recent virtual environment for inquiry is Whyville, a 2D, graphical MUVE designed in part as a virtual community for children containing a wide range of embedded scientific learning and inquiry activities (http://whyville.net). Two-thirds of Whyville's nearly two million registered users are female (Galas, 2006). Students in Whyville can participate in inquiry activities designed around biology, physics, and chemistry curricula (Simons & Clark, 2004).

One representative inquiry curriculum implemented in Whyville was the "Whypox" epidemic (Neulight, Kafai, Kao, Foley, & Galas, 2007; Galas, 2006). In the "Whypox" curriculum, students were confronted with a disease outbreak in Whyville that was first revealed as red spots and gray color on the faces of student avatars in the virtual world. In addition, students infected with Whypox found that their text-based chat was interrupted by "ah-choos" when they attempted to type messages to other students. The illness soon spread through the online community, prompting on- and offline discussions about the possible causes and means of controlling the outbreak. Students tracked the spread of the outbreak on charts in their classroom. In addition, participants were able to gather information about disease transmission in a virtual "Center for Disease Control" in the Whyville environment, and use an "Infection Simulator" to observe how diseases spread in a population (Galas, 2006).

In her study, Galas (2006) found that the Whypox outbreak provided a meaningful, engaging curriculum around which her sixth grade students could conduct authentic, collaborative scientific inquiry. Students became deeply involved in gathering data and forming hypotheses, working on the project after school, taking part in impromptu online meetings to talk about the epidemic, and writing about the outbreak for an online newspaper.

More recently, technological advances have enabled the creation of 3D MUVEs like *River City*. As with earlier text-based and 2D environments, much of the current research into educational MUVEs centers on the viability of the environments to support collaborative inquiry curriculum (e.g., Annetta & Park, 2006; Barab, Thomas, Dodge, Carteaux, & Tuzan, 2005; Clarke & Dede, 2005; Corbit, 2002). Yet very few of these environments focus on experimental aspects of inquiry in the k-12 classroom.

Design-Based Research

Our work centers on design, practice, and research. The interplay of the design, instructional strategies and learning in classroom contexts lends itself to emerging research practices that have come to be known as design-based research (DBR Collective, 2003). Design-based research is a relatively new research methodology that the scholarly community is still in the process of defining and distinguishing from other research methodologies (see DBR Collective, 2003; Barab & Squire, 2004; Collins, Joseph, Bielaczyc, 2004; Sandoval & Bell, 2004; Wang & Hannafin, 2005). In this chapter, we use the definition provided by the Design-Based Research Collective (2003): "Design-based research (Brown, 1992; Collins, 1992) is an emerging paradigm for the study of learning in context through the systematic design and study of instructional strategies and tools… design-based research can help create and extend knowledge about developing, enacting, and sustaining innovative learning environments" (p. 5).

Design-based research is an iterative process where investigators engage in design, implement in classroom settings, research the learning in context, refine theories of learning, engage in redesign and continue the cycle of implementation. During this process, both qualitative and quantitative research and analysis methods are employed. With the River City project, we conduct rigorous classroom observations, interview students, and examine student work and social interactions. We administer surveys and analyze learning outcomes. This iterative process as applied in the River City project has aided us in understanding students' inquiry learning and how MUVEs can foster learning and engagement and support higher self-efficacy.

At various points over the past 8 years, our focus has leaned in a particular direction (design, practice, or research); however, most often it leans toward practice. The bulk of our work has been conducted in classroom settings in public schools. We have worked hard to establish relationships with schools and teachers to ensure that our curriculum could be implemented and studied in natural settings. Each implementation led to new insights on student learning, design, and instructional strategies. In the following sections we describe our iterative process of design, practice, and research.

River City 2000–2002

River City began its life as the "Multi-User Virtual Environment Experiential Simulator" (MUVEES) and was the focus of a 2-year National Science Foundation (NSF)-funded research project. The original intent was to create and evaluate graphical multi-user virtual environments (MUVEs) that use digitized museum resources to enhance middle school students' motivation and learning about science. MUVEES extended the MUVE capabilities of the time in order to study the science-learning potential of immersive simulations, interactive virtual museum exhibits, and "participatory" historical situations (Dede, Salzman, Loftin, Ash, 2000). To accomplish these goals, we built our own MUVE shell based on the (now defunct) Sense8 WorldToolKit (http://www.sense8.com/).

At various times, partners in this original research were Harvard University's Graduate School of Education, the Virtual Environments Lab at George Mason University, the Smithsonian's National Museum of American History (NMAH), and Thoughtful Technologies, Inc. The development team included education researchers, science educators, instructional designers, computer scientists, museum archivists and exhibit designers, graphic artists, scientists, and middle school science teachers from both public and private schools. We documented our design process in order to offer an example to other groups developing educational multi-user virtual environments as well as evaluating and improving our own.

Design for Scientific Inquiry

Our initial design started with problem areas identified by science teachers. The teachers were interested in experimenting with an intervention that specifically addressed the most difficult parts of the curriculum, not material for which well-functioning instructional strategies and curricula were already available. For middle school, the teachers identified experimental design as the most difficult concept for students to learn and the one for which teachers were most eager to find an alternative instructional method. In particular, they suggested an activity in which students behaved as scientists while they identified a problem through observation and inference and then formed and tested hypotheses.

We developed two prototype middle school science curriculum units, each based around national science standards, content typically covered in the middle school science curriculum, and the types of investigative process skills necessary for students to do an independent science fair project. Each unit consisted of a MUVE-based curriculum centered on cooperative investigation of issues affecting residents of a virtual town. Our first curriculum prototype (the *River City* Unit) centered on content in biology and ecology and is the topic of this chapter. The second curriculum prototype (the Bicycle unit) focused on the physical and material sciences and was centered on problems of bicycle design related to Newtonian motion. The Bicycle Unit was never developed beyond the pilot stage, and thus we focus our attention on the *River City* curriculum for the rest of the chapter.

River City is based on students collaboratively investigating a virtual town with a river running through it, different forms of terrain that influence water runoff, houses, industries, and institutions such as a hospital and a university. The learners themselves populate the city, along with nonplayer characters (NPCs), digital objects that can include audio or video clips, and computer-based agents (Nelson et al., 2005). In *River City*, learners are engaged in a "participatory historical situation" in which they can apply tools and knowledge from both the past and the present to resolve an authentic problem. In this "back to the future" situation, students' mastery of twenty-first century classroom content and skills empowers them in the nineteenth century virtual world. Through data gathering, students observe the patterns that emerge and wrestle with questions such as "Why are many more poor people getting sick than rich people?" Multiple causal factors are involved, including polluted water runoff to low-lying areas, insect vectors in swampy areas, overcrowding, and the access to medical care.

Multiple teams of students can access the *River City* MUVE simultaneously, each individual manipulating an avatar through their computer. In our implementations, the class is divided into teams of two to four students, which are "sent back in time" to this virtual town. To guide the team efforts in *River City*, they are provided with a lab notebook that asks them to help the city solve its environmental and health problems, which are directly related to middle school science content. To accomplish this, the students must collaborate to share the data with their team. Teams communicate primarily through a MUVE-based text chat tool, rather than face to face. Beyond textual conversation, students can project visual "snapshots" of their current individual point of view (when someone has discovered an item of general interest) to each other and also can "teleport" to various areas or to join anyone on their team for joint investigation. In-group collaboration is visible only to other group members. Students enter *River City* multiple times over the course of the curriculum. Each time that a team reenters the town, several months of time have passed in *River City*, so that learners can track the dynamic evolution of local problems.

The main goal of the *River City* MUVE is to teach students the skills necessary for scientific inquiry, such as conducting investigations for a science fair project. The emphasis in *River City* is on front-end inquiry skills, particularly in learning how to identify a problem. Therefore, *River City* has multiple lines of potential exploration. *River City*, set in the nineteenth century, is typical of towns in the United States at that time with wealthy homes situated in the hills, a town center midway down, and tenements built in the lowlands of the town. The three main strands of illness in *River City* reflect this time period and include malaria, tuberculosis, and problems related to poor sanitation.

These three diseases were chosen to represent three different disease vectors: water-borne, air-borne, and insect-borne. They are integrated with historical, social, and geographical content to allow students to experience the realities of identifying a problem from within a content-rich environment. The first disease strand centers on the introduction of tuberculosis from outside the town, and the curriculum enables students to uncover both the cause of the introduction of the disease and the patterns that emerge of its spread throughout *River City*. The students' ability to track the spread of the disease over time is particularly interesting for this disease. The next disease, malaria, was endemic to many areas of the United States in the 1800s and follows the life cycle of its carrier, the mosquito. As a result, as the students enter *River City* over successive sessions, they are able, if this problem is of interest to them, to follow the rise and fall of new cases of malaria from summer to winter and back again. The last illness embedded in *River City* stems from drinking water contaminated by sewage. The sewage reaches the river from deliberate outflow of flush toilets newly introduced to the wealthy homes in the mountains. This contaminated water flows downstream to the swampy lands behind the tenement homes and is used by the poor as potable water. In addition, some of the city wells, used by middle class residents and hotel guests, are also contaminated from street runoff of manure.

Many students have the naive epistemic view that there are right and easily discernible answers to problems in science. In exploring *River City*, however, students are each guided in teams to make a unique hypothesis regarding one of many problems, based on their own interests. At the end of the project, they compare their research with other teams of students to discover the plethora of potential hypotheses and avenues of investigation available for exploration.

During their time in the MUVE, students answer questions in a lab notebook that guides their activities in *River City* and that teachers later use for assessment purposes. The lab notebook starts with questions that promote exploration of the environment and help students master the interface, building toward later investigations that are content specific and require completing data tables based on the water samples encountered in *River City*. At the end, students write a letter to the mayor of *River City* describing the health and environmental problems they have encountered and making suggestions for improving the life of the inhabitants.

River City contains over 50 digital objects from the Smithsonian's collection, plus "data collection stations" that provide detailed information about water samples at various spots in the world. Figure 4.1 is a screen shot depicting a "birds-eye" view of this city.

Throughout the world, students encounter residents of *River City* and "overhear" their text-based conversations with one another. These nonplayer characters (NPCs) disclose information and indirect clues about what is going on in *River City*. Students can also access clues associated with the museum artifacts that are embedded throughout *River City*. These clues as well as the ones spoken by the residents of *River City* change from season to season, helping students understand the impact of weather and time on the disease patterns.

One of the first challenges we encountered in designing *River City* was how to give students a virtual laboratory experience. As mentioned above, we use scientific inquiry in a narrow sense that refers to active investigations and processes.

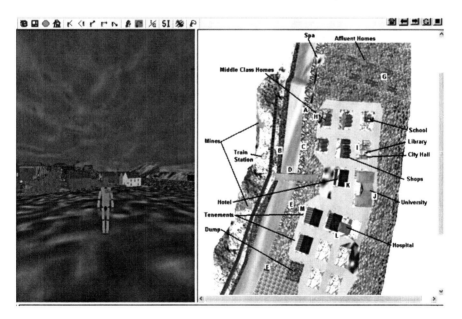

Fig. 4.1 The 2000–2002 *River City* interface showing an avatar and the city map

Our definition is based on the National Science Education Standard's definition of inquiry as a:

> ... multifaceted activity that involves making observations; posing questions; examining books and other sources of information to see what is already known; planning investigations; reviewing what is already known in light of experimental evidence; using tools to gather, analyze, and interpret data; proposing answers, explanations, and predictions; and communicating the results. (National Research Council, 1996, p. 23)

As we have described, our initial design had students making observations as they explored *River City*, listening to conversations among the computer-based residents to elicit clues and information, working with their teacher to find information from their textbook and other sources of information in their classroom, planning an investigation, and communicating the results of that investigation to their peers in a mini-research conference. However, what we were missing in this first instantiation of *River City* was the ability for students to use tools to gather, analyze and interpret data. In our first attempt to address this issue, we decided to create water-sampling stations along the river and by various wells in town that offered students access to tables of raw data about the water quality throughout town. The data included the red herring of bacteria that were set at the "background noise" level along with other bacteria that were pertinent to the diseases central to the investigation. While analysis of these predefined data tables was far from true experimentation, other components of the project did allow for all other aspects of inquiry, such as gathering data through interviewing, analyzing collected data and making inferences from that analysis. Figure 4.2 presents an example of water quality data table from 1 of 11 water-sampling stations in *River City*. The cholera levels represent the red herring while the coliform bacteria levels are the actual contamination.

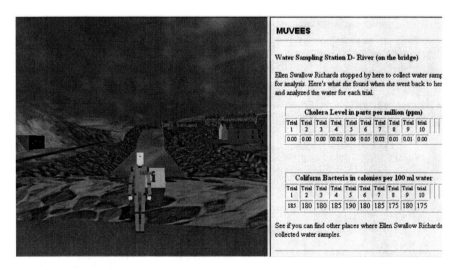

Fig. 4.2 The 2000–2002 *River City* interface showing the data table accessible from a water-sampling station

Initial Research Outcomes

In 2002, we tested our design in public school classrooms in a large urban northeastern school district. With the assistance of school administration, two classrooms that had access to the computer hardware and software required by MUVEES were identified for participation in the project. They were located in two different middle schools, each with its own racial/ethnic mix. One was a seventh grade classroom in School A, serving a population of primarily African–American and Hispanic families. School B had a large Asian population, and we worked with a sixth grade class there. Control classrooms with similar attributes were chosen in each school. In School B, the experimental and control classes were taught by different teachers; in School A, the same teacher taught both. The control curriculum was designed to match the intervention curriculum on as many characteristics as possible other than technology. The intervention lasted for a total of 3 weeks. There were 45 students in the two experimental classes, and 36 in the control, evenly split by gender. Approximately 25% of students in each class spoke English as a second language and over 75% were identified as free and reduced-lunch students.

Both qualitative and quantitative data were collected from students and teachers over the 3-week implementation period. Observational data was collected from the test classrooms throughout the project and sporadically from the control classrooms. All teachers responded to a pre- and postquestionnaire regarding their methods and comfort with technology. The test classroom teachers also wrote a narrative about their perceptions of *River City* at the end of the project.

The content tests covered three main areas: scientific method literacy, knowledge of disease transmission, and problem-solving skills. The overall raw pre- and postscores for the content test showed a 3% gain by the experimental group and a 4% gain by the control group – not a statistically significant difference.[1] Students, on average, started the project with 48% understanding of the scientific process as tested by this instrument, high for the start of a new unit. However, the results were more interesting when broken down by starting knowledge. Six of seven experimental students scoring less than 35% on the content pretest improved their content knowledge above that level, while only two of five control students did so.

Of more interest to this paper, however, was the answer to the research question of whether this intervention could help students develop and engage with scientific inquiry. We wondered whether the complexity of *River City* would be overwhelming for students. However, we found that students were able to tease apart the curricular threads in the *River City* scenario (Dede, Ketelhut, & Ruess, 2002). In our seventh grade classroom, for example, seven teams came up with five different hypotheses about the causes of disease, ranging from population density to immigration to water pollution.

---

[1] The quantitative data was analyzed with SAS. A significance level of $p < 0.05$ was used and checks for linearity, normality, and homoscedasticity were performed at various intervals. No clear violations were noted.

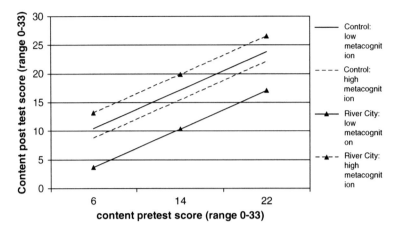

Fig. 4.3 The effect of treatment and metacognitive ability on science content posttest score ($n = 81$)

While students were able to negotiate the complex curriculum, it did seem to privilege some students more than others. We measured students' ability to be reflect on their own learning (metacognition) using the subscale, *thoughtfulness of inquiry* (Midgley et al., 2000). We discovered that the effect of the treatment varied by students' ability to be metacognitive. Figure 4.3 shows this relationship.

Figure 4.3 shows students' content posttest score, controlling for their pretest score. The dotted lines are students with high metacognition and those without, low metacognition. As can be seen, students with high metacognition in the *River City* treatment post higher posttest scores than any other group of students across all starting pretest scores. Unfortunately, the reverse is true for students with low metacognition in the *River City* treatment. Students with low metacognition in the control group do better than all other students other than the high metacognitive *River City* students. These results indicate to us that typical classroom curricula are not engaging students with high metacognitive abilities, but that *River City*'s complexity might be too much or too open-ended for students without those skills.

An interesting and unexpected finding was the effect the implementations had on students' sense that their teachers were compelling them to strive for understanding, as measured by the subscale, *Academic Press* (Midgley et al., 2000). There is a significant difference in the means between the experimental and control groups ($t = -2.64$, $p < 0.05$), with the control group beliefs increasing by 0.41 and the experimental group declining by 0.93, on average (Fig. 4.4).

At first glance, this result appears to indicate that *River City* students perceived that they were not asked to reach understanding. However, the emphasis in these questions is on the students' perceptions of how much the teacher *pressed* the students. We feel that this result is a reflection of the difference in the teacher role in the two treatments, and reflects the more autonomous nature of the experimental

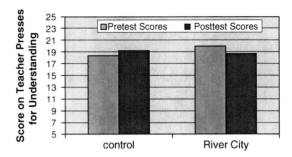

Fig. 4.4 Student perceptions of "Teacher Presses Me for Understanding"

group. This might indicate the role technology could play in supporting students' growth toward self-responsibility in learning, a crucial habit of mind for scientific inquiry. However, we caution that more research into this and effects of the intervention on students' understanding are necessary to tease out the underlying explanation for this difference.

River City 2004–2006

Designing for Inquiry

In 2004, we migrated the River City MUVE from our own custom-built platform to one built using a commercial MUVE engine from ActiveWorlds, Inc. (http://www.activeworlds.com). This update of the technology opened new avenues for design. First, use of the more modern platform allowed us to more easily embed realistic tacit visual and auditory clues throughout our virtual town; for example, students could hear coughing from residents sick with TB, and see muddy streets in the spring versus dry ones in the summer. These clues increased students' needs for careful observation and opened up the project to learners with poorer reading skills who could gather data from multimedia-based contextual clues rather than only text-based ones.

In addition, the change of platform supported the introduction of two curricular changes that improved our ability to support realistic experimentation: the use of virtual tools and the introduction of controlled experimentation. While we struggled with a lack of tools for students to gather data for analysis in the earlier version of River City, in this version we were able to create virtual microscopes through which students could see accurate models of bacteria moving across the screen (Fig. 4.5). Further, we created virtual dissecting microscopes for investigating mosquitoes caught in "bug catchers" scattered around River City. With this addition, River City now supported all aspects of the National Science Education Standards definition of inquiry.

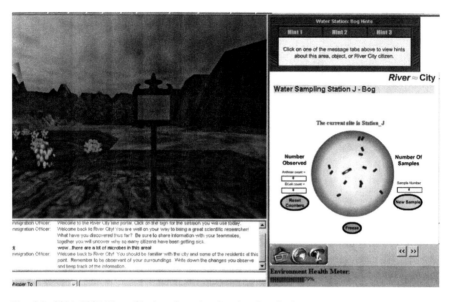

Fig. 4.5 2004–2006 *River City* interface showing the virtual microscope

The 2000–2002 River City had offered students the option to do comparison research: looking at changes over time or across areas. However, with this new version of River City, students were now able to do controlled research. The 2004–2006 River City incorporated the ability for students to affect a single change in the virtual town and then compare the data they collected with and without the change to see how that change influenced the spread of disease. To do this, we developed two experimental worlds. The first acts as the control (River City without any changes) and the second as the experimental portion (River City with one change based on students' hypothesis). For example, a team of students hypothesize that the fever and chills are related to the large population of mosquitoes that appear to be breeding by the bog. Therefore, they decide that if they drain the bog, the number of cases of fever and chills will go down because there will be fewer mosquitoes. To conduct their experiment, students first enter the control world and gather data on the illness and the bog. They then enter the experimental world, which is the exact same River City but with the bog drained. They then gather data and compare with the data they collected in the control world. In this example, students will find fewer mosquitoes, fewer cases of reported fever and chills, and learn through conversations with residents that now that the bog has been drained they are much happier. However, students will also find that the river is still polluted and that the number of residents with coughs and stomachaches has not changed.

In the second iteration of River City, we were also able to create an embedded hint system used to support students in making connections between data elements scattered in space and over time in River City. Our hint system (Fig. 4.5) tracked student interactions with residents and objects in the virtual town and offered text-based hints based on evolving event "trails" that each student produced while exploring the town. For example, students could enter the River City hospital and view an admissions chart. When doing so, the hints system would offer guidance about how to interpret the data on the chart based on where an individual student had visited previously. If a student had talked with town residents living near a polluted bog in the tenement district, for example, the hints system would ask the student if any of the patients admitted to the hospital had come from that part of town (Nelson, 2007).

This version of River City (http://muve.gse.harvard.edu/rivercityproject/) was implemented across the United States in urban, suburban, and rural school districts. Approximately 3,000 students used this River City in their science classrooms over the 2 years that this version was active. In nearly all cases, each teacher implemented River City with at least half of their classes while a paper-based control curriculum was implemented in the others. Thus, each teacher implemented both curricula, helping to control for differences due to teaching, professional development as well as school.

Outcomes Related to Scientific Inquiry

With the major changes to the inquiry aspects of this version of River City, we were particularly interested to see what impact these changes had on students' inquiry skills and efficacy. Below we list the major inquiry-based outcomes from the series of implementations throughout 2004–2006:

- Students used both tacit and explicit clues in determining the extent of the problems in River City: "We think many things are going on. There are coughs, stomach aches, mosquitoes, dump near the tenements, debris in the river and streets, and probably even more!!" (Galas & Ketelhut, 2006).
- Students in River City with low self-efficacy gained significantly more on the scientific inquiry portion of the content test than did those in the control curriculum; students with high self-efficacy, however, do better in the control curriculum (Ketelhut, Clarke, Nelson, & Dukas, 2008).
- Students increased their use of the virtual tools throughout the project, on average, and the amount they access these tools is directly related to increased gains on the posttest content score (Ketelhut, 2007; Ketelhut & Dede, 2007).
- When asked to list the three things they liked the best, students listed scientific inquiry 50% of the time and the virtual tools specifically 33% of the time (Ketelhut & Nelson, in press).
- Students who used the embedded hints system extensively saw significantly higher score gains on science and inquiry measures than those who used the hints system less, or those who did not use the system ($p < 0.05$) (Nelson, 2007).

River City **2006–2008**

Powers

As illustrated in the findings above, our movement to the custom-built platform using a commercial MUVE engine showed promising results for delivering authentic inquiry learning in classroom settings. Our current series of studies focus on what it takes to bring the *River City* environment to scale in hundreds of classroom across the United States. Research has documented that in education, unlike other sectors of society, the scaling of successful programs from a few settings to widespread use across a range of contexts is very difficult (Dede, Honan, & Peters, 2005). Yet, if virtual scientific inquiry curricula are to be successful, small research projects must show success at scaling up. As we have scaled, our design process has evolved to include features that are flexible enough to use in a wide variety of contexts across a spectrum of learners and teachers.

Findings from our previous studies revealed that students who started the project with low self-efficacy outperformed students who started the project with high self-efficacy (Ketelhut et al., 2008). As we scaled, we knew we needed to adapt our design to include features that would keep high-achieving students engaged in the inquiry learning throughout the curriculum. In 2006, we developed an additional storyline we call "Powers." Powers is influenced by a feature of videogame design that allows players to secretly unlock content during game play. In *River City*, the content that is unlocked is directly linked to the curricular objectives and the *River City* narrative. In order to unlock the content, students must complete a series of curricular objectives linked to inquiry and data gathering.

When teams of students complete curricular goals (a combination of events) they are teleported to a secret mansion in *River City* that contains historical information related to a previous epidemic in *River City*. Students can read about children of their age who used to live in *River City*. They can view a researcher's journal about a previous disease outbreak and view CAT scans of people's lungs to see if they are diseased. We are currently conducting research to determine if the inclusion of powers keeps all students engaged, regardless of their prior academic achievement and starting self-efficacy in science.

Online Student Lab Book

In 2007, we developed an online student lab book that is integrated in the River City environment. This allows students to keep their focus directed at the screen at all times rather than switching their attention back and forth between a paper-based lab book and the computer screen. The development of the online lab book required a redesign of the right hand interface into a student workspace. Objects clicked in the world had to be redirected and access to the tools such as the online microscope had

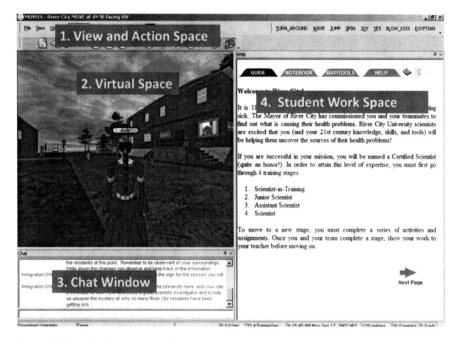

Fig. 4.6 *River City* interface showing the new student workspace

to be redesigned. Figure 4.6 shows the design of the online lab book and redesign of the virtual space. We implemented this online lab book in late fall 2007 and are just starting to conduct design-based research on its efficacy of use and help in student learning. Thus, for this chapter, we will limit our discussion to the design features.

The new online lab book contains four tabs: Guide, Notebook, Map/Tools, and Help (Fig. 4.7). The Guide contains the curriculum that students follow as they work in River City. It is the same curriculum that was delivered via the paper-based lab book used to support student learning in previous years, yet slightly modified for the online delivery. This guide keeps students' placement in the curriculum. For example, if a student logs out in the middle of a season, when they log back in the guide opens on the page students were last on.

The Notebook is where students record the data they gather in River City. It is designed to help them organize and categorize their data. For example, when students enter data in their notebook, they have to indicate what type of data it is (observation, inference, general science notes, prediction). Students can then sort their data stored in the notebook by the time period they were visiting (season) or type of data (observation, inference, etc.). The notebook also includes a search capability.

The Map/Tools contains the various tools students use as the explore River City: the online microscope, the environmental health meter, and interactive map. The function of these tools is the same as in previous years; however, using them and

Fig. 4.7 *River City* interface showing the online materials located in the student workspace

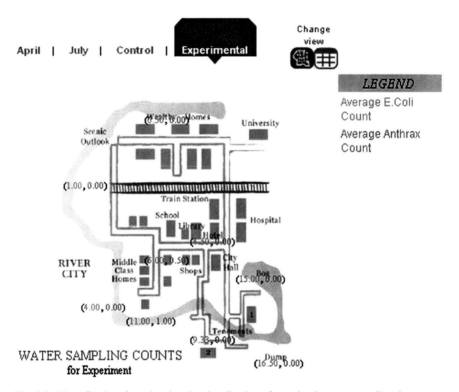

Fig. 4.8 *River City* interface showing the visualization of a student's water-sampling data

storing data are quite different. Students can now view their saved water-sampling data and bug catcher counts in two ways. They can view their data visually by examining a map of River City with the readings superimposed on their location (Fig. 4.8) or in a data table format.

The Help tab provides information about how to use the student workspace and the various tools located in the tabs. This feature ensures that students have access to "just-in-time" help when working through the curriculum. All four of these features, Guide, Notebook, Map/Tools, and Help, have been particularly designed to support students in gathering and interpreting data in River City.

Conclusion

River City was initiated to explore the affordances of MUVEs for delivering middle school science inquiry curriculum and to investigate the impact MUVE-based curricula could have on student engagement in learning science. The design-based research approach used with *River City* cycled between design, implementation, evaluation, and redesign. In each iteration, we discovered methods to improve the implementation process, aspects of virtual inquiry and learning outcomes. As part of our emphasis on developing insights about how to design MUVEs for learning, we were able to make several discoveries about their potential in K-12 classrooms. First, MUVEs appear to be motivating in a sustained way (beyond an initial novelty effect). In addition, MUVEs seem to have a strong impact on learning for students identified as low performers in more traditional curricula. Three girls from the 2000–2002 implementations offer a case in point. These girls were intrigued with our initial presence in the classroom; but, by the time the pretesting was concluded, they had reverted to their previous inattentive and disruptive behaviors. In fact, for the first day or two of the intervention, they groaned whenever we entered the room. Two weeks later, these girls were still inattentive to their teacher, but had become highly engaged in the virtual world of *River City*. They were working hard on interpreting their data and finishing the project, demanding that the researchers read their final report immediately. This example was not isolated. During the 2004–2006 implementations, a similar situation occurred. On the second day of the implementation, a student, whose teacher had been ignoring him, called one of us over, claiming to have solved the mystery of why people were becoming ill. His teacher had told us previously that this student was failing the course and would most likely not engage with the project or be able to interpret any observations he might make. However, contrary to the teacher's expectations, this student was able to give a very insightful interpretation of the data available to him at that stage of the implementation. We have many similar anecdotes from teachers that reiterate lower performing students becoming and remaining engaged with the *River City* curriculum, often to the surprise of the teacher.

Overall this research strongly suggests that virtual scientific inquiry-based environments can have a viable and valuable role as a platform for realistic science inquiry curriculum in the classroom. Our work to date represents an initial attempt to determine how well they promote scientific inquiry learning. The data is promising, if provisional. Still, it clearly suggests that future research into the effectiveness of MUVEs for learning in general and for learning science inquiry in particular is warranted.

We have also learned much on the technical strengths and weaknesses of MUVEs in the classroom. In order to support chat for collaboration and send data back and forth from our servers, computers running *River City* must be connected to the Internet. This often sparked concerns from technology administrators (and sometimes parents), and left the project vulnerable to bandwidth and filtering issues. For some schools, this problem was never solved. In addition, *River City* has suffered the basic issues associated with any technology-based curriculum implemented in public schools, including aging hardware in labs, difficulties in scheduling computer time, system instability, and so on.

From its inception, the *River City* Project has been extending MUVE capabilities in order to study the science-learning potential of immersive simulations, interactive virtual museum exhibits, and "participatory" historical situations, particularly for low-performing students who are turned off to school and skeptical about their ability to learn. This research to date demonstrates that MUVEs are viable tools allowing learner-centered, collaborative inquiry learning that can provide an alternative to more conventional kinds of inquiry-based science instruction.

Acknowledgments This material is based upon work supported by the National Science Foundation under Grant Nos. 9980464, 0296001, 0202543, 0310188, and 0532446. Any opinions, findings, and conclusions or recommendations expressed in this material are those of the authors and do not necessarily reflect the views of the National Science Foundation. The authors wish to acknowledge and give a special thank you to Chris Dede, the Principal Investigator on the River City grants. We would also like to acknowledge and thank the rest of the River City team: Catherine Bowman, Edward Dieterle, and Geordie Dukas for their collaboration throughout River City's evolution.

References

Annetta, L. & Park, J.C. (2006). *Video games in science: A model for students and teachers creating 3D role playing games.* Paper presented at the Annual Conference of the Society for Information Technology and Teacher Education, Orlando, FL.

Barab, S. A., & Squire, K. D. (2004). Design-based research: Putting our stake in the ground. *Journal of the Learning Sciences, 13*(1), 1–14.

Barab, S., Thomas, M., Dodge, T., Carteaux, R., & Tuzan, H. (2005). Making learning fun: Quest Atlantis, a game without guns. *Educational Technology Research & Development, 53*(1), 86–107.

Bowers, A. (1987). Creative C.O.W. or a moo is worth a thousand words. *Pointer, 32*(1), 9–13.

Brown, A. (1992). Design experiments: Theoretical and methodological challenges in creating complex interventions in classroom settings. *The Journal of the Learning Sciences, 2*(2), 141–178.

Bruckman, A. (1996). Finding one's own space in cyberspace. *Technology Review, 99*(1), 48–54.

Bruckman, A. (2000). *Uneven Achievement in a Constructivist Learning Environment.* Paper presented at the International Conference on Learning Sciences, Ann Arbor, MI.

Chinn, C., & Hmelo-Silver, C. (2002). Authentic inquiry: Introduction to the special section. *Science Education, 86*, 171–174.

Clarke, J., & Dede, C. (2005). *Making learning meaningful: An exploratory study of using multi-user environments (MUVEs) in middle school science.* Paper presented at the American Educational Research Association Conference, Montreal, Canada.

Collins, A. (1992). Toward a design science of education. In E. Scanlon & T. O'Shea (Eds.), *New directions in educational technology* (pp. 15–22). Berlin: Springer Verlag.

Collins, A., Joseph, D., & Bielaczyc, K. (2004). Design research: Theoretical and methodological issues. *The Journal of the Learning Sciences, 13*(1), 15–42.

Corbit, M. (2002). Building virtual worlds for informal science learning (SciCentr and SciFair) in the active worlds educational universe (AWEDU). *Presence: Teleoperators & Virtual Environment, 11*(1), 55–67.

Crosier, J. K., Cobb, S., & Wilson, J. R. (2002). Key lessons for the design and integration of virtual environments in secondary science. *Computers and Education, 38*(1), 77–97.

DeBoer, G. E. (1991). *A history of ideas in science education: Implications for practice*. New York: Teachers College Press.

Dede, C., Honan, J. P., & Peters, L. C. (eds). (2005). *Scaling up success: Lessons learned from technology-based educational improvement*. San Francisco: Jossey-Bass.

Dede, C., Ketelhut, D., & Ruess, K. (2002). Motivation, usability, and learning outcomes in a prototype museum-based multi-user virtual environment. In P. Bell, R. Stevens & T. Satwicz (Eds.), *Keeping learning complex: The Proceedings of the Fifth International Conference of the Learning Sciences (ICLS)*. Mahwah, NJ: Erlbaum.

Dede, C., Nelson, B., Ketelhut, D., Clarke, J., & Bowman, C. (2004). Design-based research strategies for studying situated learning in a multi-user virtual environment. *Proceedings of the 2004 International Conference on Learning Sciences* (pp. 158-165). Mahweh, NJ: Lawrence Erlbaum.

Dede, C., Salzman, M., Loftin, R. B., & Ash, K. (2000). The design of immersive virtual environments: Fostering deep understandings of complex scientific knowledge. In M. J. Jacobson & R. B. Kozma (Eds.), *Innovations in science and mathematics education: advanced designs for technologies of learning* (pp. 361–414). Mahwah, NJ: Lawrence Erlbaum.

Design-Based Research Collective. (2003). Design-based research; an emerging paradigm for educational inquiry. *Educational Researcher, 32*(1), 5–8.

Fanderclai, T. L. (1995). MUDs in education: New environments, new pedagogies. *Computer Mediated Education Magazine, 2*(1), 8.

Falsetti, J. (1995, March 26-April 1). *What the heck is a MOO? And what's the story with all those cows?* Paper presented at the Annual Meeting of the Teachers of English to Speakers of Other Languages, Long Beach, CA.

Galas, C. (2006). Why whyville? *Learning and Leading with Technology, 34*(6), 30–33.

Galas, C., & Ketelhut, D. J. (2006). *River City*, the MUVE. *Leading and Learning with Technology, 33*(7), 31.

Herzog, H. (1998). *MUDs and MOOs in higher education*. Retrieved April 30, 2007, from http://css.psu.edu/news/nlfa98/mudsmoos.html

Ketelhut, D. J., Clarke, J., Nelson, B., & Dukas, G. (2008). Using multi-user virtual environments to simulate authentic scientific practice and enhance student engagement. In L. A. Annetta (Ed.), *Serious educational games: From theory to practice*. Rotterdam, The Netherlands: Sense Publishers.

Ketelhut, D. J., & Nelson, B. (in press). Designing for Real-World Scientific Inquiry in Virtual Environments. *Educational Research*.

Ketelhut, D. J. (2007). The impact of student self-efficacy on scientific inquiry skills: An exploratory investigation in *River City*, a multi-user virtual environment. *Journal of Science Education and Technology, 16*(1), 99–111.

Ketelhut, D. J., & Dede, C. (2007). Alternative assessments of students' understanding of scientific inquiry via a multi-user virtual environment. *Distributed Learning and Collaboration (DLAC-II) Symposium*, Singapore.

Klahr, D., Triona, L. M., & Williams, C. (2007). Hands on what? The relative effectiveness of physical versus virtual materials in an engineering design project by middle school children. *Journal of Research in Science Teaching, 44*(1), 183–203.

Marshall, J., & Dorward, J. (2000). Inquiry experiences as a lecture supplement for preservice elementary teachers and general education students. *American Journal of Physics, 68*, S27–S36.

Midgley, C., Maehr, M. L., Hruda, L. Z., Anderman, E., Anderman, L., Freeman, K. E., et al. (2000). *Manual for the patterns of adaptive learning scales (PALS)*. Ann Arbor, MI: University of Michigan.

National Research Council. (1996). *National science education standards: Observe, interact, change, learn*. Washington, D.C.: National Academy Press.

National Research Council. (2005). *America's lab report: Investigations in high school science.* Washington, D.C.: National Academies Press.

National Society for the Study of Education. (1932). *A program for teaching science: Thirty-first yearbook of the NSSE.* Chicago: University of Chicago Press.

Nelson, B. (2007). Exploring the use of individualized, reflective guidance in an educational multi user virtual environment. *The Journal of Science Education and Technology 16*(1), 83–97.

Nelson, B., & Ketelhut, D. J. (2007). Designing for real-world inquiry in virtual environments. *Educational Pyschology Review, 19*(3), 265–283.

Nelson, B., Ketelhut, D. J., Clarke, J., Bowman, C., & Dede, C. (2005). Design-based research strategies for developing a scientific inquiry curriculum in a multi-user virtual environment. *Educational Technology, 45*(1), 21–27.

Neulight, N., Kafai, Y. B., Kao, L., Foley, B., & Galas, C. (2007). Childrens' participation in a virtual epidemic in the science classroom: Making connections to natural infectioius diseases. *Journal of Science Education and Technology, 16*(1), 47–58.

Roehrig, G., & Luft, J. (2004). Constraints experienced by beginning secondary science teachers in implementing scientific inquiry lessons. *International Journal of Science Education, 26*(1), 3–24.

Rotbain, Y., Marbach-Ad, G., & Stavy, R. (2008). Using a computer animation to teach high school molecular biology. *Journal of Science Education & Technology, 17*(1), 49–58.

Sandoval, W. A., & Bell, P. L. (2004). Design-based research methods for studying learning in context: Introduction. *Educational Psychologist, 39*(4), 199–201.

Simons, K., & Clark, D. (2004). Supporting inquiry in science classrooms with the web. *Computers in the Schools, 21*(3/4), 23–36.

Smith, A., & Hall, E. H. (1902). *The teaching of chemistry and physics in the secondary school.* New York: Longmans, Green and Co.

Spencer, H. (1860/1896). *Education: Intellectual, moral, and physical.* New York: D. Appleton and Co.

Trindade, J., Fiolhais, C., & Almeida, L. (2002). Science learning in virtual environments: A descriptive study. *British Journal of Educational Technology, 33*(4), 471–488.

Triona, L. M., & Klahr, D. (2003). Point and click or grab and heft: Comparing the influence of physical and virtual instructional materials on elementary school students' ability to design experiments. *Cognition & Instruction, 21*(2), 149–173.

Wallace, J., & Louden, W. (2002). Introduction to 'laboratories'. In J. Wallace & W. Louden (Eds.), *Dilemmas of science teaching* (pp. 36–37). New York: RoutledgeFalmer.

Wang, F., & Hannafin, M. J. (2005). Design-based research and technology-enhanced learning environments. *Educational Technology Research and Development, 53*(4), 5–23.

Windschitl, M. (2004). Folk theories of "inquiry:" How preservice teachers reproduce the discourse and practices of an atheoretical scientific method. *Journal of Research in Science Teaching, 41*(5), 481–512.

Yang, K., & Heh, J. (2007). The impact of internet virtual physics laboratory instruction on the achievement in physics, science process skills and computer attitudes of 10th-grade students. *Journal of Science Education & Technology, 16*(5), 451–461.

Zacharia, Z. C. (2007). Comparing and combining real and virtual experimentation: An effort to enhance students' conceptual understanding of electric circuits. *Journal of Computer Assisted Learning, 23*, 120–132.

Chapter 5
Design Perspectives for Learning in Virtual Worlds

Michael J. Jacobson, Beaumie Kim, Chunyan Miao, Zhiqi Shen, and Mark Chavez

Overview

We live in a time when the first day revenues from a top selling computer game have exceeded those of any motion picture ever made. Virtual online communities such as Second Life have millions of "virtual inhabitants" and even a thriving real money economy in which approximately US $450 million was spent in 2008. The highly interactive and multiuser engagement in the current generation of commercially available computer games has attracted millions of users around the world and created a large economic market that is driving further development in this area. Regarding the potential of digital media and computer games for education, even the popular press (e.g., Business Week, WSJ, Wired, Fast Company, Business 2.0, and Economist) has published featured pieces about this topic over the past few years.

However, as is discussed below, a critical look at current empirical research on learning with 3D computer games suggests equivocal support that such environments inherently or automatically facilitate learning of subject-specific content knowledge. The challenge for using virtual worlds for learning[1] – as Chris Dede

M.J. Jacobson (✉)
Centre for Research on Computer-supported Learning and Cognition (CoCo),
The University of Sydney, Australia
e-mail: michael.jacobson@sydney.edu.au

B. Kim
Learning Sciences Laboratory, National Institute of Education, Nanyang Technological University, Singapore

C. Miao, Z. Shen, and M. Chavez
Nanyang Technological University, Singapore

---

[1] Various terms are used to describe 3D games and virtual environments for use in learning contexts, such as *serious games, multiuser virtual environments, immersive environments*, and so on. We prefer the use of *virtual worlds for learning* in this chapter to stress the purpose of these systems in educational contexts in contrast to implicit views of "games" as an entertainment outlet.

M.J. Jacobson and P. Reimann (eds.), *Designs for Learning Environments of the Future: International Perspectives from the Learning Sciences*, DOI 10.1007/978-0-387-88279-6_5, © Springer Science+Business Media, LLC 2010

(personal communication) has noted – is that unlike standing next to a fire where one automatically gets warm, being in a virtual learning world or game does not necessarily mean learning will occur.

As part of an investigation into this challenge, this chapter describes a program of research that is exploring pedagogical dimensions for designing virtual worlds for learning. The design and research work involving *Virtual Singapura* is discussed, which is a virtual world for learning science inquiry skills. The chapter first discusses issues in the literature related to learning content-specific knowledge in immersive virtual worlds and game environments, and pedagogical design approaches for learning in virtual worlds. Next, the design of *Virtual Singapura* is described in terms of its scenario for science inquiry learning, behaviors of the intelligent agents representing nineteenth-century characters, and the associated guided inquiry curriculum materials and research materials. Results of two classroom-based studies involving *Virtual Singapura* are reported, followed by a discussion of issues that emerged from these research findings.

Learning in Virtual Worlds and Game Environments

The potential of utilizing the representational, collaborative, and motivational aspects of virtual worlds to help achieve substantive education learning goals has been of interest to researchers exploring the technologies of learning for a number of years. Research into learning with 2D simulations and games has been ongoing since the late 1950s (Gredler, 2004). Surprisingly, however, even though there has been extensive development of 2D simulations and games for over 40 years, Gredler notes that most developers "report only sketchy anecdotal evidence or personal impressions of the success of their particular exercise" (p. 576). She goes on to comment that few research projects have documented enhanced posttest skills of students using games or of students' problem-solving strategies employed when using simulations.

By the mid-1990s, several researchers began to explore how immersive 3D visualizations or virtual reality (VR) technologies might be adapted for use in the development of 3D simulations for learning (Dede, 1995; Dede et al., 1994; Dede, Salzman, Loftin, & Ash, 2000; Dede, Salzman, & Loftin, 1996; McLellan, 2004; Psotka, 1994; Winn, 2002; Winn, Windschitl, & Hedley, 2001). Overall this research – which typically involved specialized VR equipment in which the learner used stereoscopic head-mounted displays (HMD) with sound and perhaps haptic devices for kinesthetic feedback – suggested that appropriately designed and used virtual learning environments may provide "value-added" learning over 2D educational technologies when content is controlled for. However, the higher cost of these technologies, both in terms of the computational resources required and the specialized ancillary equipment such as stereoscopic LCD shuttered HMD units or glasses has no doubt limited their more extensive use in precollege educational and home environments. Consequently, these research findings, while theoretically important, have had little practical impact on regular classroom practices.

More recently, the educational and research communities have become increasingly interested in systems sometimes referred to as "3D" games, which actually simulate a 3D environment displayed on a 2D computer screen (sometimes call 2.5D to differentiate from true visually immersive virtual experiences that run on currently available multimedia- and Internet-capable computers in schools and homes). The highly interactive and multiuser engagement in the current generation of commercially available computer games has attracted millions of users around the world to these environments and created a large economic market that is driving further technological and design developments in this area. Further, academics such as Gee (2003), and educational researchers such as Squire and associates (Squire, 2002, 2005; Squire et al., 2003), have recently argued that the affordances of highly interactive game-like systems are well suited to support many of the recommendations emerging from learning sciences and educational research related to how people learn. Indeed, Squire (2005) has written that the question is not "whether educators *can* use games to support learning, but *how* we use games most effectively as educational tools."

However, a critical look at the research to date on computer games and learning suggests that the case for how games support learning remains equivocal. In looking at two reviews of research on computer games and learning, it is interesting to note that the learning outcomes are discussed in very generic terms. For example, McFarlane, Sparrowhawk, and Heald (2002) note that while games provide a forum for learning knowledge and skills when playing a game, there is a mismatch between the content in commercial games and the curriculum content recognized as valuable in traditional school settings. In a more recent review of the literature, Kirriemuir and McFarlane (2004) consider issues such as the impact of violence in games, gender images in games, and the displacement of other activities by games. However, the discussion of research into learning outcomes associated with the use of commercial games in classroom settings found that whereas games were perceived to be motivational and helpful in fostering collaboration, teachers found that the amount of irrelevant information in commercial games wasted limited lesson time.

There are two notable indirect findings (i.e., not specifically discussed by either sets of authors) in both of these literature reviews of learning with games. First, the game systems that are discussed in these reviews represent commercially available games, so that the main purpose of these systems was not educational. Consequently, it is not surprising that many teachers felt there was nonrelevant material in the commercial games. Second, neither of these reviews reported empirical findings of significant learning gains in the regular curriculum content. This second point is also consistent with an observation made by Squire et al. (2003) that "very little empirical study has been done on how these games are used, and the existing research has failed to yield a useful research framework."

More recent research into learning in 3D games, multiuser virtual environments (MUVE), and virtual worlds (the term preferred for the *Virtual Singapura* research discussed in this chapter) has shifted to designing systems that are aligned with specific content, rather than attempting to repurpose existing commercially available games. For example, Squire, Barnett, Grant, & Higginbotham (2004) conducted a study in which 61 students used a game, SUPERCHARGED, to learn science content related to electrostatics, compared to 35 students in the control condition that did not use the game. Students in the experimental condition scored significantly higher on items related to electrostatics on the posttest compared to the control condition and no significant gender differences were found. Both the posttest and the qualitative interviews, however, revealed that most students did not construct understandings of the more complex electrostatic concepts in the SUPERCHARGED game and that certain misconceptions about charged particles in an electric field persisted. Other qualitative findings were that both boys and girls were initially eager to play the game, but that many boys lost interest by the second day once they felt they had "beat" the game. Interestingly, girls were less interested in "playing-the-game-for-points" mode and instead explored the game as a simulation in which they collaboratively worked to record their actions and to share their results with student peers.

A more extended program of research, the *Quest Atlantis* (QA) project employs an educational multiuser virtual environment that allows students to travel in a virtual space to perform in class or after school educational activities, talk with other students and mentors, and build virtual identities (Barab, Thomas, Dodge, Carteaux, & Tuzun, 2005). Research involving QA has consistently documented the motivational aspects of students engaged in QA "quests" (Barab, Dodge et al., 2007; Barab et al., 2005), which is consistent with the findings involving commercial computer games used in the classrooms discussed above. Interestingly, this research also found that students responded to the narrative aspects of the immersive experience more so than the "game-like" features (Barab et al., 2005), which is consistent with the findings of Squire et al. (2004) for the girls in that study. Unlike the research involving commercial computer games, however, there is a growing number of studies involving QA that are documenting significant learning gains in a variety of subjects, such as social studies (Barab, Dodge et al., 2007), and science (Barab, Warren, & Ingram-Goble, 2006; Barab, Zuiker et al., 2007).

Another long-term program of research into content learning with a 3D virtual environment is the *River City* MUVE project. We refer the reader to the extended discussion of design and learning research related to the *River City* project in the Ketelhut, Clark, and Nelson chapter (this volume). Of relevance to themes in the review of literature on learning with virtual environments, the *River City* project is another example of the explicit design of a virtual environment to be closely aligned with subject-specific knowledge, in this case, with a focus on science inquiry skills, health and diseases, ecology, and biology. Significant findings of learning content knowledge and inquiry skills have been found, as well as the motivational efficacy of the *River City* MUVE for a broad range of students, including those students struggling with motivation, self-worth, and lack of science content knowledge (Dede, Clarke, Ketelhut, Nelson, & Bowman, 2005b; Ketelhut, Dede, Clarke, Nelson, & Bowman, 2007).

The pedagogical designs of the educationally successful virtual learning environments discussed here – and others not considered here for brevity, such as the research of Shaffer, Squire, Halverson, and Gee (2005) and Steinkuehler (2004) – are explicitly or implicitly guided inquiry approaches based on a Vygotskian social constructivist model of learning-by-doing. For example, the guided social constructivist approach that has been primarily used for *River City* (Dede, Clarke, Ketelhut, Nelson, & Bowman, 2005a; Ketelhut et al., 2007) consists of a science inquiry curriculum that begins with relatively small scale or structured activities and progress to more complex and less structured activities over approximately 4 weeks, such as conducting scientific experiments in the virtual *River City*. Online resources, a printed laboratory book, and class talks by the teacher outside of the MUVE provide other scaffolding or structure in *River City* during the initial and middle portions of the curriculum, but this structure is faded by the time of the culminating experiments the students conduct as they investigate their team's hypotheses about what is causing the virtual citizens of *River City* to become sick. The learning activities or "quests" in *Quest Atlantis* also typically employ a guided or scaffolded inquiry approach that is intended to "bring together two traditionally disparate forces – the motivation of free play and the rigor of academics…" (Barab et al., 2005, p. 96).

In conclusion, recent research exploring the nature of learning with multiuser virtual worlds and 3D game environments has documented interesting educationally relevant outcomes, such as their motivational power and the opportunity to help develop important skills (e.g., collaboration) (Gee, 2003; Steinkuehler, 2004). However, there remain concerns about depth of learning about subject-specific knowledge and skills in virtual learning environments as well as the ability of students to apply and use this knowledge in new situations and contexts (Dede et al., 2005a).

Design Considerations for a Virtual World for Learning

The main goals of the ongoing research reported in this chapter are to explore the learning of challenging knowledge and skills in virtual worlds and the ways in which students may transfer their knowledge to novel problem contexts and to future learning (Bransford & Schwartz, 1999) outside of the virtual experiences. Undertaking research of this type, however, requires attention to a number of design issues that span different areas of specialization. In this section we use the *Virtual Singapura* (VS) project as a case study to discuss designing for: (a) situated and contextualized learning, (b) virtual pedagogy, (c) intelligent adaptive virtual interactions, and (d) virtual aesthetic experiences.

Designing for Situated and Contextualized Learning

The classroom-based research with VS investigates how a "virtually authentic" context might be engaging and meaningful for students as they develop science inquiry skills such as questioning, forming hypotheses, collecting data, data analysis, and hypothesis revision, as well as learning important science content knowledge about biology, communicable diseases, ecology, and human environmental impact. As part of the design research methodology of the project, the research team has worked closely with teachers in two Singapore secondary schools to get their perspectives and suggestions during the initial development phase of creating VS as well as during the classroom-based research in which their students used the VS multiuser virtual environment. It was hoped that using virtual nineteenth-century artifacts about Singapore such as historical buildings, agents representing different ethnic groups in Singapore (e.g., Chinese, Malay, Indian, Westerners), and historic period photographs would make this science inquiry environment relevant and motivating for Singapore students.

The basic scenario for VS was inspired by the fictional nineteenth century River City MUVE research (Dede et al., 2005b; Ketelhut et al., this volume). As VS was initially intended for use in Singapore secondary science classrooms, the teachers who collaborated with the research team as part of the design research methodology we employed suggested that a Singapore context for science inquiry might be more interesting for their students than the American centered River City MUVE. Our design team elected to base the VS scenario more tightly on historical research information about disease epidemics in nineteenth-century Singapore and about the cultural practices and conditions of the period, in contrast to the more fictitious scenarios of River City or Quest Atlantis. The scenario for VS has twenty-first century Singapore students go back in time to help the Governor of Singapore, Sir Andrew Clarke, and the citizens of the city figure out what is causing the illnesses and to propose viable nineteenth-century solutions to stop the epidemics. The cholera epidemic of 1873–1874 is used as the main source theme for VS, with historically based information about tuberculosis and malaria integrated into the scenario of the virtual science inquiry experiences of the students.

When students teleport back to nineteenth-century Singapore, they arrive at the Boat Quay on the Singapore River and then use their avatars (computer-generated characters on the screen that they control and communicate through) to explore portions of the historical city that include the Tan Tock Seng Hospital (Chinese Pauper Hospital), St. Joseph's Institution (one of the first schools in Singapore), a traditional Chinese Medical Hall in the merchant area by the Marina, tenement houses in Chinatown, marsh, and houses in the wealthy European neighborhood (see Fig. 5.1). As the twenty-first century student scientists investigate the causes of the diseases, they will visit various locations in the city, meet computer-generated VS residents (i.e., agents), inspect digital objects such as historical pictures to obtain information; and obtain air, water, and insect samples at selected data collection stations. The students communicate with team members using the group-chat function and they may also chat with the various nineteenth-century agents they meet, such as the doctor and nurse in the hospital (see Fig. 5.2), the wife of the traditional Chinese doctor, coolies on the street, a researcher at the medical school, the poor mother of a sick child, and so on.

Another history of science theme that was embedded in the VS scenario was the prevalent nineteenth-century theory that cholera was an air-borne disease rather than one transmitted due to feces-contaminated water, which was not widely

Fig. 5.1 Screen shot of student who is accessing the navigational map of *Virtual Singapura* along with the online "virtual microscope" developed by Dede's group at Harvard University

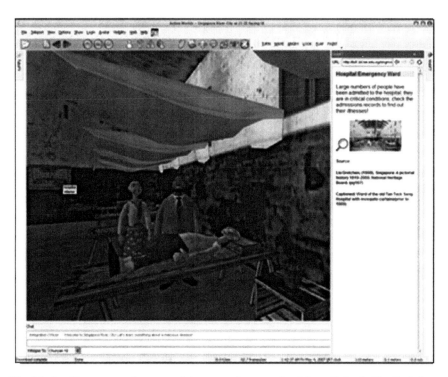

Fig. 5.2 Intelligent agent characters of the nurse, doctor, and a sick coolie in the Tan Tock Seng Hospital with a historical picture of the hospital on the right side of the screen

accepted until the late nineteenth century (for an interesting account of nineteenth-century scientific views of cholera and the impact of cholera epidemics, see Johnson, 2006). By including this history of science theme, our intent was to illustrate that science does not consist of fixed and static "facts," but instead involves initial tentative theoretical understandings and knowledge that changes over time. The revision of theories is thus inherently part of the scientific process, but one that secondary students do not often have the opportunity to experience. We also hoped that the historical contexts for VS could provide teachers with opportunities to extend the primary science inquiry focus of the current VS curriculum to include nineteenth-century historical and social issues that were important in Singapore and in other port cities around the world during that period.

The students experience how the early Chinese and European immigrants formed ethnic town areas, which we call Chinatown and European town in VS. The Chinatown population consisted mainly of laborers, commonly known as coolies, who lived in overcrowded and unhygienic quarters. Due to these poor and unhealthy living conditions, coolies were extremely vulnerable to diseases, and significant death rates were common in this area. In contrast, the European quarter had a relatively small population of rich European traders who lived in spacious and comfortable houses. Within the context of this complex historically based environment, VS allows students to engage in science inquiry activities related to understanding why and how the virtual citizens of VS become sick with diseases such as cholera, malaria, and tuberculosis.

Designing for Virtual Pedagogy

The curriculum of VS is intended to be aligned with the Singapore secondary science syllabus, in particular with knowledge and skills related to science inquiry that are just now being explicitly taught in 2008 at the secondary level. Students learn to identify problems and to suggest a hypothesis for a problem of interest, identify relevant dependent and independent variables, gather data, and to discuss if their hypothesis was confirmed or not and to provide an explanation for that outcome.

Pedagogically, the VS Student Lab Book exemplifies a guided inquiry approach (Dede et al., 2005a; Ketelhut et al., 2007; Tinker, 2007) in which students are initially scaffolded (e.g., experience a structured set of activities) while they are learning science inquiry skills, and over the course of the unit, the structure or scaffolding is gradually reduced (i.e., this is a "high-low-structure" pedagogical approach, see below). As a team, students collaboratively obtain information, collect data, and discuss their findings. Working together with peers not only helps students to see different perspectives, but also allows them to "divide and conquer" the tasks at hand. Information is available from interactions with the intelligent agents and from clickable informative objects (e.g., pictures, library books, and hospital admissions chart) in VS. For example, when students click on a picture in the interior of the hospital, a panel appears on the right side of the screen and provides historical information as well as clues related to different things that are going on in VS related to the health issues in the city (Fig. 5.2). Individually, students write reflections and interim reports to the Governor, which provide teachers and researchers with formative insights into students' understanding of the scientific inquiry process and their thoughts on the causes of different diseases and their transmission.

The Student Lab Book functions as a road map to guide learners to advance through three levels: Level One – Junior Scientist, Level Two – Assistant Scientist, and Level Three – Scientist. Each of these levels consists of class objectives and goals for students to accomplish in their scientific inquiry activities in the VS world. In Level One, as Junior Scientists, students apply more everyday ways of doing inquiry, such as making inferences based on observations, using their senses (e.g., seeing and hearing) as research tools for exploring VS, sharing gathered information with teammates, and making educated guesses about possible causal factors. In Level Two, students, as Assistant Scientists, learn to apply more formal scientific inquiry process and tools to conduct a research experiment. Virtual researcher tools, such as the air and water sampling stations and insect catcher/counter, are embedded in VS for students to compare the levels of different disease concentrations or number of insects from one area to another. The progression from Level One to Two provides students with the experience of shifting learning perspectives from subjective inferences to more formal science inquiry-based reasoning. Finally, in Level Three, students conduct their experiments about what was causing people to get sick in *Virtual Singapura*. There were six independent variable conditions that were developed for VS that the student teams could select from: (a) clean resident's residencies, (b) change to the rainy season (main VS world is set in the low rain season in Singapore), (c) drain the swamp, (d) close all wells and build new ones, (e) build new tenement buildings, and (f) change the practices of the night soil coolies. The teams would state what their hypothesis was (e.g., closing contaminated wells and building new ones would lower the number of people getting cholera), decide what dependent variables for which to collect data (e.g., collect water samples and count the number of hospital patients sick with cholera in the main VS world and in the VS world with the clean wells), and then interpret the data to see if their hypothesis was confirmed. The students then individually wrote up their online reflections to the Governor about what they found and what they recommended, and each team gave presentations to the entire class.

Designing for Intelligent Adaptive Virtual Interactions

The design of adaptive synthetic characters is a challenging problem in the field of artificial intelligence and education, and there has been little research to date into the use of intelligent agent techniques to model synthetic characters in immersive virtual worlds for learning (see, for example, Holmes, 2007). A focus of this portion of our research is to explore how the functionality of intelligent agents might enhance the learning outcomes of students in their virtual world experiences. The intelligent agents in *Virtual Singapura* are designed using the Goal Net architecture, which is a set of algorithms for modeling the goals of agents in multiagent virtual worlds developed by members of the Emerging Research Lab at Nanyang Technological University in Singapore (Shen, Miao, & Cai, 2007; Shen, Miao, & Gay, 2006). A Goal Net is composed of *goals* and *transitions*. Goals represent the objectives that an agent needs to pursue, and transitions specify the relationship between two goals. Each transition is associated with a task list that defines the possible tasks the agent needs to perform in order to move between two goals. A Goal Net thus defines all the possible paths by which a goal can be reached or achieved from another goal. In addition, a Goal Net may consist of *atomic goals* and/or *composite goals*. An atomic goal is a primitive that cannot be further decomposed, whereas a composite goal can be split into subgoals connected via transitions. A complex Goal Net thus can be recursively decomposed into a hierarchical structure consisting of composite goals and atomic goals, which simplifies the goal modeling process across different levels of abstraction. Finally, the Goal Net architecture connects input and output goals using four types of transition relations: *sequence, choice, concurrency,* and *synchronization.* The combination of the different types of relations and connections between goals defines all possible goal pursuit paths. The selected path is dynamically determined in real time with the goal selection algorithms as part of the runtime environment.

In our research, the Goal Net architecture has been extended to interoperate with the Active Worlds virtual world server as part of the pilot VS project (see below). The use of agents with goal nets has been initially tested in the VS world in relatively simple yet functional ways, such as increasing the range of queries and informational responses a synthetic character may "understand," helping students navigate in the virtual landscape, or answering various forms of questions students commonly ask virtual characters, such as: *Who are you? Are you sick? Where am I? Where should I go next after I explore this area?*

For another example of how the intelligent agents behave in VS, Dr. Rajabali and Nurse Siti follow goal net rules to move around and visit the various patients in the hospital for 5–10 s each and to occasionally come together themselves (see Fig. 5.2). When a student's avatar approaches either of them, at a certain distance they will turn to the avatar and begin a greeting, as shown in this initial conversation between Dr. Rajabali and a student who visits the hospital for the first time:

Hi there, June! I believe this is your first visit at the hospital. Many of the patients have very bad diarrhea, and some of their bodies had turned blue from dehydration. As my medicine is not working, I am reexamining my patients' symptoms to come up with other cures. Perhaps you should talk to my patients, too.

When this student visits the hospital for the second or third time,[2] Dr. Rajabali's responds in this way:

[2] We developed three different paraphrased versions for each response option, so there would be a two out of three chance a subsequent response would be slightly different than the first response, or that a second student approaching an agent would get a slightly different greeting than the previous student.

Hello again! The situation has not improved. I hope you are able to find out what is causing my patients to be sick. Feel free to look around or talk to the people here.

The agent "knows" that this is the first or subsequent time a student visited this particular location, and thus can adaptively provide context and situation-specific information to the student. The agents in different VS "sets" (i.e., the virtual locations we have developed) also keep track of the information resources (e.g., artifacts, pictures with captions) each student has accessed in these various areas, and agents may provide suggestions to a student, such as to check important resources that may not have been accessed during previous visits. In addition, by primarily having the agents initiate the interactions with avatars, the design team intended to constrain the range of likely questions a student might ask, and thus to minimize the number of responses to be authored for each synthetic character. Log files record all interactions between students and the agents in our studies, and we plan to review these logs to identify commonly asked additional questions that responses will be authored for and then programmed into future versions of the virtual world.

The research reported in this chapter represents our early technology development and research steps to integrate and to use intelligent agent technologies in a virtual learning world. In the discussion of future research, we consider new directions we plan to explore for ways in which intelligent agents might support innovative pedagogical trajectories for learning in virtual world experiences.

Designing for Virtual Aesthetic Experiences

In designing the aesthetic and visual appearance of the VS virtual world, we chose to use the look of Cibachrome prints and illustrations of nineteenth century Singapore. The goal was to immerse the user in the look of the era as seen from the twenty-first century within the limitations of the Active Worlds DirectX 7 graphics engine. Our team resourced photographs in the National Archives of Singapore, photographed the existing buildings from the era, and studied the costumes and hairstyles of men, women, and children from this historical period.

The short development timeline for 20 agent characters used in *Virtual Singapura* was a challenge met by redesigning models sourced from a library of character models. These models were modified to reflect the cultural and ethnic milieu of nineteenth century Singapore as well as the costuming and hairstyles of the era. The Nanyang Technology University art team utilized character assets and the motion and gestures provided by the Active Worlds environment. In doing so, we minimized the labor that would normally be devoted to the design, animation, and rigging of 3D characters. However, while this is not an optimal approach when creating original art assets, the emphasis within the research team for this project was to create an engaging aesthetic experience in the virtual world to support the learning sciences and agent research, rather than on artistic novelty per se.

Research

Two studies have been conducted to date involving the *Virtual Singapura* (VS) science inquiry unit. In this section, we provide an overview of these studies (for additional information, see Jacobson, Kim, Lee, Lim, & Low, 2008).

Virtual Singapura Study 1

VS study 1 was a pilot study involving the initial implementation of the VS environment, supporting materials, and assessments to explore ways in which this virtual environment might help students to learn science inquiry skills. The study was implemented over ten class periods, each 50 min, for Secondary One (grade 7) students in an all boys Singapore school during August 2007. Three classes with a total of 104 students went through the VS science inquiry program based on historical epidemics in nineteenth-century Singapore. They worked collaboratively in teams of four on the various problems and science inquiry activities in the Student Lab Book (see above), answered online and off line questions during these classes, and came up with group presentations to their respective classes on their hypotheses related to the causes of diseases in VS.

The students also completed a pretest and a posttest, which consisted of both multiple choice and open-ended items. In addition to the tests, pre- and postsurveys were administered that contained affective measures derived from the Attitude toward Science and Adoption of Science Values scales of the *Test of Science-Related Attitudes* (TOSRA) by Fraser (1978). The survey items asked the students' perceptions about "feeling like a scientist," working in teams, and learning in the VS science inquiry unit. All of these items were measured with seven-point Likert scales (1–7 representing the negative and positive ends of each item). Interviews of a group of the students and of all participating teachers were conducted at the end of the VS unit.

Given that the pretest and posttest were of unequal lengths, the scores on the parallel items from the two tests were compared instead. It was found that the mean score on the posttest ($M=0.75$, SD$=0.12$) was significantly lower than on the pretest ($M=0.78$, SD$=0.12$; $t(209)=2.89$, $p<0.01$), although the effect size was moderate ($d=0.40$). However, the Likert scale responses on both the Attitude towards Science and Adoption of Science Values scales were significantly higher ($p<0.05$) on the posttest than the pretest.

The main qualitative data consisted of interviews conducted with one team of four students from each of the three VS classes, as well as with the three VS teachers. Briefly, these interviews suggest that the students found VS to be very engaging and, more important, that they felt it fostered different types of learning than is typical in science classes:

...so we don't feel bored...because the teachers just like (gave) us all the notes...then we just copy down and all that, but in 'Virtual Singapura,' we get to carry out experiments ourselves, so we understand better.

...it ('Virtual Singapura') was very interesting as we not only get information from our teachers... we get to conduct experiments by ourselves, and when there were different outcomes from the others, it was like very interesting...

We all learn how to use our information we gathered to err... like conduct experiments, form a hypothesis, and err...find the outcome of the experiment...

...the process of learning while you're playing is quite fun...you can learn better.

The teachers overall had positive comments about the use of this approach to help students learn about scientific inquiry and science content. A science education teacher who had been part of the design research team from the start of the project expressed her impressions this way:

I think to have the virtual world is a very good idea, because they use their own senses; it is online… they get to ask questions…they get to figure things out for themselves…it is much better than teachers telling them. I really like the way they learnt how to write the hypothesis statements. They learnt how to construct a hypothesis or educated guess. They tried different ways to prove themselves correct or wrong. A few of them went on the wrong direction when they tried to do certain experiment and nothing happened, I could see the disappointment on their faces, and I am so happy to see that not because they were disappointed but because they really wanted to know the answers. They did not turn to their classmates for answer; they worked among the group themselves to find the answer as to what could they do differently…I liked it.

It can be seen in these short interview excerpts that both the students and this teacher regarded VS as a learning environment in which the students had more ownership and responsibility for their learning. The distinction between a fundamentally learner-centered approach of VS and of didactic teaching that is common in Singapore is one both the students and the teacher noted. In addition, both the students and the teachers regarded VS as a clearly more motivating and engaging way to learn compared to one in which students would just "copy down notes," as one boy commented. Clearly the students and this teacher (as well as the other teachers, not quoted here) felt the students were learning important subject knowledge and skills and that the experience was an engaging one.

Overall, the qualitative findings are consistent with the higher scores on the Attitude toward Science and Adoption of Science Values scales. However, the lower scores on the science content and inquiry oriented posttest are puzzling given the clear indications the students were motivated and engaged in their learning activities, which generally is correlated with increased learning outcomes. One possible reason may be that the students were not motivated during the VS study 1 posttest as this was not a "grade counting" test given the experimental context of this study. Assuming, however, that the students were reasonably conscientious in their work on the posttest, there appear to be two other main factors to explain the lower posttest results. First, only 10 of the 40 computers in the lab could run the VS program simultaneously due to bandwidth limitations, and even those computers responded very slowly at times. Consequently, it was necessary to group four students per team to share one computer. This was hardly an ideal situation, as often only one or two students seemed actively engaged with the virtual activities at any given moment. Second, it may be that the students were in fact learning about science inquiry skills in the context of the virtual world, but that they were unable to apply or to transfer these new understandings to the paper-and-pencil-based context of the posttest. In the next section, we discuss the follow-up study that was designed to explore issues raised in this initial research involving the VS science inquiry unit.

Virtual Singapura Study 2

After completing the VS study 1 in September 2007, teachers at the participating school approached the research team about using VS in a science education module for the new grade seven cohort of students (nine classes) that was entering this all boys secondary school in Singapore. The school agreed to provide additional time in the main computer lab so that we could accommodate the additional students. Even though the teachers were clearly pleased with the engagement and outcomes of the initial pilot study, the research team was interested in taking advantage of this opportunity to investigate possible reasons for the mixed learning findings in the earlier VS study. In preparation for this second study, we made changes in the design based on teachers' suggestions and our observations and interest. Table 5.1 summarizes the changes, which were mainly focused on the pedagogical considerations of the design. VS study 2 focused on three main research questions. First, what are the technical infrastructure conditions that would be necessary to deploy the intelligent agent and virtual world architecture our team had used to develop VS on a wider scale in a secondary school setting in Singapore? Second, would there be enhanced engagement and learning from the VS science inquiry unit if all students had individual access to VS with a computer? Third, might a post-VS classroom-based activity enhance the ability of students to apply or to transfer knowledge and skills experienced in the virtual world to a new, nonvirtual world context?

To explore the first two research questions, the project provided a dedicated 10 megabit high speed Internet connection to the computer laboratory where the VS study 2 was held, which was approximately 10–15 times faster than the standard Internet bandwidth provided in Singapore schools at the time the study was run. This allowed each student to individually run the VS program, control his own avatar, complete the online individual tasks, and to interact with teammates on the online collaborative activities in the VS science inquiry unit. Concerning the second research question, it was hoped that this additional interaction and engagement for all students would enhance learning gains at the end of the VS science inquiry unit.

The third research question represented a new direction for VS research related to the issue of learning for transfer in a virtual world. Dede et al. (2005a) have observed with respect to learning in virtual and game environments that "no studies have yet established the transfer of skills mastered in gaming to life situations" (p. 1). At the time the VS study 2 was conducted in 2008, our research team was not aware

Table 5.1 Design changes in the two *Virtual Singapura* studies

Design consideration	Study 1 design features	Design changes in study 2
Situated and contextualized learning	• Nineteenth century Singapore disease epidemics • Sir Andrew Clarke, the governor's request • Synthetic characters sharing their difficulties, observations, and hypotheses (according to historical information) • Learners as problem solvers	No major changes
Virtual pedagogy	• Guided inquiry • Leveling up as scientists • Reflective questions and reporting to the governor • Most of the tools and information online • Virtual experiments (one experiment is chosen by the group)	• Fewer guiding questions • Selected online tools also made available in the printed lab book (e.g., hospital records) • Virtual experiments (one asked by the governor, another chosen by the group) • Pedagogy outside of VS (i.e., analogical encoding)
Intelligent adaptive virtual interactions	• Synthetic characters adaptively responding to the virtual learner avatars • Four students interacting with agents using one computer	• No major change in the agent interactions • Each student interacting with agents using his own computer • Group members communicating through chat
Virtual aesthetic experiences	• Nineteenth century Singapore setting • Synthetic characters with different ethnic groups and traditional costumes	No major changes

of any studies of learning in virtual or game worlds that had empirically addressed this challenge. As background for how we approached this question, we view transfer as an indication of deep learning and understanding that is reflected in the ability of learners to use their knowledge in new ways or to further advance their understandings and learn in the future.[3] Recently, a perspective about the mechanism of

---

[3] Theoretical framings in the learning and cognitive sciences of the construct of "transfer" have received considerable attention over the past two decades, as the review by Lobato (2006) provides. In this chapter, we align with the definitions of transfer provided by (a) the United States National Academy of Science (Bransford, Brown, Cocking, & Donovan, 2000) defined as the "ability to extend what has been learned in one context to new contexts" (p. 51) and (b) preparations for future learning (Bransford & Schwartz, 1999).

transfer – analogical encoding theory (Gentner, Loewenstein, & Thompson, 2003) – has been proposed that is a variation of the influential structure-mapping theory proposed by Gentner. In analogical reasoning, a set of correspondences is highlighted between the shared relational structures of two analogs that might have different surface features, with a person's knowledge of the source analog (hopefully) leading to understanding of the target analog. With analogical encoding, however, a learner may only partially understand two cases, but the process of comparing two cases that share an underlying principle or concept helps the learner focus on the structural commonalities rather than the idiosyncratic surface features. It is further postulated that the process of analogical encoding promotes schema abstraction and thus enhances learning, recall, and transfer. Empirical research involving analogical encoding learning activities has demonstrated significant enhanced learning and transfer for participants in the analogical encoding "contrast and compare" condition in contrast to comparison treatments such as sequentially studying cases (Gentner et al., 2003; Thompson, Gentner, & Loewenstein, 2000). There has also been recent work on the design of a virtual game-based system based on principles of analogical encoding (Williams, Ma, Feist, & Prejean, 2007).

Our research team elected to design an intervention based on analogical encoding theory (Gentner et al., 2003) for the students to complete *after* going through all of VS science inquiry classes but before the posttest. Two short text problem-solving scenarios were developed that differed in terms of their "surface" features but each shared solution approaches involving science inquiry principles. The first inquiry problem, *Purpura Nautica*, concerns the historical challenge James Lind experienced on the HMS Salisbury in trying to determine the cause of the disease killing numerous sailors in which they had teeth and hair loss, sunken eyes, and often death. The second inquiry problem, written to have highly contrasting surface features, concerned a market researcher interested if a certain word in the subject line of a mass distributed email advertising an event might be interpreted as "spam" and thus not read by the intended recipient.

Three different teacher lead treatment conditions were developed: (a) Contrast and Compare, (b) Advise–Advise, and (c) Content Revision. In the Compare and Contrast experimental condition, students were asked to reflect on the things that they had learned from using VS, to contrast and compare the two cases to determine if there were common principles, and then to write their solutions to each of the problem scenarios. The other two treatments were comparison conditions designed to be similar to relatively common school-based learning tasks. In the Advise–Advise comparison condition, students were asked to read the two problem scenarios and then to write their "advice" about how each of them should be solved. Content Revision was the second comparison condition, and students answered a set of questions that were related to the information presented in the two problem scenario. There are no single "correct" solutions to these problems, but each of them is best solved using scientific inquiry principles, such as formulating a hypothesis, identifying appropriate dependent and independent variables, collecting data, and interpreting results.

It was expected, based on the findings of VS study 1, that the students might only partially understand the science inquiry principles they learned during the activities involving *Virtual Singapura*. Based on analogical encoding theory, it was hypothesized that students in the Contrast and Compare treatment would abstract or construct an understanding of the structural similarities across the cases, that is, principles of science inquiry, in a manner not cognitively tied to the surface features of the two cases or to the VS virtual world. Thus it was hypothesized that students in the Contrast and Compare experimental condition would have a higher performance on a posttest science inquiry transfer problem that had not been previously studied than students in the two comparison conditions.

Materials

Consistent with the design research methodology employed in the program of research, quantitative and qualitative information from the prior study as well as feedback from the teachers was used to iteratively revise the materials, activities, and assessments for VS study 2. The VS program itself was not substantively changed for this study, although we elected to disable a couple of Active Worlds avatar characters available for the students to select, such as the young male avatar with shades riding a motor scooter (clearly not appropriate for the nineteenth century scenario of VS), and the "alien" and "bird" avatars. The VS Student Lab Book was slightly revised in two ways. First, the daily sequence of activities was shortened to nine class periods (rather than ten in VS study 1), which was done by removing selected tasks that did not seem valuable in the initial implementation, although the content coverage remained the same.

Second, and of more importance, the description of the major task for the final science inquiry experiment the student teams were to undertake was changed based on our classroom observations in VS study 1. Recall that the student teams in VS study 1 were asked to select one of six different experimental settings, articulate a hypothesis, collect data to see if their hypothesis was confirmed or not, and then to explain why it was or why it was not. What we qualitatively observed was that if the teams felt the data was not consistent with their hypothesis, this meant they had chosen the wrong experimental setting and that they had the "wrong answer." They would then select a second or even a third experimental setting to try to get the "right answer." For example, if a team selected "close all wells and build new ones" experiment (which would involve collecting water samples from the main VS world, and then collecting data from new wells about a month after the old wells were closed), then they would find out that the same wells in the Chinese Rickshaw tenement area of Singapore were *still* polluted. The design team had intended that the students reflect on this finding, which would disconfirm their hypothesis, and to perhaps realize that some of the virtual characters in VS and information in embedded pictures discussed how the night soil coolies, who carried buckets of human waste to the farms, were seen to wash these buckets in the wells. This historically documented practice contributed to cholera outbreaks in Singapore that were more common in the dry season (when the water tables were quite low) than in the rainy season, when tuberculosis was more common (presumably as more people were inside, particularly in the cramped tenements the coolies lived in).

To address this problem, the design team changed the final online task in this way: "The Governor has requested that your team investigate a public health question he has for Virtual Singapura." The teacher would then explain that the Governor had tried six different public health projects and that the student research teams were to select one of the projects and to run an experiment to see which, if any, public health projects were successful. (As there were approximately nine to ten teams in each class, some of the projects had two teams running experiments, which actually stimulated some of the discussions during the final team presentations.) Our hope was that the students would not feel a *personal* investment in the particular experiment if the hypothesis was not confirmed, as they were not being judged about whether their findings were "the right answer" as to why people were getting sick in VS. We did not observe any of the student teams trying to run other experiments (as in VS study 1), and instead, they seemed focused on trying to understand how the data explained if the particular public health project was successful or not, which was the intended task.

VS Study 2 Method and Results

Three hundred thirty five grade seven students, all boys with mean age of 13, took part in this study. Of these, 27 students did not complete all of the assessments (pretest, posttest, and surveys), so the final data analysis involved 308 participants. During this implementation, each student had access to a computer and interacted with his teammates through online chatting, unlike in the pilot study when four students had to share a single computer.

For the class in which the three analogical encoding treatment conditions were administered, three classes were assigned to each of the three conditions: Contrast and Compare (107 students), Advise–Advise (98 students), and Content Revision (103 students). In each of these conditions, the students spent about 20 min going through the two cases (see Appendix 1) and attempting to answer questions that were posed. Teachers then spent the remaining class time going through the cases, discussing, and sharing suggested solutions consistent with the three strategies associated with the three treatment conditions. Three teachers, A, B, and C took part in the study, and each taught three classes. They facilitated all the science inquiry lessons and the three analogical encoding treatment conditions.

In the assessment results, the overall pretest and posttest scores revealed no significant differences, unlike in the VS study 1 where there was a significant decrease in the posttest performance compared to the pretest. To assess the effectiveness of the analogical encoding treatment conditions, we looked at the performance on open-ended pretest and posttest problem-solving scenarios that were to be solved using science inquiry principles (these items were similar to the two scenarios used in the analogical encoding treatments, see Appendix). The responses to the items were coded using a 16-point rubric by two raters; interrater percentage agreement was 97–100%. A one way (Problem-Solving Group) Analysis of Covariance (ANCOVA) was conducted to test for differences in the performance on the posttest inquiry problem, controlling for corresponding pretest inquiry problem. Although the mean scores were in the predicted direction, with the Contrast and Compare condition performing at a higher level than the other two comparison conditions (Contrast and Compare ($n = 107$): $M = 0.20$, $SD = 0.14$; Advise–Advise ($n = 98$): $M = 0.18$, $SD = 0.16$; Content Revision ($n = 103$): $M = 0.19$, $SD = 0.14$), the results of the ANCOVA did not reveal a significant group effect.

Since the teachers facilitated each of the classroom analogical encoding treatments, performance on the posttest inquiry problem was further examined with Teacher as a factor. A two way (Teacher and Analogical Encoding Group) ANCOVA was conducted to determine if there were any differences in the posttest performance, controlling for the performance on the pretest inquiry problem. There was no significant group effect, but a significant Teacher ($F(2,298) = 8.02$, $p < 0.001$, $\eta^2 = 0.05$) and Teacher by Analogical Encoding Group interaction effects were found ($F(2,298) = 9.29$, $p < 0.001$, $\eta^2 = 0.11$). As shown in Table 5.2, the means of inquiry problem scores of teachers A and B were in the expected directions, whereas the mean scores for teacher C were not. Teacher C was the least experienced of the three teachers, so an additional ANCOVA was run selecting for the two experienced teachers, A and B, which involved 209 students. A one way (Analogical Encoding Group) Analysis of Covariance (ANCOVA) was conducted on the posttest inquiry problem, which revealed a significant group effect ($F(2,208) = 4.20$, $p < 0.05$, $\eta^2 = 0.04$)[4] whereby students in the Contrast and Compare group performed at a significantly higher level than the two comparison groups.

As in VS study 1, students in this study completed the same instrument based on the Fraser (1978) *Test of Science-Related Attitudes* (TOSRA). For the science attitudes, paired *t*-tests revealed that there were significantly lower ($p < 0.05$) attitudes toward science and less adoption of science values by the postsurvey compared to

Table 5.2 Posttest means and estimated marginal means on posttest science inquiry problem-solving scenario

| Teacher | Analogical encoding group | | | | | |
| | Means (SD) | | | Estimated marginal means (SE) | | |
	Control ($n=103$)	Advise–advise ($n=98$)	Compare contrast ($n=107$)	Control ($n=103$)	Advise–advise ($n=98$)	Compare contrast ($n=107$)
A	0.19 (0.13)	0.21 (0.15)	0.22 (0.15)	0.19 (0.02)	0.20 (0.02)	0.22 (0.02)
n	32	35	37	32	35	37
B	0.15 (0.10)	0.25 (0.18)	0.25 (0.15)	0.16 (0.02)	0.25 (0.02)	0.26 (0.02)
n	37	33	35	37	33	35
C	0.24 (0.17)	0.08 (0.08)	0.21 (0.09)	0.24 (0.02)	0.08 (0.03)	0.12 (0.08)
n	34	30	35	34	30	35

[4] A partial $\eta^2 = 0.01$ is considered a small effect size, 0.06 medium, and 0.14 a large effect size.

the presurvey, which was surprising given the significant increase on these scales pre-to-post in the VS study 1.

A new Likert scale item was added to the VS study 2 postsurvey that asked about the students' perceptions of learning with *Virtual Singapura*. The results were largely positive as more than 75% of the students liked using the program in the range of 5–7 of 7 ($M = 5.43$, SD = 1.29). This survey response is also consistent with the overall positive comments about learning with VS that were made by students in the exit interviews.

Concerning perceptions of the final online activities, the teachers reported having a concern about the students collecting data in two experiments that resulted in student complaints and made implementation even more packed given the available time. One of teachers made this comment during her interview:

> ...we should have a more thorough explanation of what is it they actually go through that two times, that two trials. Because when I actually tried to explain to them, some of them did not really understand why is it they have to actually go on to take test on the water samples and... they do it twice, so when they actually did the second time, they were like complaining to me, 'Eh, I'm doing the same thing again.' But after it takes some time to explain to them and stuff like that, they kind of get it...

The student interviews about this issue were interesting. For example, students mentioned that their favorite activities were doing the experiments, which we did not hear from the previous interviews with the VS study 1 students. To probe the concern of the teachers about doing two experiments, we asked students whether or not they preferred doing just one experiment. We found that many students in fact felt this was a useful set of activities: "We prefer more [experiments];" "It's like better so we can check more hypotheses to see which one is correct;" and "two is better than doing one."

It is interesting that the students came to value doing two experiments and no longer had any complaints during the interview. We also see here the important role of the teacher as a facilitator or coach to help the students persevere, which in turn resulted in a better long-term learning outcome from the students' perspective of their experiences in VS. This is clearly a different teacher role than traditional didactic instruction, but illustrative of vital facilitative ways in which teachers will likely help students in future learning environments such as virtual worlds.

Finally, based on qualitative classroom observations, the students in VS study 2 seemed to make higher quality presentations about their research findings to their peers and teachers than in the previous study even though these students had just started secondary school (VS study 1 students were at the end of the second term for secondary one). For example, some of the presenting teams were asked to explain how the data they reported actually related to the hypothesis that was proposed, or to justify how data collected about water quality in the wells impacted diseases when there was no data reported on patient symptoms from the hospital (see Appendix 2 for excerpts of this classroom discussion). Still another student team was carefully questioned about why they believed draining the marsh (which only reduced the number of malaria carrying mosquitoes in VS) would impact the cholera microbe counts in the drinking water wells located in completely different locations of the city.

VS Study 2 Discussion

The first research question concerned the type of technical infrastructure that would be necessary to deploy the intelligent agent and virtual world architecture of *Virtual Singapura* in a regular school setting. The technical data we collected indicated that the higher bandwidth the project team provided into the school's main computer lab was in fact necessary for the VS program to run at an appropriate speed and for each student in the computer lab to be able use the program and to engage in the virtual world learning activities. Whereas this high bandwidth requirement for the intelligent agent VS program may limit its wider scale use in the short term, it is generally expected that the next generation broadband speed that schools will have access to will be increased to the levels that programs such as VS require. Another solution to this issue would be to locate servers for the intelligent agent and virtual world engines at individual schools, which would be cost effective given the current low cost of high performance computer servers and the typical high speed internal networks most schools have (typically 100 times faster than the external Internet connection). Another advantage of this solution is that the servers would be inside the firewalls nearly all schools have, which are often strictly setup to protect students from accessing inappropriate websites but with the unintended consequence of blocking access to external servers for various virtual world systems such as Second Life that could be used for educational purposes.

The second research question dealt with levels of engagement and learning that might result if all students had individual access to VS with a computer, in contrast to the four to a computer situation in VS study 1. Based on our qualitative observations of the students in the VS study 2, it was clear that there was much less off-task behavior in this enactment of the VS science inquiry unit. The students indicated they like using VS on a postsurvey item, and comments in the student and teacher interviews suggested both engagement and positive views of learning with VS.

Concerning the issue of enhanced learning being associated with the one-to-one computer access, the results are less clear. We were disappointed that there were no significant learning gains demonstrated on the main posttest items compared to the pretest. Comparing this finding to the VS study 1, where there was a significant *decrease* in the posttest performance, suggests that there may have been a small efficacy for the one-to-one computer access. Members of the research team also felt the presentations by the student teams seemed to be at a higher level than in the first study. Still, given clear indications the students were motivated and engaged in the guided inquiry activities, the lack of demonstrated gains on the main posttest assessments was disappointing.

The third research area investigated a post-VS classroom-based activity that might enhance transfer of knowledge and skills experience in the virtual world to nonvirtual settings and contexts. It was found that students receiving the experimental analogical encoding treatment scored significantly higher on the main posttest problem-solving transfer task that required specifying an appropriate scientific hypothesis, dependent and independent variables, and expected outcomes than the students in the other two conditions, which was in the theoretically predicted direction. Whereas the effect size for this finding is moderately small, we believe future research is warranted to explore this theory-based classroom pedagogical approach that accompanies pedagogies of virtual worlds.

Also related to the third research area into transfer of learning, it was interesting that often it was not the teacher who provided critical comments after the team presentations, but rather the fellow students in the class. Indeed, these questions were quite aligned with the types of science inquiry skills and ways of thinking we wished the students to learn. In addition, the team presentation activity was "outside" of the virtual world, and thus shows the potential anchoring value of such classroom experiences to help foster learning through collaboration and reflection about the experiences students had been involved with "inside" the virtual world. Thus future research might explore the potential value of learning in virtual worlds in terms of "preparations for future learning," which is an important direction for research on transfer (Bransford & Schwartz, 1999), and also to explore the importance of reflective learning "outside" of the virtual world to foster deeper learning experiences.

Future Research

Overall, the findings from the two studies involving the use of *Virtual Singapura* and the VS science inquiry unit provide useful technical, implementation, and learning findings. The technical and implementation implications are important, such as the need for adequate bandwidth, but relatively easy to systemically explore and to address if there is sufficient school or educational system interest. The VS project represents one of the first to integrate an intelligent agent architecture with a virtual world to explore ways in which adaptive synthetic characters might enhance the learner's experience in a virtual world and perhaps to enhance learning as well. The positive findings of student engagement and motivation are consistent with virtual- and game-based learning research reported by others (e.g., Barab et al., 2005; Dede et al., 2005a; Gee, 2003; Ketelhut, Clarke, & Nelson, 2009).

In terms of future advances in the computational architecture of the VS virtual world, we are interested in enhancing the functionality of agents to have an awareness of locations (where), situations (what happened), and contexts (how) (Cai, Miao, Tan, & Shen, 2008) to enhance their ability for social collaboration in order to further support student learning in the virtual environment (Yu, Shen, & Miao, 2008b). In addition, authoring tools such as a "scenario designer" and an "agent factory" are being developed to support the generation of agents in virtual worlds (Cai, Shen, & Miao, 2007; Yu, Shen, & Miao, 2008a). These agent development tools are intended to be easy to use by nonprogrammers and will be integrated into virtual worlds such as a new version of *Virtual Singapura* so that researchers and teachers (rather than programmers) can create agents and build scenario based goal nets according to research or curriculum needs. In addition, new functionality is being developed to support knowledge mining, dynamic inference, and action selection, which will greatly enhance the research data that will be obtained in the project and in turn provide information to inform the iterative enhancement of agents in future studies.

The mixed learning findings, however, are problematic in ways that may require theoretical rethinking of the pedagogical designs for virtual worlds for learning. For example, the only significant learning gain documented in either of these studies – the higher performance on a challenging transfer problem on the posttest – involved an innovative pedagogical intervention based on analogical encoding theory (Gentner et al., 2003) that was implemented *outside* of the virtual learning experiences. Although a provisional finding that needs further investigation, it broaches a broader issue of the types of pedagogical experiences that might evoke successful learning outcomes in what generally have been found to be engaging and motivational experiences for learners. We next consider a new framework for the design of pedagogical experiences for virtual (and non-virtual) learning environments that we plan to explore in future research.

The metaphor mentioned above that learning in a virtual world is not like automatically getting warm standing next to a fire alludes to the issue of how to design or to structure virtual worlds so that learning in fact does occur. Structure may be conceived in a variety of forms, such as structuring a problem, scaffolding, instructional assistance, providing tools or expert help, worksheets or scripts, and so on (Puntambekar & Hübscher, 2005). This issue of structure is also central to recent discussions of the *Assistance Dilemma* (Koedinger & Aleven, 2007), which has been articulated in the context of the timing of when and how to provide structure (i.e., assistance) in intelligent tutoring systems. Other researchers have extended the issues of the timing of structure associated with the Assistance Dilemma to learning in collaborative computer environments (Kapur & Rummel, 2009). In this section, we argue that the issues of the timing of structure are also of particular relevance to research into learning with virtual worlds in which students collaborate via interactions with each other through avatars as well as with synthetic agents.

We propose that there are three main paradigms for how and when to structure pedagogical activities involving virtual worlds.[5] First, the pedagogical activities may be relatively open ended and consist of *low or minimal structure*. However, minimally structured "discovery learning" environments generally do not result in successful learning outcomes (Mayer, 2004), and so we expect low structure activities in virtual worlds will generally not be effective for learning. One might regard having students use commercial game software as an example of this paradigm as there is little explicit structure provided that links information in the game scenario with subject-specific knowledge and skills associated with formal educational curricula. As discussed earlier, research has found relatively little learning of

---

[5] In this chapter, we focus on educational virtual worlds in particular, although clearly the issue of the design of structure in trajectories of learning activities is of relevance to all learning environments, whether they are technologically based or not.

school-oriented content with commercial games (Kirriemuir & McFarlane, 2004; McFarlane et al., 2002).

Second, virtual worlds may be designed with *high-to-low structure* pedagogically trajectories, whereby learners initially experience guided or scaffolded activities, with the structure gradually "faded" or removed over time as students are presumed to become more independently knowledgeable or skilled. This second approach seems to be commonly used in learning research to date involving virtual worlds specifically designed for educational settings. The research discussed in this chapter involving *Virtual Singapura*, as well as the program of research with *River City* (Ketelhut et al., 2009) and *Quest Atlantis* (Barab et al., 2005) have primarily used a guided inquiry approach based on a Vygotskian social constructivist model of learning-by-doing.

The third pedagogical structure paradigm is *low-to-high structure*, which is perhaps best exemplified in research into *productive failure* (PF) (Kapur, 2008; Kapur & Kinzer, 2009). Recently, Kapur and associates have been conducting a program of research exploring the possibility that under certain conditions engaging learners to persist, struggle, and even fail at tasks that are ill-structured and beyond their current abilities may in fact be an exercise in failure that yields longer-term productive learning gains. The productive failure hypothesis was first tested through a series of classroom-based quasi-experimental studies conducted with approximately 300, 11th-grade science students across seven Indian schools. Student triads solved either ill-structured (IS) or well-structured (WS) problems in an online chat environment. After group problem solving, all students individually solved WS problems followed by IS problems. Compared to WS problem-solving groups, IS groups initially had difficulties in defining and solving the problems and demonstrated poor group performance in the short term. However, the IS participants subsequently outperformed their counterparts in the well-structured condition on individual transfer measures, suggesting a delayed or latent productivity in learning resulted from the initial failure. A second study has replicated the research design and findings in three other schools (Kapur & Kinzer, 2009).

Other research has investigated a productive failure approach for using an agent-based modeling (ABM) and visualization environment for learning important physics concepts related to electricity (Jacobson, Kim, Pathak, & Zhang, 2009). The "non-productive failure" (NPF) group received an initial problem to solve involving the use of an electricity ABM with a set of structured worksheet steps whereas the "productive failure" (PF) group worked on the problems without any structure provided. Both groups then worked on a second problem involving an electricity ABM, but this time a worksheet (i.e., a structured activity) was provided to both groups. Both groups then worked on a third problem involving the electricity ABM, but with neither group receiving any worksheet provided structure. It was found after four sessions with four different electricity ABMs that the PF group scored significantly higher on the posttest compare to the NPF group, which actually decreased slightly from the pretest to the posttest. Overall, the findings in the ABM study of productive failure are consistent with those of Kapur and associates, which is important given the different content domain and the use of a visually oriented computer-modeling environment as the medium for the learning activities.

Briefly, Kapur (2008) has argued that from a theoretical perspective, it is likely that the low prior knowledge of novice students impedes their ability to understand the importance and value of domain-specific concepts, representations, and methods that might be presented during high structure activities such as direct instruction or as part of scaffolding provided during problem-solving tasks. Second, and related, when domain-specific concepts, methods and representations are presented in a organized manner during direct instruction or other structured activities, students may not understand why particular concepts, representations, and methods are being used or why they were organized in particular ways (Chi, Glaser, & Farr, 1988; Schwartz & Bransford, 1998).

In contrast, the initial failure and the delay of structure in PF conditions may result in students noticing and appreciating the relevance and value of key concepts, representations, and methods when exposed to them in subsequent direct instruction or structured problem-solving activities. Further, the activation of a range of prior knowledge by a student (which may be incomplete and even inaccurate) in the initial failed problem activity followed by the experience of a problem structured with appropriate concepts, representations, and methods might lead to knowledge abstraction and construction that perhaps are similar to cognitive processes proposed in analogical encoding theory (Gentner et al., 2003). Consequently, the process of productive failure may help students better discern and construct understandings of the concepts, representations, and methods from the structured activity so that they perform at a higher level on subsequent problems as well as on tests of conceptual understanding and knowledge transfer.

We believe there has been no research to date to systematically explore the premise that appropriately designed initial *failures* in virtual worlds as part of low structure activities, where learners may struggle as they think about and attempt to solve problems, might lead to longer-term and deeper learning effects than pedagogical approaches that initially provide higher structure that is reduced or faded over time. Consequently, a productive failure perspective has interesting implications for the sequencing of pedagogical structure in a virtual learning world. In addition, there may be important implications for how intelligent agent technologies might be designed and used in virtual world for learning. In a virtual learning world designed with a *high-to-low structure* pedagogical trajectory, such as guided inquiry, the initial learning tasks are structured so that students would be expected to succeed, with intelligent agents designed to intervene or to provide scaffolding if the learner showed difficulty with a given task. Over time, the task difficulty would increase and the degree of scaffolding or structure provided would be gradually faded or reduced. Put another way, the design of intelligent agents in *high-to-low structure* pedagogical trajectories – whether in learning activities in virtual worlds or in ITS – is to help students to *initially succeed,* with the assumption that there will be longer-term productive learning gains as well.

In *low-to-high structure* pedagogical sequences, however, the role of intelligent agents is reversed; agents would be designed to insure that students *initially fail.* A central premise of productive failure is that the initial learning activity must be challenging enough that learners struggle and pursue a range of approaches for completing the activity or solving the problem. If a learner can easily accomplish the activity, then there is likely to be little additional learning gained from a subsequent structured experience, as shown in research by VanLehn, Siler, and Murray (2003). Agents may thus be designed to have three main roles in a low-to-high structure virtual world. First, agents could monitor solution profiles and if the learner seems to easily accomplish the task or solve the problem, then a more difficult task would be provided. Second, agents could be designed to support *persistence* in the solving of a challenging task as quickly giving up would mean that prior knowledge and/or naïve conceptions may not be activated, with the result that the learner would not benefit from a subsequent structured experience. Third, agents could be designed to provide "structure" (i.e., scaffolding, direct instruction) following the low-structure activity in which the learner struggled and failed.

Our research group is planning new research to investigate productive failure (PF) designs for pedagogical activities in virtual worlds. The initial studies will explore PF designs without agents, with these findings then being used to inform how the intelligent agents would be programmed. Subsequent PF studies with intelligent agents in virtual learning worlds will then be conducted. We anticipate students learning in virtual worlds designed with low-to-high structure pedagogical sequences will demonstrate enhanced long-term learning gains compared to students using high-to-low structure approaches. We also view analogical encoding based activities as a type of structure that may be provided in trajectories of learning experiences that may have cognitive benefits in terms of fostering the ability of students to transfer their understandings constructed in virtual worlds to new settings and learning contexts. Given the preliminary findings the enhanced transfer problem-solving performance of the analogical encoding treatment in VS study 2, we are planning future research in this area.

Conclusion

In conclusion, it is hoped that over time, the program of design research discussed in this chapter will contribute to our understanding of how motivationally powerful immersive virtual worlds might be designed to help students to deeply learn conceptually challenging knowledge and skills. In addition, this project hopes to make a contribution to early research efforts into how intelligent agent technologies might be used to augment and enhance learning in immersive virtual worlds. Envisioning that future of learning environments will include virtual worlds augmented with intelligent agents in various ways seems a likely future. We hope that theoretical and research perspectives such as those discussed in this chapter might inform these design and development efforts both for the virtual world technologies themselves and for the overall formal and informal learning environments in which they will be used.

Acknowledgments This project was funded by two research grants from the Singapore Ministry of Education through the Learning Sciences Laboratory to the chapter authors. Special thanks are extended to Chris Dede, Diane Jass Ketelhut, and Brian Nelson for their feedback on this project and providing access to technology and research resources of the Harvard River City project. Diana Ang, Seo Hong Lim, June Lee, Lynn Low, and the participating teachers greatly contributed to this research. We are also grateful to the Singapore National Archives and the National Museum of Singapore for their assistance in obtaining historical information and pictures used in *Virtual Singapura*.

Appendix 1

Case texts used in the analogical encoding treatment conditions:

1. Purpura nautica

During the Age of Discovery, scurvy became a disease among sailors. The disease was often referred to as *Purpura nautica*, as sufferers had purple (*purpura*) blotches under their skins. They would also have teeth and hair loss, sunken eyes, paleness, blindness, and most would die. In 1747, James Lind, the surgeon aboard HMS *Salisbury*, was faced with many cases of scurvy and a high death rate. He thought that the disease was related to a lack of ascorbic acid, which is found in citrus fruits, but had to prove it. What Lind did next changed the history of scurvy. As a scientist, what do you think he did?

2. Is it good to be special?

The shoe company *Steps* decided to run a free webinar (a type of web conference) to get people to be aware of shoe comfort, and be interested in *Steps*' footwear. E-mails would be sent to invite people to the webinar. When drafting the e-mails, the marketing manager noted an interesting claim, that the word "special" should not be in e-mails' subject lines. E-mails with "special" in their subject lines were avoided by people as they were seen as spam. The manager was keen to test this claim, and to find out whether differences in subject lines mattered to whether people would attend the webinar. As a market researcher, what should she do?

Appendix 2

Conversations after a presentation regarding missing supporting data:

1. All Presenters: (after presenting the last slide) So we will now take your questions.

2. Teacher: Okay, any questions?
3. Audience 1: How about the number of patients who fell ill due to the illness? The number of patients?
4. Teacher: Can you go back to your graph again?
5. Presenter 1: Our graph would be regarding the number of bacteria in the wells…?
6. Audience 1: Then how about the number of patients? (pause)
7. Presenter 1: We don't have the graph.
8. Audience 1: Is this illness that's causing the patient to? When you say, you know, when you say symptoms, but what about the number of patients...
9. Presenter 2: No, no… When...
10. Audience 1: …(that bacteria really) causes the illness...?
11. Presenter 1: This is the… for the…
12. Audience 1: The patients, according to the number of patients who want to (claim from this)? We do not know whether it significantly went down. So the… (how to know) would be this?
13. Presenter 2: Okay, maybe we didn't really write it down here, but anyway diarrhea would significantly decrease from 35-7, 2 digits to 1 digit. Wow. Yeah.
14. Audience 1: How about the rest, like the, can you go to your graph.
15. Teacher: Can you go back to your previous slide. Previous slide.
16. Audience 1: What, how about the fever and all that? And the rest...
17. Presenter 2: Tuberculosis will also significantly decrease but I guess we put didn't put it inside here… Sorry.

References

Barab, S., Dodge, T., Tuzun, H., Job-Sluder, K., Jackson, C., Arici, A., et al. (2007). The Quest Atlantis Project: A socially-responsive play space for learning. In B. E. Shelton & D. Wiley (Eds.), *The educational design and use of simulation computer games* (pp. 161–188). Rotterdam, The Netherlands: Sense Publishers.

Barab, S., Thomas, M., Dodge, T., Carteaux, R., & Tuzun, H. (2005). Making learning fun: Quest Atlantis, a game without guns. *Educational Technology, Research, and Development, 53*(1), 86–107.

Barab, S., Warren, S., & Ingram-Goble, A. (2006). *Academic play spaces: Designing games for education.* San Francisco, CA: Paper presented at the annual meeting of the American Educational Research Association.

Barab, S., Zuiker, S., Warren, S., Hickey, D., Ingram-Goble, A., Kwon, E.-J., et al. (2007). Situationally embodied curriculum: Relating formalisms and contexts. *Science Education, 91*(5), 750–782.

Bransford, J. D., Brown, A. L., Cocking, R. R., & Donovan, S. (eds). (2000). *How people learn: Brain, mind, experience, and school* (expandedth ed.). Washington, DC: National Academy Press.

Bransford, J. D., & Schwartz, D. L. (1999). Rethinking transfer: A simple proposal with multiple implications. In A. Iran-Hejad & P. D. Pearson (Eds.), *Review of research in education* (Vol. 24). Washington, DC: American Educational Research Association.

Cai, Y., Miao, C., Tan, A. H., & Shen, Z. (2008). *Context modeling with evolutionary fuzzy cognitive map in interactive storytelling.* Paper presented at the IEEE International Conference on Fuzzy Systems (FUZZ2008), 2008 IEEE World Congress on Computational Intelligence, Hong Kong, China.

Cai, Y., Shen, Z., & Miao, C. (2007). *G-MADE: A hybrid interactive storytelling architecture.* Paper presented at the 2007 AAAI Symposium on Intelligent Narrative Technologies, Arlington, VA

Chi, M. T. H., Glaser, R., & Farr, M. J. (eds). (1988). *The nature of expertise.* Hillsdale, NJ: Lawrence Erlbaum Associates.

Dede, C. (1995). The evolution of constructivist learning environments: Immersion in distributed, virtual worlds. *Educational Technology, 35*(5), 46–52.

Dede, C., Clarke, J., Ketelhut, D. J., Nelson, B., & Bowman, C. (2005a). *Fostering motivation, learning, and transfer in multi-user virtual environments.* Paper presented at the annual meeting of the American Educational Research Association, Montreal, Canada.

Dede, C., Clarke, J., Ketelhut, D. J., Nelson, B., & Bowman, C. (2005b). *Students' motivation and learning of science in a multi-user virtual environment.* Paper presented at the annual meeting of the American Educational Research Association, Montreal, Canada.

Dede, C., Loftin, R. B., Regian, J. W., Salzman, M., Calhoun, C., & Hoblit, J. (1994). The design of artificial realities to improve learning Newtonian mechanics. *Proceedings of the East-West International Conference on Multimedia, Hypermedia, and Virtual Reality, Moscow, Russia.*

Dede, C., Salzman, M., Loftin, R. B., & Ash, K. (2000). The design of immersive virtual learning environments: Fostering deep understandings of complex scientific knowledge. In M. J. Jacobson & R. B. Kozma (Eds.), *Innovations in science and mathematics education: Advanced designs for technologies of learning* (pp. 361–413). Mahwah, NJ: Lawrence Erlbaum Associates.

Dede, C., Salzman, M. C., & Loftin, R. B. (1996). *Early research results from using virtual reality to enhance science education.* Paper presented at the annual meeting of the American Educational Research Association, New York, NY.

Fraser, B. J. (1978). Development of a test of science-related attitudes. *Science Education, 62*(4), 509–515.

Gee, J. P. (2003). *What videogames have to teach us about learning and literacy.* New York: Palgrave Macmillan.

Gentner, D., Loewenstein, J., & Thompson, L. (2003). Learning and transfer: A general role for analogical encoding. *Journal of Educational Psychology, 95*(2), 393–408.

Gredler, M. E. (2004). Games and simulations and their relationship to learning. In D. H. Jonassen (Ed.), *Handbook of research for educational communications and technology* (2nd ed., pp. 571–581). Mahway, NJ: Lawrence Erlbaum Associates.

Holmes, J. (2007). *Designing agents to support learning by explaining Computers & Education, 48,* 523–547.

Jacobson, M. J., Kim, B., Lee, J., Lim, S. H., & Low, S. H. (2008). *An intelligent agent augmented multi-user virtual environment for learning science inquiry: Preliminary research findings.* Paper presented at the annual meeting of the American Educational Research Association, New York, NY.

Jacobson, M. J., Kim, B., Pathak, S. A., & Zhang, B. (2009). *Learning the physics of electricity with agent-based models: Fail first and structure later?* Paper presented at the 2009 Annual Meeting of the American Educational Research Association, San Diego, CA.

Johnson, S. (2006). *The ghost map: The story of London's most terrifying epidemic–and how it changed science, cities, and the modern world.* New York: Riverhead Books.

Kapur, M. (2008). Productive failure. *Cognition and Instruction, 26*(3), 379–424.

Kapur, M., & Kinzer, C. (2009). Productive failure in CSCL groups. *International Journal of Computer-Supported Collaborative Learning, 4,* 21–46.

Kapur, M., & Rummel, N. (2009). *The assistance dilemma in CSCL.* Symposium presented at the 8th International Conference on Computer Supported Collaborative Learning, Rhodes, Greece.

Ketelhut, D. J., Clarke, J., & Nelson, B. C. (2009). The development of River City, a multi-user virtual environment-based scientific inquiry curriculum: Historical and design evolutions. In M. J. Jacobson & P. Reimann (Eds.), *Designs for learning environments of the future: International learning sciences theory and research perspectives.* New York: Springer.

Ketelhut, D. J., Dede, C., Clarke, J., Nelson, B., & Bowman, C. (2007). Studying situated learning in a multi-user virtual environment. In E. Baker, J. Dickieson, W. Wulfeck & H. O'Neil (Eds.), *Assessment of problem solving using simulations* (pp. 37–58). Mahwah, NJ: Taylor & Francis, Inc.

Kirriemuir, J., & McFarlane, A. (2004). *Literature review in games and learning. Report 8.* Bristol, UK: FutureLab.

Koedinger, K. R., & Aleven, V. (2007). Exploring the assistance dilemma in experiments with cognitive tutors. *Educational Psychology Review, 19*(3), 239–264.

Lobato, J. (2006). Alternative perspectives on the transfer of learning: History, issues, and challenges for future research. *Journal of the Learning Sciences, 15*(4), 431–449.

Mayer, R. (2004). Should there be a three-strikes rule against pure discovery learning? The case for guided methods of instruction. *American Psychologist, 59*(1), 14–19.

McFarlane, A., Sparrowhawk, A., & Heald, Y. (2002). *Report on the educational use of games.* Cambridge: TEEM.

McLellan, H. (2004). Virtual realities. In D. H. Jonassen (Ed.), *Handbook of research for educational communications and technology* (2nd ed., pp. 461–497). Mahway, New Jersey: Lawrence Erlbaum Associates.

Psotka, J. (1994). *Immersive tutoring systems: Virtual reality and education and training.* Retrieved from http://198.97.199.60/its.html.

Puntambekar, S., & Hübscher, R. (2005). Tools for scaffolding students in a complex environment: What have we gained and what have we missed? *Educational Psychologist, 40*(1), 1–12.

Schwartz, D. L., & Bransford, J. D. (1998). A time for telling. *Cognition and Instruction, 16*(4), 475–522.

Shaffer, D. W., Squire, K. D., Halverson, R., & Gee, J. P. (2005). *Video games and the future of learning,* accepted for publication.

Shen, Z., Miao, C., & Cai, Y. (2007). *Agent augmented game development.* Paper presented at the 2nd Annual Microsoft Conference on Game Development, Orlando, FL.

Shen, Z., Miao, C., & Gay, R. (2006). *Goal-oriented methodology for agent-oriented software engineering.* Paper presented at the IEICE Transaction on Information and Systems.

Squire, K. (2005). Changing the game: What happens when video games enter the classroom? *Innovate: Journal of Online Education, 1*(6). Retrieved from http://www.innovateonline.info/index.php?view=article&id=82.

Squire, K., Barnett, M., Grant, J. M., & Higginbotham, T. (2004). *Electromagnetism supercharged! learning physics with digital simulation games.* Paper presented at the International Conference of the Learning Sciences, Los Angeles, CA.

Squire, K., Jenkins, H., Holland, W., Miller, H., O'Driscoll, A., Tan, K. P., et al. (2003). Design principles of next-generation digital gaming for education. *Educational Technology and Society, 43*(5), 17–23.

Squire, K. D. (2002). Rethinking the role of games in education. *Game Studies, 2*(1). Retrieved from http://www.gamestudies.org/0102/squire/.

Steinkuehler, C. A. (2004). *Learning in massively multiplayer online games.* Paper presented at the International Conference of the Learning Sciences, Los Angeles, CA.

Thompson, L., Gentner, D., & Loewenstein, J. (2000). Avoiding missed opportunities in managerial life: Analogical training more powerful than individual case training. *Organizational Behavior and Human Decision Processes, 82*(1), 60–75.

Tinker, R. (2007). How do students learn from models? Case studies in guided inquiry. *@ Concord, 11*(1), 14-15.

VanLehn, K., Siler, S., & Murray, C. (2003). Why do only some events cause learning during human tutoring? *Cognition and Instruction, 2*(3), 209–249.

Williams, D., Ma, Y., Feist, S., & Prejean, L. (2007). The design of an analogical encoding tool for game-based virtual learning environments. *British Journal of Educational Technology, 38*(3), 429–437.

Winn, W. (2002). Learning in artificial environments: Embodiment, embeddedness and dynamic adaptation. *Technology, Instruction, Cognition and Learning, 1*, 87–114.

Winn, W., Windschitl, M., & Hedley, N. (2001). *Learning science in an immersive virtual environment.* Paper presented at the American Educational Research Association (AERA) Annual Meeting 2001, Seattle, WA.

Yu, H., Shen, Z., & Miao, C. (2008a). A goal oriented development tool to automate the incorporation of intelligent agents into interactive digital media applications. *ACM Computers in Entertainment, 6*(2), Article 24.

Yu, H., Shen, Z., & Miao, C. (2008b). *Transforming learning through agent augmented virtual world.* Paper presented at the 8th IEEE International Conference on Advanced Learning Technologies, Santander, Cantabria, Spain.

Chapter 6
Learning to Learn and Work in Net-Based Teams: Supporting Emergent Collaboration with Visualization Tools

Peter Reimann and Judy Kay

Introduction

Collaboration in virtual teams and communities is becoming part of the K-12 curriculum ("twenty-first century skills" – see, e.g., iN2015 Education and Learning Sub-Committee, 2007; West Virginia Department of Education, 2007) and also increasingly well-established in university education (Resta & Laferriere, 2007). Not only do we see an increase in the frequency of employing group learning in educational settings, but also see a qualitative change taking place: the expectations as to the outcomes of collaborative learning have changed from a focus on improving individual learning (via motivational and cognitive processes) to also include gains with respect to shared knowledge (e.g., groups producing artifacts useful for others) and gains in social capital (e.g., students becoming integrated into social networks).

It is not that we have to force students to do things together. In their life outside of schools, today's young people spend an increasing amount of time using so-called social media such as Facebook, MySpace, or Second Life (in addition to using the equally social IM, SMS, phone, and e-mail services). create and share music, pictures, movies, homework, and experiences all the time.

This chapter is about creating and sharing knowledge and epistemic practices. With Scardamilia and Bereiter, we regard the knowledge challenge to be the central educational challenge of the twenty-first century: "how to develop citizens who not only possess up-to-date knowledge but are able to participate in the creation of new knowledge as a normal part of their lives" (Scardamalia & Bereiter, 2003). Due to the rapid adaption of information technologies in developing countries, tasks of

P. Reimann (✉)
Centre for Research on Computer-supported Learning and Cognition (CoCo),
University of Sydney, Sydney, NSW 2006, Australia
e-mail: peter.reimann@sydney.edu.au

J. Kay
School of Information Technologies, University of Sydney, Sydney, NSW 2006, Australia

M.J. Jacobson and P. Reimann (eds.), *Designs for Learning Environments of the Future:*   143
International Perspectives from the Learning Sciences, DOI 10.1007/978-0-387-88279-6_6,
© Springer Science+Business Media, LLC 2010

many kinds can now be allocated to a globally distributed workforce, creating pressure in high-income countries to retain only knowledge- and service-intensive (nonroutine) economic activities. While information and communication technologies are for part "responsible" for the rapid growth of global competition for performing tasks (for pay) that require basic to medium skill levels, information and communication technologies are also part of the answer to the resulting knowledge challenge: "The same technologies that make innovative and creative thinking critical skills for the future also make it possible for students to prepare for that future" (Shaffer, 2008, p. 37). Computers and communication networks can connect students to resources, tools, and communities that are necessary to develop the skills, knowledge, values, mindsets (Shaffer speaks of "epistemic frames") required for complex, nonroutine, knowledge-rich problem solving.

Specifically, networked computers can be used to make collaborative learning easier to conduct, and more sustained and integrated with life in- and outside of formal educational settings. While it can be hard to manage collaborative learning from a teacher's perspective, at least for large classes (in university courses, often comprising hundreds of students), learning management systems have made it considerably easier to deal with the logistics, and tools such as LAMS (http://www.lamsfoundation.org/) that specializes in forms of team learning offer even more support. And while it is very hard in face-to-face groups to keep track of individual contributions (with problematic consequences for motivation and group dynamics), when collaboration is conducted through networked computers, students' individual contributions can easily be recorded and set in relation to each other. Thus, through technology we have fairly direct access to students' socially distributed practices, to the tools and artifacts (such as chats, forums, shared whiteboards, wikis) used in these practices, and to the products of their collaborative work, such as texts, models, programs.

The role that and product type artifacts play for knowledge and creation and learning has in particular been recognized in the "trialogic" framework (Paavola & Hakkarainen, 2005): "Trialogue means that by using various mediating artifacts (signs, concepts, and tools) and mediating processes (such as practices, or the interaction between tacit and explicit knowledge) people are developing common objects of activity (such as conceptual artifacts, practices, products, etc." (p. 546). This view that learning is not adequately described by the acquisition and/or the participation metaphor (Sfard, 1998), but that a third dimension needs to be taken into account: learning as artifact creation. Artifacts are always social in nature, not only because they are frequently created in a collaborative fashion, but also because they are intended for subsequent use by others. Once created, artifacts, in the form of concepts (such as a scientific theory), tools, and practices, enable people to engage in activities were not at their command before – Engeström (1987) speaks of learning as an "activity-producing activity." This third metaphor for learning is better suited than the acquisition and the participation metaphor to accommodate notions of innovation and knowledge building (Scardamalia & Bereiter, 2006).

Since knowledge can reside in peoples' minds, in their practices, and in the tools and artifacts they create and use, learning means not only increase individual knowledge and skill, but can also take the form of improving upon social practices (such as forms of team work) and of creating or modifying tools and artifacts. Working together, for the purpose of learning, makes address all three forms, and indeed is a for practice improvement, such as improving on general and specific team skills.

Attending to "team skills" is not only important when the goal is to teach such skills directly, but a basic level of functioning as a group is a prerequisite for successful collaborative learning in general, as it is for working together (Arrow, McGrath, & Behrdal, 2000; Kreijns, Kirschner, & Jochems, 2003). While productive group collaboration can be "designed" to some extent from the outside, e.g., by setting up roles and workflows ("scripting" the collaboration, see (Kollar, Fischer, & Hesse, 2006), there are limits to this, in particular as we move to long-term collaboration (weeks and months instead of minutes and hours) and as collaboration skills themselves become the learning goal.

Long-term group work among students can take various forms. Examples are knowledge-building communities (Lee, Han, & van Aalst, 2006), problem-based learning (Zumbach, Hillers, & Reimann, 2003), and design-based learning (Kolodner et al., 2003). While knowledge-building communities can be seen as working with declarative knowledge directly by creating artifacts that represent ideas, theories, explanations and their relations, the pedagogy behind problem-based and design-based learning addresses learning and knowledge creation indirectly: students are engaged working on a task, the artifacts created are typically task-related (e.g., a design sketch), and learning is seen as occurring as a "side effect" of working on the task. In any case, for groups of students working together as a team for some time, not only do they need to get their task done (e.g., knowledge building, problem solving, design), they also need to manage their interaction, establish and maintain common ground, keep the group stable, and take care of individual members' concerns (McGrath, 1991). These collaboration management aspects mean that teams need to engage in ongoing learning about how to manage themselves.

To appreciate the complexity of teamwork, the conceptual framework suggested by Arrow et al. (2000) is illustrative. They describe groups as involving the elements members, tasks, and tools, and comprising six networks of relationships between these three elements: (a) the network between team members (social relationships, e.g., affiliation), (b) tasks (i.e., dependencies), and (c) tools (e.g., flow of data between various software tools), and furthermore (d) the role network between tools and members, (e) the labor network between members and tasks, and (f) the job network between tools and tasks. Each of these networks needs to be initially established, and then continuously elaborated, enacted, maintained (e.g., monitored), and modified. In the framework of Arrow and colleagues, this is called the "coordination cycle." An elaboration of one or more of the networks is often necessary because typically not everything a team needs to have and know in order to get started with its work (enactment phase) is provided from the outside. The task may be given to the team, but it may need identification of subtasks. Group membership may be specified from the outset, but roles may need to be identified by the team.

Elaborating, maintaining, and modifying (improving) these networks does not get easier when the team members interact (mainly) with each other and the task mediated by communication technology. "Virtual" teams face additional challenges resulting from too little information: the lack of social awareness (Bodker & Christiansen, 2006), lack of common ground (Clark & Brennan, 1991), lack of transactive memory (Wegner, 1986), lack of social control and, hence, increased tendency for free-riding (Albanese & Fleet, 1985), lack of experience with the communication technology, and so on. At the same time, virtual teams suffer from too much information: too many postings, e-mail messages, and parallel activities that are hard to monitor and to make sense of (Fussell et al., 1998).

These complexities of team work in general and of virtual teams in particular need to be addressed, certainly in cases where the goal is to develop team "skills" amongst students, but also for supporting groups for the benefit of subject-matter learning and knowledge development. Our research aims at developing and analyzing computational methods for visualizing aspects of team performance to help virtual learning teams with their production tasks and to help them to become better in their coordination tasks, i.e., to develop team skills.

We have been studying teams in the context of university courses (advanced undergraduate and graduate level) performance involves substantial collaboration, over several weeks if not months, where the primary goal for student teams is to create a shared artifact (such as wiki pages, programs, and models) and where the learning occurs in the context of working on the task and reflecting on one's performance. We use the term "team learning" to signal that under such circumstances students need to act very much like a "real" team, where this includes making substantial investments in managing team processes. In an educational context, such learning teams can be expected to (a) produce useful artifacts that constitute a contribution to socially shared knowledge (e.g., a problem solved), (b) to learn individually about the domain the problem is contextualized in, and (c) to learn individually about the team members and to develop knowledge and skill about collaboration management. On the group level, we can expect learning to occur (d) by improved team effectiveness, such as improved coordination of members' activities, and in general, changes in group work practices.

An example is the case where students work as a software team that needs to collaborate over several months to build a system for a client, using the Extreme programming method (Beck, 1999) for the broad software development process and Java as the programming language. In this case, by the end of their project students can be expected to (a) have produced a program that satisfies the requirements, (b) Java programming and know more about the domain that the program addressed, (c) have a better understanding of team members and team processes as well as improved collaboration skills, and (d) work better together as a software development team.

One cannot expect that the learning outcomes (b–d) will emerge automatically; providing students with a group task, some incentives for accomplishing the task, and collaboration tools are necessary, but not sufficient conditions for productive interactions and serious learning to occur (Kreijns et al., 2003). For learning to take place along these dimensions, group members need to be, for example, motivated and supported. Motivation can be established, for instance, making the learning goals explicit and rewarding progress; in particular, it must be clear to the team members that they are supposed to learn about team management, leadership, online collaboration, and so on, and that this learning will be rewarded. Support can be established in many forms (see Reimann, 2003), but teams must be provided with the information required for learning along all of the dimensions and they must be provided with information on team processes, in addition to the task-related information. This, then, is our basic approach to "teach" team skills: We provide groups with a challenging task, including criteria for success, a suite of authentic collaboration technologies, access to information on group performance parameters, and expectations associated with indicators for effective team work.

In this chapter, we describe a number of mirroring and feedback approaches that we have developed to support collaboration management for teams. They make use of electronic communication tools, especially, but not only, wikis, in order to create a jointly constructed knowledge artifact, such as a program or a report. All these approaches were developed, and have been tested to varying degrees, in the context of university courses at undergraduate and graduate level.

We begin with an analysis of artifact-mediated, net-based collaboration, using wikis as a paradigmatic case. Demands that this mode of collaboration impose on students are identified, based on a review of the literature on computer-supported collaborative writing and on a semiotic analysis of wiki writing. This analysis yields two central areas for support: coordination of team members, and establishment of coherence in the shared document. We then describe our first approach to supporting artifact-mediated collaboration. It targets team member coordination by measures aimed at increasing task and member awareness. The approach exploits the database of student actions as they make long-term use of an online collaboration tool. We focus on providing visualizations of participation patterns. These are intended to support reflection by team members and, especially, team leaders.

We then turn our attention to the question of how students can be supported in creating coherence amongst their collaboratively developed ideas as reflected in the shared knowledge artifacts, wiki pages in particular. Just as a sitemap can be an invaluable aid for static web sites, a new tool, WikiNavMap, provides several ways to see the structure of a wiki and to "see" or visualize the most salient features, including the parts where a particular author made contributions, the parts that were edited at different times, and the rate of development of the wiki. Importantly, it also shows how parts of the wiki are linked to each other. We have trialed this in long-term group projects. This approach to mirroring information should help students reflect on many important questions for their collaboration and progress, including whether they have covered all the topics/aspects relevant to their task.

A second approach we have developed to help students with the task of creating coherent works on the level of individual wiki pages. Using computational text analysis methods, this approach identifies and visualizes a network of concept relations. As in our first approach, we hope that mirroring information should help students to reflect on the knowledge contained in the pages and the learning with respect to domain concepts the group went through. Before we introduce these team support measures, we first the need for such support.

Collaboration Mediated by Knowledge Artifacts

We are focusing on wikis as the main collaboration medium not only because they are frequently used to accomplish work in (virtual) teams, but also because they play an interesting double role: they often operate as both the medium and the product of collaboration. As a product, they function as a knowledge object (Paavola & Hakkarainen, 2005), whereas as a medium, they function as a coordination device (Olson, Malone, & Smith, 2001).

In our research, we work with student groups that are using shared textual artifacts as a means to go about their work and to communicate their ideas, such as wiki pages and program code managed in a shared versioning file repository. This is different from the case where dedicated interaction technologies are used, such as chat, discussion boards, newsgroups, or email (e.g., Stahl, 2006). However, the use of shared artifacts of textual representations is quite typical for the communication that takes place between software developers (Ripochet & Sansonnet, 2006) or between authors of jointly written documents (Zacklad, 2006). In such groups, one finds collaboration typically being conducted through a combination of face-to-face meetings, synchronous remote communication such as phone conversations, and an asynchronous textual medium such as a wiki. The artifacts created on wikis and in version-controlled collaborative document repositories can be seen as combining work on the task with interaction and coordination functions, to the extent that such artifacts are used not only to document work, but also to coordinate team members' activities and to structure their interactions. Using such document-like artifacts is convenient because they are often part of the groups' work anyway and hence constitute little communication overhead (MacMillan, Entin, & Serfaty, 2004). For instance, software designers often use wikis to document use cases and to develop user manuals, and they use shared versioning systems to both manage the code and also to distribute tasks amongst the team members (Layman, Williams, Damian, & Bures, 2006).

This convenience factor can easily lead to problems. Due to the fact that interaction and coordination functions are not systematically separated from production tasks, and given that documents tend to grow quickly in size over a project's time, it can become hard for team members to keep track of tasks and commitments. One way to address this issue is to separate the coordination aspects from the production aspects but keep them within the same basic medium. This is, for instance, possible in systems such as Xplanner (http://www.xplanner.org) and in Trac (trac.edgewall. org), the wiki-based group support tool employed in our research.

Collaborative Computer-Supported Writing

Collaborative writing (CW) is widely performed in industry, academia, and government (Cross, 2001), and with the rise of Web 2.0 genres such as wikis and blogs, it has also become part of popular culture. Amongst the positive effects of writing documents collaboratively are learning, socialization, new ideas, and more understandable – if not more effective – documents (Phillips, Lawrence, & Hardy, 2004). However, outside of creative writing courses, writing in a collaborative manner is hardly taught and practiced in secondary and tertiary education (with exceptions, e.g., Lowry, Nunamaker, Curtis, & Lowry, 2005). The only forms of collaboration in the writing process that students might experience are typically variants of peer review (Topping, 1998), but even then the goal is still to improve upon an individually authored document.

Collaborative writing, defined by Lowry, Curtis, and Lowry (2004, p. 72) as "… an iterative and social process that involves a team focused on a common objective that negotiates, coordinates, and communicates during the creation of a common document" is a cognitively and organizationally demanding process. As a special form of group work, it involves a broad range of group activities, multiple roles, and subtasks. When performed by groups that communicate (partially or only) through communication media, the process typically involves additionally multiple tools (e.g., phone, mail, instant messaging, document management systems) that each have different use characteristics.

From a cognitive perspective, (individual) writing has been described as an "ill-structured" problem type, meaning that there is no single "correct" way to write a particular document, and that instead, the writing task has to be clarified by the writer(s) before engaging in any more targeted problem solving (Hayes & Flower, 1980). When performed in an educational context, a lecturer typically provides the writing task, writing and communication tools, and group composition, so that teams can focus on team planning and document production. Both of these are typically complex, and involve steps such as task decomposition, role definition, task allocation, milestone planning as components of team planning, and brainstorming, outlining, drafting, reviewing, revising, and copyediting as components of document production.

With respect to computer-supported collaborative writing, two areas of research, in particular, are relevant for our purpose: (a) research that analyzes CW in terms of group work processes, focusing on issues such as process loss, productivity, and quality of the outcomes (Erkens, Jaspers, Prangsma, & Kanselaar, 2005; Lowry et al., 2004); and (b) research that studies CW in terms of group learning processes by focusing on topics such as establishing common ground, knowledge building, and learning outcomes (Scardamalia & Bereiter, 1991). In the second line of research, writing is seen as a means to deepen students' engagement with ideas and the literature and for knowledge building (Scardamalia & Bereiter, 2006). In CSCL, in addition to knowledge building in asynchronous collaboration, synchronous collaborative development of argumentative structures and texts has received much attention (e.g., van Amalesvoort, Andriessen, & Kanselaar, 2007). Recent research has had a particular focus on textual data-mining techniques to enhance student writing. For instance, Williams, Calvo, & Bell (2003) applied automatic classification techniques to classify student postings based on the topic of their content. Others have applied similar techniques to classify postings by the type of contribution they make to an argument (Dönmez, Rosé, Stegmann, Weinberger, & Fischer, 2005).

Collaborative Wiki Writing: A Semiotic Analysis

Wikis, as one type of the evolving class of online documents, can be seen as the current culmination point of three trends in document production: (a) from text media to multimedia: online documents often contain nontextual materials, such as images, sound, and video; (b) from a clear separation of production and use-time to a fusion as wikis are already "published" while they are written (in some cases, such as Wikipedia, they are constantly (re-)written, so that their end state is indeterminate); (c) from single authorship to collective authorship.

Wikis have rapidly become part and parcel of learning environments in Higher Education. They are now a component of most learning management systems, for instance, and are routinely used in courses and seminars. And with the rapid spread of blogs wikis on the Internet, wikis have become part of popular culture. Although the interest in wikis has been boosted by the success of Wikipedia, this specific use of a wiki engine to orchestrate mass cooperation around an online encyclopedia is not the one most typical for (higher) education. Wikis were originally developed for fostering writing and collaboration in small teams (software development teams in particular, Leuf & Cunningham, 2001), and it is this form of use that we will be analyzing.

We focus, in particular, on situations where wiki documents are used to mediate the coordination of distributed small teams of students who are working together toward a common goal. Wikis are frequently used by teams not only because they are easy to set up and use, they also typically provide excellent support for a deep notion of document versions. The wiki can be the immediate object of students' activities (e.g., a group writing assignment), or it can play a supporting function in creating other artifacts, such as computer programs or models. In the later case, wikis are often used to explore the problem, communicate with clients outside of the team, to support coordination within the group (such as meeting agendas, minutes and other joint planning pages) and to write documentation for the program or model. In all these cases, a wiki page (or set of wiki pages; we use the singular "wiki" for ease of reference) is appropriately seen as a "document for action" (Zacklad, 2006), as "… a set of fragments contributed by various authors, the final content of which remains largely indeterminate, while its fast dissemination makes it a useful tool for conveying information, assisting decision-making and probing situations" (p. 206). We will apply Zacklad's insightful analysis of electronic documents-for-action (DofA) to the special case of collaborative wiki text authoring.

Like blogs and other documents which exist mainly online, wiki pages are characterized by certain properties that make them very different from paper-based documents, amongst them: a prolonged state of incompletion, durability, high degree of fragmentation, diverse commitments of their authors, and the evolving nature of their content (Zacklad, 2006). The two main activities performed on wiki pages are adding fragments and adding annotations. Annotation activities can be defined as all those "...activities serving to link together the fragments of DofAs with a view to achieve the common goals of a distributed collective practice" (Zacklad, 2006, p. 6). Wiki pages, produced in the context of collaborative projects, mediate (potentially widely) distributed emerging communicational transactions. They pose unique challenges regarding the coordination of these transactions and the establishment of coherence amongst the text fragments.

Coherence amongst the fragments in such documents is an emerging quality rather than being due to a specific plan or outline. Establishing coherence becomes a particular challenge, as this has to be accomplished in and through the same medium – the wiki page – that contains the fragments. Coordination of the transactions on the perennial artifact "wiki page" is mediated through the wiki medium and at the same time geared toward the wiki page, in order to make it serve its purpose(s) and to keep it coherent.

Since the transactional practices around the construction of wiki pages are distributed over space, time, and actors, groups and organizations have to find ways to effectively manage these transactions. (Zacklad, 2004) distinguishes eight (not exclusive) methods to accomplish the coordination and distribution of communicational transactions in general, with the last four being of particular relevance for print and electronic documents, including wikis: (1) standardizing the transaction situation, (2) formalizing the modes of expression, (3) mnemotechnic ritualization (such as using rhymes), (4) abstraction, (5) substitutive mediation, (6) documentarization, (7) increased recourse to techno-informational equipment, and (8) substitutive coordination. We now discuss the last four.

Substitutive mediation (5) refers to the phenomenon of separating the production of a semiotic product (e.g., an utterance of a sentence by a speaker) from the reception of that product by a receiver (a listener) by one or more intermediate media. Substantive mediation is particularly effective to help with distribution of the semiotic product (and coordination of its production) if the intermediate medium is perennial, such as a writing substrate. Documentarization (6) is an extended version of substantive mediation as it refers to endowing perennial substrates "... with specific attributes making it possible: (i) to manage them along with other substrates, (ii) to handle them physically, which is a prerequisite to be able to browse semantically among the semiotic content, and lastly (iii), to guide not only the recipients, but also the producers themselves to an increasing extent, around the substrate by providing one or several maps of the semiotic contents" (Zacklad, 2006, p. 215). For instance, the creation of a table of contents, or of an index, is an example a documentarisation process. Techno-informational equipment (7) refers to things such as filing cabinets (and their digital "equivalents") that affect the use of documents (and/or their production) without being part of the documents, while substitutive coordination (8) results from the automation performed by techno-informational equipment. The automatic indexing of a document, for instance, document retrieval technologies, and the coordination of a document production process with a workflow tool are examples of substitutive coordination.

In the case of wikis as the perennial artefact involved in groups' work, it is in particular the distinction between substitutive mediation (5) and documentarization (6) that is important. In order to make a wiki a good resource for team work, more is needed than just "writing things down"; the collectively generated fragments must be further reformulated and organized in a manner that reflects their shared meaning amongst the team members. If the artifact is supposed to be of use for others who are not part of the team, then even more documentarization work will need to be invested to turn notes into a knowledge resource.

Wikis share essential features with online newsgroups and discussion forums. Similar to those, wikis are used to conduct and store traces of a kind of polylogal (multiparty) communication. In this respect, wikis are also similar to face-to-face group communications and to chat communications, but unlike those, are not conducted synchronously. Different from online newsgroups and discussion forums, wikis lack an explicit representation for "contributions" and for the take-up of contributions in form of "responses." Thus, in terms of their affordances, wikis are more a medium for writing than a medium for discussing. However, because of their double role, at the same time the product of writing and the medium to coordinate writing activities across multiple authors, wiki pages will often contain "discussion" entries (for instance, discussions as to what to include and not include in the text) as well as substantial entries. These discussion entries have the characteristics of annotations since they refer to the text but are not (yet) a proper part of the text.

Annotations can be seen as a mechanism to deal with the main problem confronting members of groups coproducing DofAs in general and wikis in particular: the lack of information about the transactional context associated with a proposed fragment. While the transactional context is continuously and seemingly effortlessly established in face-to-face communication, mediated communication situations, and particularly those of the asynchronous kind lacking an immediate feedback/repair channel, make it much more difficult to establish context. Annotations are the main device to establish context in such situations.

Following Zacklad (2006), we can see an author contributing a free (i.e., not yet integrated) fragment to a wiki page as a basic turn, or transactional bid. The free fragment can be complete or incomplete. It is complete when participants (readers and coauthors) perceive it as a coherent micro-transaction, and incomplete otherwise. The relationship between a (complete) free fragment and the wiki page as the main semiotic product emerging in the framework of the transaction can be variable: They constitute accessory semiotic products as long as their status with respect to the page has not been clearly established. If taken up by coauthors, a fragment can either be rejected, or be (gradually) included in the main product by becoming subject to changes in the mode of expression and/or semiotic content. The uptake step is essential: "However, if free fragments are not properly articulated together as soon as they are inscribed on the substrate, the uptake process will not be possible and the DofA will not be able to efficiently sustain the emergent distributed transactions involved in the cooperative activity" (p. 221). Hence, the uptake is conditional not only on the readers' processing of the text, but also on how the fragment is introduced by the author. In peer groups, uptake will be made more complex by the fact that there is not clear attribution of specific authority to accept/ reject free fragments.

Some Conclusions About Wikis

Wikis constitute, from a semiotic perspective, a rather complex document category. They are complex not only because of the need to coordinate a multistep group writing process (Lowry et al., 2004), but also because of the need for extensive documentarization in order to create shared meaning for what is collaboratively written. Wikis, being essentially a writing medium, require substantial coordination efforts amongst the members of the team involved in creating documents in them. A particular challenge is the establishment of coherence, on the level of text (connecting fragments that take the form of sentences and paragraphs) as well as on the level of concepts (ideas, arguments). The same holds for other types of digital knowledge objects that can be authored by a number of people in a manner at least technically independent of each other, such as documents in shared repositories (e.g., Lotus Notes) or on the Web (e.g., Google Docs).

Based on our analysis of wikis as documents-for-action, they ought to be rather hard to use when the goal is to produce coherent documents. So far, systematic analysis of this issue has not been performed. We can take the increasing interest in semantic wikis (Souzis, 2005) and in visualization/navigation support for wiki sites (Reinhold, 2006) as indicative of the fact that today's standard wiki technology has recognized limitations. It is also informative in this regard to see the many social rules and the increasing user role differentiations that have been evolving around the mass-cooperation sites, notably Wikipedia.

In general, students who are not experienced in working in virtual teams and who are not experienced in authoring text or other knowledge artifacts together will need to be supported in order to produce knowledge objects of good quality, and to learn from this experience.

Below we report on our own work on providing such support, in three forms: (a) by monitoring and visualizing group members' interactions and contributions, (b) by visualizing wiki site structure, and (c) by providing information on wiki page content based on a text-statistical analysis. These measures aim at improving coordination of team members' activities and increasing document coherence. In an educational context, such as a university, students are ideally not only supported in creating knowledge artifacts collaboratively, but would also learn how to get better at this, in particular learning how to work in (partially or fully) virtualized teams and how to author collaboratively. Therefore, we will look into team skills development next.

Developing Team Skills

Providing groups with ill-structured problems (i.e., problems that require elaboration and negotiation to be defined, and for which no single correct solution exists) and mirroring/feedback information, instead of well-formed problems and strong scaffolds and guidelines, can be seen as a risky pedagogical strategy (Kirschner, Sweller, & Clark, 2006). However, when development of team skills is part of the learning goals it is necessary to provide sufficient space so that students can experience aspects of real teamwork such as breaking down a large task into subgoals, defining roles and allocating team members to roles and tasks, reacting adaptively to unforeseen obstacles, changes in the group environment as well as in members needs, etc. There might be no other way to learn to manage what sometimes looks like chaos than to experience the chaos. There is no question that students will sometimes fail to deal with the demands of dynamic group work, but failure can be productive (Kapur, 2006), in particular when followed by opportunities for reflection.

Because most of the research on collaborative learning pertains to forms of collaboration where many of the decisions concerning group composition, roles, responsibilities, and timing have been made for the group, not by the group, developing team skills as such has not been much of a research issue. There are exceptions, such as research on how training for group work in school settings affects individual learning (Yager, Johnson, Johnson, & Snider, 1986), group performance (Johnson, Johnson, Stanne, & Garibaldi, 1989), and collaborative language and behavior (Gillies, 2004; Gillies & Ashman, 1996) as well as more recent work in Higher Education (Prichard, Startford, & Bizo, 2006). But by and large, team (skills) development has received more attention in organizational psychology, in the context of work teams, and by far most of the research has been conducted on types of teams where communication and coordination breakdowns can quickly result in disaster, groups of soldiers and pilots in particular (e.g., Cannon-Bowers & Salas, 1998). In the organizational and military training research literature, we find a diversity of team-training approaches that have been developed, as well as reviews of their effectiveness (Dyer, 1984; Kozlowski & Ilgen, 2006).

Pedagogical Approaches

Team-skills training is a broad term, comprising numerous skills such as goal setting, interpersonal relations, and role clarification (e.g., Buller & Bell, 1986), and various training strategies, such as team building (Salas, Rozell, Mullen, & Driskell, 1999) and team self-correction strategies (Blickensderfer, Cannon-Bowers, & Salas, 1997). An important didactical decision is whether to teach such skills individually or practice them in teams. While research shows that team skills can to a certain extent be taught individually, highly interdependent forms of team work requires practice in team form (Kozlowski, Brown, Weissbein, Cannon-Bowers, & Salas, 2000). Focusing on teams as the learning unit, a further decision has to be made instruction and training to develop spontaneously in the context of teamwork. The consensus seems to be that any kind of team skill can be enhanced by facilitation through training, if not always qualitatively then at least in the form of an acceleration of the development process (Prichard et al., 2006).

Skills Addressed by Training

In addition to the variation in didactical approaches, one finds a variety in the topics that are addressed in team-skills education, such as goal setting, interpersonal relations, and role clarification. As Prichard and Ashleigh (2007) summarize:

> Training directed at goal setting emphasizes the setting of goals and objectives, the identification of obstacles to achieving goals, and action planning to determine how goals are to be reached and obstacles overcome. The interpersonal model focuses on the development of open communication, mutual trust, and cohesion. Role clarification models emphasize the different interacting roles that people play in a group situation and aim to increase each person's knowledge about the roles played by others. (p. 703–704)

Increasingly, these elements are combined into integrated, generic training programs (e.g., Prichard, Stratford, & Hardy, 2004).

Analogous to using analysis of experts' competence and skills identify learning goals, we suggest the factors characterizing successful teamwork in order to decide on learning goals for team skill development. This is particularly relevant when supporting team learning in a computer-based manner. In this case, aspects of individual and group work to provide feedback, given that many aspects can be recorded easily, but only few can be visualized in the shared working environment on a computer screen.

The question of what processes and components comprise teamwork and how teamwork contributes to team effectiveness has received much attention in team research. A recent review of this body of research resulted in the identification of the "Big Five" components of teamwork (Salas, Sims, & Burke, 2005). This review identifies the elements that make up teamwork, independent of the task a team has to perform:

1. Team leadership: Ability to direct and coordinate the activities of other team members, assess team performance, assign tasks, develop team knowledge, skills, and abilities, motivate team members, plan and organize, and establish a positive atmosphere.
2. Mutual performance monitoring: The ability to develop common understandings of the team environment and apply appropriate task strategies to accurately monitor team-mate performance.

3. Backup behavior: Ability to anticipate other team members' needs through accurate knowledge about their responsibilities. This includes the ability to shift workload among members to achieve balance during high periods of workload or pressure.
4. Adaptability: Ability to adjust strategies based on information gathered from the environment through the use of backup behavior and reallocation of intrateam resources. Altering a course of action or team repertoire in response to changing conditions (internal or external).
5. Team orientation: Propensity to take other's behavior into account during group interaction and belief in the importance of team's goals over individual members' goals.

Teams that enact these five elements will enjoy improved performance. However, in order to fully realize this performance improvement potential, research shows that three additional coordinating mechanisms need to be in place (Salas et al., 2005, p. 564): (a) Shared mental models: An organizing knowledge structure of the relationships among the tasks the team is engaged in and how the team members will interact; (b) Mutual trust: The shared belief that team members will perform their roles and protect the interests of their teammates; (c) Closed-loop communication: The mutual acknowledgment of the success or otherwise of an exchange of information between a sender and a receiver, irrespective of the medium.

Transfer

An important issue is the extent to which team skills can be seen as generic, i.e., independent of a specific team and task. Cannon-Bowers, Tannenbaum, Salas, & Volpe (1995) argue that team members must have both generic and specific team competencies (knowledge, skills, and attitudes) because in order to be effective, the generic aspects must be enriched by team-specific information. For instance, it is not only important that team members share information (generic), but each team member must have knowledge about the knowledge and skills other team members have (specific). One implication is that regrouping of effective teams should lead to performance loss, which has been widely demonstrated in team research (Prichard et al., 2006).

A fundamental challenge for developing team skills arises from the multilevel, dynamic, and complex nature of groups. There is general consensus amongst researchers that groups need to be conceptualized as embedded in a multilevel system that has individual, team, and organizational aspects (Kozlowski & Ilgen, 2006) as well as a wider socio-cultural context (Bonk & Cunningham, 1998). Furthermore, groups incorporate temporal dynamics involving active different time scales, ranging from the episodic to the developmental (McGrath & Tschan, 2004). And that groups share many features with other complex, open systems, in particular the fact that many group processes are emergent phenonema and that so, there are limits to their predictability. If groups are essentially complex systems, than we cannot account for group phenomena by aggregating over the individual members, the effects of interactions on the member level will not directly and linearly show effects on the group level (but be highly state dependent), and group level phenomena (such as role distribution, power structure, shared knowledge) will affect member behavior, but cannot be reduced to it (Arrow et al., 2000; Kapur et al., 2007). Furthermore, complex systems are path-dependent: How they will react to a signal from their environment depends not only on the signal and the current state of the system, but also on the "history" of the system. Time matters (Reimann, 2007).

This does not only makes comparative (e.g., experimental) research on groups problematic (because it is not quite clear what we are comparing, given that any group will be different from any other after a couple of minutes into their group existence), it also make it hard to come up with general advise on group performance, given the differences in group behavior as well as the path-dependence of the effects of the advice. One way to avoid these conceptual issues is to provide groups with information that is specific to their history and their current situation, and is hence adapted to the potentially unique information needs for each specific group at each specific point in time. To accomplish this, computational means are needed, because it is not feasible that human tutors or facilitators can deliver this kind of information just in time.

Supporting Coordination by Visualizing Interactions

We have identified the need to help students working in teams to produce knowledge artifacts with respect to two aspects: coordinating member activities and establishing coherence amongst ideas (concepts) and of the documents produced. In this section, we focus on the first aspect, supporting coordination.

Systems that support the management of distributed collaborative learning processes can be classified as mirroring tools, metacognitive tools, or guiding/coaching systems (Soller, Martínez-Monés, Jermann, & Muehlenbrock, 2005). We are interested in the first two categories, as they place the locus of the processing into the learners' hands. Mirroring tools (see, e.g., Barros & Verdejo, 2000) impose few constraints on users, but are purely performance-based and do not offer semantic interpretation or analysis of the nature of the user's intervention. In particular, mirroring approaches do not compare current performance with target performance; they do not show a gap. Mirroring is particular appropriate when information about "good" or "optimal" behavior is lacking. Metacognitive approaches build on the notion that a model of good performance (if not theory-based, then at least "best practice") is available and hence the difference between current and target performance – the "gap" – to the learners. In other words, the metacognitive approach provides students with feedback.

Functionally, visualizations of the mirroring type should be effective for enhancing team work in general and member/task coordination in particular because they contribute to task awareness and/or social awareness, depending on what is visualized. Task awareness should be increased when the visualization displays information on tasks and the degree of task completion. A typical example is a Gantt chart, often used in project management. Social awareness should be increased the type of information displayed about team members (e.g., their expertise areas; available time), the relations between members and tasks (e.g., task load, roles), and relations between members (e.g., social networks diagrams).

Visualizations for Wiki-Mediated Collaboration: Wattle Trees

We have created a set of interrelated visualizations that display a useful overview of the vast amount of information stored in electronic traces such as log files. We designed the visualization to directly support team functions (Kay, Maisonneuve, Yacef, & Reimann, 2006). In our approach, we draw upon theories of group work to define dimensions of group operation that we wish to scaffold and where we can identify sources of evidence of the ways that these are operating within a group. We track students' interaction behavior along these dimensions and provide visualizations that are mirrored back to the groups. We believe that groups gain benefit from "just" mirroring information, provided that information speaks to the right issues.

Collaboration Environment

To support their tasks and communication, groups use Trac (http://www.edgewall. com), a tool designed for programmers build software. It has three tightly integrated parts:

- A wiki for collaborative editing of web pages for general group communication, and in our case, for collaboratively creating the major report for the project;
- An issue tracking system based on so-called tickets (see Fig. 6.1), where one creates a ticket when a task needs to be done and this is allocated to a team member and, when the task has been completed, the ticket is closed;
- A browsing interface to a repository based upon the version control system called Subversion (SVN), for storing documents like source code, including any versions.

We describe our visualizations in the context of trac as it has provided most of our experience to date. Moreover, it is an authentic tool that is widely used and is representative of a substantial class of tools that such groups use: it supports

Fig. 6.1 A ticket in Trac. A ticket represents a task issued by somebody (the reporter) to somebody else or to oneself. Tickets in Trac are associated with milestones (available on a different screen), and with the due dates specified in the milestones

task management and allocation, general communication and shared text space, and is the central repository for the work produced, three important pillars for team work.

Form of Team Work

In order to illustrate our approach, we use observations from a software development project where students work in groups of five to seven over 13 weeks. Team members tend to focus on the goal of producing a software product that meets their clients' needs, rather than the group management needed to achieve this. Following the Extreme Programming (XP) approach (e.g., http://www.extremeprogramming. org), each student takes one or more of the XP roles, such as team leader (who manages the group), tracker (who tracks people's work and ensure that things are progressing as planned), the programmer (who deals with technical issues), the tester (in charge of functional testing), the doomsayer and so on. Teams meet face-to-face in order to evaluate and coordinate their work, but the main work done through the wiki and the code versioning system (SVN), both accessible in Trac.

Wattle Trees

Given our focus on helping small groups (five to seven members) manage their group processes, including communication, interaction and workload management, what information can we extract from the use of these three mediums to inform team members about these? Wiki pages are not owned by any one person but by everyone who can access the site. When several people alter the same wiki page, we regard this as an interaction. The size of each contribution is taken into account. Similarly, when a team member assigns, or reassigns a ticket to another member or closes it, we also regard this as an interaction between these members. With SVN, when members work on the same files, we also regard this as an interaction and record the size of the contribution.

Figure 6.2 shows our main visualization, which we call the Wattle Tree. (We chose this name as the Wattle tree is an Australian native plant with fluffy golden-yellow round flowers, similar to this visualization). The design goal for this vizualisation was to create a single overview of the total activity of each group member over the 3-month project, with differentiation of the different media. Essentially, it is a bird's eye view of the thousands of actions of the team over a period of time.

Each member of the team is a single wattle tree, with its vertical green stem that grows up the page, each day from the start of the project activity on Trac. Wiki-related activity is represented by yellow "flowers," the circles on the left of the trees. SVN-related activity is similarly represented, as orange flowers on the right of the trees. The size of the flower indicates the size of the contribution. Ticket actions are represented by leaves – the green lines: a dark green leaf on the left indicates a ticket was opened by the user and a light green leaf on the right indicates the user closed a ticket. The length of the left leaf is proportional to the time it remained opened. Those still open are shown at a standard, maximal size (e.g., the ones around day 41 in Fig. 6.2). Often, a good team leader will take the responsibility for opening most of the tickets. We see that the leftmost person in Fig. 6.2 has opened many tickets while the closing of tickets is more evenly distributed across the team.

Although these visualizations are intended to be meaningful for the team, rather than the outsider viewing them, there are some features we can identify in Fig. 6.2. The student at the very left has many yellow circles reflecting high wiki activity until around day 40 and they have created many tickets, indicated by the dark green lines. The second student from the left has a similar level of wiki activity and has opened many short-lived tickets and closed many tickets. Overall, these two members appear to have been the most active in management aspects at the wiki and tickets: knowledge of the group bears this out. The fourth student from the left is particularly active on SVN corresponding to a larger role in the technical development. The fifth student from the left has a hiatus from about Day 27 corresponding to little activity. This group had times when several members were ill or had other difficulties and they could see the effect of these problems in the Wattle diagram. The team member with responsibility for tracking progress could use the Wattle

Days

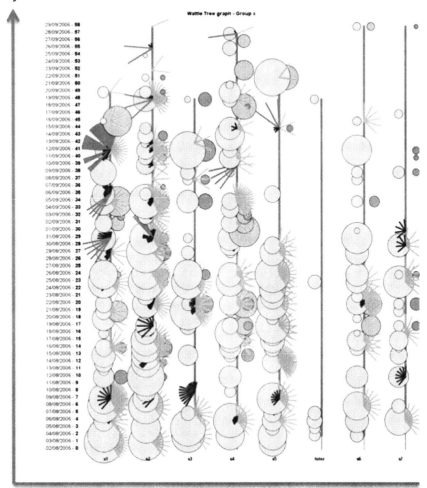

Team members

Fig. 6.2 Wattle tree diagram. Each person in the team appears as a "tree" that climbs up the page over time. The tree starts when the user first does an action on any of the three media considered. The vertical axis shows the day number and date

tree to get an overview of overall activity at a glance: they could also quickly see recent changes in activity by individuals, for example, those working on urgent or critical tasks. This serves as a starting point for delving into the details, as needed, by checking individual tickets, wiki pages and SVN documents and their histories. It also gives each individual team member a sense of how their level of activity compares with that of others in the team.

Social Network Diagrams

Wattle trees do not contain information on who issued tickets to whom, and who contributes to a wiki page. In order to visualize this kind of information, we use what we call an Interaction Network, inspired by the graphical notations used in Social Network Analysis (Scott, 1991), which aims to show relationships and flows between entities. The network is modeled as a graph, with each node representing a team member, always shown in the same, fixed position. So, for example, the person at 12 o'clock in Figs. 6.3 and 6.4 is the same in each of these visualizations. Lines between these nodes indicate interaction between these team members. We define interaction to occur when two people modify the same wiki page or SVN file or perform actions on the same ticket. The width of the edge is proportional to the number of interactions between them. For a given resource, the number of interactions is calculated as $n = \min(n1, n2)$ where $n1$ and $n2$ are the number of times user1 and user2 modified the resource.

So, for example, the interaction network for ticket interaction as depicted in Fig. 6.3 shows considerable interaction between most team members (but not the tutor). Note that some team members interact with more members of the team than others. For the tickets, we use color to indicate who initiates tickets, with blue at the node for a person who initiates more tickets. So, for example, a team leader often allocated tickets to all others and in this case, the lines from the leader are blue at the leader's end. Finally, the Interaction Diagram for the wiki shows that every member of the team interacts with every other one, including the tutor. These diagrams change over time. As we have already mentioned, this is intended to be meaningful for the team members who should know who was working on each aspect and who may have been interacting with others.

Table 6.1 briefly describes how the two visualizations relate to team success factors of the Big Five model. The aspects and behavioral markers are taken from (Salas et al., 2005). We show only those what are applicable to the visualization. When designing the visualizations, we had to balance the complexity of the display against the number of aspects presented. Importantly, we had to take account of which aspects could sensibly be inferred from the available data. So, for example, the first row indicates one role of the team leader, facilitating team problem solving. The next column briefly indicates how the interaction network can support this aspect. For example, one potentially pathological pattern occurred when one person could be seen interacting with every other team member on SVN: in this case, this person was fixing problems in all other team member's code, something that they should have been responsible for. This form of domination suggests a problem in the group. This can happen when several people have weak technical skills and they expect the top programmer to fix their code and do the difficult work. This pattern can, equally, occur when one person believes they are better than the others and that person leaps in and works on other people's code, not allowing them to complete it themselves, even though they are keen to do so and capable.

Fig. 6.3 Interaction network
based on tickets

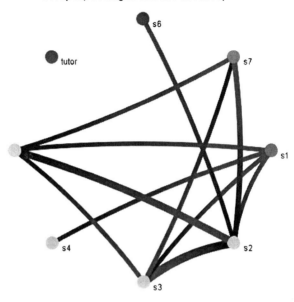

Fig. 6.4 Interaction network
based on wiki entries

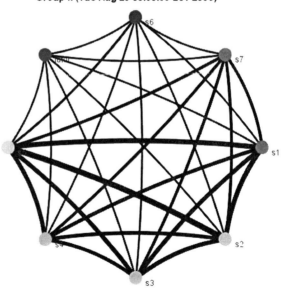

Table 6.1 Relations between the visualizations and the Big Five framework

Aspect and behavioral markers	Interaction network	Wattle tree
Team leadership		
Facilitate team problem solving	Identify potential problems, due to unexpected interactions, such as one person altering work allocated to another. Starting point for leader to ask others about what appear to be problems	Missing activity where expected points to potential problems. This can be used as a starting point for conversations and checking details
Synchronize and combine individual team member contributions		Progress of each team member and type of activity can be seen and this can help with planning of integration
Seek and evaluate information that affects team functioning	Maintain awareness of who interacts with whom and, importantly clear lack of interaction when expected	
Clarify team member roles	Comparing expected interactions with the actual points to possible problems	Can see activity types and assess if they match expectations – and then act to address problems
Engage in preparatory meetings and feedback sessions with the team		Gain an overview of progress as part of planning the meeting and deciding whether there are problems to discuss at the meeting
Mutual performance monitoring		
Identifying mistakes and lapses in other team members' actions	Identifying lack of interaction when it was expected	Indicates the periods of inactivity
Providing feedback regarding team member actions to facilitate self-correction	Unexpected patterns of interaction may indicate problems, e.g., one person correcting/amending work allocated to another	Shows overall forms of activity, such as increased work on one medium
Backup behavior		
Recognition by potential backup providers that there is a workload distribution problem in their team		Can see distribution of workload, and potential for rebalancing of workload
Shifting of work responsibilities to underutilized team members	Can see interaction on same resources when one person begins work started by another	Can see both recent long-term contribution levels by those doing little at present
Completion of the whole task or parts of tasks by other team members	As above	Can see some rebalancing

(continued)

Table 6.1 (continued)

Aspect and behavioral markers	Interaction network	Wattle tree
Adaptability		
Identify cues that a change has occurred, assign meaning to that change, and develop a new plan to deal with the changes	In new releases of the interaction overviews, can see new interactions, either confirming planned allocations or showing the unexpected	Can see unexpected patterns of activity and changes in level of use of each medium
Identify opportunities for improvement and innovation for habitual or routine practices	Can see that there is continuation of interactions that have been unproductive or start of new interactions	Can see changes/continuation of contribution levels on each medium and interpret this relative to plans
Remain vigilant to changes in the internal and external environment of the team	Quickly see unexpected changes in interaction	See unexpected patterns of activity, e.g., a person suddenly ill
Team orientation		
Taking into account alternative solutions provided by teammates and appraising that input to determine what is best	Partly visible as interaction on wiki and tickets	
Increased task involvement, information sharing, strategizing, and participation in goal setting	Each team member can see the interactions and link this to other knowledge of progress	Can see indications of chances for increased involvement, e.g., if one person was very active on the wiki, others may realize they need to check for the new information provided

This example illustrates some important aspect of our mirroring approach. Given the complexity of long-term group work on challenging tasks, the simple measures of interaction cannot possibly capture deep and subtle features of the group interaction. However, the team members have considerable knowledge of the nature of the tasks, the allocations as well as the personalities, skills and commitment and the particular circumstances of other team members. They can use this to interpret the visualizations, checking what these show against their expectations.

The third column in the table provides comments on the ways that the Wattle visualization can support the various aspects shown. Again taking the example of the first row, this visualization can either vindicate expected activity on each medium or, when a problem has occurred, it can give an early warning of this. For example, if a team member has been allocated a task, such as writing for part of the task, one would expect to see progress on this as SVN activity. If there is none visible, it points to a possible problem. The leader can use the Wattle tree to begin the discussion about this: they can simply comment that they would have expected to see such activity.

First Experiences Using the Visualizations

We report here experiences from a semester-long project course (capstone project) where teams used Trac. There were seven groups of 5–7 students in each team, with 44 students making it to the end. We began the semester with a lecture about collaboration management, introducing the visualizations. We introduced weekly meetings with the leader of each team, to discuss concerns and challenges. There were also interviews with each team at three points in the semester to monitor their response to collaboration management.

The visualizations were made available to the students on a regular basis throughout the semester, on their wiki. In both the interviews and weekly meetings with the team leaders, there was a spontaneous response to the visualizations. Three of the seven groups showed great enthusiasm for them and asked to be able to generate them on demand. (This was not possible at that stage.) The students indicated that the visualizations were helpful for the tracker (the person who has to ensure that work is progressing as intended) and the manager (who distributes the workload). There has also been spontaneous reference to the visualizations in relation to some difficulties in groups, particularly in the case of seeming occurrences of social loafing, with an individual failing to carry their fair share of work in the group.

Students have also commented that the visualizations help individuals to see the amount of work they have contributed to the group, to compare it with that of others and to provide some quantitative measurement for balancing the group workload. Notably, six of the seven groups encountered serious problems with group members (absence due to sickness or travel, social loafing and technical weakness). Three groups asked for more frequent releases of the diagrams. Some students explained that they would like to see how the diagrams change after they have contributed a fair amount of work and see how this amount compares with the others. One group mentioned that the lack of contribution from a member showed up on the Wattle Tree. The group would have liked to see the evidence. The member said he took it as a wake-up call, and intended to participate more: importantly, he did so.

Overall, our experience has indicated that these visualizations are particularly useful for providing an early warning of problems. Since we have used them, we have had none of the most dysfunctional groups we saw in the past, especially for the case of social loafing that persisted through the semester. This operates for two classes of reasons. First, it was rather difficult for teachers to identify dysfunctional groups early enough to help them recover. Second, in the past, even when teachers could see indicators of dysfunction, it was very difficult to communicate this to the students effectively. More recently, there have been spontaneous requests for the visualizations to be made available for other users of Trac.

The main negative feedback was related to the fact that the visualizations are based on simple counts of the amount of activity and there is no measure of quality. This is a very valid concern. There was also some negative feedback about the whole enterprise of monitoring activity and making this explicitly available in the visualizations. It was expressed most strongly by one student in these terms: "The virtual cybernetic monitoring of our work was counterposed by the need to set our own goals and this made for a fairly unalienated work environment but unfortunately there was also a resulting uneasy foreboding if we stopped working a while".

We certainly acknowledge the simplicity of the information presented. However, we also know that it is not really rewarding to play the system since we make no use of the visualizations for anything other than as a support for collaboration management. If a student played the system (and this did happened a couple of times, to a limited extent), perhaps creating many vacuous tickets or large quantities of low quality wiki or SVN content, the team members can readily see that if they scrutinize these. Every team member knows that this is the case. The students seem to generally be most positive about the Wattle tree: it summarizes temporal aspects and enables students to see and respond to changes. The interaction networks also seem to be important and they certainly did point to cases where an individual is isolated from the group.

From a questionnaire study, we gained the reactions as shown in Table 6.2. This shows two values, the average score on the Likert scale (from 1 to 7) first for the full cohort and then for just the seven managers. On average, most students found the visualizations somewhat informative and helpful (mean > 3.5). Notably, those in the manager role gave far stronger positive responses, around 1 point higher on the

Table 6.2 Students' reactions to the visualizations

Questionnaire item (each item scaled from 1 to 7 indicating increasing agreement)	Mean score (all/managers only)
I found the Wattle tree useful	4.7/5.8
I found the interaction network useful	3.8/4.8
I found that the combination of the diagrams helped me learn things that the individual diagrams did not…	3.8/4.5
The diagrams gave me a sense of "big picture" and/or revealed things I did not know about the members' contribution…	4.4/4.8
Without the diagrams, it would be difficult to get this overall sense of big picture…	3.9/4.8
The simplicity of the metrics used still conveys useful information…	4.1/5.0
I recommend the use of these diagrams for future offerings or other group project offerings	5.2/6.0
I/my group changed something during the semester in light of what I/we saw in the diagrams	Yes: 38% No: 62%

Likert scale for most aspects. This is reasonable, since the visualizations support the role of the managers.

For each of the items, we also allowed for open answers. These are particularly interesting for the question assessing the consequences of seeing the diagrams. Students' open answers to this item are shown in Table 6.3. Only one student (pessimists may say, the only honest one) remarked that the group began to "play" the system ("cheat the system almost"). However, even this student's behavior change may be seen as positive – they took more care to report their work on the wiki and tickets in order to be seen to be working: this, in turn, meant that the tracker could use these media without needing to wait for the next meeting. In addition, if the student claimed to have done work, Trac makes it easy to link this claim to the actual contribution, be it on the wiki or SVN. So, the tracker should have been able to thoroughly check the work had been completed satisfactorily. Many students referred to the visualizations for their reflective statements in their final reports, pointing to features in the visualizations and explaining the corresponding events.

Table 6.3 Students reporting consequences or implications of the visualizations

I/my group changed something during the semester in light of what I/we saw in the diagrams…

Yes	No
I tried to show the work I was doing better, using more tickets	Did not shed light on something unknown, so no change was warranted
Make sure to contribute and interact on these levels (cheat the system almost)	Our approach didn't really need to be changed
We update our wikis more often and are pushed to commit stuff regularly	We only got them twice. Need weekly diagrams
	Not that useful, just states the obvious
I realized that I wasn't ticketing enough work so I stepped up	There was no need of change
	Because people were lazy
I took more effort on wiki and ticket after seeing the first diagram	Again, we were not surprised/upset by what they showed. Diagrams in contribution were already known and accounted for
Roles were changed in order to cater for aspects that group members were missing. Even though group members would gravitate toward original position	
I used the Wattle tree to highlight contribution of team members	
Some members find they weren't working enough and improved	
We worked harder. Created more tickets. Did more interactive group activities	
I became more aware of my interaction with the wiki/SVN	

New Developments Based on First Experiences

We were pleased to see how such visualizations are actually used by teams. We found that our teams need to be introduced to these tools. This goes hand-in-hand with the need to motivate team members to appreciate the importance of collaboration management. Compared to former semesters (not reported here), the students in this study worked much harder on their team performance, having been shown why they need to be concerned about group maintenance and having been shown how the visualizations might help. It may have also been important that we showed them how to interpret the diagrams. Equally important may be the value of showing examples of the varied forms these visualizations tend to take in highly successful groups as well as problem groups. This might make it easier to recognize the same visual pattern when it arose in their own group.

We have subsequently been extending this approach on several fronts. When we began this work, we built the visualizations to be independent of any tool: so, for example, we built visualizations for discussion groups in WebCT and for groups using a set of different media in a Flash based online learning system. A disadvantage of this separation of the learning environment from the visualization software was that the visualizations had to be produced off-line and, hence, they were not available on demand. Rather they were generated and added to the Trac wikis at set times. We have been rebuilding the visualization software to be integrated into Trac, so that it can be used at any time, on demand.

The second design goal was to generalize the visualization so that not only Trac components such wiki pages, tickets, and SVN interactions be visualized, but any combination of the many communication methods available in courses, and external to Trac, such as discussion board entries and chat entries. A third design goal was to link the visualizations with the underlying log data in an interactive manner: when selecting a specific part of the interaction visualization with the mouse, the log data behind that component of the visualization would be rendered on the screen. This implied a redesign of the visualizations itself, as shown in Fig. 6.5.

The former Wattle Tree is now replaced by a set of "swim lanes," one for each student in a team (in Fig. 6.5, that is area A, with three students S1, S2, S3, and one tutor, T; time is in days, running from bottom to top). Color is used to represent the type of contribution (wiki, ticket, svn), per day (or other time units) and aggregated over the visualized time period (B). When the user clicks a point in one of the swim lanes that has an activity indicated (i.e., is colored), the underlying log data for that cell will be rendered on the screen (C). Since this visualization is now fully integrated into Trac, the user can further drill down by following the links to trac objects. For instance, in Fig. 6.5(C) ticket change events are shown, and clicking on each of the links will bring the user to the respective ticket.

A second line of work is addressing the limitations of the visualizations is their use of very simple measures of the numbers of lines contributed to the wiki or SVN and the gross actions on tickets. We have been exploring ways to use machine learning, clustering, and data mining to identify patterns which could augment the simple line count (Perera, Kay, Yacef, & Koprinska, 2007). Notably, our clustering

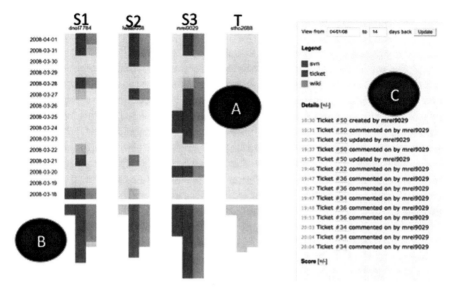

Fig. 6.5 Narcissus, an interactive form of interaction visualization. See text for explanations

approaches grouped individuals into some meaningful and valuable groups. For example, this gave one group that we would describe as having characteristics of a manager, with heavy use of ticketing and the wiki, based on a large collection of measures. Notably, successful groups had one such person and that person was the nominated manager. Problem groups had various other combinations, such as having several people with this cluster of behaviors with none being the nominated manager. We are exploring ways to use such data-mining approaches to provide additional mirroring information.

Data on students' interaction behavior are a rich source for mirroring and feedback, and particularly valuable when the learning goals comprise collaboration skills. But there is another source of information: the "product" that students generate in the course of their interactions. Mirroring, feedback, or guidance with respect to the group product will certainly be helpful for domain learning, but it is also important for the team process because, at the very least, teams need to know if/when the task is complete, and even better to what degree the task has been accomplished. For instance, if the goal is to develop a piece of software, then information on whether the software works and if the client is satisfied with the software is helpful. If the goal is to develop a written report, then information on the quality of writing and the satisfaction of the readers is helpful. In the following sections, we describe our first attempts to support teams with information on the features of their jointly authored wiki documents.

Visualizing Wiki Site Structure

The very nature of a wiki means that its structure and content will typically change over time. When the wiki is the main collaboration tool for learners, they need to be able to find the relevant parts of the wiki. On each return visit to the wiki, the learner needs to determine where to focus their attention. For example, they may need to determine where there have been changes made. If a person comes to a mature wiki project, with well-developed content, she or he needs to gain an overview of the wiki so that they can begin to get a sense of its extent and structure. A teacher is in a similar situation to the new visitor since they will typically visit intermittently and there may have been large changes in the wiki structure and content.

Static web sites address some similar problems by providing a site map. Of course, for the case of a wiki, this would fail to account for the temporal issues. In a static site map, it is not usual to indicate the level of change that has occurred on parts of the site. Nor is there the need to indicate who made recent changes to parts of the site. However, in the case of a wiki, it will often be important to have such information. For example, if students use a wiki to write an essay collaboratively, a student may want to be able to see which parts have changed since they last visited the site. It may also be important to see which parts of the wiki were edited by a particular person, perhaps to monitor responses by others.

WikiNavMap (Ullman & Kay, 2007) is an exploration of ways to support navigation in a wiki (see Fig. 6.6). It enables the user to customize the view of the wiki in terms of time and in relation to the authorship of activity on the pages. It aims to enable users to answer questions like these: Which are the pages that I have made contributions to? Which are the pages that another nominated person has made contributions to? Which are the pages associated with a certain task? Which are the pages with the most activity? Which pages changed in the last week? Which changed in a particular period of time, such as a particular month? What is the extent of the wiki? To do this, it provides a customization menu which enables the user to filter the pages, based on time and author. It also provides a complete overview, in a thumbnail and it presents a view of a larger version of the selected part of this, allowing the user to move this larger, viewed area. While these facilities give an overview, the user can see additional details via a mouse-over and then can click on the page to go to it, to see the full details of that page.

WikiNavMap has been implemented as a plugin for Trac. As shown in Fig. 6.6, each rectangular box is a wiki page. The figure shows the page for a meeting. The user has their mouse over that box, causing the display of the information about recent actions on that page. The larger the box, the more activity there has been on it. The interface allows the user to control the shade of color to indicate the time. So, for example, the user could set the deepest color to show the pages which were last altered in the last week, the next deepest colour to show older pages, changed up to a month ago, and so on. Then, the largest boxes of a particular shade are the ones that had the most activity in the corresponding time period. Tickets are shown inside a box with a fine red line border, like the one at the bottom of the figure with

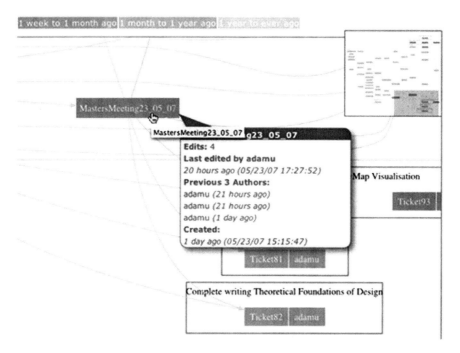

Fig. 6.6 WikiNavMap creates a dynamic visualization of a whole wiki site

Ticket 82. The tickets are grouped by their milestone, a notion supported by Trac to group tasks according to the higher-level goals of the group.

WikiNavMap plays both a navigational role, and also has the potential to increase member and task awareness (hence, affecting coordination), and helps to monitor coherence. If one filters the display to see the contributions of each team member in turn, it is easy to gain a sense of what each has contributed to the wiki. So, for example, one can set the colors to show work in the first, second, and third months of a 3-month project and then filter to show one team member. Then one can see which wiki pages and tickets this person completed work on in each month.

The display also shows lines from each page to other pages it links to. This are shown as very light lines in the display so as not to overwhelm the other information and because they can be very dense and complex. Such visualization of the hyperlinks between the wiki pages, which typically reflect semantic relations, provides the viewer not only with an idea of what topics are discussed on the pages, but also how they are related to each other. Thus, provided the links reflect content relations, the WikiNavMap visualization can be interpreted as a semantic network (Jonassen, Beissner, & Yacci, 1993) with directed, nonlabeled arcs.

Visualizing the Conceptual Structure of Wiki Page Content

In the third approach to supporting the use of wikis (as a paradigmatic collaborative writing technology) we focus directly on the conceptual content and the semantic relations. Providing information on what concepts are contained in a document and to what extent these are related to each other is helpful for individual writing, but it is particularly important for a collaboratively authored text. While an individual writer can be expected to know what concepts and ideas are in a document written by that author, on an active wiki site many changes will be made to a page, and it is hard for the writers to know at any point in time what is currently covered in the page.

In addition, both for the case of individual and collaborative writing, getting information on how the network of ideas and concepts contained in the text changes over time can be an important regulative for the writing process. In order to conceptualize such changes, one can build on a taxonomy suggested by Chi and Ohlsson (2005) for individual (declarative) learning:

- Knowing more on the same level of detail/abstractness;
- Increased density: new connection/relation identified;
- Increased consistency: errors/misconceptions identified and overcome, resulting in increased (local) consistence;
- Finer grain of representation: more details known, such as additional parts things are made of. Distinct from knowledge increment in as much as one moves down to identify which parts make up the thing/process described on the higher level;
- Greater complexity: integration of existing simpler ideas/theories/schemas;
- Higher level of abstraction, e.g., generalizing, conceptualizing;
- Shift in vantage point: a shift in perspective that allows us to see something in a new light, from a different angle;
- Identifying a dead-end line of inquiry/thought without being able to provide a better solution at this time.

Clearly, changes in conceptual knowledge are the hardest part to track and mirror automatically, even if we assume, as we do here, that text versions produced by students in the course of writing reflect changes in their declarative knowledge. Also, we assume that these types of changes are meaningful when applied to a jointly authored textual artefact – a document – not only when used to describe individual cognitive changes. Even when these assumptions hold, most of the forms of learning distinguished by Chi and Ohlsson require careful analysis on a semantic level. This cannot be accomplished computationally in full. However, techniques that are based on relations between text surface level and semantic level can be applied, and can support mirroring back to students some information about the knowledge contained in their (individually or collaboratively produced) texts. In the following, we illustrate how such an analysis can be performed, and what kind of information it yields.

Automap Analysis of Collaboratively Authored Wiki Pages

The automatic concept analysis method that we employed is based on Carley's map analysis technique (Carley, 1986, 1997) and the corresponding software, called Automap. This method is based on the assumption that peoples' mental models can be represented as concept maps (a variant of semantic networks), and that the mental models people have of a domain can be inferred from what people write about that domain. The map analysis method is predicated on the assumption that features of the text surface correspond to relations in the mental model: concepts that appear comparatively frequently in close proximity (window, e.g., within five words from each other) are treated as linked together in a statement (chain of interlinked concepts) in the mental model.

What counts as a concept needs to be defined by the analyst. Typically, and minimally, one would want to avoid treating certain words (such as the) as a concept, and one would want to treat singular and plural forms of a noun as the same concept. AutoMap provides the means to define concepts with (hierarchical) thesauri, thus accounting for concepts at multiple levels of generalization and abstraction.

Space prevents us from describing the technical details, so we confine ourselves to examples of how we use this method to provide information to students on the concept relations contained in their wiki contributions. The first example looks at a wiki page that has been coauthored by a number of students, on the topic of knowledge-building theory, based on their reading of Scardamalia and Bereiter (2006). This is one of the collectively authored wiki pages analyzed in Cai (2007), using a thesaurus of domain concepts for the learning sciences domain of approximately 300 entries. The length of the wiki analyzed was 663 words. Table 6.4 shows the basic parameters for the concept map based on the specific thesaurus.

There are 28 unique concepts and 110 unique statements in the map; the density of the map is 0.14; and the centrality of the map is 0.86. Density is calculated by dividing the number of identified links by the number of possible links. Centrality (of the map) reflects the extent to which a single concept has high centrality and the others low centrality, with a single concept's (in_degree) centrality defined as Total number of statements with concept in posterior position/Number of unique concepts per text. Figure 6.7 shows the map in a graphical format.

The value of such text statistics and displays becomes clearer when students can perform comparisons between wiki documents, as the absolute numbers do not provide much information in isolation. Comparisons are possible for instance between two pages on the same topic from different teams, or comparisons across versions. For instance, the same students produced a wiki page on another topic with more words (1,253), 55 unique concepts and 261 unique statements, with a density of 0.09 and a centrality of 0.62. In addition to comparing quantitative parameters of maps, visual inspection is useful, in particular for identifying information pertaining to specific concepts. For instance, a concept's relative centrality can be visually discerned in networks such as displayed in Fig. 6.7.

Table 6.4 Descriptive text statistics for a wiki page

Page name: "knowledge building"	
Page length	663 words
No. of concepts analyzed	
Total	105
Unique	28
No. of isolated concepts	
Total	2
Unique	1
No. of statements	
Total	162
Unique	110
Map density	0.14
Map centrality	0.86

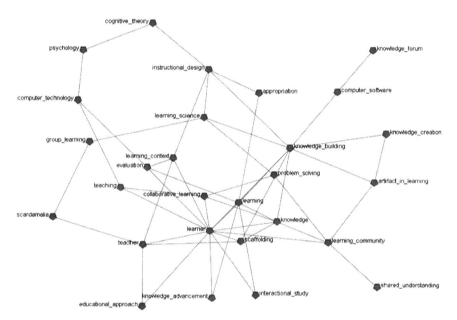

Fig. 6.7 A network view of the concepts identified in a jointly authored wiki page

Tracing a Document's Concept Structure Across Versions

An example for comparing across document versions, i.e., over time, is now illustrative as it sheds some light on the process of collaborative writing and knowledge construction. The wiki page analyzed here for the purpose of illustration went through 59 revisions, and reached a length of 4,128 words. The majority of the changes were done on the first day, 21st April, when the lecturer running the course set up a preliminary structure for the document. In the first few days the majority of the versions were written (52), after which one change was written each on the 28th and 29th, following which was a break. On the 29th of May there was another change, and then there were four final changes on the 21st July. Most of the changes were written by the author A (12), followed by B (10) and C (9). The next five authors are responsible for around four to six changes, and three authors changed the wiki only once. This, however, does not correlate directly with the number of words contributed to the page. The largest number of words were, in fact, contributed by C (743) with the majority of students contributing an average of around 500 words. The mean word increase between documents is 70, with a standard deviation of 119. This illuminates the fact that a significant portion of the changes contributed less than 10 words, and a few others were very large, around 300–400 words increase.

It is illustrative to trace the development of this page across versions. As the wiki page grows, more concepts are added, and the concepts are used in statements with other concepts, this creating links in the concept analysis. However, with more concepts, the possible number of links between concepts grows, disproportionately to the actual number of links created. The density – defined as number of identified links/number of possible links – therefore drops as more versions added, despite the fact that some concepts have a large number of links to other concepts (see Fig. 6.8). This may be typical of a knowledge document, in which there is a large number of concepts used, and a limited opportunity to link them with other concepts. There were versions in which the density increased (between 5 and 6, 15 and 16, and 20 and 21). These revisions resulted in no or just one new concept

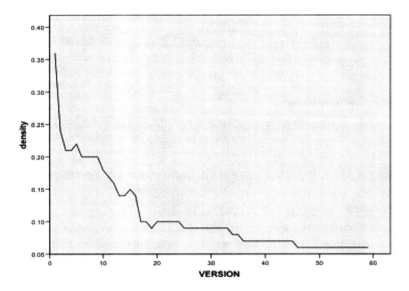

Fig. 6.8 Development of concept density over document versions

being introduced, but a substantial number of links was added. These could be instances of reevaluating, or enriching the understanding of, previously mentioned concepts. (Note that we speak rather loosely of "links added"; it needs to be kept in mind that it is not the students who are adding these links directly, but the numbers are based on an algorithm identifying such links given how students had been revising the text.)

Another useful indicator of coherence is the Variance of Concept Degree Centrality (VCDC). It measures the extent to which concepts are more central (more connected) than others:

$$VDVC = \frac{Sum(in\_degree - mean - in\_degree)^2}{No.\,of\,unique\,concepts}.$$

In looking at Fig. 6.9 we see that the VCDC value climbs sharply over time (versions). This is due to the fact that while a few concepts are very connected and central, others are very peripheral, particularly as more concepts added over time. Indeed, many of the concepts that have the most links in the last version were introduced in the first five revisions, while other concepts, with only one or two links, were introduced later in the document history. That being taken into account, this graph indicates that this particular wiki page is shaped on a few, key concepts, while mentioning a great many of peripheral ones.

It seems plausible that information such as provided in form of concept maps and/or concerning the development of concept map parameters such as density over

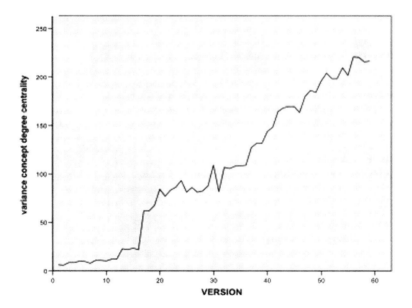

Fig. 6.9 Development of concept variance over versions

time can act as important regulators for a collaborative writing process, in particular concerning the coherence of the document. For individuals and groups to benefit from this information, the visualizations need to be made available for them, ideally on demand. Automap, as a stand-alone program, does not provide for this. We have, therefore, made the algorithm and visualization available online.

A Web-Based Program for Computing Concept Maps

An analysis similar to the Automap algorithm as described above is available on the Internet using Glosser, an online writing support environment developed at the University of Sydney (Villalon, Kearney, Calvo, & Reimann, 2008). Glosser uses text-mining techniques (based on Latent Semantic Analysis technique, Foltz, Kintsch, & Landauer, 1998) to provide student writers with information about their text on a number of dimensions, including conceptual coherence. A version of Glosser is integrated into Trac, another one can be used with Google Docs and Facebook (for more information, see http://www.weg.ee.usyd.edu.au/projects/glosser).

The Trac version of Glosser can be activated for any wiki page with a mouse click. The text of the page is then transferred to the Glosser server, which performs the text-mining analysis and renders the result to the students as shown in Fig. 6.10. In addition to the concept map visualization, Glosser currently provides information on text structure, text coherence, topics, as well as participation information. In addition, reflection questions are introduced for each of these aspects.

Discussion: Implications for Assessing Team Skills

In this chapter, we have described a number of approaches for supporting emergent collaboration, as distinct from designed collaboration, by providing mirroring and feedback information to groups in mainly graphical formats. Using wikis as a prototypical type of collaboration software, we have illustrated ways to visualize individuals' and groups' conceptual knowledge with automatically created concept maps and wiki site maps as well as various ways to visualize groups' work practices, e.g., with social network diagrams and the Wattle Tree visualization.

In the collaborative uses of wikis we studied, wikis sometimes played the role of the mediating artifact only – for instance when used by computer science students it was one of the means to develop the target activity (a software program) or by instructional design students to develop a course design – and sometimes wikis were both mediating artifact and target artifact at the same time –for instance when students create wiki pages that serve as research reports. In both cases, they were "activity-expanding" artifacts since they were intended for subsequent use: to guide

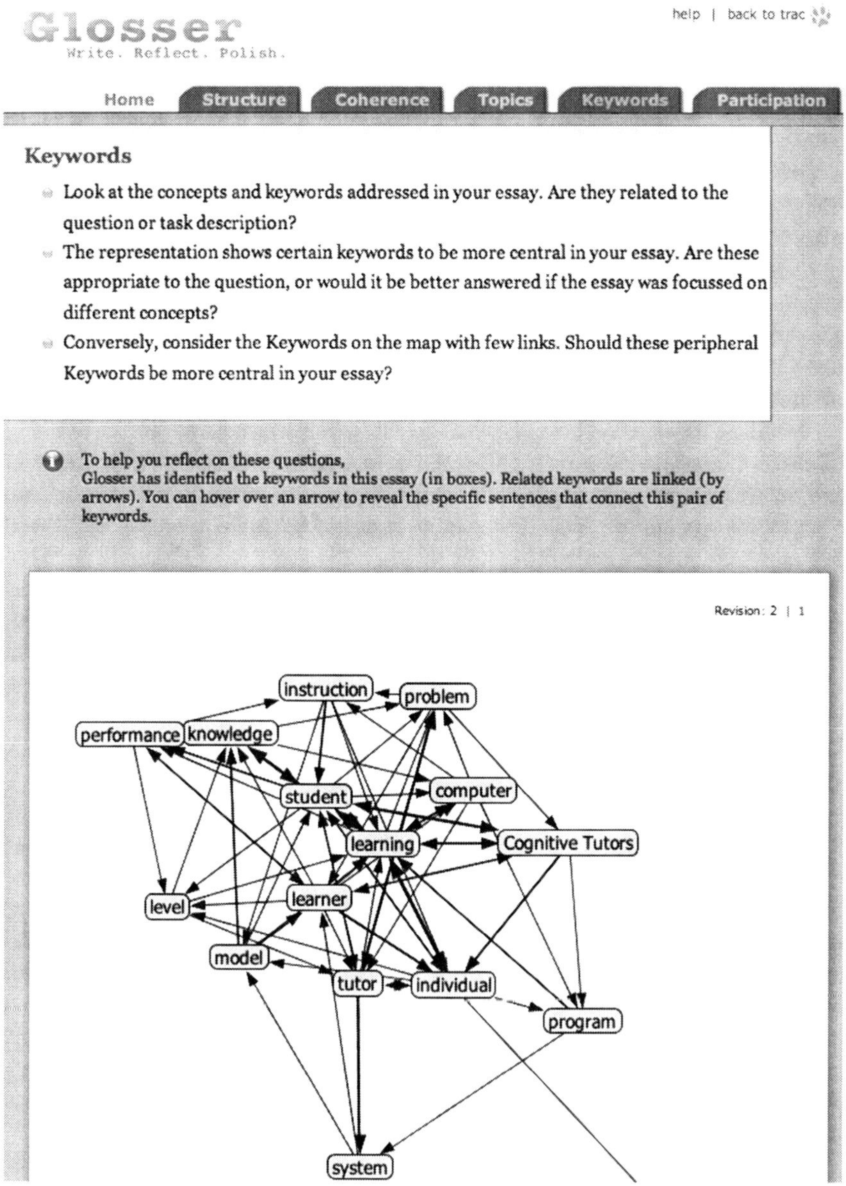

Fig. 6.10 Glosser web interface with reflection question on top and concept map on bottom

(later) action. In the case of students creating software, the software (and its design) was the tool for later use. In the case of students creating literature reviews and research reports, later use might be "knowledge building" activities (Scardamalia & Bereiter, 2003).

Reflecting further on the function of our concept map visualizations, created from students' individual and/or collective writing (see Fig. 6.7) and the wiki site visualization (Fig. 6.6), one can see that these visualizations have two functions: a pragmatic and an epistemic one. Pragmatically, visualizations such as these can make it easier to manage the challenges of producing or maintaining documents with multiple authors (who can make changes in a quasi-parallel manner): they serve a techno-informational purpose and the purpose of substitutive coordination, in Zacklad's (2006) terminology. For instance, the graphical representation of a wiki site can be seen as an automatically created index of that site, where the index reflects modification activities by the authors.

At the same time, such visualizations have an epistemic function. The concept map in Fig. 6.7, for instance, can be seen as identifying the main ideas of the text that served as the source for the concept analysis, and of the connectedness of these ideas. It shows which concepts "go together" for the author or authors. In this sense, this kind of representation of text content is closer to Popper's (1972) "World 3," the world of ideas and concepts, than to the text surface (that would belong to "World 1," the physical world). This is not a representation that says anything about how well ideas are expressed in the text, but provides an answer to the question What is this text about? What do the authors use as the main concepts and how do they see them going together?

It needs to be mentioned that the concept maps created both with Automap (Carley, Diesner, & de Reno, 2006) as well as with Glosser (the web-based implementation) are not semantic nets: The links between the nodes are unlabeled and undirected. Analogous to Social Network Analysis (Wasserman & Faust, 1994), the basis for the visualization is cooccurrence information: the strength of the association between two concepts (expressed by the thinkness of the link, for instance) is solely determined by the frequency of the two concepts occuring in the same "window" (a certain number of words, a sentence, a paragraph, etc.). Nevertheless, this cooccurrence information can provide useful information about semantic relations as well, to the extent that the text surface reflects semantic relations – that things that go together are mentioned in close proximity to each other. In a more elaborated form, Shaffer and colleagues (Shaffer, Hartfield, Svarovsky, Nash, Nutley, Bagley et al., 2009) have used a similar approach to capture learners' "epistemic frames" and to track their development over time. The drawback with their method at this stage is that students' writings (and other textual data, such as transcripts from dialogs with mentors) need to be analyzed by trained human raters in order to identify if a certain element of the epistemic frame is realized or not. In contrast, our analysis works fully automatically.

The theory of Trialogic Learning (Paavola, Lipponen, & Hakkarainen, 2004) suggests that knowledge is to be found not only in peoples' head and the artifacts they create, but also in their practices: how they go about things. Learning in this respect means to become able to participate in practices, to become part of a community of practice for instance (Wenger, 1998). Visualizations of participation behavior (e.g., Fig. 6.2) can be seen as visualizing aspects of groups' practices. They thus can play a role in knowledge creation to the extent that such visualizations help groups to reflect on their practices, with a view to improving on them. We have at least some evidence that teams engage in such activities, from our studies with software programming teams. To increase the frequency and depth of students' reflection on their team and work practices, we have begun to introduce example models of "good team work" into our groups, and work is under way to automatically identify students' work practices and to match them against these best-practice models.

Toward Assessing Team Practices and Artifacts

We have talked a lot about providing mirroring and feedback information, i.e., about formative assessment, but said nothing so far on summative feedback, on grading. While grading (and testing) may be of limited value to help with learning, they play an important role for evidence-based decision making on the level of schools and beyond, for placement and selection, and for large scale and long-term evaluations of curriculum reforms (Hickey, Suiker, Taasoobshirazi, Schafer, & Michael, 2006). Hence, any pedagogical or technological innovation needs eventually to be related to assessment in order to be integrated into an educational system (Fishman, Marx, Blumenfeld, Krajcik, & Soloway, 2004).

Again, computers can be used in various ways to help, both for assessment with a formative function (e.g., feedback on performance of a specific task) as well as a summative function (e.g., computer-based testing at the end of a school year). Computers are particularly well-suited for formative feedback, provided to the teacher and/or student directly contingent on performance – not test or exam performance, but problem-solving and decision-making performance, i.e., task performance. Such assessment is particularly important as it can affect learning while it is taking place (Shute, 2008).

Assessing group artifacts automatically is challenging, but can be done, in particular where the artifact has formal semantics. For instance, where students construct formal models such as Petri Nets (Reisig, 1985) as their products, it could be determined computationally if these nets are well-formed and able to produce the behavior required from the model. It is much harder to automatically evaluate artifacts of the computer program type with respect to their semantics (do they compute what they are supposed to compute?), but feedback on syntactic correctness can easily be provided. Moreover, current best practice, such as that advocated in Extreme Programming, require the programmer to create test cases before starting to write code. Such sets of tests can then be used for automated testing as the code development progresses, giving an ongoing form of formative feedback about the progress of the programming. If the artifacts take a textual form, a variety of methods for automatic essay scoring (Shermis & Burstein, 2003) can be employed. In particular methods that calculate similarities between documents can be used for both formative and summative feedback in a rather straightforward manner. For summative feedback, a reference solution needs to be provided in addition to students' essays. We can for instance use the text analysis methods described in the section on visualizing concept structures for assessment by calculating the similarity between a student concept map and a map computed from a reference text (e.g., expert solutions).

Similarly, assessing group performance requires normative reference models of what constitutes "good teamwork," what processes characterize a good software team, for instance. In order to develop this line of thought a bit further, one can build on concepts developed in Intelligent Tutoring Systems (vanLehn, 2007) and in Evidence-centered Assessment Design (Mislevy, Steinberg, & Almond, 1999). Assessment here takes the form of updating a student model, a qualitative or quantitative representation of the skills and knowledge in terms of which one wants to make pedagogical or evaluative decisions. In the simplest, but most frequently used form, a student model is list of variables, of attribute–value pairs. The student model is constructed and maintained by calculating values (in the simplest case, quantitative values such as counts) for the variables in the student model based on observations about task performance. The relation between task performance and student model is mediated by an evidence model (Mislevy et al., 1999) that determines which aspects of students' performance to register (i.e., it defines event categories) and how to express the consequences of registering an event instance in terms of the student model (see Fig. 6.11). For instance, a variable may be increased when a certain student behavior is noted. Table 6.1 shows the relation between certain observable behaviors in the Trac collaboration environment and concepts of the Big Five framework for teamwork can be seen as forming the basis for a simple evidence model with the Big-5 concepts as the (latent) variables in the student model.

In state-of-the-art student-modeling approaches, task-related behavior is connected to student models using a Bayesian Net (Conati, Gertner, & vanLehn, 2002), thus accounting for the fact that the relation between latent variables and observable events is typically not a deterministic ("noise free") one. While this approach is elegant and computationally effective, it requires a careful analysis of the relation between events and variables, and it works best when the event categories and relations are not only known in advance, but also stay stable.

We have begun developing an approach that does not require such a detailed understanding and representation of the task domain. Instead of modeling students' capacities in a student model made out of variables, and calculating the value of variables based on performance observations, this approach works with a holistic, graphical model of team practices (Reimann, Frerejean, & Thompson, 2009). As illustrated in Fig. 6.12, a team practice (in this case, a decision-making process) can be represented as a formal process model (in this case, a transition diagram, see

Fig. 6.11 A conceptual assessment framework (adapted from Mislevy et al., 1999)

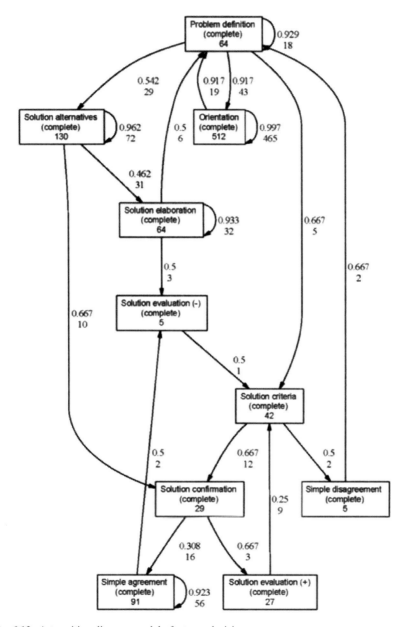

Fig. 6.12 A transition diagram model of a team decision process

Weijters, Van der Aalst, & Medeiros, 2006). To the extent that such models can be
automatically identified based on observations (event logs), they become a basis for
formative as well as summative assessment. Since methods of process mining (Van
der Aalst & Weijters, 2005) provide the practical means for automatic process

modeling, this approach becomes practically feasible. For formative purposes, groups could receive process visualizations such as shown in Fig. 6.12 to reflect upon their practices. For assessment purposes, normative process models can be represented in the same format, and the similarity between the empirical and the normative models (calculated with standard algorithms for graph comparison) can form the basis for grading.

We end this chapter, which mainly dealt with issues of mirroring and feedback, with some thoughts on assessment because with few exceptions (notably Barros & Verdejo, 2000), assessment has not been in the focus of research on computer-supported interaction analysis (e.g., Bratitsis, Dimitracopoulou, Martínez-Monés, Marcos, & Dimitriadis, 2008). Given the role assessment plays on multiple levels of any educational system (Hickey et al., 2006), this led to the current situation where state-of-the-art methods and tools developed in research on computer-supported collaborative learning are disconnected from any mainstream educational assessment practices, despite the fact that collaborative learning forms an important part of educational policies and practices. Unfortunately, what students do in the course of their collaboration with peers does not relate to how they are assessed, and the outcomes of assessment rarely affect what they will do next. Further, considerable effort currently goes into developing individually administered tests, yet for addressing other twenty-first century "skills" such as those for collaborating and for communicating mediated by technology, there is seemingly little awareness of the potential of technology to capture students' team practices and to relating this information to dimensions relevant for assessment. It is our hope that professionals developing and implementing educational assessment methods will work much more closely with those researching technology-supported learning to move education toward twenty-first century assessment, which we believe will be (perhaps paradoxically) prerequisite for any meaningful realization of twenty-first century learning.

References

Albanese, R. & Fleet, D Dv. (1985). Rational behavior in groups: The free-riding tendency. *Academy of Management Review, 10*, 244–255.

Arrow, H., McGrath, J. E., & Behrdal, J. (2000). *Small groups as complex systems: Formation, co-ordination, development and adaptation.* Thousand Oaks, CA: Sage Publications.

Barros, B. & Verdejo, F. (2000). Analysing student interaction processes in order to improve collaboration. The DEGREE approach. *International Journal of Artificial Intelligence in Education, 11*, 221–241.

Beck, K. (1999). *Extreme programming explained: Embrace change.* New York: Addison-Wesley.

Blickensderfer, E. L., Cannon-Bowers, J. A., & Salas, E. (1997). Theoretical bases for team self-corrections: Fostering shared mental models. In D. J. M. M. Beyerlein & S. Beyerlein (Eds.), *Advances in interdisciplinary studies of work teams* (Vol. 4, pp. 249–279). Greenwich, CT: JAI.

Bodker, S. & Christiansen, E. (2006). Computer support for social awareness in flexible work. *Computer Supported Cooperative Work, 15*, 1–28.

Bonk, C. J. & Cunningham, D. J. (1998). Searching for learner-centered, constructivist, and socio-cultural components of collaborative educational learning tools. In C. J. Bonk & K. S. King (Eds.), *Electronic collaborators: Learner centered technologies for literacy, apprenticeship, and discourse* (pp. 25–50). Mahwah, NJ: Lawrence Erlbaum Associates, Inc.

Bratitsis, T., Dimitracopoulou, A., Martínez-Monés, A., Marcos, J. A., & Dimitriadis, Y. (2008). Supporting members of a learning community using Interaction Analysis tools: The example of the Kaleidoscope NoE scientific network. In P. Diaz, Kinshuk, I. Aedo & E. Mora (Eds.), *The 8th IEEE International Conference on Advanced Learning Technologies (ICALT 2008)* (pp. 809-813). Washington, DC: IEEE Computer Society.

Buller, P. F. & Bell, C. H. (1986). Effects of team building and goal setting on productivity: A field experiment. *Academy of Management Journal, 29*, 305–328.

Cai, C. Y. (2007). *Extracting students' knowledge structures form their written texts through Automap approach.* Unpublished Master Thesis, University of Sydney, Sydney, Australia.

Cannon-Bowers, J. A. & Salas, E. (eds). (1998). *Making decisions under stress: Implications for individual and team training.* Washington, DC: American Psychological Association.

Cannon-Bowers, J. A., Tannenbaum, S. I., Salas, E., & Volpe, C. E. (1995). Defining competencies and establishing team training requirements. In E. S. R. A. Guzzo (Ed.), *Team effectiveness and decision making in organisations* (pp. 333–380). San Francisco, CA: Jossey-Bass.

Carley, K. M. (1986). An approach for relating social structure to cognitive structure. *Journal of Mathematical Sociology, 12*(2), 137–189.

Carley, K. M. (1997). Extracting team mental models through textual analysis. *Journal of Organizational Behavior, 18*, 533–558.

Carley, K. M., Diesner, J., & de Reno, M. (2006). *AutoMap user's guide.* Pittsburgh, PA: Carnegie-Mellon University. School of Computer Science. Institute for Software Research. Center for Computational Analysis of Social and Organizational Systems (CASOS).

Chi, M. T. H. & Ohlsson, S. (2005). Complex declarative learning. In K. Holyoak & R. G. Morrison (Eds.), *The cambridge handbook of thinking and reasoning* (pp. 371–399). Cambridge: Cambridge University Press.

Clark, H. H. & Brennan, S. E. (1991). Grounding in communication. In L. B. Resnick, J. M. Levine & S. D. Teasley (Eds.), *Perspectives on socially shared cognition* (pp. 127–149). Washington: American Psychological Association.

Conati, C., Gertner, A., & vanLehn, K. (2002). Using Bayesian networks to manage uncertainty in student modelling. *User Modelling and User-Adapted Interaction, 12*(4), 1573–1391.

Cross, G. A. (2001). *Forming the collective mind: A conceptual exploration of large-scale collaborative writing in industry.* Cresskill, NJ: Hampton.

Dönmez, P., Rosé, C., Stegmann, K., Weinberger, A., & Fischer, F. (2005, May 30-June 04). *Supporting CSCL with automatic corpus analysis technology.* Paper presented at the 2005 Conference on Computer Support For Collaborative Learning: Learning 2005: the Next 10 Years! Computer Support for Collaborative Learning, Taipei, Taiwan.

Dyer, J. C. (1984). Team research and team training: State-of-the-art review. In F. A. Muckler (Ed.), *Human factors review* (pp. 285–323). Santa Monica, CA: Human Factors Society.

West Virginia Department of Education (2007). *21st Century learning skills and technology tools: Content standards and objectives for WV Schools.* Available from http://wvde.state.wv.us/policies/p2520.14_ne.pdf

Engeström, Y. (1987). *Learning by expanding: An activity-theoretical approach to developmental research.* Helsinki: Orienta-Konsultit Oy.

Erkens, G., Jaspers, J., Prangsma, M., & Kanselaar, G. (2005). Coordination processes in computer supported collaborative writing. *Computers in Human Behavior, 21*, 463–486.

Fishman, B., Marx, R. W., Blumenfeld, P., Krajcik, J., & Soloway, E. (2004). Creating a framework for research on systemic technology innovations. *The Journal of the Learning Sciences, 13*(1), 43–76.

Foltz, P. W., Kintsch, W., & Landauer, T. K. (1998). The measurement of textual coherence with latent semantic analysis. *Discourse Processes, 25*(2–3), 285–307.

Fussell, S. R., Kraut, R. E., Lerch, F. J., Scherlis, W. L., McNally, M. M., & Cadiz, J. J. (1998). *Coordination, overload and team performance: Effects of team communication strategies.* Paper presented at the Proceedings of the 1998 ACM conference on Computer supported cooperative work, Seattle, WA

Gillies, R. (2004). The effects of cooperative learning on junior high school students during small group learning. *Learning and Instruction, 14*, 197–213.

Gillies, R. & Ashman, A. (1996). Teaching collaborative skills to primary school children in classroom-based work groups. *Learning and Instruction, 6*, 187–200.

Hayes, J. R. & Flower, L. S. (1980). Identifying the organization of the writing process. In L. W. Gregg & E. R. Steinberg (Eds.), *Cognitive processes in writing* (pp. 3–30). Hillsdale, NJ: Erlbaum.

Hickey, D. T., Suiker, S. T., Taasoobshirazi, G., Schafer, N. J., & Michael, M. A. (2006). Balancing varied assessment functions to attain systemic validity: Three is the magic number. *Studies in Educational Evaluation, 32*, 180–201.

iN2015 Education and Learning Sub-Committee. (2007). *Empowering learners and engaging minds, through infocomm*. Singapore: Ministry of Education.

Johnson, D. W., Johnson, R. T., Stanne, M. B., & Garibaldi, A. (1989). Impact of group processing on achievement in cooperative groups. *Journal of Social Psychology, 130*, 507–516.

Jonassen, D. H., Beissner, K., & Yacci, M. (1993). *Structural knowledge: techniques for representing, conveying, and acquiring structural knowledge*. Hillsdale, NJ: Lawrence Erlbaum.

Kapur, M. (2006). *Productive failure: A hidden efficacy of seemingly unproductive production*. Paper presented at the Cognitive Science Conference, Vancouver, Canada.

Kapur, M., Hung, D., Jacobson, M. J., Voiklis, J., Kinzer, C. K., & Victor, C. D.-T. (2007). Emergence of learning in computer-supported, large-scale collective dynamics: A research agenda. *Proceedings of the International Conference on Computer-supported Collaborative Learning (CSCL2007)*, New Brunswick, NJ.

Kay, J., Maisonneuve, N., Yacef, K., & Reimann, P. (2006). The big five and visualisations of team work activity. In M. Ikeda, K. D. Ashley & T. Chan (Eds.), *Intelligent tutoring systems. Proceedings of the 8th International Conference, ITS 2006* (pp. 197-206). Jhongli, Taiwan: Springer.

Kirschner, P. A., Sweller, J., & Clark, R. E. (2006). Why minimal guidance during instruction does not work: An analysis of the failure of constructivist, discovery, problem-based, experiental, and inquiry-based teaching. *Educational Psychologist, 41*(2), 75–86.

Kollar, I., Fischer, F., & Hesse, F. W. (2006). Collaboration scripts - a conceptual analysis. *Educational Psychological Review, 18*, 159–185.

Kolodner, J. L., Camp, P. J., Crismond, D., Fasse, B., Gray, J., Holbrook, J., et al. (2003). Problem-based learning meets case-based reasoning in the midlle-school science classroom: Putting learning by design into practice. *The Journal of the Learning Sciences, 12*(4), 495–547.

Kozlowski, S. W. J., Brown, K. G., Weissbein, D. A., Cannon-Bowers, J. A., & Salas, E. (2000). A multi-level perspective on training effectiveness: Enhancing horizontal and vertical transfer. In S. W. J. Kozlowski & K. J. Klein (Eds.), *Multilevel theory, research, and methods in organizations* (pp. 157–210). San Francisco, CA: Jossey-Bass.

Kozlowski, S. W. J. & Ilgen, D. R. (2006). Enhancing the effectiveness of work groups and teams. *Psychological Science in the Public Interest, 7*(3), 77–124.

Kreijns, K., Kirschner, P., & Jochems, W. (2003). Identifying the pitfalls for social interaction in computer-supported collaborative learning environments: A review of the research. *Computers in Human Behavior, 19*(3), 335–353.

Layman, L., Williams, L., Damian, D., & Bures, H. (2006). Essential communication practices for extreme programming in a global software development team. *Information and Software Technology, 48*, 781–794.

Lee, E. Y. C., Han, C. K. K., & van Aalst, J. (2006). Students assessing their own collaborative knowledge building. *International Journal of Computer-Supported Collaborative Learning, 1*(1), 57–88.

Leuf, B. & Cunningham, W. (2001). *The wiki way*. Englewood Cliffs, NJ: Prentice Hall.

Lowry, P. B., Curtis, A., & Lowry, M. R. (2004). Building a taxonomy and nomenclature of collaborative writing to improve interdisciplinary research and practice. *Journal of Business Communication, 41*(1), 66–99.

Lowry, P. B., Nunamaker, J. F., Jr., Curtis, A., & Lowry, M. R. (2005). The impact of process structure on novice, virtual collaborative writing teams. *IEEE Transactions on Professional Communication, 48*(4), 341–364.

MacMillan, J., Entin, E. E., & Serfaty, D. (2004). Communication overhead: the hidden cost of team cognition. In E. Salas & S. M. Fiore (Eds.), *Team cognition* (pp. 61–82). Washington, DC: American Psychological Association.

McGrath, J. E. (1991). Time, interaction, and performance (TIP). *A Theory of Groups. Small Group Research., 22*(2), 147–174.

McGrath, J. E. & Tschan, F. (2004). *Temporal matters in social psychology: Examining the role of time in the lives of groups and individuals.* Washington, DC: American Psychological Association.

Mislevy, R. J., Steinberg, L., & Almond, R. G. (1999). *Evidence-centered assessment design.* Available from http://www.education.umd.edu/EDMS/mislevy/papers/ECD_overview.html

Olson, G. M., Malone, T. W., & Smith, J. B. (eds). (2001). *Coordination theory and collaboration technology.* Mahwah, NJ: Lawrence Erlbaum.

Paavola, S. & Hakkarainen, K. (2005). The knowledge creation metaphor - An emergent epistemological approach to learning. *Science & Education, 14,* 535–557.

Paavola, S., Lipponen, L., & Hakkarainen, K. (2004). Models of innovative knowledge communities and three metaphors of learning. *Review of Educational Research, 74*(4), 557–576.

Perera, D., Kay, J., Yacef, K., & Koprinska, I. (2007). *Mining learners' traces from an online collaboration tool.* Paper presented at the Educational Data Mining Workshop at Artificial Intelligence and Education, Marina del Ray, CA.

Phillips, N., Lawrence, T. B., & Hardy, C. (2004). Discourse and institutions. *Academy of Management Review, 29*(4), 635–652.

Popper, K. (1972). *Objective knowledge: An evolutionary approach.* Oxford, UK: Clarendon Press.

Prichard, J. S. & Ashleigh, M. J. (2007). The effects of team-skills training on transactive memory and performance. *Small Group Research, 38,* 696–726.

Prichard, J. S., Startford, R. J., & Bizo, L. A. (2006). Team-skills training enhances collaborative learning. *Learning and instruction, 16*(3), 256–265.

Prichard, J. S., Stratford, R. J., & Hardy, C. (2004). *Training students to work in teams: Why and how?* York, UK: LTSN Psychology.

Reimann, P. (2003). How to support groups in learning: More than problem solving. In V. Aleven et al. (Eds.), *Artificial Intelligence in Education (AIED 2003). Supplementary Proceedings* (pp. 3-16). Sydney: University of Sydney.

Reimann, P. (2007). Time is precious: Why process analysis is essential for CSCL. In C. Chinn, G. Erkens & S. Puntambekar (Eds.), *Minds, minds, and society. Proceedings of the CSCL 2007 conference* (Vol. 8, pp. 598-607). New Brunswick, NJ: ISLS.

Reimann, P., Frerejean, J., & Thompson, K. (2009). Using process mining to identify models of group decision making processes in chat data. In C. O'Malley, D. Suthers, P. Reimann & A. Dimitracopoulou (Eds.), *Computer-supported collaborative learning practices: CSCL2009 conference proceedings* (pp. 98-107). International Society for the Learning Sciences.

Reinhold, S. (2006). *WikiTrails: augmenting Wiki structure for collaborative, interdisciplinary learning.* Paper presented at the 2006 international symposium on Wikis, Odense, Denmark

Reisig, W. (1985). *Petri nets. An introduction.* Berlin: Springer.

Resta, P. & Laferriere, T. (2007). Technology in support of collaborative learning. *Educational Psychology Review, 19*(1), 65–83.

Ripochet, G. & Sansonnet, J.-P. (2006). Experiences in automating the analysis of linguistic interactions for the study of distributed collectives. *Computer Supported Cooperative Work, 15,* 149–183.

Salas, E., Rozell, D., Mullen, B., & Driskell, J. E. (1999). The effect of team building on performance: An integration. *Small Group Research, 30,* 309–329.

Salas, E., Sims, D. E., & Burke, C. S. (2005). Is there a "Big Five" in teamwork? *Small Group Research, 36*(5), 555–599.

Scardamalia, M. & Bereiter, C. (1991). Higher levels of agency for children in knowledge building: A challenge for the design of new knowledge media. *The Journal of the Learning Sciences., 1*(1), 37–68.

Scardamalia, M. & Bereiter, C. (2003). Knowledge building. In J. W. Guthrie (Ed.), *Encyclopedia of education* (2nd ed.). New York: Macmillan.

Scardamalia, M. & Bereiter, C. (2006). Knowledge building: Theory, pedagogy, and technology. In R. K. Sawyer (Ed.), *The Cambridge handbook of the learning sciences* (pp. 97–115). New York: Cambride University Press.

Scott, J. (1991). *Social network analysis: A handbook.* London: Sage.

Sfard, A. (1998). On two metaphors of learning and the dangers of choosing just one. *Educational Researcher, 27*(2), 4–13.

Shaffer, D. W. (2008). Education in the digital age. *Digital Kompetanse, 3*(1), 37–50.

Shaffer, D. W., Hatfield, D., Svarovsky, G. N., Nash, P., Nutly, A., Bagley, E., et al. (2009). Epistemic Network Analysis: A prototype of 21st-Cenntury assessment of learning. International Journal of Learning and Media, 1, 33–53.

Shermis, M. D. & Burstein, J. C. (eds). (2003). *Automated essay scoring: A cross-disciplinary perspective.* Hillsdale, NJ: Lawrence Erlbaum.

Shute, V. J. (2008). Focus on formative feedback. *Review of Educational Research, 78*(1), 153–189.

Soller, A., Martínez-Monés, A., Jermann, P., & Muehlenbrock, M. (2005). From Mirroring to Guiding: A Review of State of the Art Technology for Supporting Collaborative Learning (preprint). *International Journal of Artificial Intelligence in Education, 15* (4), 261–290.

Souzis, A. (2005). Building a semantic wiki. *IEEE Intelligent Systems, 20*, 87–91.

Stahl, G. (2006). Sustaining group cognition in a math chat environment. *Research and Practice in Technology Enhanced Learning, 1*(2), 85–113.

Topping, K. (1998). Peer assessment between students in colleges and universities. *Review of Educational Research, 68*(3), 249–276.

Ullman, A. & Kay, J. (2007). *WikiNavMap: A visualisation to supplement team based wikis Conference on Human Factors in Computing Systems, CHI '07 extended abstracts on Human factors in computing systems* (pp. 2711–2716). San Jose, CA: ACM Press.

van Amalesvoort, M., Andriessen, J., & Kanselaar, G. (2007). Representational tools in computer-supported collaborative argumentation-based learning: How dyads work with constructed and inspected argumentative diagrams. *Journal of the Learning Sciences, 16*(4), 485–521.

Van der Aalst, W. M. P. & Weijters, A. J. M. M. (2005). Process mining. In M. Dumas, W. M. P. van der Aalst & A. H. M. ter Hofstede (Eds.), *Process-aware information systems: Bridging people and software through process technology* (pp. 235–255). New York: Wiley.

vanLehn, K. (2007). Intelligent tutoring systems for continous, embedded assessment. In C. A. Dwyer (Ed.), *The future of assessment: shaping teaching and learning.* Mahaw, NL: Erlbaum.

Villalon, J., Kearney, P., Calvo, R. A., & Reimann, P. (2008, July 1-5). *Glosser: Enhanced feedback for student writing tasks.* Paper presented at the 8th IEEE International Conference on Advance Learning Technologies (ICALT), Santadar, Spain.

Wasserman, S. & Faust, K. (1994). *Social network analysis: methods and applications.* Cambridge, UK: Cambridge University Press.

Wegner, D. M. (1986). Transactive memory: A contemporary analysis of the group mind. In B. Mullen & G. R. Goethals (Eds.), *Theories of group behavior* (pp. 185–205). New York: Springer.

Weijters, A. J. M. M., Van der Aalst, W. M. P., & Medeiros, A. K. A. d. (2006). *Process mining with the heuristics miner-algorithm. BETA Working Paper Series WP 166.* Eindhoven, NL: Eindhoven University of Technology.

Wenger, E. (1998). *Communities of practice: Learning, meaning, and identity.* Cambridge: Cambridge University Press.

Williams, K., Calvo, R. A., & Bell, D. (2003, July 20-24). *Autmoatic categorization of questions for a mathematics education service.* Paper presented at the 11th World Conference on Artificial Intelligence in Education, Sydney, Australia.

Yager, S., Johnson, R. T., Johnson, D. W., & Snider, B. (1986). The impact of group processing on achievement in cooperative learning groups. *Journal of Social Psychology, 126*, 389–397.

Zacklad, M. (2004). *Processus de documentarisation dans les Documents pour l'Action (DopA): statut des annotations et technologies de la coope´ration associe´es.* In Le nume´rique : Impact sur le cycle de vie du document pour une analyse interdisciplinaire. Available from http://archivesic.ccsd.cnrs.fr/sic_00001072.html

Zacklad, M. (2006). Documentarisation processes in documents for action (DofA): The status of annotations and associated cooperation technologies. *Computer Supported Cooperative Work, 15*, 205–228.

Zumbach, J., Hillers, A., & Reimann, P. (2003). Supporting distributed problem-based learning: The use of feedback in online learning. In T. Roberts (Ed.), *Online collaborative learning: theory and practice* (pp. 86–103). Hershey, PA: Information Science Publishing.

Chapter 7
Learning Mathematics Through Inquiry: A Large-Scale Evaluation

Ton de Jong, Petra Hendrikse, and Hans van der Meij

Introduction

It is currently widely accepted that learning for understanding can only take place when learners adopt an approach in which they process learning material in an active way and engage in "deeper" processes such as asking questions, searching for structures and creating abstractions (e.g., Jonassen, 1991; Mayer, 2002; Novak, 1998; von Glaserfeld, 1987). In their seminal book *How People Learn*, Bransford, Brown, and Cocking (1999) showed that active learning positively affects the construction of understanding and contributes to the development of transferable knowledge. Grabinger (1996) further emphasized that this way of learning and knowledge creation also stimulates learners to connect new information to their existing, personal knowledgebase and that learners need to have new information situated in real or realistic contexts to foster transfer. This view is contrasted with former approaches in which conveying information to learners was seen as the main form of instruction and in which context-free knowledge was seen as the goal to be reached. In an overview of differences between deep and surface approaches to learning in science, Chin and Brown empirically distinguish a number of key learning processes including searching for causally coherent explanations and question asking that characterize good students (Chin & Brown, 2000). The importance of active learning has also been recognized in much earlier work. Dewey (1916), for example, already stressed the importance of "doing" science, mathematics, and history to gain understanding of these domains. "Doing" means that learners abstract, discover, and prove. In Bruner's work as well, learning is seen as an active

T. de Jong (✉) and H. van der Meij
Faculty of Behavioural Sciences, Department of Instructional Technology, University of Twente,
P.O. Box 217, 7500 AE Enschede, The Netherlands
e-mail: a.j.m.dejong@utwente.nl

P. Hendrikse
Faculty of Behavioural Science, Teacher Training Department, University of Twente,
7500 AE Enschede, The Netherlands

M.J. Jacobson and P. Reimann (eds.), *Designs for Learning Environments of the Future:*   189
International Perspectives from the Learning Sciences, DOI 10.1007/978-0-387-88279-6_7,
© Springer Science+Business Media, LLC 2010

process in which learners develop new ideas based on prior knowledge (Bruner, 1973; Bruner, Goodnow, & Austin, 1956). Bruner's work partly had its origin in mathematics learning, which is the topic of this chapter

In this chapter, we specifically examine such approaches to learning mathematics. We have seen a shift from a more procedure-oriented view of teaching mathematics to one of helping learners to think mathematically in order to engage in meaningful activities and to understand relationships between mathematical concepts (Bransford et al., 1999; Schoenfeld, 2006). This shift is seen in a change of emphasis from traditional algorithmic problems to insight problems. According to Van Streun (1989), mathematics teachers make a distinction between "routine" problems and "thinking" problems. Routine problems can be solved with the use of algorithms and without much dependency on insight or understanding (see Schoenfeld, 1985; van Streun, 1989). As long as the learner can classify the problem in the correct class, problem solving will take place almost automatically. However, when problems become more complex or when classes of problems are not self-evident, then an algorithmic approach loses its effectiveness. In teaching, a decision should thus be made to either instruct and practice algorithms with satisfactory performance on routine problems, or to adopt a more time consuming, insightful approach to support the construction of more flexible knowledge that can be applied to thinking or transfer problems (Gravemeijer et al., 1993). Cobb and McClain (2006) make a similar distinction by pointing out that statistics education traditionally aims at teaching routines whereas a more conceptual stance that focus on "big ideas" is also needed.

Contemporary approaches in mathematics seek to design conditions that stimulate and support learners to engage in active learning processes that yield conceptual knowledge. One of these is the Realistic Mathematics Education (RME) movement based on the work of Freudenthal (1991). Another approach is inquiry learning in which learners actively investigate mathematical relationships (Pea, 1987). An example of a highly successful implementation of inquiry learning in the field of mathematics is the Jasper series (Cognition and Technology Group at Vanderbilt, 1992, 1997). More recent approaches often use ICT (information, communication, and technology) to facilitate more conceptual learning (Bottino, Artigue, & Noss, 2009; Noss & Hoyles, 2006). These approaches capitalize on the interactive and dynamic capacities of ICT (Atkinson, 2005). Among these, the use of microworlds or simulations (often in the form of applets as in the ESCOT project (Underwood et al., 2005)) has been influential (Kuhn, Hoppe, Lingnau, & Wichmann, 2006). Applets have been developed that support an inquiry approach in science learning (de Jong, 2006a) and there have been some uses of applets in conjunction with computer-supported collaborative learning (Staples, 2007). An example of a computer-based inquiry learning environment for mathematics is SimCalc (Roschelle & Kaput, 1996; Roschelle & Knudsen, this volume). In SimCalc, students can manipulate formulae and observe the consequences of their changes in a number of ways such as animations, tables, and graphs. Another research project that has explored inquiry approaches for using technology to enhance the learning of mathematics is Cabri Géomètre

(Balacheff & Sutherland, 1994; Falcade, Laborde, & Mariotti, 2007; Laborde, 2002), which is a microworld that allows learners to directly manipulate geometrical objects and to observe the effects of their manipulations (Falcade et al., 2007). Yet another example of an inquiry environment in mathematics is PIE (Probability Inquiry Environment) (Vahey, Enyedy, & Gifford, 2000) that focuses on probability theory. Students can manipulate simulations and view their effects in dynamic representations.

We observe, however, that whereas an increasing number of studies have been documenting the effectiveness of technology-enabled inquiry approaches for science learning (Linn, Lee, Tinker, Husic, & Chiu, 2006) research on the effectiveness of (technology-enabled) inquiry for mathematics education are still scarce and often anecdotal. Research on mathematics learning has tended to focus on charting inquiry processes (Linn et al., 2006) although the recent study by Rasmussen and Kwon (2007) found that learners who followed an inquiry approach based on RME scored higher on items assessing mathematical "thinking" or conceptual knowledge than a traditional control group and performed equally on the measures of "routine" mathematical knowledge. A study of learning mathematical ideas with a technology-enabled inquiry approach has been recently completed by Eysink et al. (2009). This research compared the effects of different technological learning environments for learning about probability and found that inquiry learning was the most successful in developing deeper conceptual knowledge.

A general finding in the inquiry literature is that learners need support and that an appropriate balance between guidance and freedom needs to be found (de Jong, 2006b). As Freudenthal has stated: "Guiding means striking a delicate balance between the force of teaching and the freedom of learning" (Freudenthal, 1991, p. 55). Many of the aforementioned learning environments (e.g., many applets, Cabri Géomètre) concentrate on providing students with the opportunity to simulate and manipulate objects or phenomena. Not all of these environments, however, offer the necessary instructional support for these activities. An exception can be found in recent developments in SimCalc Mathworld (Roschelle & Knudsen, this volume). As a response to this issue, in the current study we have developed, over a number of iterations, a set of software-based learning environments to support mathematical inquiry activities. These learning environments give students many opportunities for investigation and exploration, but also provide embedded instructional support for their inquiry. We discuss next a large-scale evaluation of these newly developed learning environments that were compared with a traditional form of teaching.

Basic Setup of the Inquiry Learning Environment

The study focused on students learning about functions in mathematics. More specifically, it treated topics such as linear formulas, parallel lines, domain and range, and solving equations and inequalities. The study used the "Getal and Ruimte"

(Numbers and Space) method, which is widely used in secondary mathematics education in the Netherlands.

We developed a series of four inquiry environments using SimQuest software (van Joolingen & de Jong, 2003), which is an authoring tool for creating simulations with integrated instructional support that may consist of, for example, explanations and assignments. The four learning environments provided the learner with four different concrete contexts for exploring mathematical ideas about functions: Mobile Phones, Windmills, Tsunami,[1] and Benefit Concert. These learning environments were aligned with relevant chapters of the Numbers and Space method.

Figure 7.1 displays a screenshot from Windmills showing the interactive, dynamic, and graphical components of the learning environment (see the left and middle parts of the screen). Students can manipulate values of variables and observe the consequences of these manipulations in a graphical, numerical, and pictorial ways. The right side of the screen displays assignments, such as a task description, and provides students with guidance on how to operate the interactive parts of the environment. After completing an assignment, students receive feedback on their performance.

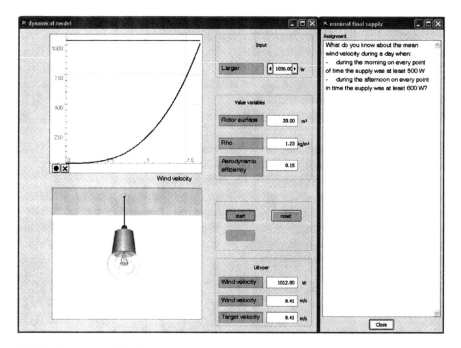

Fig. 7.1 Screenshot of SimQuest Windmill application

---

[1] This application was developed before the tsunami of December 2004 took place.

Development of the Learning Materials

The SimQuest applications serve a central role in the learning materials developed for this study. As mentioned above, each SimQuest application had a specific context to link mathematics to a real world problem (e.g., buying a mobile phone) that may be interactively explored in the simulation of the context. Learners can manipulate variables and then observe the results in various representations, such as graphs, animations, and output fields. The interactive parts are embedded in an instructional environment. SimQuest applications provided learner support through the sequencing of assignments and models as well as explanatory texts. The assignments followed a specific structure and generally started with an introductory text to provide the context and explain the variables, to pose a problem-solving question, and to introduce the interactive part. In addition, the underlying models increased in complexity by adding variables, with each model progression level having its own interface and set of assignments. Topical themes were directly visible for students; however, the degree of complexity was not.

The experimental materials and SimQuest applications were iteratively developed based on the results of a series of preliminary studies that involved 77 students, 41 girls and 36 boys, from secondary education (average age 15–16). Students had different profiles, with 36 students taking predominant courses from the cultural and social sciences (e.g., law, history and geography), and 41 students primarily taking science courses (e.g., mathematics and physics). Participants in the first two preliminary studies had already been taught the subject matter; participants in the third had not. Three mathematics teachers also participated in the third preliminary study. Data in all three preliminary studies was collected through interviews, think-aloud protocols, observations, and log data.

During this development process, we focused on the elicitation and support of learning activities such as abstracting, structuring, evaluating, interpreting, and proving. For example, structuring assignments sometimes invited students to examine differences in results between two different situations and elaborations often promoted reevaluations of how results could have been calculated. In addition, we stimulated and supported students to communicate using the language of mathematics (e.g., in presenting formulas). We found in the third preliminary study that students frequently engaged in these desired learning activities, such as in attempts to formulate a solution process in abstract, general terms or when students began to look at certain situations (structuring) in order to be able to show that a proposition is true (proving).

The basic design decisions for the four SimQuest applications were refined over the course of these studies in three main ways. First, the context of each initial application was used throughout the set of assignments the students completed. In the revised applications, a series of assignment contexts went through transitions in which concrete content gradually became more abstract. That is, students started with a familiar and realistic concrete context that then was translated into a mathematical context. The new mathematical context was further generalized and again a mathematical view on this general information was taken. Second, the goal of the assignments shifted from constructing equations and concepts to exploring their properties. Third, assignments were extended with subassignments to provide additional support for students who failed on the original assignment. These subassignments were shaped according to the following design.

- Step 1: consider which variable(s) you are going to change and what output you are going to look at.
- Step 2: what are the different possibilities for the values of the variable(s)?
- Step 3: try out the different possibilities.
- Step 4: look back at the process. What can you conclude?

Every subassignment consisted of two components, one that asked the student for a possible approach and one that gave an exemplary elaboration. Fourth, additional support outside of the computer-based SimQuest materials was provided so that the revised materials also included classroom conversations on key topics (e.g., Cobb & McClain, 2006) and requesting students to make subject-matter overviews (e.g., Horton et al., 1993). The classroom conversations allowed special support (such as evaluating, interpreting, and reasoning) that is hard to elicit and support in an online learning environment. In these conversations, students would need to verbalize their ideas and "defend" these against others. As a result, they were encouraged to reflect and think more deeply about what they had done. Students could also be confronted with new and alternative viewpoints, possibilities, and relations to consider. One of the interlocutors in these conversations was the teacher who also can bring in the socio-cultural aspects of the mathematics profession.

The preliminary studies also made it clear that students needed a way to structure the information they received. For this reason we asked the students to make a paper-based subject-matter overview that was *not* to report the outcome of a calculation, but rather to describe what they learned from an assignment and how that knowledge related to the mathematical domain. The overview was intended to stimulate students to draw abstract and general conclusions and to help them to structure different domain elements.

Finally, the third preliminary study indicated that teachers needed support as well. Therefore, for the large-scale study we developed a teacher guide that described a scenario on how to deal with the various information sources (e.g., SimQuest environment, tools, textbook) in all the lessons on functions. The guide described how teachers could alternate between the textbook and SimQuest simulations in such a way that they would be coordinated with each other by roughly dividing each lesson into the four phases: orientation, introduction, processing, and recapitulation. We then indicated which parts of the applications could be used in each phase of each lesson. The final sequence that was developed had these components: (a) introduction by the teacher, (b) students work with the SimQuest materials alone or in groups, (c) whole class conversation (intended to foster processing), and (d) completion of a topic or subtopic, creation of a subject-matter overview consisting of a short description of important findings (intended to foster recapitulation and reflection).

Method

Subjects

In this study, the experimental condition used the inquiry materials (i.e., SimQuest applications, classroom conversations, and subject-matter overviews), whereas for the control condition, "standard" didactic lessons were given (e.g., teacher led questions and answers). Eleven schools from across the Netherlands participated in the study. The experiment started with 470 students in 20 classes. However, due to illness and absentees, the final dataset consisted of 418 students (206 male and 212 female). The students came from secondary education classes and ranged in age from 15 to 16. Of these students, 155 had an "M-profile" (cultural and social science) and 263 had an "N-profile" (science). The N-profile attracts students who are primarily interested in science and technology topics, whereas the M-profile students tend to focus on courses in culture, economics, and society. Students in the N-profile on average have stronger background knowledge in science than students in the M-profile, which is not surprising as the N-profile curriculum contains more science elements. The division of classes over conditions was not arbitrary; schools had chosen to place classes in the experimental or in the control condition, often based on practical reasons. Seven classes (140 students) were in the control condition and 13 classes (278 students) were in the experimental condition. The division of gender and of M- and N-profiles over conditions is shown in Table 7.1. Chi-square analyses showed that gender and profiles were not divided evenly across the two conditions. The control condition contained more students from the N-profile and more male student participated in the control condition, which was probably due to the historical trend that the M-profile attracts more female than male students.

Table 7.1 Posttest scores (adjusted)

Condition	Profile	Gender	Number	Mean	SE
Control	M	Male	21	23.51	1.95
		Female	19	22.35	2.06
	N	Male	55	30.30	1.24
		Female	45	32.58	1.36
	Total		140	27.19	0.86
Experimental	M	Male	42	25.19	1.40
		Female	73	23.72	1.10
	N	Male	88	32.15	0.95
		Female	75	28.78	1.03
	Total		278	27.46	0.57
Total			418	27.32	0.50

Test

The pretest used in this study assessed relevant prior mathematical knowledge. The pretest, which had a maximum score of 40, consisted of four main questions and 14 subquestions on first-degree and second-degree equations and geometry. Students were allowed a maximum of 20 min to complete the pretest, which was found to have a Cronbach's α reliability of 0.74.

The posttest consisted of six main questions that split into 15 items that covered the topics of linear functions, investigating functions, equations and inequalities, and applications (e.g., optimizing a surface). Six items from the posttest measured procedural knowledge, six other items measured conceptual knowledge. It was hypothesized that the control group would perform better on the procedural items whereas the experimental group was expected to score higher on the conceptual items. The remaining three items measured a combination of conceptual and more technical – procedural – knowledge. No predictions were given for those three items.

The maximum score on the posttest was 63. Because in some schools different classes participated in the experiment and not all classes took the test at the same time, four different versions of the posttest were developed. Items on the different versions of the posttest differed in appearance but not in content. The students' score on the posttest was counted as an actual mark for their school examination. The Cronbach's α reliability of the posttest was 0.68.

Procedure

Teachers in the experimental condition attended an introductory meeting a few months before the start of the series of lessons where they worked with the four SimQuest simulations. They also received a schema for 12 lessons that described the materials from the textbook and the simulations that should be covered in each lesson. Prior to the start of the lesson series, the teachers received the teacher guide and a software manual plus CD with the instructions and software for installing the simulations. In the first lesson, the students were introduced to the software, and a member of the research team was present in the lesson to assist with software installation and to answer students' questions. The pretest was administered in the second lesson, and the actual activities for the experimental and control conditions began in the third lesson, continuing to the end of the implementation. The lessons for the experimental condition had a general format of introductions in which the software was used for demonstration purposes, after which students worked with the software and on exercises from the textbook. There were also classroom conversations that were sometimes held after students had individually worked with the software in order to discuss their findings or to discuss the main issues of a series of problems. Each topic ended with a summary and the students completed a subject-matter overview. The posttest was taken around a week to 10 days after the last lesson. Teachers in the participating schools were free to follow their own insights and organization in implementing the program that led to considerable differences between schools. For example, the number of lessons on subtopics could differ between two and four, and lesson length varied between 45 and 60 min. In addition, the availability of computer rooms, data projectors, and other technical facilities varied considerably between schools that influenced the students' time on task. Because the use of a computer program in mathematics lessons was new to the teachers, the lessons often took more time than anticipated, which led some teachers to cover less of the domain than originally intended.

Results

The control group scored significantly higher on the pretest ($M = 19.98$, SD$=6.58$) than the experimental group ($M = 14.56$, SD$=7.37$). A regression analysis, using the enter model,[2] gave a significant model for *pretest* scores with the factors of Condition, Gender, Profile, and their interactions ($F_{7, 410} = 14.14$, $p < 0.001$). The factor Condition was significant (df$=410$, $t = -6, 57$, $p < 0.001$), as was the factor Profile (df$=410$, $t = 4.92$, $p < 0.001$) in favor of the N-profile. Gender was not significant and there were no interactions.

On the overall (uncorrected) *posttest* score, the control group again outperformed the experimental group. However, the average relative difference (absolute difference/total number of points) between both groups decreased from 13.6% to 6.3%, which indicates that the two groups have come closer together. Given the significant difference between the two conditions on the pretest, these scores were used as a covariate for additional analyses. An enter model regression gave a significant model ($F_{8,409} = 25.361$, $p < 0.001$) for the posttest scores with the factors Condition, Profile, Gender, and the interactions between these three factors using the pretest as a covariate. The factor Condition was not significant ($n = 418$, df$=409$, $t = 0.260$, $p > 0.05$), whereas the factor Profile was significant ($n = 418$, df$=409$, $t = 7.01$, $p < 0.001$, Cohen's $d = 0.73$, one-sided test).[3] Gender was not found to be a significant factor ($n = 418$, df$=409$, $t = -0.93$, $p > 0.05$). There were no significant interactions. Table 7.1 shows the posttest scores (adjusted with the pretest scores) for the control and the experimental group with a further division into gender and profile.

---

[2] In order to run a regression analysis, one of the optional models has to be chosen. The different options are: enter, stepwise, remove, backward, and forward. The enter model is also called forced entry model. All variables specified are entered into the model in a single step. This model is generally used (when there are no specific expectations).

[3] One-sided tests are performed for specified predictions (e.g., the control condition performs better on procedural items). All other tests are two-sided.

We also compared the performance of the conditions on conceptual and procedural items for which the data are displayed in Table 7.2. A regression analysis (enter model) gave a significant model for *procedural* items ($F_{8,409} = 17.380$, $p < 0.001$) with the factors Condition, Profile, Gender, and their interactions with pretest scores as covariate. Students in the control condition outperformed the experimental condition students ($n = 418$, df $= 409$, $t = -1.687$, $p = 0.046$, Cohen's $d = -0.18$, (one-sided test). There was a trend for girls to score higher on the procedural items in the control condition ($n = 418$, df $= 409$, $t = -1.777$, $p = 0.076$, Cohen's $d = -0.19$, two-sided test). For *conceptual* items, a regression analysis (enter model) also resulted in a significant model ($F_{8,409} = 10.858$, $p < 0.001$) with the factors Condition, Profile, Gender, and the four interactions over these factors with pretest score as covariate. There was no significant difference between conditions ($n = 418$, df $= 409$, $t = 0.466$, $p = 0.321$, one-sided test), but there was a trend for boys to outperform girls ($n = 418$, df $= 409$, $t = -1.835$, $p = 0.067$, Cohen's $d = -0.19$). There was also a trend for an interaction between condition and profile ($n = 418$, df $= 409$, $t = -1.751$, $p = 0.081$, Cohen's $d = -0.18$, two-sided test): M-profile students performed better in the experimental condition while the N-profile students scored higher in the control condition.

As stated earlier there were considerable differences between schools. Therefore, we also explored the data of two more or less comparable classes (both classes come from the same school, have an N-profile, one is in the control condition, the other in the experimental condition). A regression analysis (enter model) yielded a significant model for *posttest* scores with the factors Condition, Gender, and their interaction with pretest scores as covariate ($F_{4, 39} = 7.11$, $p < 0.001$). There was a trend for students in the experimental Condition to score higher ($n = 44$, df $= 39$, $t = 1.90$, $p = 0.065$, Cohen's $d = 0.61$). Gender was not significant, nor was the interaction between gender and condition. The pretest significantly influenced the results on the posttest ($n = 44$, df $= 39$, $t = 4.99$, $p < 0.001$, Cohen's $d = 1.60$, one-sided test) and there were no significant interactions.

Table 7.2 Posttest scores (adjusted percentages) and SE (of the adjusted scores) on conceptual and procedural items

Condition	Profile	Gender	Number	Procedural		Conceptual	
				Mean	SE	Mean	SE
Control	M	Male	21	0.55	0.04	0.55	0.07
		Female	19	0.59	0.04	0.41	0.07
	N	Male	55	0.63	0.03	0.73	0.04
		Female	45	0.71	0.03	0.75	0.05
	Total		140	0.62	0.02	0.61	0.03
Experimental	M	Male	42	0.54	0.03	0.59	0.05
		Female	73	0.53	0.02	0.53	0.04
	N	Male	88	0.64	0.02	0.73	0.03
		Female	75	0.62	0.02	0.66	0.04
	Total		278	0.58	0.01	0.63	0.02
Total			418	0.60	0.01	0.62	0.02

A regression analysis (enter model) didn't give a significant model for *procedural* items ($F_{4, 39} = 1.99$, $p = 0.114$) with the factors Condition, Gender, and their interaction with pretest scores as covariate. A regression analysis (enter model), gave a significant model for *conceptual* items with the factors of Condition, Gender, and their interaction with pretest as covariate ($F_{4, 39} = 3.48$, $p = 0.016$). There was a trend for students in the experimental Condition to score higher ($n = 44$, df $= 39$, $t = 1.59$, $p = 0.060$, Cohen's $d = 0.51$, one-sided test). Gender was not significant, nor was the interaction between gender and condition.

Discussion and Conclusion

In this work, we have developed a set of computer-based inquiry learning environments for mathematics. The materials were developed iteratively over a range of preliminary studies. Besides the computer materials, there was an instruction booklet and a teacher manual with guidelines for the setup of a series of lessons, for classroom discussions, and for creating subject-matter overviews. In addition, the teacher manual explicitly linked the new material to the existing textbook. The material was not confined to a single lesson or a limited part of a topical domain but covered a series of 12 weeks of lessons on all the topics of functions treated in the textbook. Once developed, we tested the materials by "letting them loose" in a larger set of schools of a divers nature and compared the results with achievements in traditional classrooms that just followed the textbook.

The large-scale study that we conducted showed that implementing the program in schools led to a wide diversity of usages, dependent on local organization, structures and facilities. Schools differed considerably in their implementation efforts, sometimes shortening the program due to time constraints (many teachers in the experimental condition dropped the creation of subject-matter overviews), sometimes skipping computer exercises due to problems with the facilities (e.g., computers that were out of order, projectors that did not function or were not available). Of course, this threatens the experimental rigor, but it should also be recognized that the materials are likely to be used in these ways in everyday practices. In any case, we can safely conclude that the implementation of the experimental condition was not optimal in many schools.

Even under these challenging conditions the learning results of the experimental group on the posttest were encouraging. After correcting for pretest scores, the outcomes in the experimental condition equal the outcomes in the control condition in which students received the type of instruction they were used to and in which no major practical problems occurred. Exploratory analyses of two classes, one control and one experimental, that were more or less comparable for these external conditions, points even more strongly in this direction as posttest scores turned out higher for the experimental group.

Students from the control group turned out to score significantly better on procedural items for which, primarily, mastery of techniques is important. These students also executed the test at a higher pace and succeeded to reach the end of the test more frequently (in the control group 82.9% of the students made one of the last questions, in the experimental group 67.3% did). This suggests that these students had automated their knowledge more, which was what we expected. In contrast, students in the experimental groups had higher scores (corrected for pretest scores) on conceptual (insight) items. This is in line with the idea that the experimental material focused more on building insight than the traditional material. Although the latter difference between conditions did not reach significance it was in the predicted direction. These results fit into a more general trend that is emerging from research (see, e.g., Rasmussen & Kwon, 2007).

An interesting finding in this study concerns the gender differences. Overall, and regardless of prior knowledge, girls performed better in the traditional classroom setting whereas boys profited more from the inquiry setting. One possible explanation for this effect is self-efficacy, that is, the students' handling of the inquiry environment may have been affected by their competency beliefs about learning mathematics in a more open-ended, guided inquiry learning manner. On the influence of gender on mathematics, the literature is equivocal. Some studies found no differences between girls and boys in self-efficacy beliefs toward mathematics (e.g., Chen & Zimmerman, 2007) whereas others report relevant gender differences. For example, Meece, Glienke, and Burg (2006) found that boys report higher interest and competency beliefs in mathematics than girls and Frenzel, Pekrun, and Goetz (2007) found that girls feel more insecure in mathematics than boys even when their knowledge is on the same level. To our knowledge, only few studies on the impact of gender on (guided) inquiry learning have been conducted. In an older study, Gennaro and Lawrenz (1992) found that girls performed better on inquiry tasks than boys. A similar finding is reported by Timmermans, Van Lieshout, and Verhoeven (2007) who compared guided instructions with prescribed, direct instruction. On the former, girls performed better and felt more at ease than boys. It is clear that more work needs to be done to unravel the relation between gender and inquiry learning in general and mathematics inquiry learning in particular.

An obvious question is how the implementation can be improved. One important constraint was the structure and quality of the textbook. We had to work in a set curriculum and therefore took the textbook of the schools as our starting point for developing the SimQuest applications. This turned out not to be optimal; among others because equations seemed to come "out of the blue." Whenever possible, learning materials should be simultaneously developed to realize a better integration of textbooks and the interactive materials (see chapter by Roschelle & Knudsen, this volume). Another important factor that we could not alter in the present study was the time available for this series of lessons. The realistic class situation required accommodating the existing time schedule for learning the topic of functions. However, having learners investigate mathematics themselves invariably costs more time. In the current situation, it may have demanded too much time. A different time schedule maybe necessary when students engage in inquiry learning, certainly when they do this for the first time. The third factor that clearly limited the implementation concerns the access to computer facilities. In many schools, it was difficult to use computer applications comfortably in the lessons. Even in schools with a good computer infrastructure, problems repeatedly emerged due to organizational obstacles. In other words, a hefty check on computer facilities and organizational embedding is needed to ensure that these conditions do not form an obstacle.

Overall, the results of this study confirm a set of recent studies that indicate that traditional didactic teaching approaches achieve lower-order learning outcomes, whereas learner-centered and inquiry approaches, often enabled by technology, allow students to construct deeper and more conceptual understandings and enhanced problem-solving abilities. This justifies efforts to further investigate the conditions under which these types of learning experiences can be optimized.

Acknowledgements We gratefully acknowledge the Netherlands Organisation for Scientific Research (NWO) for funding this study (Project Number 411-01-063). We also thank Henri Ruizenaar, a mathematics teacher, who contributed extensively to the development of the research materials.

References

Atkinson, R. K. (2005). Multimedia learning of mathematics. In R. E. Mayer (Ed.), *Cambridge handbook of multimedia learning* (pp. 393–408). Cambridge, UK: Cambridge University Press.

Balacheff, N. & Sutherland, R. (1994). Epistemological domain of validity of microworlds - The case of Logo and Cabri-Geometre. *Lessons from Learning, 46*, 137–150.

Bottino, R. M., Artigue, M., & Noss, R. (2009). Building European collaboration in technology enhanced learning in mathematics. In N. Balacheff, S. Ludvigsen, T. de Jong, S. Barnes, & A. Lazonder (Eds.), *Technology enhanced learning - Principles and products* (pp. 73–89). Berlin: Springer Verlag.

Bransford, J. D., Brown, A. L., & Cocking, R. R. (eds). (1999). *How people learn: Brain, mind, experience, and school*. Washington, D.C: National Academy Press.

Bruner, J. (1973). *Going beyond the information given*. New York: Norton.

Bruner, J., Goodnow, J., & Austin, A. (1956). *A study of thinking*. New York: Wiley.

Chen, P. & Zimmerman, B. (2007). A cross-national comparison study on the accuracy of self-efficacy beliefs of middle-school mathematics students. *Journal of Experimental Education, 75*, 221–244.

Chin, C. & Brown, D. E. (2000). Learning in science: A comparison of deep and surface approaches. *Journal of Research in Science Teaching, 37*, 109–138.

Cobb, P. & McClain, K. (2006). Guiding inquiry-based math learning. In R. K. Sawyer (Ed.), *The Cambridge handbook of the learning sciences* (pp. 171–186). Cambridge: Cambridge University Press.

Cognition and Technology Group at Vanderbilt. (1992). The Jasper series as an example of anchored instruction: Theory, program, description, and assessment data. *Educational Psychologist, 27*, 291–315.

Cognition and Technology Group at Vanderbilt. (1997). *The Jasper project; Lessons in curriculum, instruction, assessment, and professional development*. Hillsdale, NJ: Lawrence Erlbaum Associates.

de Jong, T. (2006a). Computer simulations - Technological advances in inquiry learning. *Science, 312*, 532–533.

de Jong, T. (2006b). Scaffolds for computer simulation based scientific discovery learning. In J. Elen & R. E. Clark (Eds.), *Dealing with complexity in learning environments* (pp. 107–128). London: Elsevier Science Publishers.

Dewey, J. (1916). *Democracy and education. An introduction to the philosophy of education.* New York: MacMillan.

Eysink, T. H. S., de Jong, T., Berthold, K., Kollöffel, B., Opfermann, M., & Wouters, P. (2009). Learner performance in multimedia learning arrangements: an analysis across instructional approaches, *46*, 1107–1149.

Falcade, R., Laborde, C., & Mariotti, M. (2007). Approaching functions: Cabri tools as instruments of semiotic mediation. *Educational Studies in Mathematics, 66*, 317–333.

Frenzel, A. C., Pekrun, R., & Goetz, T. (2007). Girls and mathematics - A "hopeless" issue? A control-value approach to gender differences in emotions towards mathematics. *European Journal of Psychology of Education, 22*, 497–514.

Freudenthal, H. (1991). *Revisiting mathematics education: China lectures.* Dordrecht, the Netherlands: Kluwer Academic Publishers.

Gennaro, E. & Lawrenz, F. (1992). The effectiveness of take-home science kits at the elementary level. *Journal of Research in Science Teaching, 29*, 985–994.

Grabinger, R. S. (1996). Rich environments for active learning. In D. H. Jonassen (Ed.), *Handbook of research for educational communications and technology* (pp. 665–692). New York: Simon & Schuster Macmillan.

Gravemeijer, K., van den Heuvel-Panhuizen, M., van Donselaar, G., Ruesink, N., Streefland, L., Vermeulen, W., et al. (1993). *Methoden in het reken-wiskundeonderwijs, een rijke context voor vergelijkend onderzoek (No. SVO-6010).* Utrecht: Freudenthal-instituut.

Horton, P. B., McConney, A. A., Gallo, M., Woods, A. L., Senn, G. J., & Hamelin, D. (1993). An investigation of the effectiveness of concept mapping as an instructional tool. *Science Education, 77*, 95–111.

Jonassen, D. H. (1991). Objectivism versus constructivism: Do we need a new philosophical paradigm? *Educational Technology: Research & Development, 39*, 5–14.

Kuhn, M., Hoppe, U., Lingnau, A., & Wichmann, A. (2006). Computational modelling and simulation fostering new approaches in learning probability. *Innovations in Education and Teaching International, 43*, 183–194.

Laborde, C. (2002). Integration of technology in the design of geometry tasks with Cabri-Geometry. *International Journal of Computers for Mathematical Learning, 6*, 283–317.

Linn, M. C., Lee, H.-S., Tinker, R., Husic, F., & Chiu, J. L. (2006). Teaching and assessing knowledge integration in science. *Science, 313*, 1049–1050.

Mayer, R. E. (2002). Rote versus meaningful learning. *Theory Into Practice, 41*, 226–232.

Meece, J. L., Glienke, B. B., & Burg, S. (2006). Gender and motivation. *Journal of School Psychology, 44*, 351–373.

Noss, R. & Hoyles, C. (2006). Exploring mathematics through construction and collaboration. In R. K. Sawyer (Ed.), *The Cambridge handbook of the learning sciences* (pp. 389–409). Cambridge: Cambridge University Press.

Novak, J. D. (1998). *Learning, creating and using knowledge: Concept map^{TM} as facilitative tools in schools and corporations.* Mahwah (NJ): Lawrence Erlbaum Associates, Inc.

Pea, R. D. (1987). Cognitive technologies for mathematics education. In A. H. Schoenfeld (Ed.), *Cognitive science and mathematics education* (pp. 89–122). Hillsdale, NJ: Erlbaum.

Rasmussen, C. & Kwon, O. N. (2007). An inquiry-oriented approach to undergraduate mathematics. *The Journal of Mathematical Behavior, 26*, 189–194.

Roschelle, J. & Kaput, J. (1996). SimCalc MathWorlds for the mathematics of change: Composable components for calculus learning. *Communications of the ACM, 39*, 97–99.

Roschelle, J., & Knudsen, J. (this volume). From new technological infrastructures to curricular activity systems: advanced designs for teaching and learning. New York: Springer

Schoenfeld, A. H. (2006). Mathematics teaching and learning. In P. A. Alexander & P. H. Winne (Eds.), *Handbook of educational psychology* (2nd ed., pp. 479–510). Mahwah, NJ: Lawrence Erlbaum Associates.

Schoenfeld, A. H. (1985). *Mathematical problem solving.* New York: Academic Press.

Staples, M. (2007). Supporting whole-class collaborative inquiry in a secondary mathematics classroom. *Cognition and Instruction, 25*, 161–217.

Timmermans, R. E., Van Lieshout, E., & Verhoeven, L. (2007). Gender-related effects of contemporary math instruction for low performers on problem-solving behavior. *Learning and Instruction, 17*, 42–54.

Underwood, J. S., Hoadley, C., Lee, H. S., Hollebrands, K., DiGano, C., & Renninger, K. A. (2005). IDEA: identifying design principles in educational applets. *Etr&D-Educational Technology Research and Development, 53*, 99–112.

Vahey, P., Enyedy, N., & Gifford, B. (2000). Learning probability through the use of a collaborative, inquiry-based simulation environment. *Journal of Interactive Learning Research, 11*, 51–84.

van Joolingen, W. R. & de Jong, T. (2003). SimQuest: Authoring educational simulations. In T. Murray, S. Blessing & S. Ainsworth (Eds.), *Authoring tools for advanced technology educational software: Toward cost-effective production of adaptive, interactive, and intelligent educational software* (pp. 1–31). Dordrecht: Kluwer Academic Publishers.

van Streun, A. (1989). *Heuristisch wiskunde-onderwijs: Verslag van een onderwijsexperiment.* Groningen.

von Glaserfeld, E. (1987). Learning as a constructive activity. In C. Janvier (Ed.), *Problems in the representation in the teaching and learning of mathematics* (pp. 3–17). Hillsdale, NJ: Lawrence Erlbaum.

Chapter 8
Scaffolding Knowledge Communities in the Classroom: New Opportunities in the Web 2.0 Era

Vanessa L. Peters and James D. Slotta

Technology for the Twenty-First Century Classroom

Computer and information technologies have transformed nearly every dimension of society, including business, government, science, and engineering. The changes within these organizations reflect the emergence of a "Knowledge Society," where we come to rely on processes of knowledge creation and advancement over those of labor, industry, or mechanical production (Drucker, 1959; Bereiter & Scardamalia, 1996). Yet in spite of such twenty-first century movements, the education sector of society remains largely unchanged, with classrooms still closely resembling those of the mid-twentieth century (Becker, 1999). A number of scholars have remarked on the slow uptake of technology-enhanced methods in the classroom (e.g., Tyack & Cuban, 1995; Cuban, 2001). As diSessa (2000) observes, "Few can or should claim that computers have influenced the cultural practices of school the way they have other aspects of society, such as science or business. Just look at texts, tests, and assignments from core subjects. They really have changed little so far" (p. 3). The conservatism observed by these scholars has persisted despite efforts from the learning sciences community to transform classroom culture from one that is teacher dominated, to one where students assume autonomy over their own learning. Given the knowledge-oriented, technology-infused workplaces in which students will participate, it is important that schools integrate technology meaningfully into the curriculum, and develop new methods of instruction that emphasize collaborative knowledge construction.

However, any substantive change made to school curricula will require a corresponding significant change in teachers' practices. Integrating new, technology-based innovations into one's classroom practice is not easy. Teachers rely on familiar methods not because they lack incentive for improving student learning,

V.L. Peters (✉) and J.D. Slotta
Ontario Institute for Studies in Education, University of Toronto, 252 Bloor Street West, Toronto, Ontario M5S 1V6, Canada
e-mail: vlpeters@gmail.com

M.J. Jacobson and P. Reimann (eds.), *Designs for Learning Environments of the Future: International Perspectives from the Learning Sciences*, DOI 10.1007/978-0-387-88279-6_8, © Springer Science+Business Media, LLC 2010

but because these methods fit within the complex ecology of their classroom and school community. Teachers' methods must also accommodate the mandated curriculum subject content, which is usually assessed through conventional measures. Thus, the successful adoption of any newly designed curriculum will require a continued serious investment of time and intellectual energy from teachers, administrators, and other school personnel who are directly involved with student achievement (Cuban & Usdan, 2003). Ideally, teachers' involvement would begin in the early stages of the curriculum design process. Too often, teachers learn the details of new methods or materials at roughly the same time they are implementing them (Glenman & Melmed, 2000), leaving them little time to consider how to best integrate the innovations into their broader curriculum.

Many teachers do see technology as a means of supporting new pedagogical practices. However, even when they have access to educational technologies such as SMART Boards, Clickers, or Internet-enabled computers, they often lack knowledge of how these innovations can be effectively used for learning and instruction. Thus, teachers face a steep learning curve in adopting new technologies for curriculum or assessment within their classroom. Whereas on one hand they should not be expected to design such innovations on their own, on the other, there are generally few ways in which someone else could do it for them. In order for curriculum innovations to really succeed in a classroom, the teacher's must be involved in their design and customization for specific contexts. This requires research from the learning sciences, as well as targeted professional development programs that include in-service supports for teachers as they embark on the voyage of transforming classrooms into knowledge communities.

It has never been more important for educators to embrace new technologies, in order to help students learn the skills and practices required of knowledge workers (Scardamalia, 2000). This chapter will explore the implications of Web 2.0 technologies for supporting new forms of curriculum and assessment in classrooms, and the impact of a co-design method in engaging teachers in the process of transforming their curriculum. We begin with a short summary of the key features of Web 2.0, followed by a review of research from the learning sciences that could be relevant to educators who wish to apply these technologies. We then describe a theoretical model for designing curriculum that emphasizes collaborative knowledge construction, and a methodology of co-design. Two studies are then presented in which this model was applied in developing a high school biology curriculum, followed by a discussion of the outcomes of our curriculum. We close with a discussion of implications and next steps.

The Emergence of Web 2.0

Following the economic collapse of the dot-com bubble in 2001, several pioneers of the Internet, including Tim O'Reilly (2007), observed that far from collapsing, the Web was becoming even more important to society. In 2003, they coined the term "Web 2.0" to refer to a new generation of Internet-based applications that were functionally distinct from those of the previous era. These are technologies that push the boundaries of how we think about collaboration and communication, and are perhaps best exemplified in the way in which web content is produced and consumed. Whereas earlier web applications emphasized individual production and mass consumption (i.e., an individual creates a web site which is then read by many), Web 2.0 emphasizes mass production and mass consumption (i.e., users are both producers and consumers – see Alexander, 2006).

Interactivity and social networking are typical of Web 2.0 resources, with millions of people around the globe connecting through social networking applications such as MySpace and Facebook. Another recent social networking service that allows users to aggregate photo, video, and chat applications is called Tagged (http://www.tagged.com). Social elements of Internet applications have allowed the transformation of our online experience. Many people now maintain "blogs," a periodic narrative typically authored by a single individual but with comments on blog entries given by the community of subscribers. Podcasts serve a similar function, but are presented in an audio or audio-visual format instead of simple text. Using a simple syndication service (RSS), users can subscribe to blogs, podcasts, or other web sites and receive automated notification whenever content has been added or updated. Google now offers a "reader" service that allows individuals to subscribe to any number of such publications (see http://reader.google.com). Thus, a fundamental feature of Web 2.0 is the connection of individuals into social networks. Even now, new features are being added, such as enabling the interconnection of cell phone and other hand held computers within such networks, as exemplified by the social messaging application called Twitter (see http://www.twitter.com) which has spurred a global conversation with the question: "What are you doing?"

Another important characteristic of Web 2.0 applications is their support of collaborative editing. Wikis, including the well-known Wikipedia, are ongoing artifacts that are written, edited, and maintained by any number of contributors. Many wiki applications are available free of charge on Web sites, enabling any group or organization to engage in collaborative writing and thereby harnessing the combined contributions and insights of all members. Some of the earliest research into wiki usage was conducted in educational settings. As an extension of Ward Cunningham's "WikiWikiWeb," Guzdial (1998) developed "CoWeb," an educational wiki-based collaboration tool for use by students, educators and researchers. The open-authoring capabilities of CoWeb supports a number of important pedagogical objectives, as students develop their own knowledge through creating public artifacts (Papert & Harel, 1991), and increase their level of student agency (Scardamalia & Bereiter, 1991). Thus, another essential aspect of Web 2.0 is the aggregation of contributions from the distributed audience. Rather than rely on a single source authority to create the content that is consumed by the masses, Web 2.0 relies on "The Wisdom of Crowds" (Surowiecki, 2004).

Many web applications have been created that draw on the aggregated input of their visitors. Amazon bookseller (http://www.amazon.com) was one of the first web sites to demonstrate the power of aggregated visits through its use of recommender systems: what other books you would like. Based on your selection of a book to purchase, Amazon is able to quickly correlate your choice with those of others who chose the same book (as well as your own past history of purchases) and recommend a set of other books that you might enjoy. This illustrates how patterns of use and preference can be another form of aggregation (not just aggregated content). The YouTube video sharing community demonstrates this capability through its "popularity" index – where the most viewed videos are recommended in the display, and a new set of videos is recommended based on patterns of popularity and coselection. News aggregators such as Digg (http://www.digg.com) simply report all of the most popular news items, as rated by viewers. In this way, Web 2.0 applications employ a social feedback mechanism to actually provide an essential aspect of their functionality.

A final related characteristic of Web 2.0 is that of social tagging and "folksonomies" – collaborative and dynamic categorizations of web sites. Anyone who has used an electronic subject index is acquainted with the idea of searching through resources using tags or keywords. However, unlike traditional indexing, the keywords (or "tags") in a folksonomy are not defined by information specialists or librarians, but by users themselves. There is no hierarchal organization of tags in a folksonomy. Users are free to assign them into overlapping categories of their choice, and have the option of sharing their repository of keywords with other users (Alexander, 2006). Folksonomies are extensively used in social bookmaking services such as Delicious and BibSonomy – applications that provide tools that help users semantically organize their favorite web sites. Tag activity within a folksonomy can also be represented with "tag clouds" – visual structures that arrange search terms according to defined categories or frequency of use. Folksonomies are used extensively in photo management applications such as Flickr and Picasa, and are a standard feature in many new and emerging web applications such as photosynth (http://www.photosynth.net/) and taggraph (http://www.taggraph.com), which employ folksonomies to achieve remarkable user experiences.

New Opportunities for Teaching and Learning

The knowledge-oriented media associated with Web 2.0 present exciting new opportunities for educational research (Ullrich et al., 2008). Indeed, scholars have begun exploring how Web 2.0 can be productively used for learning and instruction. Wikis, for example, provide a collaborative structure that enables students to learn from both their individual and collaborative efforts. When coauthoring a document, students' individual contributions are a first step toward social collaboration (Aguiton & Cardon, 2007). Students working in a wiki cannot predict how their contributions will be received, nor can they predict how the coauthored document will evolve. Negotiating the content for a collaborative document can prompt the type of peer exchange that has been shown to foster student learning (e.g., Webb & Palincsar, 1996; Palincsar, 1998). Bryant, Forte, and Bruckman (2005) demonstrated that participants adopt new goals as they become more involved in the authoring process, shifting their focus from one of personal contribution to one of growing concern for the shared artifact. Students can also socially tag their wiki entries, resulting in folksonomies that make them accessible to a wider audience, which can encourage students to make more thoughtful and conscientious contributions (Wheeler, Yeomans, & Wheeler, 2008). Thus, wikis can provide educators with a powerful tool for fostering new philosophical outlooks and accepted forms of practice within the classroom (Papert, 2000).

The studies mentioned above are just the beginning of what will likely become an interesting new thread within the research literature. At the 2008 meeting of the International Society of the Learning Sciences, we convened a panel (Peters & Slotta, 2008) to address the new affordances of Web 2.0 technologies for research. Just as students and teachers can benefit from the opportunities provided by collaborative technologies, researchers can also gain new opportunities to support complex models of learning and instruction. There is still much to discover about how emerging technologies can be leveraged in ways that are compatible with theories of learning. In response to society's increasing dependence on knowledge and technical innovation, educational researchers can help to determine effective pedagogical approaches that support collaborative knowledge construction in the classroom. In the next section, we review research from the learning sciences that is relevant to our own theoretical perspective, ending with a description of a new pedagogical model that guides our designs of innovative Web 2.0 curriculum.

Scaffolding Knowledge Communities and Inquiry

Fostering a Knowledge Community

One strand of the learning science research literature that is clearly relevant to the successful integration of Web 2.0 approaches is the one concerned with "knowledge communities." In this research tradition, students collaborate with their peers and teachers to develop a shared understanding of their goals for learning and the process by which they will meet those goals (Brown & Campione, 1996; Scardamalia & Bereiter, 2003; Hakkarainen, 2004). For example, in the research program called Fostering Community of Learners (FCL), Brown and Campione (1996) carefully choreographed an elementary classroom, selectively presenting materials to small groups of students with different areas of expertise, so that the students and teachers within the classroom grew as a "knowledge community." The key components of FCL – student driven research, jigsawed information sharing, and performance of consequential tasks – provide structure and support for students' collaborations within the learning community. When combined, these components form a potent pedagogical strategy that fosters critical reflection and deep understanding of disciplinary content. An important theoretical contribution of FCL is the notion of diverse expertise. In their classroom implementations of

FCL, Brown and Campione (1996) found that students came to highly value the contributions of their peers. These contributions were not always about content, but were often related to using the computers or managing the group (Collins, Joseph, & Bielaczyc, 2004). A related innovation called crosstalk involves students presenting their preliminary findings to the entire class, producing a peer-review of ideas that often resulted in students developing a new line of inquiry (Bielaczyc, 2006).

A related approach known as knowledge building emphasizes the production and improvement of ideas that are shared within a community (Scardamalia & Bereiter, 1991, 2003; Brown & Palincsar, 1989). Students are given exclusive responsibility for the high-level processes of knowledge construction: generating new ideas, building on classmates' ideas, and synthesizing ideas into higher-level concepts. Unlike a traditional cognitive view of learning, which is concerned with individual cognitive development, knowledge building results in the creation or modification of public knowledge. Public, in this sense, means that the knowledge is available to other group members to be worked upon and improved. At times, knowledge building may involve disagreement in terms of what constitutes advancement of an idea, and how the limits of understanding should be defined. In a knowledge-building environment, such issues are dealt with jointly by group members, and not arbitrated by any external authority.

Through maintaining a shared and sustained focus, members of knowledge communities work jointly to arrive at new meanings and understandings. In this way, ideas are subject to multiple revisions and refinements that ultimately result in an improvement of the original. One of the most important measures of success in a knowledge community approach is whether students are working toward a common goal. This feature separates knowledge communities from other approaches such as project-based learning, guided discovery, or scaffolded inquiry (discussed next), which may rely on collaborative activities and real-world content to encourage the social construction of knowledge, but have a tendency to result in what Scardamalia and Bereiter (2003) call "shallow constructivism" (p. 1370). In a knowledge community approach, students work collaboratively in developing a community-owned knowledge base. In turn, this process supports individual students to develop as autonomous learners (Bereiter & Scardamalia, 1989). The teacher is considered a learning partner and facilitator, not an expert who is the principal source of knowledge. Rather, students develop expertise by asking questions and negotiating personal understandings through their own line of inquiry.

In general, it is quite challenging for teachers or researchers to coordinate a knowledge community approach in any classroom. As Kling and Courtright (2003) observe, "developing a group into a community is a major accomplishment that requires special processes and practices, and the experience is often both frustrating and satisfying for many of the participants" (p. 221). Thus, while this research tradition has earned great respect among scholars, it has been difficult to extend into K-12 classrooms where there is such a strong focus on the coverage of curriculum standards. This is particularly true of secondary science, where teachers are faced with substantial content expectations and traditional assessments, and are thus reluctant to embrace the wholesale changes required to enact a knowledge community model (Rico & Shulman, 2004; Whitcomb, 2004; Gardner, 2004). Teachers in these settings are typically under great pressure to ensure that the students develop an understanding of a wide range of topics, presenting unfavorable conditions for a knowledge community approach (Slotta & Peters, 2008). Thus, despite the acclaim given to the knowledge community approach in research reviews (e.g., Bransford, Brown, & Cocking, 2000), the instructional method has not been widely adopted by teachers, particularly at the secondary level.

Scaffolded Inquiry

Another strand of learning science research is that of scaffolded inquiry, where students learn by interacting with carefully designed "scaffolded" learning materials and negotiating ideas with their classmates. A number of prominent pedagogical approaches have been developed for scaffolded inquiry, most of which are deeply committed to incorporating collaborative activities (e.g., Krajcik, Blumenfeld, Marx, & Soloway, 1994; Edelson, Gordin, & Pea, 1999; Linn & Hsi, 2000; Quintana et al., 2004; Slotta & Linn, 2009). However, while scaffolded inquiry may be deeply collaborative, the perspective of learning remains focused on the individual learner. Guided by cognitive and constructivist frameworks, scaffolded inquiry materials are carefully scripted to guide students from one reflective activity to the next. All student work in such activities is collected by researchers for purposes of analysis of students' understanding. Specific research studies typically investigate questions related to the effectiveness of different curriculum designs, and how they enable students to develop a deep personal understanding (Linn & Eylon, 2006; Slotta & Linn, 2009).

Great progress has been made in the approach of scaffolded inquiry, perhaps because many more studies have examined this approach than that of knowledge communities. Indeed, it is relatively straightforward to design and enact a well-controlled investigation of scaffolded inquiry. One feature that is quite common to such investigations is the use of scaffolding technologies that guide students through the curriculum sequence, prompt for reflections, and provide rich multimedia materials. Several scaffolding environments have been developed over the past decades for science inquiry, including BioKIDS (Songer, 2006), BGuILE (Reiser et al., 2001), Inquiry Island (White et al., 2002), Knowledge Integration Environment (KIE) (Bell, Davis, & Linn, 1995) and WISE (Slotta, 2004). These environments were designed to enable teachers to more easily enact complex forms of inquiry instruction, demonstrating the powerful enabling role of technologies (e.g., see Roschelle, Knudsen, & Hegedus, this volume). Such work has given rise to several general frameworks for scaffolded inquiry, such as those of Quintana et al. (2004) and Linn and Eylon (2006).

Still, despite the relative success of such approaches in classroom studies, there has been little uptake of these innovations by teachers in regular classrooms

(Blumenfeld, Fishman, Krajcik, Marx, & Soloway, 2000; Borko & Putnam, 1995; Cuban, 2001). While they may be more straightforward than a knowledge community approach, scaffolded inquiry methods are still quite challenging for teachers to adopt (Slotta & Linn, 2009). They generally demand a deeper treatment of topics, and thus more curriculum time for any given topic than most teachers are allowed – particularly in secondary science. In general, rich new models of collaboration and inquiry are challenging for teachers, who must tailor their course curriculum to provide room for some topics to be covered in greater depth than others. This tailoring process requires teachers to fully understand the nuances of the innovative materials (including any scaffolding technologies) to ensure that they are properly enacted. However, because researchers generally develop these materials, teachers may not find them straightforward to interpret or adapt.

The Knowledge Community and Inquiry Model

In order for teachers to adopt inquiry and knowledge community approaches, we must find a way to include them in the design of the curriculum, ensuring that a balance is held between implementing specific pedagogical models and covering the required content. Science textbooks cover more topics than any other subject, resulting in a curriculum that can be described as being "a mile wide and an inch deep" (Schmidt, McKnight, & Raizen, 1997, p. 62). Science teachers are required to cover specific content matter (e.g., cellular function, collision theory, organic compounds), making it difficult to design learning activities where students can pursue a deep understanding of science topics as a community of learners. Any science lesson or unit must be able to fit within a tight schedule of content coverage, with outcomes that are assessable by conventional measures. Teachers must feel that that every class period is used productively, and that their lessons are in alignment with the science topics outlined in the curriculum expectations (Penuel, Fishman, Gallagher, Korbak, & Prado-Lopez, 2008).

How can we help teachers adopt innovative, research-based approaches into their secondary science classrooms? Although research has explored avenues for adding inquiry-based and collaborative knowledge construction to the curriculum, teachers have not readily embraced either of these approaches. Inquiry has often been too rigidly designed and inflexible, requiring specific practices and materials that may not fit with the existing curriculum. Collaborative knowledge construction is often too open-ended, making it difficult for teachers to target specific learning outcomes. What is needed is a way to help teachers design and adopt rich inquiry-oriented curriculum that connects deeply to science content expectations, and supports teachers and students in their enactment of new methods.

In an effort to make headway on these problems, Slotta and his colleagues have developed the Knowledge Community and Inquiry (KCI) model that combines collaborative knowledge construction with scripted inquiry activities to target specific curriculum learning objectives (Slotta, 2007; Slotta & Peters, 2008). The model produces curriculum designs that begin with a collaborative knowledge construction phase where students explore and investigate their own ideas as a community of learners and create knowledge artifacts that are aggregated into a knowledge base. This community knowledge base then serves as a resource for subsequent scaffolded inquiry activities, where students are engaged in collaboration and reflection. To adhere to the spirit of knowledge communities, such inquiry activities should not be completely predetermined (i.e., before the knowledge construction phase), as the ideas and interests of the students should help to determine the focus of any inquiry (Scardamalia & Bereiter, 1996). Common themes, ideas or interests should emerge, reflecting the "voice" of the community. The instructor must listen to this voice and respond by designing activities that reflect students' interests. The latter process is critical, but also pedagogically challenging to execute, since the inquiry activities must also address the content expectations and learning goals of the curriculum.

It is no easy task to design activities that responds to community interests while addressing learning goals and adhering to time constraints. In the KCI model, scaffolded inquiry activities are co-designed by teachers and researchers only after the knowledge construction phase is well underway, building upon the themes they identify within the knowledge base. Students then draw upon the elements from their community knowledge base to complete the scaffolded inquiry tasks that are directly connected to assessable content-learning outcomes. KCI curricula can only be developed through close collaboration between researchers and teachers to ensure a carefully controlled flow of collaborative knowledge construction and scaffolded inquiry activities that are specifically designed to address specific learning objectives (Slotta & Peters, 2008).

A Co-design Community for Curriculum Development

The success of any research-based curriculum will critically depend on the teacher's understanding of the theoretical basis of that curriculum. Teachers would be unlikely to succeed in implementing any complex forms of curriculum for which they were not involved in the design. Moreover, it would be impossible for any researcher to create truly engaging curriculum materials without continuous input from the teacher(s) that will be enacting that curriculum. In order to design curriculum that meets the researchers' objectives while fulfilling the teacher's curriculum requirements, a collaborative model of development must be pursued.

One approach where all learning materials and pedagogical activities are developed collaboratively by researchers and teachers is that of co-design. Roschelle, Penuel, and Shechtmen (2006) employed a co-design method for a study in which they worked closely with stakeholder groups to produce an innovative curriculum for secondary school science. They describe co-design as "a highly facilitated, team-based process in which teachers, researchers, and developers work together in defined roles to design an educational innovation, realize the design in one or more prototypes, and evaluate each prototype's significance for addressing a concrete educational need" (p. 606). Co-design has a number of features that are common with other user-oriented design methods such as participatory design and user-centered design, which also emphasize the importance of input from the stakeholders of the design innovation. Like design-based research (Brown, 1992; Collins, 1999), co-design involves the continuous refinement of a design innovation that addresses an educational objective. Co-design, however, is more specified as it involves a number of well-defined process steps that are necessary for implementation.

Penuel, Rochelle, and Shechtman (2007) discuss tensions that are typical of a co-design approach. The process of delineating a new curriculum brings to light an individual's assumptions and expectations not only about their own role in the design process, but also those of other team members. Each stakeholder group, including teachers, researchers, and technology developers, often use their own specific terminologies to describe their intentions for the innovation. Also, each member of the co-design team may be relatively unfamiliar with the challenges and perspectives of the other members, which can lead to appearances of insensitivity or lack of appreciation for their efforts. For example, a teacher who is unaware the logistics behind software development may appear demanding and unrealistic when requesting a new technology feature from a programmer. Prior to commencing the project, Penuel et al. (2007) recommend that the design team review the process steps and objectives of co-design, including identifying a concrete innovation challenge, negotiating a flexible curricular objective and establishing defined roles for all members of the co-design team.

Study 1: Physiology of Human Diseases

To conduct this research, we established a partnership with the science department of an urban high school in a large Canadian city. A number of meetings were held with school administrators and science teachers to discuss our collaboration, and two biology teachers expressed interest in co-designing a technology-enhanced curriculum. The following two studies detail the KCI curriculum that resulted from this collaboration, including classroom trials and evaluation. The goal of this research is to investigate the KCI model in terms of its capability to engage students in a knowledge community while also supporting scaffolded inquiry that targets specific learning goals.

Design Research

We chose a design research approach, with the expectation that we would conduct our research within a classroom context to evaluate our curriculum's fit to the KCI model. Collins (1999) discusses a number of issues in design research that distinguish it methodologically from traditional experimental studies. One important distinction concerns the role of the researcher. In experimental studies, the researcher makes all the decisions regarding the design and analysis of the study. Design experiments, on the other hand, entail close collaborations between the researcher and the various stakeholder groups involved in the study, which in the current study included teachers, students and school administrators. In addition, research variables cannot always be controlled in design experiments, particularly since the intervention itself changes over the course of the study. Still another challenge is the voluminous datasets that are typically collected, usually from both qualitative and quantitative methods. It has been argued that because of these challenges, design studies lack a strong theoretical foundation and do not generate findings for the purpose of extending a theory (diSessa & Cobb, 2004). Other scholars (e.g., Edelson, 2002; Bell, 2004; Hoadley, 2004) suggest that design-oriented research can be conducted with empirical rigor, resulting in credible arguments and evidence-based claims. The design research method is appropriate for this case, as it is well-suited to co-design of materials, and is focused on the evaluation and improvement of the curriculum in order to achieve the KCI model.

Embedding Technology Scaffolds

In this study, a wiki-based environment provided technological functionality for collaborative knowledge construction as it enabled students to easily access and edit one another's ideas, reorganize pages to capture emerging themes, and link pages to establish connections between related ideas. We designed a new hybrid wiki environment to improve control over student accounts, editing permissions, and other features. Although it was important to preserve the open-ended feeling of collaborative editing that typifies wikis, it was equally important to have a simple and structured way for students to create wiki pages as a knowledge resource. The result was the development of a special web form (using the Ruby on Rails technology environment) to create new wiki pages, including the collection of metadata. Whenever students wished to create a new wiki page for a certain purpose, we created a web form that allowed them to type the name and overview of the page, as well as to provide basic metadata. This form then generated a new wiki page that was properly linked, with prespecified headers and the required authoring and access permissions. For example, in creating wiki pages about human diseases (our first topic), students would click on a link called "Add New Disease Page" that would pop up a web form as shown in Fig. 8.1. Once completed, this web form would generate a new wiki page that students could then proceed to edit in the usual fashion (i.e., using the normal wiki editing).

Participants

The co-design team included two biology teachers from the participating high school, two researchers, and occasional participation from the school principal, vice principal of curriculum, as well as the school technology coordinators. Student

Fig. 8.1 "New Disease Page" script

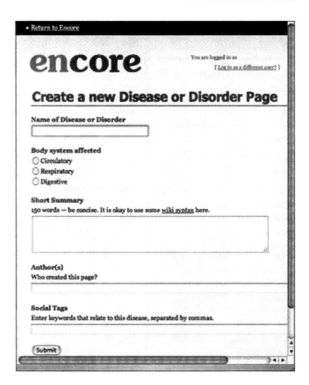

participants included 102 grade-ten students who were distributed into four sections of an intermediate-level biology class (two sections per teacher).

Design

Our co-design team held weekly meetings over a period of 4 months to develop the curriculum. During these meetings, we used our own wiki space to record minutes and document the evolving curriculum. Along the way, the teachers learned about the various theoretical ideas underlying KCI, and the researchers learned about the specific content and assessment requirements for the grade-ten biology curriculum. The result was a 1-week lesson on human diseases that fit within a larger unit on internal systems and regulation. The course syllabus allocated 40 h of class time to this unit; approximately 20 of these hours were spent covering the KCI curriculum.

All four biology classes completed the human disease lesson, which began with a knowledge construction activity where students were sorted into three groups for different human body systems (circulatory, respiratory, and digestive). Students could choose to specialize in any disease or disorder that interested them, provided it was within their assigned system. Students then formed small groups based on their shared interests in a disease or disorder, discussing amongst themselves what they already knew or had heard about their disease. Using wireless laptops (one for every two students), these same groups then created a wiki-based "Disease page" using our customized New Page script, which was presented to students as a web link within the wiki.

After the new page had been created using the New Page script (e.g., the "Pleural Effusion" disease of the respiratory system), it was accessible to all students from all four sections of the class. These disease pages comprised the knowledge base that would be used in later inquiry activities. Figure 8.2 displays the top portion of the Pleural Effusion page. Because there were four class sections of students working on these pages, they were ultimately quite well-developed with links to many outside web sites, images, and resources.

If students from the second class section (i.e., ones that met after the first class had already started creating disease pages) wanted to specialize in a disease or disorder that was already in the wiki, they were instructed to continue working on the same page rather than start a new one. This avoided redundant entries in the wiki, and helped cultivate a sense of community among the four classes. Students in the third and fourth classes contributed to the wiki in the same fashion, resulting in a single knowledge repository that would later be used by all 102 students. In this way, students from the four class sections were able to divide up the

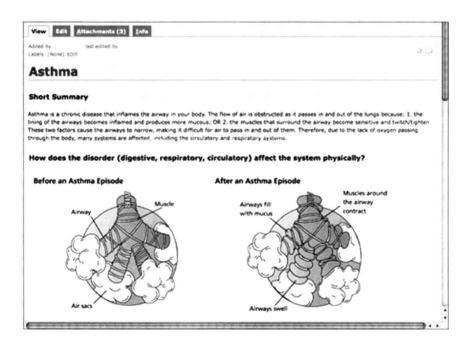

Fig. 8.2 A respiratory disease page

knowledge base into three main areas (respiratory, circulatory, and digestive diseases) for which they created and jointly edited all the major diseases. Of course, this meant that students who had specialized in one of the disease areas would not be familiar with diseases from the other two, but this was an intentional element of the design, and presumed to be one of its strengths. The teachers instructed students that they would need to "do a good job creating their disease pages, and to trust that their peers were doing the same," as they would need to rely on one another's work in subsequent activities.

After the knowledge base was constructed, we engaged students in a scaffolded inquiry activity where they were encouraged to use their peers' work in an authentic and purposeful way. This activity took the form of a "Challenge Case," which involved creating a fictitious case study of a patient who presents a number of symptoms to their physician for a diagnosis. Students created challenge cases for the same disease or disorder they had worked on when creating the knowledge base, but then solved the challenge cases created by their peers. To engage students with the wider community resource, they were instructed to choose a case that was not in the same area as the disease for which they had created a wiki page (i.e., if a student created a wiki page about a respiratory disease, they had to solve a challenge case involving either the circulatory or digestive systems).

Analysis and Findings

In evaluating the validity of the curriculum, in terms of adhering to the KCI model, we asked the following questions: Did students actively participate in constructing a community knowledge resource? Did students rely on the knowledge base to conduct the scaffolded inquiry activities? Did the curriculum cover the required biology content? Did students engage deeply in the activities, and did they demonstrate conceptual understanding of the science topics? We were also interested in students' and teachers' experiences with the curriculum, including the teachers' perceptions of the co-design process.

We found that the curriculum was successful in engaging students in coauthoring a community knowledge resource. Between the four classes, students created 23 comprehensive wiki pages about diseases of the three body systems, with an average of four authors and 15 revisions per page (see Fig. 8.3). Each of these pages was run through Copyscape©, a web-based utility that compares web pages to check for instances of plagiarism. From all 102 students and nearly 500-page revisions, there were four instances of plagiarism that warranted concern. When solving their challenge cases, students did indeed use their peers' disease pages as the primary resource. The researchers had wondered whether students might prefer to use just Google when solving the challenge cases, but classroom observations and web logs revealed that they almost universally relied upon their community resource base – presumably because it was so directly relevant to the inquiry domain.

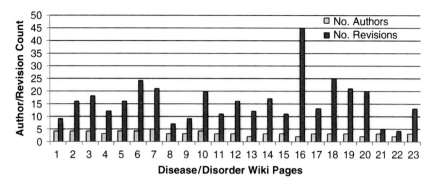

Fig. 8.3 Disease/disorder wiki pages: authors and revisions

Both of the teachers felt the wiki lesson helped students develop deeper understandings of how the three internal systems interconnect, which was an important
learning objective in the curriculum. On the final exam, students were able to make
connections between diseases of the three body systems (such as why hemophiliacs
are more susceptible to respiratory illness). One of the teachers, Patricia, described
how the curriculum addressed the content standards: "When I was doing my mark-
ing, I was actually pretty surprised… with this lesson they definitely covered the
[Canadian Education] Ministry content, and they ended up learning a lot more
about how the different physiological systems interact." One student, Cynthia,
described her understanding of blood clots in a poststudy interview:

> Well, I thought it was interesting to learn how many different diseases are connected to the
> blood – from sickle cell anemia to missing proteins that cause hemophilia since the blood
> can't clot properly. The wiki stuff we did showed me how fragile our body is, but also how
> well it can adapt to problems.

To gauge student achievement, we compared the students' exam scores with those
of students from the previous 2 years, who received the regular human disease
curriculum that consisted of lectures and a lab (Table 8.1). To control for differ-
encs in teaching style, we only used classes that had the same teacher for each of
the three academic years. We compared the performance of these three groups on
the physiology section of the final exam, which used similar open-ended questions in all 3 years (e.g., a question might ask students to describe how a disease
in one body system affected the biological processes of another). An analysis of
variance was conducted to compare the mean scores among the three groups.
Those who participated in the wiki lesson had higher physiology scores than
students who had been taught with the regular curriculum (Fig. 8.4). This difference was significant, with a value of $F(2,96)=7.236$, $p=0.001$, $\eta^2=0.13$. The
scores on the remainder of the final exam (i.e., with the physiology section
excluded) did not differ significantly across the 3 years. This suggests that there
were no baseline differences, for example, in the student populations, or the difficulty
of exams overall.

Table 8.1 Means and standard deviations of final exam scores for physiology curriculum

Biology final exam	Mean	SD
2004–2005		
Physiology section	82.65	12.86
Rest of exam	68.18	7.58
2005–2006		
Physiology section	83.35	13.84
Rest of exam	66.54	5.95
2006–2007		
Physiology section	91.60	8.58
Rest of exam	67.24	6.68

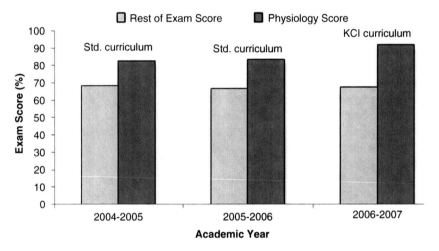

Fig. 8.4 Students' final exam scores

When interviewed, both teachers indicated that they felt positive about the experience, which had been time-consuming, but that the workload had not been too overwhelming. However, Laura did admit feeling apprehensive before beginning the unit, and expressed her concern about not covering all the required material:

> We weren't going to do [the activity] just for the sake of doing it. We're very much classroom teachers. If it's not going to help the kids learn really well, we're not interested in it. But it worked. I mean, we put a lot of time into negotiating things, but I think it ended up being a really good quality lesson.

Overall, the teachers felt the KCI human disease curriculum was a good use of class time, they were able to obtain the required assessments, and addressed all subject content expectations. The co-design team agreed to plan another unit for grade-ten students the following year, which would be our second iteration of the curriculum.

Evaluating Our Success with KCI

Although the first implementation of the KCI curriculum was encouraging, a number of problems became apparent after reviewing the students' work. During the challenge case activity, students used their community resource (the repository of wiki pages) to solve their case studies. However, when doing so, they did not engage with the material with any depth. Students consulted each other's disease pages to arrive at a diagnosis, but they did not extend the ideas any further, nor did they synthesize the material. Thus, the lesson did not fully achieve an important objective of the KCI model: to engage students in making interconnections between their ideas in the scaffolded inquiry activities and the content of the community knowledge base. We suspected that future versions of the curriculum would need to make such connections more explicit by scaffolding students' collaborative processes, and engaging them more deeply with their peers' work.

The assessment of the curriculum was also a concern for students. In a poststudy interview, a number of students expressed disappointment that the disease pages were not formally graded, and felt that their efforts should have been rewarded. Several students also expressed annoyance at not receiving more explicit and direct instructions when creating their disease pages. In the words of one student:

> I thought we were going to get a rubric for this assignment that we did, why didn't we get a rubric? All we got were a few comments about what to include in the wiki – how are we supposed to know what to write without a rubric? And the whole wiki thing was worth 5% of our final grade – that's a lot, considering we were only given two class periods to work on it.

Collectively, the findings from the first implementation of the KCI model illustrated areas in which the curriculum needed improvement. A number of refinements were required to meet the researchers' objectives, including more integration with the activities into the existing curriculum. To achieve this, the next iteration of the curriculum would need to be longer, with activities that could be formally assessed.

Study 2: Canadian Biodiversity

Encouraged by the results of the first study, the co-design team developed a new KCI curriculum in the following school term with a new cohort of 114 grade-ten biology students, in four separate classes. The co-design team remained the same, with one additional science teacher joining the group (one of the teachers from the first study taught two classes, the other two teachers each taught one). The school principal and vice principal also attended a small number of the co-design meetings; they felt our research partnership complemented the strategic vision for the school, which included more integration of technology into the curriculum. The topic of this second curriculum was Canadian Biodiversity, and included a section on Practices for Sustainable Living. The KCI portion of the curriculum was approximately 60 h, or 8 weeks of class time, interspersed over the duration of the broader 14-week unit.

Design

The teacher of each of the four biology classes began the unit by placing students into one of eight Canadian biome groups. Working in these groups, students were free to choose a geographical region from Canada for which they would create a wiki "Ecozone Page" (Fig. 8.5). A New Page script, similar to the one used in the previous iteration, was designed to create ecozone pages with a structure that linked to the curriculum standards (e.g., with headers for the eubacteria and archeabacteria in the ecozone). Students across the four classes contributed to this wiki repository, adding to and editing their peers' ecozone pages. Again, the four classes created a single knowledge repository that would be used by all 114 students for subsequent activities. Over the 8-week unit, students were given a total of six full class periods to complete their ecozone pages, with unfinished pages assigned as homework.

In small groups, students then created a "Biodiversity Issue" page, which described a problem or issue that was threatening their ecozone. Students were able to draw on the expertise they had gained from building their ecozone page to create a detailed description of the causes and implications of the issue. We designed another New Page script (Fig. 8.6), that specified the expected content, in the form of headers with small, italicized instructional prompts, to be included in the Biodiversity Issue page (e.g., discussing the protista, fungi, and plantae of an ecozone). Since ecozones overlap geographically, students were asked to make

Fig. 8.5 Temperate forest ecozone page

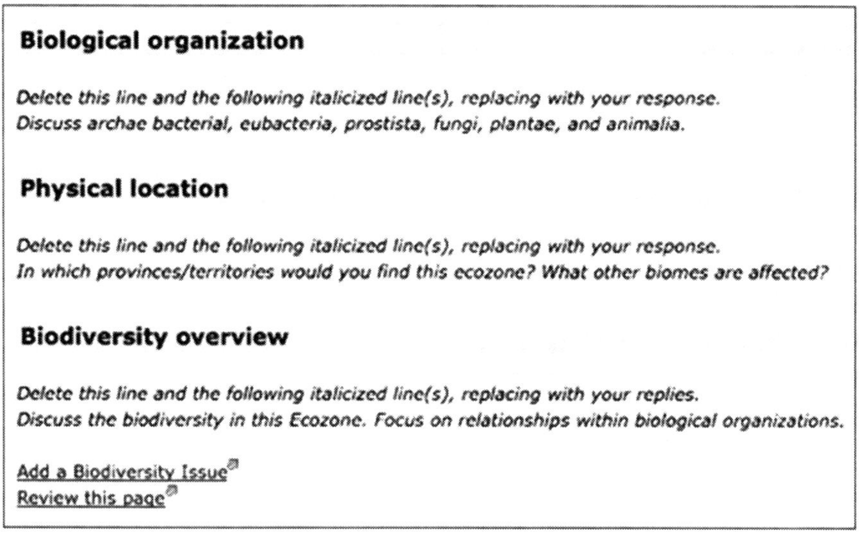

Biological organization

Delete this line and the following italicized line(s), replacing with your response.
Discuss archae bacterial, eubacteria, prostista, fungi, plantae, and animalia.

Physical location

Delete this line and the following italicized line(s), replacing with your response.
In which provinces/territories would you find this ecozone? What other biomes are affected?

Biodiversity overview

Delete this line and the following italicized line(s), replacing with your replies.
Discuss the biodiversity in this Ecozone. Focus on relationships within biological organizations.

Add a Biodiversity Issue[⌐]
Review this page[⌐]

Fig. 8.6   Specified biology content in a New Page script

connections between regions, including how the biological factors of one ecozone can influence the biology of another. Students were also asked to include links to their peers' wiki pages that they referenced, embedded in a description of how the content was related.

In the second iteration, an increased effort was given to ensure the activities reflected the voice of the student community. To this end, a "critical juncture" phase was added to capture students' interests and incorporate them into the KCI curriculum. After the Biodiversity Issue pages were completed, the researchers and teachers met to review the content and identify students' interests as represented in their wiki pages. The team identified five major themes: habitat loss and destruction, invasive species, climate change, pollution, and the demands of growing urban populations. These five themes became the topic for the final phase of the curriculum: a scaffolded inquiry activity where students produced an individual research proposal.

The purpose of the individual research proposal was to encourage students to make real-world connections among the ideas and concepts presented in the knowledge base (the ecozone and biodiversity issue pages), including the implications for Canada and their local school community. The teachers asserted that the activity would need to be an individual one so students would have the opportunity to receive an individual grade within the biodiversity unit. In their research proposal, students were asked to outline a current environmental problem in Canada, including a detailed plan of how to address and remedy the situation. Students were asked to connect their proposals to as many ecozone and biodiversity issue pages as possible, including links to all referenced pages. A final New Page script was developed to specify the aspects that should be included in their proposal: project summary, biodiversity impacts, biodiversity specifications, and possible root cause of the problem.

Analysis and Findings

Once again, we evaluated our curriculum in terms of its success in implementing the KCI model. Did students create a rich community knowledge base? Was the knowledge base important to their inquiry tasks? Was the inquiry guided by the emergent themes within the knowledge base? Similar sources of data were available for this iteration as for the previous one: student wiki pages, final research projects, and performance on the final exams, as well as interviews of students and teachers.

The second KCI curriculum was successful in engaging students in the creation of a coauthored resource base. Altogether, students created 36 biome and ecozone pages, the majority of these had three or four contributing authors (Fig. 8.7). Although students actively edited their disease pages in the physiology curriculum, they were much more engaged with revisions in the Biodiversity unit. More class time dedicated to the wiki and a longer unit overall resulted in more edits to the wiki. Interested to find out what kind of edits students were making, we created an algorithm that calculated changes made to the text of a wiki page (i.e., words that were either added, deleted, or changed). For each page revision (each time a page was opened and saved), there was an average of 74 word edits. A significant positive correlation between the number of word edits and page revisions ($r(35)=0.90$, $p < 0.0001$) suggests that students were actively authoring content throughout the

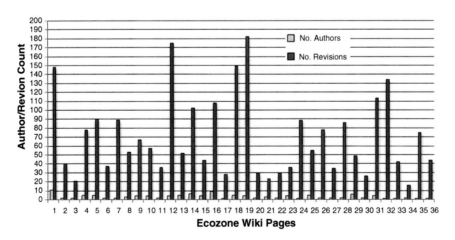

Fig. 8.7 Ecozone pages: authors and revisions

Biodiversity unit, rather than just formatting their wiki or working on the aesthetics. Asked, mid-study, about her thoughts on creating a wiki as part of her Biodiversity unit, Lily, commented:

> It was just a more interactive, more fun way to do [the unit] instead of just getting the notes. Because that's what we usually do for pretty much every unit. We have the projector up and it's just notes that we copy down.

Unlike the disease pages from first study, students were told that their ecozone pages would be formally evaluated. Although this likely provided students with some added incentive, it also appeared to be a cause of frustration, especially since they were not provided with a detailed grading rubric beforehand. One student, Teresa explained her frustration as follows:

> There should have been a restriction on length. If the wiki had to be a certain length, say 5 pages or something, then everybody would do 5 pages and it would have been fine. But since nobody knew how much to do, well, the overachievers went and did like 10 pages, and then everybody else freaked and did 10 pages, then the overachievers would do, like, 10 more pages. So no matter how hard you work, you were never done!

Still, the efforts students put into their ecozone pages appeared to have positive effects on their learning. Using the same teacher's two classes, we performed a correlation test on the relationship between students' exam scores and their ecozone page evaluation score. Student work on the ecozone pages were evaluated in terms of the specific biology content that was included in the wiki. Ecozone pages that included the content specified in the New Page script were awarded higher grades. The teacher also assessed the pages for accuracy and completeness. We found a significant positive correlation between the Ecozone Page scores and the biodiversity exam scores ($r(49) = 0.39$, $p < 0.0036$).

As we did in the first study, we compared students' final exam scores with those of students from the previous 2 years. Again, we compared only students who had the same teacher in all 3 years (Table 8.2). Again, there was a significant difference among all 3 years between the mean scores of the biodiversity section of the final exam $F(2, 113) = 7.133$, $p = 0.001$, $\eta^2 = 0.11$ (Fig. 8.8). The scores on the remainder of the final exam (i.e., with the biodiversity section excluded) did not improve across the 3-year span.

Table 8.2 Means and standard deviations of final exam scores for biodiversity curriculum

Biology final exam	Mean	SD
2005–2006		
Biodiversity section	85.57	9.37
Rest of exam	81.55	9.19
2006–2007		
Biodiversity section	83.83	17.28
Rest of exam	83.44	6.94
2007–2008		
Biodiversity section	92.93	7.98
Rest of exam	79.69	8.80

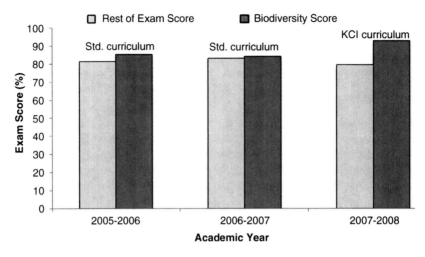

Fig. 8.8 Students' biodiversity exam scores

In the final interviews, we were interested in learning about students' perspectives of the learning process with the KCI curriculum, particularly in terms of the wiki component. Although some students expressed a sense of competition when working on their ecozone pages, others enjoyed being able to see what their peers had produced. In Alice's words:

> I kinda liked looking at other peoples' wiki pages, I thought that was a good exercise because it kind of trained you to assess how other people convey their information and you kind of just got more ideas about how you could improve your page as well, and it was good to just be able to think about it and give people constructive criticism. I don't know, I just thought that part was neat.

Another student, Jocelyn, described her ecozone page as an ongoing artifact, even though she had finished her assignments for the Biodiversity unit. Instead, she described how she felt compelled to keep updating her work. She explains:

> I don't think the wiki was a one-time thing where you're like, 'oh, I'm finished and I can stop working on it.' Like, I know for me, I'd have to go back and edit it once and a while because I'd come across some new piece of information or I'd read something and I'm like, 'oh well, I have to edit something back on my page,' or something like that. So it ended up being a really long-term thing – I even worked on it way after it was due.

We also interviewed the school vice principal, who oversees curriculum development in consultation with the subject department heads. For the researchers, part of the value of the KCI model is its flexibility in terms of subject matter and teacher enactment. Since the co-design approach ensures that teachers are deeply involved in the design of the materials, they can essentially take over when time comes to enact the curriculum. As teachers become more involved in co-design, their understanding of and familiarity with the researcher's pedagogical model (in this case, KCI) becomes more secure. It was this aspect of co-design that the school vice principal alluded to in his interview:

> The important thing for me is if we're going to introduce a new intervention or technology, then it needs to be sustainable. Because in the beginning I think the researchers have more expertise in terms of the technology, but now our teachers are getting there, too. They're more confident and comfortable using it, and now they're enabled to a point where they can do a new curriculum and sustain it, and share it with their colleagues. If this falls apart because it's totally dependent on the researchers to make it work, then there's not much value in it for us.

Design Challenges and Recommendations

After completing the second iteration, we had the opportunity to reflect on the different implementations of the KCI curriculum. We noticed there were a number of difficulties with the Biodiversity curriculum that we did not have in the first study with the Human Physiology unit. For example, the extended knowledge construction activity from the 8-week curriculum was somewhat problematic. In the Physiology unit, students' work on the disease pages was limited to two class periods over the course of a week. In the Biodiversity unit, students worked on their ecozone and biodiversity issue pages for over 8 weeks, with some students working over the December break. These knowledge construction activities dominated the second curriculum considerably, leaving comparatively little time for the final activity, the individual research proposal. Many students felt overburdened with the amount of time it took to create their community resource. Since there was a considerable amount of detailed information in their wiki pages, students were also worried about having to memorize the content for their final exam. The teachers quelled their concerns by posting messages on the class list serve, but they too had apprehensions about the wiki pages, in terms of the time it would take to grade them. To address these issues, the next iteration of the curriculum will combine the Biodiversity Issue activity with the Individual Research Proposal to alleviate some of the wiki work and lessen the time constraints for both teachers and students. In general, KCI curriculum designs must guard against demanding too much authoring from students, and must be cautious about the amount of curriculum time they demand of teachers.

We also noted the potential for improving the designs of scaffolded inquiry. In the Biodiversity curriculum, we provided students with a starter page with some appropriate headers and hints for their research proposal. However, it would be more desirable to engage students with a series of steps for reflecting about their proposal topic, searching for resources, exchanging ideas with peers, and developing several versions of the proposal. This sequence of activities could involve a number of distinct inquiry steps and various tools, including concept mapping tools and collaborative groups. Of course, this would further add to the complexity of the design and would need to be balanced in terms of the workload for students and teachers.

We noticed the co-design approach was more challenging during the second iteration of the curriculum. This was largely due to the number of co-design meetings that were required throughout the design process, which proved to be too much for the teachers. Although we had the experience of the Human Physiology curriculum behind us, the Biodiversity unit still required ongoing co-design meetings through its implementation. Adding a third teacher only contributed to the difficulty of scheduling meetings during the school term. Since the teachers had varied school schedules, it was difficult to find meeting times during the day when no teacher was in a classroom. Meetings that took place over the lunch hour were often interrupted by students, or were truncated so that teachers could use the time for grading or preparing for their next class. In a poststudy interview, one of the teachers, Laura, described her experience of the co-design meetings as follows:

> It was really hard to make the meetings. Really hard. There had to be an outside force telling me we need to meet. And it had to be me saying if we don't meet, I'm shafting somebody's research. And so many times I was dragging my heels thinking, 'I have so many more important things to do.' But those meeting were really important. And they were essential to making this work.

In both iterations of the KCI curriculum, researchers as well as teachers had hoped to make productive use of the wiki data logs (i.e., for analysis and assessment). One of the advantages of a wiki is that it preserves all saved versions in a historical archive. Any previous version can easily be restored, along with users' editing activity. Such functionality has the potential for providing teachers with a powerful tool for assessing group work, and is the kind of tool our teachers expressed an interest in employing. In previous studies, researchers have used data logs to create visualizations for quantifying students' individual wiki contributions (Kay, Yacef, & Reimann, 2007) and for facilitating navigation and content flow (Ullman & Kay, 2007). Still, the voluminous data generated by web logs can be quite daunting, and more research is required before teachers can use such sources to assess the quality of students' wiki contributions. We are currently engaged in efforts to design analytic tools for such purposes.

Conclusion

This chapter provides the first empirical support for the Knowledge Community and Inquiry model. The work reported here demonstrates that the model can result in effective designs that engage students in a knowledge community, while also enabling structured inquiry activities that address content expectations. The co-design process was also confirmed as an effective approach, as it provided an engaging experience for the researchers and teachers, and resulted in two iterations of successful design. It is worth noting that this kind of curriculum is a rare event in research or classroom practice, where four students in different sections of a class collaborate together to create a useful knowledge resource, and then separately work on technology-enhanced inquiry projects that draw upon that resource. It was felt by the teachers and researchers that this project had positive outcomes, and that students had learned in ways that none of us had experienced before.

The teachers' commitment to the KCI curriculum was essential for ensuring that students were engaged with the materials and actively participating. This commitment also enabled them to adopt new methods of knowledge construction and collaborative inquiry, which were supported by a technology (i.e., the wiki) that was new to the teachers. These teachers responded enthusiastically to the new methods, and are currently engaged in designing a new global climate curriculum that is yet another iteration of the model. Further, they continue to enact the physiology and biodiversity units, which are now a core part of their curriculum. This study demonstrates that knowledge community methods can be successfully designed for high school science classrooms, and provides support for the KCI model as an effective mechanism for embedding such methods into curriculum activities. This work thus responds to an ongoing challenge of how to make community-based learning activities and scaffolded inquiry more relevant for secondary teachers, and opens up possible avenues for future research and theoretical models.

Acknowledgments The authors gratefully acknowledge the support provided by the Social Sciences and Humanities Research Council of Canada (SSHRC).

References

Aguiton, C. & Cardon, D. (2007). The strength of weak cooperation: An attempt to understand the meaning of Web 2.0. *Communication & Strategies, 65*(1), 51–65.

Alexander, B. (2006). Web 2.0: A new wave of innovation for teaching and learning? *EDUCAUSE Review, 41*(2), 32–44.

Becker, H. (1999). *Internet use by teachers.* Irvine, CA: Center for Research on Information Technology and Organizations, University of California. Retrieved December 28, 2008 from http://www.crito.uci.edu/TLC/FINDINGS/internet-use/.

Bell, P. (2004). On the theoretical breadth of design-based research in education. *Educational Psychologist, 39*(4), 243–253.

Bell, P., Davis, E. A., & Linn, M. C. (1995). The knowledge integration environment: Theory and design. *Proceedings of the Computer Supported Collaborative Learning Conference (CSCL '95)* (pp. 14-21). Mahwah, NJ: Lawrence Erlbaum.

Bereiter, C. & Scardamalia, M. (1989). Intentional learning as a goal of instruction. In L. B. Resnick (Ed.), *Knowing, learning, and instruction: Essays in honor of Robert Glaser* (pp. 361–392). Hillsdale, NJ: Lawrence Erlbaum.

Bereiter, C. & Scardamalia, M. (1996). Rethinking learning. In D. R. Olson & N. Torrance (Eds.), *The Handbook of education and human development: New models of learning, teaching and schooling* (pp. 485–513). Cambridge, MA: Basil Blackwell.

Bielaczyc, K. (2006). Designing social infrastructure: Critical issues in creating learning environments with technology. *Journal of the Learning Sciences, 13*(3), 301–329.

Blumenfeld, P., Fishman, B. J., Krajcik, J., Marx, R. W., & Soloway, S. (2000). Creating usable innovations in systemic reform: Scaling up technology-embedded project-based science in urban schools. *Educational Psychologist, 35*(3), 149–164.

Borko, H. & Putnam, R. T. (1995). Expanding a teacher's knowledge base: A cognitive psychological perspective on professional development. In T. R. Guskey & M. Huberman (Eds.), *Professional development in education: New paradigms and practices* (pp. 35–65). New York: Teachers College Press.

Bransford, J. D., Brown, A. L., & Cocking, R. R. (eds). (2000). *How people learn: Brain, mind, experience, and school*. Washington, DC: National Academy Press.

Brown, A. L. (1992). Design experiments: Theoretical and methodological challenges in creating complex interventions in classroom settings. *Journal of the Learning Sciences, 2*(2), 141–178.

Brown, A. L. & Campione, J. (1996). Psychological theory and the design of innovative learning environments: On procedures, principles, and systems. In L. Schauble & R. Glaser (Eds.), *Innovations in learning: New environments for education* (pp. 289–325). Mahwah, NJ: Erlbaum.

Brown, A. L. & Palincsar, A. (1989). Guided, cooperative learning and individual knowledge acquisition. In L. B. Resnick (Ed.), *Knowing, learning and instruction: Essays in honor of Robert Glaser* (pp. 393–451). Hillsdale, NJ: Lawrence Erlbaum.

Bryant, S., Forte, A., & Bruckman, A. (2005). Becoming wikipedian: Transformation of participation in a collaborative online encyclopedia. *Proceedings of GROUP International Conference on Supporting Group Work* (pp. 1-10), Sanibel Island, FL.

Collins, A. (1999). The changing infrastructure of educational research. In E. C. Lagemann & L. S. Shulman (Eds.), *Issues in education research: Problems and possibilities* (pp. 289–298). San Francisco: Jossey-Bass.

Collins, A., Joseph, D., & Bielaczyc, K. (2004). Design research: Theoretical and methodological issues. *Journal of the Learning Sciences, 13*(1), 15–42.

Cuban, L. (2001). *Oversold and underused: Computers in the classroom*. Cambridge, MA: Harvard University Press.

Cuban, L. & Usdan, M. (Eds). (2003). *Introduction: Learning from the past. In Powerful reforms with shallow roots: Improving America's urban schools* (pp. 1–15). New York: Teachers College Press.

diSessa, A. A. (2000). *Changing minds: Computers, learning, and literacy*. Cambridge, MA: MIT Press.

diSessa, A. A. & Cobb, P. (2004). Ontological innovation and the role of theory in design experiments. *Journal of the Learning Sciences, 13*(1), 77–103.

Drucker, P. F. (1959). *Landmarks of tomorrow*. New York: Harper & Brothers.

Edelson, D. C. (2002). Design research: What we learn when we engage in design. *Journal of the Learning Sciences, 11*(1), 105–121.

Edelson, D. C., Gordin, D. N., & Pea, R. D. (1999). Addressing the challenges of inquiry-based learning through technology and curriculum design. *Journal of the Learning Sciences, 8*(3/4), 391–450.

Gardner, H. (2004). Discipline, understanding, and community. *Journal of Curriculum Studies, 36*(2), 233–236.

Glenman, T. K. & Melmed, A. (2000). Challenges of creating a nation of technology-enabled schools. In R. Pea (Ed.), *Technology and learning* (pp. 48–79). San Francisco: Jossey-Bass.

Guzdial, M. (1998). *Collaborative websites to support an authoring community on the web*. Retrieved November 23, 2008 from http://guzdial.cc.gatech.edu/papers/.

Hakkarainen, K. (2004). Pursuit of explanation within a computer-supported classroom. *International Journal of Science Education, 26*(8), 979–996.

Hoadley, C. M. (2004). Methodological alignment in design-based research. *Educational Psychologist, 39*(4), 203–212.

Kay, J., Yacef, K., & Reimann, P. (2007). Visualisations for team learning: small teams working on long-term projects. In C. Chinn, G. Erkens & S. Puntambekar (Eds.), *Minds, mind, and society. Proceedings of the 6th International Conference on Computer-supported Collaborative Learning (CSCL 2007)* (pp. 351-353). New Brunswick, NJ: International Society of the Learning Sciences.

Kling, R. & Courtright, C. (2003). Group behavior and learning in electronic forums: A sociotechnical approach. *The Information Society, 19*(3), 221–235.

Krajcik, J. S., Blumenfeld, P. C., Marx, R. W., & Soloway, E. (1994). A collaborative model for helping science teachers learn project-based instruction. *Elementary School Journal, 94*(5), 483–497.

Linn, M. C. & Eylon, B. S. (2006). Science education: Integrating views of learning and instruction. In P. A. Alexander & P. H. Winne (Eds.), *Handbook of educational psychology* (2nd ed., pp. 511–544). Mahwah, NJ: Lawrence Erlbaum.

Linn, M. C. & Hsi, S. (2000). *Computers, teachers, peers: Science learning partners.* Mahwah, NJ: Lawrence Erlbaum.

O'Reilly, T. (2007). What is Web 2.0: Design patterns and business models for the next generation of software. *Communications & Strategies, 65*(1), 17–21. Available at SSRN: http://ssrn.com/abstract=1008839.

Palincsar, A. S. (1998). Social constructivist perspectives on teaching and learning. *Annual Review of Psychology, 49*, 345–375.

Papert, S., & Harel, I. (1991). *Situating constructionism* (pp. 1–11). New York: Ablex Publishing.

Papert, S. (2000). Computers and computer cultures. In R. Pea (Ed.), *Technology and learning* (pp. 229–246). San Francisco: Jossey-Bass.

Penuel, W. R., Roschelle, J., & Shechtman, N. (2007). Designing formative assessment software with teachers: An analysis of the co-design process. *Research and Practice in Technology Enhanced Learning, 2*(1), 51–74.

Penuel, W. R., Fishman, B. J., Gallagher, L. P., Korbak, C., & Prado-Lopez, B. (2008). The mediating role of coherence in curriculum implementation. *Proceedings of the Biennial International Conference of the Learning Sciences (ICLS)*. Utrecht, The Netherlands: International Society of the Learning Sciences, Inc.

Peters, V. L., & Slotta, J. D. (2008). Building wiki-based pedagogical scripts for knowledge communities. *International Perspectives in the Learning Sciences: Cre8ing a learning world. Proceedings of the Eighth International Conference for the Learning Sciences – ICLS 2008* (pp. 237-244). Utrecht, The Netherlands: International Society of the Learning Sciences, Inc.

Quintana, C., Reiser, B. J., Davis, E. A., Krajcik, J., Fretz, E., Duncan, R. G., et al. (2004). A scaffolding design framework for software to support science inquiry. *Journal of the Learning Sciences, 13*(3), 337–386.

Reiser, B. J., Tabak, I., Sandoval, W. A., Smith, B. K., Steinmuller, F., & Leone, A. J. (2001). BGuILE: Strategic and conceptual scaffolds for scientific inquiry in biology classrooms. In S. M. Carver & D. Klahr (Eds.), *Cognition and instruction: Twenty-five years of progress* (pp. 263–305). Mahwah, NJ: Lawrence Erlbaum.

Rico, S. A. & Shulman, J. H. (2004). Invertebrates and organ systems: Science instruction and 'Fostering a Community of Learners'. *Journal of Curriculum Studies, 36*(2), 159–181.

Roschelle, J., Knudsen, J., & Hegedus, S. (2010). From new technological infrastructures to curricular activity systems: Advanced designs for teaching and learning. In M. J. Jacobson & P. Reimann (Eds.), *Designs for learning environments of the future.* Springer.

Roschelle, J., Penuel, W. R., & Shechtman, N. (2006). Co-design of innovations with teachers: Definition and dynamics. *Proceedings of the Biennial International Conference of the Learning Sciences* (pp. 606-612), Bloomington, IN.

Scardamalia, M. (2000). Social and technological innovations for a knowledge society. In S. Young, J. Greer, H. Maurer, & Y. S. Chee (Eds.), *Proceedings of the ICCE/ICCAI 2000: Volume 1. Learning Societies in the New Millennium: Creativity, Caring & Commitments* (pp. 22–27). Taipei, Taiwan: National Tsing Hua University.

Scardamalia, M. & Bereiter, C. (1996). Adaptation and understanding: A case for new cultures of schooling. In S. Vosniadou, E. de Corte, R. Glaser & H. Mandl (Eds.), *International perspectives on the design of technology: Supported learning environments* (pp. 149–163). Mahwah, NJ: Lawrence Erlbaum.

Scardamalia, M. & Bereiter, C. (1991). Higher levels of agency for children in knowledge building: A challenge for the design of new knowledge media. *Journal of the Learning Sciences, 1*(1), 37–68.

Scardamalia, M., & Bereiter, C. (2003). Knowledge building. In *Encyclopedia of education* (2nd ed., pp. 1370–1373). New York: Macmillan Reference.

Schmidt, W. H., McKnight, C. C., & Raizen, S. A. (1997). *A splintered vision: An investigation of U.S. science and mathematics education.* Norwell, MA: Kluwer Academic Publishers.

Slotta, J. D. (2007). Supporting collaborative inquiry: New architectures, new opportunities. In J. Gobert (Chair), Fostering peer collaboration with technology. *Symposium conducted at the biennial Computer Supported Collaborative Learning (CSCL) Conference,* New Brunswick, NJ.

Slotta, J. D. (2004). The Web-based inquiry science environment (WISE): Scaffolding knowledge integration in the science classroom. In M. C. Linn, P. Bell & E. Davis (Eds.), *Internet environments for science education* (pp. 203–232). Mahwah, NJ: Lawrence Erlbaum Associates.

Slotta, J. D. & Linn, M. C. (2009). *WISE science: Web-based inquiry in the classroom.* New York: Teachers College Press.

Slotta, J. D., & Peters, V. L. (2008). A blended model for knowledge communities: Embedding scaffolded inquiry. *International Perspectives in the Learning Sciences: Cre8ing a learning world. Proceedings of the Eighth International Conference for the Learning Sciences – ICLS 2008* (pp. 343-350). Utrecht, The Netherlands: International Society of the Learning Sciences, Inc.

Songer, N. B. (2006) BioKIDS: An animated conversation on the development of curricular activity structures for inquiry science. In R. Keith Sawyer (Ed.), *Cambridge Handbook of the Learning Sciences* (pp. 355–369). New York: Cambridge University Press.

Surowiecki, J. (2004). *The wisdom of crowds: Why the many are smarter than the few and how collective wisdom shapes business, economies, societies and nations.* New York: Anchor Books.

Tyack, D. & Cuban, L. (1995). *Tinkering toward utopia.* Cambridge, MA: Harvard University Press.

Ullman, A. J., & Kay, J. (2007). WikiNavMap: A visualisation to supplement team-based wikis. *Proceedings of the Conference on Human Factors in Computing Systems: CHI '07 extended abstracts on human factors in computing systems* (pp. 2711–2716). New York: ACM Press.

Ullrich, C., Borau, K., Luo, H., Tan, X., Shen, L., & Shen, R. (2008). Why Web 2.0 is good for learning and for research: Principles and prototypes. *Proceedings of the International World Wide Web Conference* (pp. 705-714), Beijing, China.

Webb, N. M. & Palincsar, A. (1996). Group processes in the classroom. In D. Berliner & R. Calfee (Eds.), *Handbook of educational psychology* (1st ed., pp. 841–873). New York: Macmillan.

Wheeler, S., Yeomans, P., & Wheeler, D. (2008). The good, the bad and the wiki: Evaluating student-generated content for collaborative learning. *British Journal of Educational Technology, 39*(6), 987–995.

Whitcomb, J. A. (2004). Dilemmas of design and predicaments of practice: Adapting the 'Fostering a Community of Learners' model in secondary school English language arts classrooms. *Journal of Curriculum Studies, 36*(2), 183–206.

White, B., Frederiksen, J., Frederiksen, T., Eslinger, E., Loper, S., & Collins, A. (2002). Inquiry island: Affordances of a multi-agent environment for scientific inquiry and reflective learning. In P. Bell, R. Stevens & T. Satwicz (Eds.), *Proceedings of the Fifth International Conference of the Learning Sciences (ICLS).* Mahwah, NJ: Erlbaum.

Chapter 9
From New Technological Infrastructures to Curricular Activity Systems: Advanced Designs for Teaching and Learning

Jeremy Roschelle, Jennifer Knudsen, and Stephen Hegedus

What is an "advanced design" of a technology for learning?

For some researchers, the word "advanced" may conjure images of the latest technology. Indeed, it is a common pattern in learning technology research to undertake design studies that investigate the learning potential of the novel technologies (Bell, Hoadley, & Linn, 2004; Barab & Squire, 2004; Dede, 2004). Often the long-term residue of this research lies in its contribution to learning theory (diSessa & Cobb, 2004; Edelson, 2002); contributions to large-scale practice tend to be short lasting and infrequently adopted (Roschelle & Jackiw, 2000).

We argue that the failure of much design research to contribute to large-scale practice emerges from a design flaw: designers fail to notice the infrastructural character of technology and form an unrealistic image of how infrastructure transforms classroom practice. We overestimate the power of technology alone and the proportion of teachers who can realize its potential without extensive guidance. Our minds too often race with thoughts of the power of technology to change classroom practice and underestimate the powerful set of forces in classrooms that conspire to marginalize technological potential (Kaput & Thompson, 1994).

In this chapter, we suggest a different meaning of "advanced design" that is arising in our long-term program of research and development within the SimCalc research program. We suggest that an "advanced design" should offer a plan for bridging the gap between new technological affordances and what most teachers need and can use. We draw attention to three different foci of design in two different SimCalc projects: (a) design of representational and communicative infrastructure (b) design of curricular activity systems, and (c) design of new classroom practices and routines.

J. Roschelle (✉) and J. Knudsen
SRI International, 333 Ravenswood Ave, Menlo Park, CA 94306, USA
e-mail: Jeremy.Roschelle@sri.com

S. Hegedus
University of Massachusetts, Dartmouth, 200 Mill Road, Fairhaven, MA 02719, USA

M.J. Jacobson and P. Reimann (eds.), *Designs for Learning Environments of the Future: International Perspectives from the Learning Sciences*, DOI 10.1007/978-0-387-88279-6_9, © Springer Science+Business Media, LLC 2010

We particularly emphasize curricular activity systems because we are finding that attention to this focus of design has been critically important in our ability to measure learning outcomes at the scale of hundreds of teachers. (Classroom practices and routines are very important too, but research has yet to reduce the vast number of free parameters to a comprehensible design space for replicable classroom practices).

Our chapter begins by briefly reviewing the mission and progress of the SimCalc research program (Roschelle, Kaput, & Stroup, 2000). An important theoretical trend in the project has been the identification of its core technological aims as "infrastructural" (Kaput, Noss, & Hoyles, 2002; Kaput & Hegedus, 2007; Kaput & Schorr, 2008). We review the meaning of this term and the implausibility of jumping from infrastructural technology to scalable, robust effects in classroom practice. We then introduce the concept of a "curricular activity system" as a design emphasis that has emerged in our work on scaling up. To illustrate these concepts, we describe two different curricular activity systems at play within the research program; each supports a different classroom realization of the SimCalc vision (and is funded as a separate project). In closing, we recommend that researchers who aspire to "advanced designs" adopt a view that allows for focused work at the infrastructural, curricular, and classroom routine levels.

About the SimCalc Research Program

The mission of the SimCalc program is to "democratize access to the mathematics of change and variation" (Kaput, 1994). In a chapter in the prior book in this series (Roschelle et al., 2000), we argued that "change" will be a central phenomena of the twenty-first century and therefore that the mathematics of change and variation will become a centrally important strand of mathematics for all students to learn. We argued that the present "layer cake" approach to the mathematics curriculum, in which these important mathematical ideas are restricted to a Calculus layer that is icing on the layer cake of high school algebra, geometry and trigonometry layers is problematic. New approaches are needed and these approaches must introduce the mathematics of change and variation earlier, taking advantage of results in the learning science and the affordances of new technology.

The main software product of the SimCalc program is called SimCalc MathWorlds® (hereon referred to as MathWorlds) and is available at http://kaputcenter.umassd.edu. MathWorlds supports learning about rate and accumulation (Roschelle & Kaput, 1996) by connecting students' experience of animated motion to mathematical functions, which are portrayed in algebraic, graphical, verbal, and tabular representations (Kaput & Roschelle, 1998). A distinctive feature of MathWorlds is that students can define piecewise linear functions graphically and then "execute" the functions resulting in observed motion in an animated "world." The characters and background in the world can contextualize students' experience within familiar experiences and can provide a setting in which mathematical phenomena have more meaning for learners.

As is the case with other "dynamic mathematics" products, such as The Geometer's Sketchpad, TinkerPlots, Fathom, and Cabri Geometre, the software design is strongly rooted in the nature of the mathematics and draws upon "direct manipulation" human–computer interaction paradigms to achieve executable, interactive visualizations of important mathematical concepts (Hegedus, Moreno, & Dalton, 2007).

Our earlier chapter (Roschelle et al., 2000) referred to the representational features of MathWorlds as emerging from a triangulation of perspectives on student learning, technological capabilities, and mathematical epistemology. From detailed development work on student learning, we focused on students' strong abilities to connect graphs to motions, their facility in reasoning intervals of time in graphs and motions, and the power of story telling to inform mathematics learning. The technical capabilities of MathWorlds include most importantly the ability to create "executable representations" (Hegedus, Moreno et al., 2007), representations that control animations and thus have easily perceived links between actions and consequence. Related to this, MathWorlds links representations dynamically ("hot links") so that when a student makes a change in one representation (e.g., increasing the slope of a position graph) they instantly see the corresponding change in another representation (e.g., the rate increases on a velocity graph). From the perspective of mathematical epistemology, the SimCalc team took an approach of "reconstructing subject matter" (Roschelle et al., 2000) – for example, by introducing piecewise functions much earlier in the curriculum, increasing the status and role of graphs (vis-à-vis more traditional algebraic symbols), and returning the phenomenology of motion to its historic place in the development of the mathematics of change and variation. Later, in the section on networked MathWorlds, we will see how these three perspectives were revisited and expanded with the incorporation of network connectivity as an infrastructural element.

The SimCalc research program and its software have been evolving over more than a decade of research, spanning at least eight major funded research projects. In order to contextualize what we have learned about "advanced design for learning technologies," it is worthwhile to recall where we began. In particular, in the early practice of SimCalc design and research, there was a rapid (one might even say feverish) interplay between levels we will soon define as separate. Jim Kaput, the project founder, might describe a new software feature to the developers one morning, write a new curricular lesson plan to exploit the feature that evening, and spontaneously engage in a new pedagogical practice with the lesson plan and feature in class the next day. When watching Jim work, it was easy to see the transformative potential of technology; Jim himself was a whirlwind of transformation that cut across his technological, curricular, and teaching practices. It goes without saying that Jim was fairly unique in this regard; it would be very unrealistic to expect most teachers to follow Jim's model. Further, because the SimCalc Project is deeply committed to scaling up, it has been important to figure out how to design for lasting and democratic access to the mathematical learning opportunities Jim so powerfully envisioned. This involved stabilization of opportunistic development without constraining the ability to generate new activities in the future. Such decision could be said to stabilize the element of the infrastructure.

Representational, Display, and Connectivity Infrastructure

As the SimCalc Project engaged with more and more teachers, Kaput and his colleagues came to articulate the role of the software as infrastructural, stating that their goal was:

> …to provide a framework that helps us to understand the gradual, manifold evolution of the roles of technology in mathematics education. The underlying idea is that changes over the long term amount to a process in which technology is gradually becoming "infrastructural." (Kaput & Hegedus, 2007, p. 173)

Their framework focused on the affordances of "ubiquitous forms of technology in schools" including graphing calculators, sensors and probes, laptop and desktop computers, and digital display technologies such as projectors. Indeed, these forms of technology are becoming fairly common in mathematics classrooms across the world. The SimCalc team also considered networking technologies to be on the cusp of becoming ubiquitous in classrooms such that teachers and students could instantly exchange mathematical objects appearing on their individual devices.

Kaput and colleagues were careful to distinguish between the raw materials and the capabilities that form an infrastructure. By analogy, roads and rails – not concrete and iron – form our transportation infrastructure. They viewed "infrastructure" as the foundational facilities needed for the functioning of a community, in this case, for the function of the classroom mathematical community. Three aspects of the technological infrastructure were highlighted (Kaput & Hegedus, 2007):

1. Representational infrastructure, which provides new ways for students to express, visualize, compute, and interact with mathematical objects.
2. Display infrastructure, which allows for both private (e.g., on a handheld) and public (e.g., projected) views of mathematical representations.
3. Connectivity infrastructure, which allows for rapid communication of mathematical objects among classroom participants and supports operations that distribute, collect, and aggregate student work.

Over time, new capabilities were added to MathWorlds software to integrate these three aspects. These capabilities assume that the students have a personal display and the teacher has a projected display. The new connectivity features of MathWorlds (Hegedus & Kaput, 2003; Kaput & Hegedus, 2002; Hegedus, Dalton, Moniz, & Roschelle, 2007) give teachers flexible capabilities to:

- Set up a classroom roster and cluster students into groups.
- Distribute a configured document to students, giving them a particular "setup" for an activity.
- Control which mathematical functions and representations can be viewed and edited by participants on their handheld or laptop devices.
- Collect (or have students submit) their work to the teacher's machine.

- Hide and show student contributions on the public display, often in meaningful clusters (e.g., by group or by the role in a group).
- Yield control of the main display to a particular students' device.

Each of these infrastructure elements is important because of its deep linkage to the architecture of learning. Display infrastructure is essential for creating shared attention to mathematical objects, and shared attention is a precondition for learning in any social setting, such as a classroom (Barron, 2000). Representational infrastructure is important because how people think (cognition) and come to know (epistemology) are deeply conditioned by the available representations (Kaput, 1992). Papert (2004), for example, has pointed out how difficult it would be to teach students multiplication if we still represented numbers using Roman Numerals; multiplication is much more tractable in the Arabic place value system. Connectivity infrastructure is important because it supports classroom discourse and participation (Hegedus, Moreno et al., 2007), and learning sciences researchers emphasize the importance of discourse and participation in students' development of mathematical meaning (Cazden & Beck, 2003; Cobb, Yackel, & McClain, 2002; Hicks, 1995).

Finally, it is important to note that the MathWorlds infrastructure supports the construction of more specific curricula by way of software documents. A document is a software file that users can "open" or "save." Documents configure all the elements of the infrastructure to enable the enactment of a particular activity while minimizing the amount of time teachers and students spend in preparation. Documents also avoid the need for teachers to master the full set of capabilities of the software, by presenting a narrower set of features, a set tuned to the specific learning goals of an activity. Documents give MathWorlds the advantages of a more open-ended tool (like a graphic calculator) while also appearing ready-at-hand to teachers, like very specific virtual manipulatives or applets.

The Character and Limits of Infrastructural Design Research

Educational researchers who want to study the "advanced design" of learning technologies face the challenge of justifying work that will not have immediate impact. Describing such work as aimed at infrastructure helps to set appropriate expectations. Research on new infrastructure is never undertaken for immediate benefit. Over the long term, however, infrastructural changes can yield sweeping transformations when cleverly exploited through additional layers of design and change in practice.

In infrastructural research with network capabilities, the SimCalc Project's core philosophy was to focus on mathematical content, asking: what types of mathematics can be discovered in new and innovative ways using classroom connectivity? This research attends to the principle that "technologies and tools co-constitute both the material on which they operate and the conditions, particularly social conditions, within which such operations occur" (Kaput & Hegedus, 2007, p. 173). Hence, design research clarifies the most fertile and generative aspects of the technology; less useful capabilities are pruned. Simultaneously, curricular targets are refined.

Infrastructural research can also have the theory-building character often attributed to design research (e.g., Edelson, 2002; diSessa & Cobb, 2004). Hence, SimCalc researchers have theorized about the importance of "identity" in connected class-rooms (Hegedus & Kaput, 2004; Hegedus & Penuel, 2008; Kaput & Hegedus, 2002): students can project their mathematical object (and, hence, something that represents themselves) into a public display space. Vahey, Tatar, and Roschelle (2007) examined the importance of transactions between private spaces (only visible to a student) and public spaces (visible to the whole classroom). Stroup advanced the notion that classroom connectivity makes mathematics learning more playful and generative (Stroup, Ares, & Hurford, 2005).

A limit in infrastructural research is that its usefulness depends greatly on the skills and knowledge of teacher users, as well as the particular classroom routines those teachers are comfortable employing (Fishman, 2006). For a new infrastructure to result in transformation of how mathematics is taught in a society, teacher-user communities have to inhabit the infrastructure and fill it with the activities worth doing. They are unlikely to do so if the infrastructure clashes with the comfort zone of their classroom routines and mathematical knowledge.

Although we see the view of technology as infrastructure as empowering, we also worry about two design traps. The first trap is imagining that infrastructure itself will transform educational practice. The trap arises because infrastructure dramatically underspecifies what happens in a classroom among teachers and learners. This can result in false conclusions that the infrastructure "doesn't work" when in fact, a particular realization of classroom activity around the infrastructure did not work. Designers who stop at the infrastructure level, however, have very little control over the classroom realization of their intentions.

The second trap is relying on the availability of "reform-oriented" teachers, who presumably will be ready to tap the potential of new infrastructure. A vast amount of money is directed toward teacher professional development and one might imagine that once teachers have grown through this process, they will be ready to seize new infra-structural affordances and transform their classrooms. Unfortunately, this approach has problems. For instance, it is unclear that there is a single concept of a reform-oriented teacher; rather the goals of teacher professional development tend to loosely overlap around weakly specified beliefs, attitudes, and practices (Ball et al., 2009; Cohen & Ball, 1999). It is thus unlikely that coupling an infrastructure with a particu-lar pool of "reform-oriented" teachers will result in a particular direction of transforma-tion when new technological infrastructure becomes available. In addition, designing effective curricula is hard. Although it is true that a small percentage of teachers can design effective curricula, many more teachers lack either the time or skill to do so.

Thus, we argue that infrastructural design and research, alone, is unlikely to produce desired impacts across a wide variety of classrooms, even if teachers have been pre-pared through good quality but general-purpose teacher professional development.

The Need for Curricular Activity Systems

Kaput was fond of saying "new technology without new curriculum isn't worth the silicon it's written in" (Halverson, Shaffer, Squire, & Steinkuhler, 2006). Similarly, we find that teachers are increasingly attuned to the accountability demands of their environment. Simply put, new technologies must address the core curriculum or face certain marginalization. Infrastructures, however, are not particularly "curricular" in character; they may be designed to a view of the subject matter that transcends the peculiar "school" notions of mathematics of a particular educational regime. Such was the case with MathWorlds; it was designed to address the "mathematics of change and variation" which we argued was important mathematics even if it was not directly obvious in today's school mathematics standards (Kaput & Roschelle, 1998). Curriculum is thus required to bridge the chasm between infrastructure and what teachers need (Ball & Cohen, 1996).

The word "curriculum" connotes either a framework of teaching objectives or a specific textbook that fulfills such a framework. As the work of the SimCalc Project has evolved, we have begun to design "curriculum" in both senses to complement the representational, display, and connectivity infrastructure, and also to bias teaching and learning with MathWorlds in the right directions.

We call the object of our design efforts a "curricular activity system." In this phrase, the word "curricular" is meant to convey that we take seriously the need for a learning progression that addresses important mathematics. The progression has to occur over a meaningful number of instructional hours and cover mathematical constructs that lead the learner onward. We chose the word "activity" because the object of our design is not a "lesson" or a "presentation" or a "problem set" – the commonplace objects of curricular design. Instead we design activities that we intend teachers and students to enact and participate in. The responsibility for supporting such activities is distributed across software, paper curriculum, teacher guides, and teacher training workshops. We are appropriately cautious in realizing that we cannot control the exact enactment of an activity. By activity, thus, we do not mean the colloquial sense of "what students and teachers are doing," but rather we think of an activity in terms of its objective (for the participants), available materials, the intended use of tools, the roles of different participants, and the key things we would like the participants to do and notice. Finally, we use the word "system" because our design aims to engineer an aligned set of related components that coherently support the desired curricular activities. Thus teacher training, curriculum materials, software documents, and so on are all designed together with a singular eye toward enabling classroom realization of our intended activities.

The need to design a curricular activity system has been emergent in our work, particularly as we have attempted to go from small-scale implementation of SimCalc designs (e.g., by Kaput himself or with a few teachers) to implementations involving tens and hundreds of teachers. Building on the work of David Cohen and colleagues (Cohen, Raudenbush, & Ball, 2003), we realized that an ambitious but weakly specified innovation would have little chance of success at scale. While some teachers might understand and implement our intentions, many others might distort the intended use of our infrastructure such that the intended learning gains become unlikely. Indeed, even within a curricular activity system, teachers do not "implement" classroom activities uniformly and unfortunate choices may occur (e.g., we had one teacher who decided that students did not need any hands-on experience with the MathWorlds software). Nonetheless our success in getting quantifiable results with curricular activity systems encourages us to think that this is an important target of design (Roschelle et al., 2007; Tatar et al., 2008).

The "target" of design follows from the learning science principles related to each infrastructural technology (see Table 9.1). Displays afford shared attention, but shared attention to what? We argue that a curricular activity system should afford shared attention to rich mathematical tasks. Hence, one facet of curricular activity system design should be the specification of rich mathematical tasks. We see the representational capabilities of technology as critical to emphasizing mathematical connections. These connections are (a) between students' prior knowledge and mathematical abstractions; (b) among representations of mathematics; and (c) forward and backward along learning progressions within mathematics. The design facet should therefore be knowledge building and learning progressions. Connectivity mediates participation and discourse, relating to a curricular activity system design facet that seeks to foster mathematical argumentation and participation in mathematical practices.

Below, we document examples of two curricular activity systems, each of which builds on the SimCalc technological infrastructure in different ways and is funded as a separate research project. The first draws on the representational and display infrastructure; the latter includes these infrastructural components and adds an emphasis on connectivity infrastructure. In both, we emphasize the rich mathematical tasks, the orientation to learning progressions and knowledge building, and the opportunities for mathematical argumentation and rich mathematical practices.

Example 1: Scaling Up SimCalc

The Scaling Up SimCalc research project investigated, through a randomized experiment, whether a wide variety of teachers could use SimCalc to support their students' learning of conceptually complex mathematics (Roschelle, Tatar,

Table 9.1 Design approach connects technological capability to research on learning

Technological capability	Design approach	Research on learning
Projected displays	Deep mathematical tasks	Enabling shared attention
Linked multiple representations, including animations	Learning progression from more experiential to more abstract mathematics	Emphasizing mathematical connections
Classroom connectivity	Overlapping social and mathematical structures	Engaging student participation in mathematical argumentation

Shechtman, & Knudsen, 2008). This project used MathWorlds in its computer software (not the graphing calculator application) form and did not use the connectivity infrastructure, as this was still under development. Because we were interested in scaling up to a wide variety of teachers, we planned to work simultaneously with over 100 teachers each year. To avoid the "assumption of reform teachers" pitfall, our materials needed to provide supports for teachers who were weak in some areas and they needed to be compatible with pedagogies considered "traditional" as well as "reform oriented." We expected that many of these teachers would be first time users of technology and that pedagogical styles would vary on the spectrum from "traditional" to "reform-oriented." We also wanted to avoid the design trap of under-specifying our intervention by relying too heavily on the representational infrastructure to carry the curriculum. So the complementary resources – student and teacher materials and professional development – had to do much of the specifying, while still providing rich mathematical tasks in which students could experience and be expressive with SimCalc's dynamic representations. These requirements led to the basic components of our curricular activity system: a 2-week replacement unit with a student workbook, brief teacher notes, and software files correlated to the workbook pages. We decided to focus on a replacement unit because replacement units are relatively easy to adopt and offer more breadth and depth than a single lesson. Professional development completed the Scaling Up curricular activity system. Just defining these components helped us in clearly specifying the experiment's "treatment."

Mathematics Content and Learning Progression

The SimCalc representational and display infrastructure has been tested in design experiments with mathematics content ranging in level from middle school through first-year university courses and including topics in algebra, trigonometry, precalculus and calculus courses. A first step in going from an infrastructure to a curricular activity system is to choose a more focused curricular target.

Consideration of the needs of our intended study participants, students and teachers in Texas, led to the selection of a curricular focus. Texas teachers needed materials that addressed their state's accountability requirements, were consistent with locally recommended practices, and used the technology available to them. In Texas' high-stakes testing environment, our curriculum needed to address important state standards – and not just any of the standards, but the ones teachers focused on in preparing students to pass the state test. Because many teachers were following rapidly paced instructional calendars, our unit needed to be short enough to fit in. Texas also has a diversity of students and so we needed to factor in considerations for their needs as well. For example, we needed to lower typical barriers for students who were learning English and for students with low reading levels.

Finding the best intersection of Texas needs and SimCalc offerings was not easy. A signature feature of earlier SimCalc work was exploring the representation of rate in both velocity and position graphs. Prior research gave us strong reasons to believe that we could produce a large learning gain by focusing learning on this SimCalc sweet spot. However, velocity graphs do not fit into Texas middle school standards; it would be hard to convince teachers to spend time teaching velocity graphs and hard to define a fair control condition. After much discussion, we discarded the idea of including velocity graphs and instead focused on a function-based approach to rate and proportionality.

Traditionally, rate and proportionality are taught as separate topics each clearly in the middle school "number" strand. Students are taught to choose appropriate values from a word problem to set up an equation of the form $a/b = c/d$. By filling in three numbers, a fourth can be found using cross multiplication. But implicit in this proportional relationship – and explicit in "rate" problems – is a rate of change which can define a function of the form $y = kx$ where k is the constant of proportionality. With this approach, students are preparing for entry into algebra and later on into calculus, where rates of change are a central topic and are treated algebraically. Moreover, this approach follows naturally from MathWorld's dynamically linked representations of objects in motion and their distances. Rates of change can be identified with slopes of lines that represent the object's speed. This approach leads to a qualitative comparison of different speeds, which can then support analysis of functions tied to their algebraic form.

Fortunately, education leaders in Texas were already advocating that teachers use a function-based approach to teaching proportionality. Texas leaders were also providing professional development, helping teachers consider the standard proportion word problems in a new light. So our curriculum and mathematical approach clearly helped Texas education leaders with one of their goals while remaining true to SimCalc's focus on the mathematics of change and the representation of rate in graphs, tables, equations, and narrative.

With our topic specified, we began to design a learning progression, beginning with simple motion and linear functions, and then developing rich tasks that could develop cognitively complex concepts and skills. The unit had two halves, united by a theme, *Managing the Soccer Team*. Within this theme, lesson-specific activities provided support for understanding the mathematics.

The first half addressed constant speed, comparing simple line graphs and their associated representations. The unit's first activity introduces a single character moving at a constant speed. The character's motion is linked to a graph of time versus position so that as the character moves, the graph builds – with the graph's steepness representing the rate of change or speed of the character. Over the next several activities, complexity develops: Students analyze graphs of characters moving at different speeds and from different starting positions; they recognize faster runs, earlier starting times and races that end in ties through their graphical representations. Students build from the connection between the graph and the situation, to include tables and equations. Culminating this first half, students are asked to translate among graphical, tabular, symbolic and narrative representations of functions of the form, $y = kx$, where time is x, a character's position at time x is y, and the character's speed is k.

The second half moved on to multirate linear functions, where characters in the simulation took on more interesting behavior – e.g., stopping, running backward, and then forward again – all controlled by piecewise linear graphs. The tasks in this half present more challenging mathematics – characters moving at different speeds in a single trip, represented by multisegment line graphs. It was at this point that we moved beyond the state standards for seventh grade. Students learn to interpret horizontal as a stopped motion and a negative slope as a "backward" motion. Through a set of problem-solving activities, students are asked to predict what a simulation or graph will look like, to check their prediction by running the software, and to explain the results in light of the prediction – a routine used across many SimCalc activities.

Overall Support for Teachers and Students

Going from an infrastructure to a curricular activity system requires providing much more support to teachers and students and aligning this support around the key mathematical ideas.

Several features of *Managing the Soccer Team* were aimed at helping a wide variety of teachers to implement the unit. In prior work, we found that teachers often use student materials as their main lesson guide. So we made sure that any crucial information for teachers was not buried in a teaching guide that they might never open. Instead, the student workbook prompts can serve as a kind of "script" for the lesson, though not a prescriptive one. The teacher, then, is not required to develop a sequence of questions and activities to support a learning progression that is likely new to her – but she is free to adapt, edit, and add to the lesson.

Although we did not count on teachers using them, our teaching notes provided simple lesson plans to complement the structure built into the unit – including a page-by-page guide for the "big" mathematical idea for each lesson. Suggested timelines helped teachers figure out how to complete the unit to fit their pacing chart requirements. Lesson planning documents helped teachers make a more detailed "map" of what they intended to do, including specifying what material in their regular curriculum they would "replace" with our unit. In addition, to help the teachers, the Texas standards covered by the unit were listed in the front of the teacher book.

Other features of the unit were designed to address the needs of a wide variety of students. Numbers used in the activities were, for the most part, realistic, so that students could use their knowledge of speed and prices in the real world to gage the correctness of their answers. The text used simple sentence structure and consistent vocabulary, never going beyond a fifth grade reading level, in order to accommodate those with low-level reading skills and to assist English learners in making sense of the context and the mathematics. To help guide and organize students' activities, the workbook used graphical conventions to indicate various kinds of activities and content. For example, definitions appeared inside boxes on the page, as did other critical content information. The amount of white space left after a question indicated the type and length of an expected answer. Simple graphics served as implicit indices for the activities. Even the fact that the workbook contained all the student activities physically bound together provided another organizational aid to students. Lastly, we used as much color as we could afford in reproducing thousands of workbooks, an attempt to appeal to the aesthetic sense of youth who live in a media rich – and colorful – world.

A 3-day teacher workshop was designed to support teachers' effective implementation of the unit. We did not try to change teachers' practices, but instead aimed at providing teachers with a mental image of the unit as a whole and a detailed experience of the unit as learners. The workshop used a standard "teacher-as-learner" approach, providing teachers with an opportunity to experience our intended activities for themselves. We modeled and highlighted use of "predict, check, explain" with students and encouraged teachers to let students use the software. In addition, the workshops provided time for teachers to practice and "play" with the software, to boost their comfort with computer technology. We gave particular focus to the "mathematics knowledge for teaching" that underlies and goes a bit beyond the mathematics students are to learn. Although teachers are familiar with the procedures for calculating using proportional relationships, many middle school teachers are less aware of the critical connections among proportionality and rate, the connections across representations, and how exploring proportionality can become a first step toward algebra.

Design Decisions: From Infrastructure to a Curricular Activity System

A comparison of a "traditional" SimCalc activity with an activity from the Scaling Up unit will illustrate some of our design decisions as we adapted core SimCalc activities for our Scaling Up curricular activity system.

"Sack Race" is a widely used SimCalc activity in which students are asked to create a graph that represents "an exciting sack race" and produce a narrative matching their graph. Using a MathWorlds file that has one character traveling at a constant speed over the course of the race, students create graphs for another character so that it slows down, speeds up, goes backward, and catches up – or any combination of these. By creating different graphs in the software, and trying them out in the simulation, students can explore how different parts of a "multirate linear function" affect the speed and direction of the character. Playfulness is encouraged in students' narration of their race. For example, as their character's race is played out, students often say something like: "Now he has fallen down and can't get up. Finally he struggles to his feet but takes off much more slowly than before."

The resources supporting this activity can be downloaded from the SimCalc website and include one MathWorlds file, an activity sheet and several pages of teacher notes. The original description of Sack Race was follows:

> This is our first 'performance' activity. Its primary focus should be on slope as rate of change and piecewise functions. This activity allows exploration of multiple types of slope; i.e., positive slope, negative slope, or zero slope for students to build their understanding of varying rate. This activity also allows for exploration of intersections of linear functions

leading to an understanding of solutions to systems of equations. There is no one correct answer to this activity and students should focus on what conditions determine a correct answer...Students' creativity will set the tone for the discussion. You may choose specific students to display their graph and discuss their story one at a time. You want students to pick out the correlation between the action and the function. For example, if someone reads a story where his or her Actor stops, there should be a segment with a zero slope. Students will be excited to share even when their stories are incorrect, be sure to encourage a positive environment for corrections.

The original teacher notes for this SimCalc activity provide guidance in how to structure the lesson for this activity. There are three parts to the lesson: a whole class introduction, individual or group work time, and a whole class discussion of a sampling of students' work. For the introduction, teachers are told to "...decide on as much or as little detail as you wish for an introduction. You should at least introduce adding and manipulating segments to control Actor B's function..." For individual or group work time, the teacher is advised: "This is your opportunity to monitor group progress and determine what students are thinking and/or struggling with. Try not to answer questions directly, give students ways of using the motion to answer their questions."

Teachers create their own lesson plan aligned with this advice. Creating a lesson plan of this sort requires extensive teacher knowledge, some of which would likely be developed over time when using SimCalc materials. Just creating the demonstration MathWorlds file requires design decisions that invoke knowledge of mathematics, theories of learning, and knowledge of students' current levels of understanding. For example, one point of this lesson is that "backward" motion is represented in the graph by segments with negative slope. How should this idea figure into the whole class introduction? Should the teacher leave it out altogether so that students can discover it later? Should it be present in the teachers' demonstration MathWorlds file, without a lot of explicit discussion? Or should the teacher demonstrate and elicit an explanation of backward motion before students do their own work? If so, what is the right introduction? Should the teacher show a segment that is "slanting downward" and ask students what it could mean? Or should she show a backward motion and ask what it is?

In the Scaling Up unit, we include an activity with similar mathematical goals to those of "Sack Race." This activity, called "On the Road" (see Fig. 9.1), differs from the original by being substantially more structured for the teacher and her students. In "On the Road," students are presented with a series of trips between Abilene and Dallas, Texas. Each trip is made by bus and van and each trip is fraught with difficulties: bus breakdowns, forgotten items and bad traffic. The first problem in the activity, shown in Figs. 9.1 and 9.2, asks students to compare the trip of a bus and a van by comparing their graphs on a by-then familiar time versus position graph. This problem introduces a single object moving at two different speeds, but constrains the direction of motion to the familiar moving forward.

The next two problems introduce horizontal lines and then downward slanting lines (all without a formal definition of slope). Once these three ideas have been introduced sequentially, then students work in groups on problems of greater com-

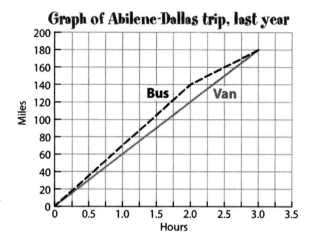

Fig. 9.1 A portion of the student workbook page for the "On the Road" activity

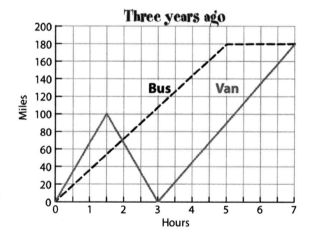

Fig. 9.2 More of the "On the Road" activity, from the student workbook

plexity, combining these different types of motion and their representation graphs. The most complex of these is shown in Fig. 9.2, below.

Relative to the original "Sack Race," we see that designing a curricular activity system involved several additional layers of specification. Both activities fit our notion of a "rich mathematical task," in that comparing the two motions draws forth a set of connected mathematical ideas about slope and rate. But whereas "Sack Race" leaves it to the teacher to find appropriate times and questions to address all the relevant mathematics, "On the Road" sequences the mathematics to start with a simpler situation and build toward the more complex situation. The sequence is structured to direct the teacher's and students' shared attention to relevant aspects of the task in a manageable progression. For example, question 4.a "What did the van do after traveling for one and a half hours?" directs attention to the contrast between positive and negative slopes.

Both activities also engage multiple representations, including narrative, graphs, and motions. The "On the Road" version, however, specifically cues useful knowledge building practices. For example, question 2.a. asks the students to make predictions from the graph before they run it. Note that the question specifically asks students to think about "speed." One problem with a rich context (e.g., the sack race) is that children tend to dwell on aspects of the story that are irrelevant to the mathematics. In the original, teachers are left to direct students to the mathematically relevant features; the curricular activity system version supports the teacher by including a specific prompt to look at speed. Further, in both questions 2 and 4, the prompts also support the SimCalc routine, "predict, verify, explain." Student discussion is also specifically scaffolded by prompts in the teacher guide. Mathematical argumentation is encouraged by prompts in the teacher guide, by the questions asked of the students, and by the training that was given to teachers in the summer workshop.

Results

Overall, in our Scaling Up SimCalc project we collected data from 95 seventh grade teachers, half in the control group and half in the SimCalc group. We found statistically significant differences between classrooms that used SimCalc and those that used existing curriculum for the topic of rate and proportionality (Roschelle et al., 2007). Students in classrooms where teachers used SimCalc's integration of curriculum, software, and professional development had higher learning gains. The gains were higher, specifically on the more advanced aspects of mathematical understand that SimCalc sought to cultivate; students learned about the same amount on the simpler mathematics measured on the Texas state test.

Our findings for both the seventh and eighth grade experiments are presented in detail elsewhere (Roschelle et al., 2007; Roschelle, Tatar, Shechtman, Hegedus et al., 2008). Here, we focus on the specific indicators of the success of the "On the Road" activity in the seventh grade curriculum. Teachers overwhelmingly rated "On the road" their favorite lesson in the unit. In postunit debriefing interviews, we also found that teachers frequently talked about this activity as a highlight. Further, we found high learning gains on test items that are closely related to "On the Road." Consider the test item in Fig. 9.3

This item targets a common misconception – that the point of intersection on a graph is the time at which the objects are traveling at the same speed. Choosing answer B is an indicator that a student may have this misconception. The correct answer is C, because the objects have the same speed when their graphs have the same slope. On the pretest, only 23% of students got this item correct – and this is about the percentage that would be produced by random guessing. On the posttest, 55% of students who had been in classrooms using SimCalc got the item right, a statistically significant gain. In comparison, only 38.5% of students in non-SimCalc classrooms got the item right at posttest and more students (55%) chose the misconception-based distracter, answer B.

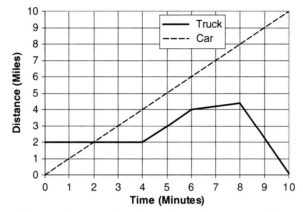

When are the car and truck traveling at the same speed?

    A. Between 1 and 4 minutes

    B. At 2 minutes

    C. Between 4 and 6 minutes

    D. Between 6 and 8 minutes

Fig. 9.3 A test item targeting the concept that parallel slopes (not an intersection point) indicate when two objects travel the same speed

On the basis of these results, we argue that the design of the curricular activity system around the "On the Road" activity worked with a wide variety of teachers and students.

Example 2: SimCalc Classroom Connectivity Project

Continuing in the learning progression described in Example 1 (e.g., proportionality and linear function), the next set of mathematical topics occurs in Algebra I (e.g., writing and manipulating linear functions, solving simultaneous equations, etc.). A look at SimCalc's "advanced technology" for Algebra I, however, affords more than a look at additional content because the team working on Algebra I also used new infrastructural capabilities. Consequently, this second example provides a look at a different embodiment of a curricular activity system. It is also different because students used graphing calculator hardware – not computers – connected by the TI-Navigator wireless network.

    In addition to two infrastructural aspects of technology leveraged previously, representations and public displays, the SimCalc Classroom Connectivity Project (Hegedus, Dalton et al., 2007) leverages network connectivity among students' devices and the teacher's public display. Within-classroom networks are emphasized rather than connecting to outside-of-class resources over the Internet. Thus, the roots of SimCalc's approach to connectivity are more closely related to prior work on student response systems (a.k.a. "clickers") than to other forms of networked eLearning (Hegedus & Penuel, 2008). Like the work on clickers, the SimCalc Classroom Connectivity Project builds on the opportunity to connect students within a classroom so that they may respond in real-time to a teacher's queries and have their "responses" instantly (and often anonymously) collected and posted to a public display, where they become the focus of classroom discussion. As in certain response system work (Roschelle, Penuel, & Abrahamson, 2004), the major focus is on transforming classroom participation to dramatically increase students' roles in a meaningful classroom discourse. Unlike most of the work on clickers, however, which is content-neutral (the clickers accept only multiple choice responses), the SimCalc connectivity work depends on richer functionality to allow students to construct and contribute mathematical objects, not just select from predetermined multiple-choice responses. These capabilities lead to a *participation infrastructure,* permeated by mathematical considerations, that complements and extends the earlier representational infrastructure.

The rationale for attending to participation infrastructure draws upon the three perspectives (learner, technological, and epistemological) in parallel to the earlier rationale provide for representational infrastructure.

From a learner-centered perspective, the rationale for focusing on participation infrastructure aims to address the sense of alienation that many students experience in typical mathematics courses. Rather than feeling empowered by their inclusion in Algebra classes under the banner of "Algebra for All," many students experience Algebra as affirming their disenfranchisement from mathematics. This outcome, obviously, runs counter to the SimCalc mission of democratizing access to important mathematics.

Ethnographical studies of high school students (Davidson & Phelan, 1999; Phelan, Davidson, & Yu, 1998) reveal a world of alienation with strongly negative responses to standard practices (Meece, 1991) and strong sensitivity to interactions with teachers and their strategies (Davidson, 1999; Johnson, Crosnoe, & Elder, 2001; Skinner & Belmont, 1993; Turner, Thorpe, & Meyer, 1998). Negative responses, particularly as they are intimately connected with self image and sense of personal efficacy, can be deeply debilitating, both in terms of performance variables (Abu-Hilal, 2000) as well as in the ability to use help when it is available (Harter, 1992; Newman & Goldin, 1990; Ryan & Pintrich, 1997). On the other hand, students exhibit consistently positive responses to alternative modes of instruction and content (Ames, 1992; Boaler, 2002; Mitchell, 1993). A recent review by the National Mathematics Advisory Panel (Geary et al., 2008) focused attention on the connection between participation structures and the achievement gap. Evidence suggests that Black and Hispanic students learn particularly well in classrooms that stress a more communitarian outlook and in which they experience the teachers as caring about each child personally (e.g., Fullilove & Treisman, 1990; Ladson-Billings, 1995). More interactive and social classroom participation structures, thus, are seen as a potentially important tool for closing achievement gaps.

A complementary epistemological perspective attends more strongly to mathematics as constructed socially, through argumentation. A watershed event for this perspective with respect to the infrastructure of network connectivity occurred at a 2002 Psychology in Mathematics Education, North America meeting where Stroup led a symposium on the potential interplay of mathematical and social spaces in a connected classroom (Stroup et al., 2002). The symposium emphasized the idea of aligning how students belong to the classroom as a social collective with how each student's mathematical contributions belong to a higher order mathematical object. For example, each student can contribute a single point that fits the equation $y = 2x$ and their collective construction, graphed on the shared public display, will be a line with a slope of 2. Likewise, each student can contribute a function in the form $y = 2x + b$ with a different value for b and their collective construction, graphed on the shared public display, will be a family of mathematical functions, all with a slope of 2 and parameterized by variation in the y-intercept. An emerging epistemological design principle, then is to overlay mathematical variation onto the social structure of the classroom – mathematically coherent displays arise from socially coherent individual participation. The contrast to the earlier clicker-based approach could not be more stark: clickers emphasize an epistemology of consensus on the right answer; the newer capabilities emphasize the dialectic emergence of coherent mathematical constructions through social argumentation about mathematics that arises from systematically varied individual contributions. Just as mathematical considerations permeate the design of the representations in the earlier version of MathWorlds, mathematical considerations permeate the design of the social infrastructure in the connected version of MathWorlds. A classroom experience that interconnects the social and the mathematical has the potential for increasing students' sense of identity, agency, and belonging because their mathematical contributions remain identifiable in the collective, carry their agency, and belong to the larger group construct.

Technologically, therefore, the right infrastructure needs to do more than collect and display students' mathematical contributions in juxtaposition. In particular, it must make the contributions part of a collective mathematical construction. The newer versions of MathWorlds add a few key features to accomplish this. First, connected MathWorlds provides facilities to collect student contributions into a common motion animation. For example, if each student contributed a function $y = 2x + b$, the common animation might look a parade of characters moving at the same speed but with different starting positions. Second, the representational contrasts can be spread out socially in the classroom, for example, so that students contribute a function using Algebraic symbols but see their contribution expressed on the public display as a graph or an animation. Hence, the principle of multiple representations (Goldenberg, 1995) becomes socially distributed in a networked classroom rather than distributed over adjacent windows on the same display. Third, it provides tools for hiding and showing coherent collectives of student work, so that the teacher can focus on comparing and contrasting student work in ways that focus on the relevant mathematics.

Per our central argument, this participation infrastructure remains just that – an infrastructure. And thus it would be unlikely to see transformation in classrooms, even with reform-oriented teachers, without working toward an "advanced design" – that is a design which leverages the new infrastructure in appropriate curricular activity systems.

Algebra I Curricular Activity System Overview

The Classroom Connectivity (CC) curriculum activity system for Algebra I builds upon the lessons learned from the seventh and eighth grade work reported in Example 1. As in Example 1, the mathematical learning progression was designed with close attention to the overlap between state standards and MathWorlds capabilities. In this case, the target state was Massachusetts and about half the topics in the Algebra I standards for Massachusetts were directly amenable to a SimCalc focus, so these conventional topics became the focus of the learning progression. The learning progression built on the succession of topics found in textbooks used in Massachusetts, such as the progression from graphing linear equations to writing linear equations and to solving systems of linear equations. Also, as in the case with the Texas work, the "system" included a student curriculum book, a teacher edition and teacher professional development, with many of the same considerations as discussed earlier.

One new and important element in the CC Algebra I materials is the inclusion of more extensive dialog prompts in the teacher edition. Teachers are deliberately guided to engage their classroom with questions that focus on (a) the activity (b) the connections among multiple representations and (c) the central mathematical ideas of key lessons. This practice aligns with the enhanced emphasis on argumentation in the networked SimCalc classroom. Because the logic of the learning progression and the teacher supports has already been discussed in Example 1 – and not to diminish the role of this logic in the overall curricular activity system – we focus Example 2 on three kinds of activity structures that have emerged to leverage the connectivity infrastructure and support the epistemological alignment of mathematical and social structure in classroom enactment.

The "Where Am I?" Activity

In this activity structure (Hegedus & Kaput, 2002), each student privately constructs a mathematical function in one representation (e.g., an expression for a linear function) and then contributes their function to a collective class representation. Students then participate as a group in trying to find their mathematical objects in a public, collective representation (e.g., an animation where each dot moves according to a student contribution).

Early SimCalc investigations revealed a powerful drive for students to "find themselves" in the collective animation, where students see and talk about contributed functions as extensions of personal identities. Thus, students' attention is drawn to the collective display. Further, the only way to self-identify is to pay attention to the mathematically relevant attributes of the animation, such as the start position and speed of a moving dot. In a classroom discussion, students might, for instance, notice that there is a group of dots that all move at the same speed. The teacher could hide all the other dots and focus on these. Using MathWorlds capability to leave "marks" at positions that are 1 second apart, the class could work to quantify the speed of this subset of dots and discuss which variable, m or b, is related to the speed. This creates a trajectory from (a) self-identification with a mathematical object to (b) focus of attention on mathematically relevant attributes of the animation and onward to (c) the connection between the perceptual attributes of a motion and the mathematical abstractions of slope and intercept. Hence, instantiating systematic variation socially in the curricular activity system becomes the organizing structure that allows for classroom enactments that personally engage each student, focus their attention on the relevant public mathematics, and move from personal to more abstract mathematics.

Research analyses of SimCalc activities have conceptualized "identity as a form of mediated action" to capture this phenomena (Hegedus & Penuel, 2008). In particular, classroom conversations have many deictic references that connect a person's name and a public mathematical object. The aspect of identity highlighted here is less one's attributions to self in relationship to community (a broader, more cultural view of identity) and more one's projections of self in relationship to the microcommunity constituted in the classroom. One might think of this as a small "i" form of identity that could nonetheless powerfully contribute to a big "I" form of Identity as an adult who feels ownership of the cultural tools of algebra. Indeed, one case study tracked "X" a student who was initially invisible in class, but who became "famous" through the public activity of tracking down his unique identity in the animation, and consequently became a more frequent and vocal participant in the classroom (Kaput & Hegedus, 2002).

Parameterized Variation Activities

A second genre of networked SimCalc activities systematically organizes mathematical variation in a classroom so that the collection of functions submitted by students form a family of functions (Hegedus & Kaput, 2004; Hegedus & Kaput, 2003; Hegedus & Kaput, 2002; Kaput & Hegedus, 2002). These activities rely on a surprisingly simple and robust social idiom, called "counting off" in the United States. To "count off," each student announces a successive number, thus claiming that number. Working in groups of 4, for example, students can count off numbers from 1 to 4. In some SimCalc activities, groups are also assigned numbers, such that each student has a unique pair of numbers, a group number and a count-off number. Once students have their numbers, a teacher can begin a networked SimCalc activity by asking each student to make a function that uses these uniquely assigned numbers (Fig. 9.4).

One particularly profound use of this capability contrasts functions with the same slope versus functions with the same y-intercept. Imagine that each student has made a unique linear function $f(x) = g \times x + c$, where g and c are a student's group and count-off numbers, respectively. Using simple networked SimCalc capabilities, a teacher can collect these functions, display them in a graph, and animate moving actors according to them. Further, the teacher can choose settings

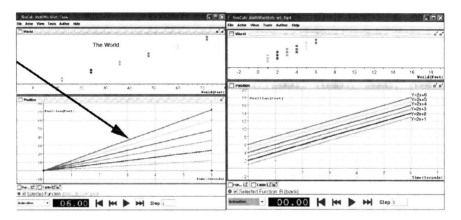

Fig. 9.4 Contrasting lines with the same y-intercept versus lines with the same slope

that highlight all students with an equal group number or all students with an equal count-off number.

In classroom practice, these capabilities are deployed with opportunities for cycles of prediction, reflection, and feedback. For example, before showing a graph of all the functions with the group number (and hence, slope) of 2, the teacher should ask students to predict what the graph will look like. Likewise, before animating these graphs as moving characters, the teacher should ask students to predict what the motion will look like. Further, when collecting students' work it is rare that everyone in the classroom made the correct function for their assigned numbers. Hence, cycles of reflections and feedback are appropriate.

The visual and animated results of family-of-function constructions are quite striking and memorable. A collection of functions with the same slope but different y-intercepts appears as parallel lines and the motion looks like a series of actors following each other in lock-step (because they move at the same speed). In contrast, a collection of functions with the same y-intercept, but different speeds, appears as a "fan" or "spray" of lines emanating from a point. The characters start at the same place but spread apart because they move at different speeds. Indeed, research data show that students remember and recall these patterns. A "fan" can become an iconic representation for "different slopes, same intercept" and parallel lines can become an iconic representation for "same slope, different intercepts." Likewise, "spreading apart" and "marching in lock-step" can become easily remembered correlates of these icons (Piaget, 1970, we note, theorized that "speed" arises as a concept for children in relationship to their perception of "catching up" and "spreading apart" behaviors). Hence, these motion representations are likely deeply connected to the relevant everyday concepts). For example, the SimCalc CC project reports the case study of Erin, who says "we're sandwiching at 12 feet" when asked to predict what would happen if all students make functions with different slopes that intersect at the point (6,12). The same report shows four instances of students' spontaneous gestures in class, using their fingers or other line-like objects to show spread or parallelism.

These mnemonics are important because students have difficulty remembering the different meanings of m and b in $y=mx+b$. Increasing either m or b can be superficially described as "moving up" which misses the difference between "tilting up" and "shifting up." Notice what has happened here, relative to earlier generations of dynamic graphing software. In early generations of software, a mouse drag could be used so that an individual student could see how a changing parameter affected a single line. Now, with networked MathWorlds, a classroom can see how systematic variation in a parameter results in a family of functions. Instead of being contained within an individual eye-hand coordination loop, a group now participates in coordinating the production of a family of functions. Further, social parameterization produces an iconic figure and animation, making it easier (we think) for students to remember the different meanings of "m" and "b." Research within the SimCalc CC Project has begun to quantify the impact of socially distributed parameterization by tracking the increased number of student-to-student conversation sequences, relative to student-to-teacher sequences (Hegedus & Penuel, 2008). Student-to-student conversation sequences would likely increase when variation is distributed between students, rather being contained within the control of the only student with the mouse.

Mathematical Performance Activities

A third kind of activity, a mathematical performance, engages students in using mathematics expressively (Hegedus & Kaput, 2004; Hegedus & Kaput, 2003; Hegedus & Kaput, 2002; Kaput & Hegedus, 2002). Working privately at first, students create a personally meaningful use of mathematics to express a story. The students can then send their mathematics to the teacher via the connectivity infrastructure. The teacher can choose particular students to perform (e.g., tell the story) of their mathematics.

In one such activity, a pair of students position their actors a symmetrical distance away from a meeting point and have to coordinate the creation of a pair of linear functions that will result in a motion animation that shows the actors meeting at the same time at the designated place (Fig. 9.5). The teacher can show successful or unsuccessful meetings and engage students in telling the story of what they had to do to arrange a meeting (since the distance and time to the meeting point are the same, the students need to create functions that model motions of the same speed but opposite direction).

Research on this activity structure suggests that it shares aspects of both prior activities. Organizing students' work as mathematical seems to powerfully engage the identity between a student and the public display of his or her work. Further, different pairs of students naturally vary in *how* they solve the problem (e.g., use different times and speeds), which can result in mathematical debate among students

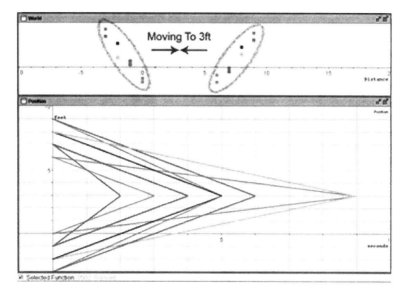

Fig. 9.5 Graphs of functions that converge at 3 feet, but at different times

in the classroom about what was the same and different among their approaches. From such a debate, students can generalize the connections among the equation, graph, and motion form of functions with the same speed by opposite direction.

Results

Research using the connectivity infrastructure is at an earlier stage than the research using only the representational and display infrastructure but is on a similar trajectory toward scale. In a pilot quasi-experiment, a district volunteered seven classrooms of students ($n = 133$) to use SimCalc and the remaining eight classrooms of students formed a comparison group ($n = 184$). The main effect was statistically significant and showed that students in the SimCalc group had a higher gain on items related to linear functions, slope as rate, proportion, linear variation, seeing across representations, and graphical interpretation, with a medium effect size (Hegedus, Dalton et al., 2007). SimCalc students did especially well, in contrast to the comparison group, on an item that asked students to identify how a position graph represents a change in direction in the corresponding motion. This gain conceivably follows from mathematical performance activities, such as the one described above, which may powerfully address common graph-as-path misconceptions.

The research team is also pursuing classroom changes other than those found via assessments of mathematical content knowledge. For example, as described in the context of the activities above, the team is also searching for methodological refinements that can capture the impact of a networked SimCalc curricular activity system on classroom participation, student identity, and mitigation of students' sense of alienation from mathematics (Hegedus & Penuel, 2008). Promising indicators include the ratio of student-to-student versus student-to-teacher conversational exchanges; an increase in student control of the conversational floor and teacher use of "revoicing" and other facilitation moves; use of deictic markers that connect personal identity and mathematical abstractions. Further, the team is conducting a scale up study looking specifically at longitudinal impacts of participation in networked SimCalc classrooms (using computers and calculators), which might move beyond local engagement to influence on students' proclivity for continuing onward in science, mathematics, technology and engineering studies, and careers.

Discussion

We have presented two design examples from the SimCalc Project, arguing that elaborating a curricular activity system to leverage infrastructure is what makes these designs advanced. In both examples, infrastructure was a target of initial research and emerged from the triangulation of learner-centered, technology-centered, and discipline- or epistemology-centered perspectives, as recapitulated in Table 9.2. An additional common infrastructural element is the use of computer projects to allow a shared, public display. Across the two examples, we have described what elaborating a curricular activity system entails.

Table 9.2 Representational and connective infrastructure from three intersecting perspectives

Perspective	Representation infrastructure	Connectivity infrastructure
Learner-centered	Building on learners' strengths including: • Making sense of motion • Reasoning about intervals • Connecting graphical and linguistic representations	Building on learners' strengths including: • Making sense of motions of groups of actors • Communicating with gestures and informal argument • Identifying with one's contribution in a collective representation
Technology-centered	Presenting new cognitive experiences using: • Executable representations • Dynamically linked representations • Simulated motion	Presenting new social experiences using: • Sharing mathematical objects • Spreading multiple representations across people • Family-of-function-based aggregations of student work
Epistemology-centered	Developing meaning by connecting algebraic symbols and: • Graphs • Piecewise functions • Motions	Developing meaning by connecting algebraic symbols and: • Graphs of families of functions • Relative motions among actors • Parameterized variation

At the heart of our design efforts, the first design focus is always the specification of rich mathematical tasks with an overall learning progression. In our view, these tasks emphasize mathematical connections that are both locally important in terms of the specific curricular objectives but also of longitudinal importance in students' ongoing mathematical development. Rich mathematical tasks often involve multiple representations and involve students in making meaning across representations. Further, within rich mathematical tasks students often have opportunities to practice earlier mathematical skills (for example, identifying point in a Cartesian graph) and procedures (calculating values of mathematical expressions). In the seventh grade curriculum used in the Scaling Up SimCalc project, the "On the Road" activity was a signature mathematical task. Indeed, teachers often commented on this specific activity in the debriefing interviews we conducted after their SimCalc teaching was finished for the year. In the Algebra curriculum used in the SimCalc CC project, the exploration of families of functions with equal slope versus a common point of intersection formed the basis of some of the signature activities. In both cases, these specific tasks occurred as part of a longer-term learning progression that led up to these concepts and built further upon them.

A second design focus is on materials to support teachers and students. It is important to note that these materials are often based on very traditional infrastructure – paper. We continue to find many benefits to a paper workbook to accompany our activities. Some representations (e.g., writing equations, making tables, sketching graphs) continue to be easier for students and teachers to produce in paper form than using a mouse and keyboard. Further, paper extends the real estate available for activities. Instead of overcrowding computer screens, work can extend to extra work surfaces. Indeed, we find that teachers commonly project the MathWorlds display on a screen that is next to their whiteboard, allowing them to work across both the computer display and their whiteboard at the front of the classroom. It is also easier for teachers to markup and comment on student work in paper form. The paper materials provide structure to the activities by introducing the activity and highlighting key concepts, terms, and procedures and by organizing the activity according to some key driving questions. For the teacher, the teacher guide supports enactment of activities by suggesting key questions for classroom discussions. In the SimCalc CC work, for example, the teacher guide offers suggestions for different aspects of the classroom dialog, including a focus on the meaning of the activity, the connections across multiple representations, and essential mathematical ideas of the lesson.

We further consider teacher workshops to be a component of the curricular activity system design, because these workshops are designed to align with and emphasize the enactment of the classroom activities. Consequently, much of the time in teacher workshops is dedicated to working through the student materials, but with commentary and reflection on a teacher level. As these workshops are relatively short in duration and tightly scoped, we tend to think of them as teacher training (to enact the curricular activity system) rather than teacher professional development (with a broader aim in long-term transformation of teaching practice).

The detailed design work involves providing enough structure to enable a broad population to enact the activities without draining the opportunity to struggle with important mathematics out of the activities. As Hiebert and Grouws (2007) argue, two ways that teachers can make a difference in mathematics teaching is to (a) make concepts an explicit focus of classroom discussions and activities, and (b) allow students to struggle with important and meaningful mathematics. In the first example, our design balanced structure and struggle by organizing a progression from simple to more complex mathematics within the activity, but not providing a recipe or procedure for solutions. In the second example, we discussed three specific activity designs, "Where Am I?", Parameterized Variation, and Mathematical Performances, each of which provides substantial structure for classroom enactments but still preserves core conceptual struggles as work for students to do.

We have suggested that recent work in the SimCalc Project has benefited from the growing realization that much of our technology is infrastructural in character and requires the further design of curricular activity systems in order to yield better teaching and learning at scale. The two projects use different combinations of infrastructural features and curricular design principles, making clear that there is not a necessary 1:1 correspondence between a representational infrastructure and a curricular activity system. Further, there is not a 1:1 correspondence between a curricular activity system and how teaching and learning is enacted in particular classrooms. Nonetheless, we have seen that designing a curricular activity system on top of an infrastructure yields enough specificity that a wide variety of teachers can achieve learning gains for students.

We wish to distinguish a curricular activity system from other forms of midlevel design. A curricular activity system is not a web-based repository of teacher-contributed lessons. While such repositories can allow sharing of favorite lessons, they lack the coherent learning progression that we believe is important to strong mathematical growth. A curricular activity system is also not a set of lesson plans or a set of problems, because the design focus is on enacting a classroom *activity*, not on the content of lessons or practicing problem solving. Finally, a classroom activity system is not a technology application. Rather, we have found that the necessary system requires a mix of kinds of materials (e.g., software, paper, teacher guides) and kinds of processes (including teacher workshops but also forms of coaching and peer support) that use the technology infrastructure, but without being exclusively technologically reliant.

Before closing this discussion, we also note that we have focused less on the design of classroom practices and routines, not because we consider these less important but rather because we consider aspects of interventions need much additional research. We do advocate certain classroom moves, for example, asking students to predict what they will see before running the MathWorlds animation or asking students to explain their answers. In general, all aspects of the SimCalc Project value extended mathematical argumentation in the classroom. Overall, however, current research does not provide sufficient guidance to anticipate how to design classroom practices and routines that could scale up to larger numbers of teachers with bounded quantities of professional development.

Conclusion

The central contention of our chapter has been that an advanced technology for learning earns its label not because it uses "advanced technology" but rather because it advances designs for learning. Further, we attend to scaling up as a key goal for advanced technology for learning. Thus, the field needs to become aware of features of its initial designs that may be workable at a small scale but insufficient to structure enactment by a wide variety of teachers across a diversity of school settings. Our work in the SimCalc program suggests that scaling up requires understanding the contributions of different levels of design to successful implementation. At one level, advanced technologies for learning should begin with the identification of new infrastructural capabilities that could profoundly alter students' opportunity to learn. We have argued that these infrastructural capabilities emerge from the joint consideration of students' strengths as learners, specific features of technology, and an epistemological quest for more productive learning progressions that nonetheless honor disciplinary subject matter. At another level, advanced technologies for learning include the design of curricular activity systems. These systems specify rich mathematical tasks within a particular learning progression and include key supports beyond the technology that contribute to successful enactment. A key tension at the curricular activity system level is providing enough structure to make good enactments likely without detracting from a focus on concepts and the opportunity for students to struggle meaningfully with important mathematical ideas. At yet another level, we see long-term teacher professional development as being dialectically coupled to the design of advanced technology for learning. Better enactments are certainly possible when teachers experience carefully designed curricular activity systems that contribute to the vitality of professional development experiences.

Overall, we doubt that mathematics and science education can be improved sufficiently through independently acting, single-factor interventions. Instead, compound interventions are needed and these will include elements designed at different levels of removal from local contexts. Infrastructure, by its very nature, should be designed to provide key capabilities that can be powerfully leveraged in ways that will offer value in many different venues over a long period. Infrastructural design efforts are both important and incomplete with respect to achieving deep educational transformation. We have identified curricular activity systems as another level that is somewhat removed from the specifics of each individual school, teacher, and student but which can provide common structures that make successful enactments likely. Finally, we suspect that improving teaching and learning will always also have a profoundly local aspect, which involves professional development and leadership development at the school level. Thus, we are not recommending an either-or approach to design, but rather that innovators recognize and act more explicitly on their opportunities to create value for teachers and learners at multiple, overlapping levels.

Acknowledgments We thank Corinne Singleton for her work on an earlier draft of this chapter. This material is based in part upon work supported by the National Science Foundation under Grant Numbers 0437861 and 033710. Any opinions, findings, and conclusions or recommendations expressed in this material are those of the author(s) and do not necessarily reflect the views of the National Science Foundation.

References

Abu-Hilal, M. (2000). A structural model for predicting mathematics achievement: Its relation with anxiety and self-concept in mathematics. *Psychological Reports, 86*, 835–847.

Ames, C. (1992). Classrooms, goals, structures, and student motivation. *Journal of Educational Psychology, 84*, 261–271.

Ball, D. L. & Cohen, D. K. (1996). Reform by the book: What is – or might be – the role of curriculum materials in teacher learning and instructional reform. *Educational Researcher, 25*(9), 6–8.

Ball, D., Roskam, A., Morris, A., Hiebert, J., Suzuka, K., Lewis, J., et al. (2009). Improving mathematics teaching and teacher education through "specification". *Paper presented at the National Council of Teachers of Mathematics Research Precession, Washington DC, April, 21*, 2009.

Barab, S. & Squire, K. (2004). Design-based research: Putting a stake in the ground. *The Journal of the Learning Sciences, 13*(1), 1–14.

Barron, B. (2000). Achieving coordination in collaborative problem-solving groups. *The Journal of the Learning Sciences, 9*(4), 403–436.

Bell, P., Hoadley, C. M., & Linn, M. C. (2004). Design-based research in education. In M. C. Linn, E. A. Davis & P. Bell (Eds.), *Internet environments for science education* (pp. 73–85). Mahwah, NJ: Lawrence Erlbaum Associates.

Boaler, J. (2002). *Experiencing school mathematics*. Mahwah, NJ: Lawrence Erlbaum Associates.

Cazden, C. B. & Beck, S. W. (2003). Classroom discourse. In A. C. Graesser, M. A. Gernsbacher & S. R. Goldman (Eds.), *Handbook of discourse processes* (pp. 165–197). Mahwah, NJ: Lawrence Erlbaum Associates.

Cobb, P., Yackel, E., & McClain, K. (eds). (2002). *Communicating and symbolizing in mathematics: Perspectives on discourse, tools, and instructional design*. Mahwah, NJ: Lawrence Erlbaum Associates.

Cohen, D. K., & Ball, D. L. (1999). *Instruction, capacity, and improvement* (No. CPRE Research Report No. RR-043). Philadelphia, PA: University of Pennsylvania, Consortium for Policy Research in Education.

Cohen, D. K., Raudenbush, S., & Ball, D. L. (2003). Resources, instruction, and research. *Educational Evaluation and Policy Analysis, 25*(2), 1–24.

Davidson, A. (1999). Negotiating social differences: Youth's assessments of educators' strategies. *Urban Education, 34*, 338–369.

Davidson, A. & Phelan, P. (1999). Students' multiple worlds: An anthropological approach to understanding students' engagement with school. In T. C. Urdan (Ed.), *Advances in motivation and achievement: Role of context* (Vol. 2, pp. 233–283). Stamford, CT: JAI Press.

Dede, C. (2004). If design-based research is the answer, what is the question? A commentary on Collins, Joseph, and Bielaczyc; diSessa and Cobb; and Fishman, Marx, Blumenthal, Krajcik, and Soloway in the JLS special issue on design-based research. *The Journal of the Learning Sciences, 13*(1), 105–114.

diSessa, A. A. & Cobb, P. (2004). Ontological innovation and the role of theory in design experiments. *The Journal of the Learning Sciences, 13*(1), 77–103.

Edelson, D. C. (2002). What we learn when we engage in design. *Journal of the Learning Sciences, 11*(1), 105–121.

Fishman, B. (2006). It's not about the technology [Electronic Version]. *Teachers College Record.* Retrieved July 6, 2006 from http://www.tcrecord.org.

Geary, D.C., Berch, D.B., Boykin, A.W., Embretson, S., Reyna, V., Siegler, R., et al. (2008). *Report of the task group on learning processes*. Retrived July 17, 2008 from http://www.ed. gov/about/bdscomm/list/mathpanel/report/learning-processes.pdf.

Goldenberg, P. (1995). Multiple representations: A vehicle for understanding understandings. In D. N. Perkins, J. L. Schwartz, M. M. West & M. S. Wiske (Eds.), *Software goes to school* (pp. 155–171). New York, NY: Oxford University Press.

Halverson, R., Shaffer, D., Squire, K., & Steinkuehler, C. (2006). *Theorizing games in/and education*. Bloomington, IN: Paper presented at the seventh International Conference on Learning Sciences.

Harter, S. (1992). The relationship between perceived competence, affect, and motivational orientation within the classroom: Process and patterns of change. In A. Boggiano & T. Pittman (Eds.), *Achievement and motivation: A social-developmental perspective* (pp. 77–114). New York: Cambridge University Press.

Hegedus, S., Dalton, S., Moniz, R., & Roschelle, J. (2007). *SimCalc classroom connectivity project 2: Understanding classroom interactions among diverse, connected classroom technologies* (No. 1:1). North Dartmouth, MA: University of Massachusetts.

Hegedus, S., & Kaput, J. J. (2002). *Exploring the phenomenon of classroom connectivity*. Paper presented at the 24th Conference for the North American Chapter of the International Group for the Psychology of Mathematics Education, Athens, GA.

Hegedus, S. J. & Kaput, J. (2003). *The effect of a SimCalc connected classroom on students' algebraic thinking*. Honolulu, HI: Paper presented at the Psychology in Mathematics Education conference.

Hegedus, S. J. & Kaput, J. J. (2004). *An introduction to the profound potential of connected algebra activities: Issues of representation, engagement and pedagogy*. Bergen, Norway: Paper presented at the Eighth Conference of the International Group for the Psychology of Mathematics Education.

Hegedus, S., Moreno, L., & Dalton, S. (2007). *Technology that mediates and participation in mathematical cognition*. Paper presented at the 5th Congress of the European Society for Research in Mathematics Education (CERME), Larnaca, Cyprus.

Hegedus, S. J. & Penuel, W. R. (2008). Studying new forms of participation and identity in mathematics classrooms with integrated communication and representational infrastructures. *Educational Studies in Mathematics, 68*(2), 171–183.

Hicks, D. (1995). Discourse, learning, and teaching. *Review of Research in Education, 21*(1), 49–95.

Hiebert, J. & Grouws, D. A. (2007). The effects of classroom mathematics teaching on students' learning. In F. K. Lester (Ed.), *Second handbook of research on mathematics teaching and learning* (pp. 371–404). Charlotte, NC: Information Age Pub Inc.

Johnson, M. K., Crosnoe, R., & Elder, G., Jr. (2001). Students' attachment and academic engagement: The role of race and ethnicity. *Sociology of Education, 74*, 318–340.

Kaput, J. (1992). Technology and mathematics education. In D. Grouws (Ed.), *A handbook of research on mathematics teaching and learning* (pp. 515–556). New York: Macmillan.

Kaput, J. (1994). Democratizing access to calculus: New routes using old roots. In A. Schoenfeld (Ed.), *Mathematical thinking and problem solving* (pp. 77–155). Hillsdale, NJ: Erlbaum.

Kaput, J., & Hegedus, S. J. (2002). *Exploiting classroom connectivity by aggregating student constructions to create new learning opportunities*. Paper presented at the 26th Conference of the International Group for the Psychology of Mathematics Education, Norwich, UK.

Kaput, J. & Hegedus, S. (2007). Technology becoming infrastructural in mathematics education. In R. Lesh, E. Hamilton & J. Kaput (Eds.), *Foundations for the Future in Mathematics Education*. Mahwah, NJ: Lawrence Erlbaum Associates.

Kaput, J., Noss, R., & Hoyles, C. (2002). Developing new notations for a learnable mathematics in the computational era. In L. D. English (Ed.), *Handbook of international research in mathematics education* (pp. 51–75). Mahway, NJ: Lawrence Erlbaum Associates.

Kaput, J. & Roschelle, J. (1998). The mathematics of change and variation from a millennial perspective: New content, new context. In C. Hoyles, C. Morgan & G. Woodhouse (Eds.), *Rethinking the mathematics curriculum*. London, UK: Falmer Press.

Kaput, J. & Schorr, R. (2008). Changing representational infrastructures changes most everything: The case of SimCalc, Algebra, and Calculus. In K. Heid & G. W. Blume (Eds.), *Research on the impact of technology on the teaching and learning of mathematics: Volume 2, cases and perspectives* (pp. 211–253). Charlotte, NC: Information Age Publishing.

Kaput, J. J. & Thompson, P. W. (1994). Technology in mathematics education research: The first 25 years in the JRME. *Journal for Research in Mathematics Education, 25*(6), 676–684.

Ladson-Billings, G. (1995). Toward a theory of culturally relevant pedagogy. *American Educational Research Journal, 32*(3), 465.

Meece, J. (1991). The classroom context and student's motivational goals. In M. Maehr & P. Pintrich (Eds.), *Advances in motivation and achievement* (Vol. 7, pp. 261–285). Greenwich, CT: JAI Press.

Mitchell, M. (1993). Situational interest: Its multifaceted structure in the secondary school mathematics classroom. *Journal of Educational Psychology, 85*, 424–436.

Newman, R. & Goldin, L. (1990). Children's reluctance to seek help with school work. *Journal of Educational Psychology, 82*, 92–100.

Papert, S. (2004). Will going digital improve or transform education? [Electronic Version]. *New futures for learning in the digital age.* Retrieved July 30, 2008 from http://fundamentalchange. carolstrohecker.info/documents/ImproveOrTransform.pdf.

Phelan, P., Davidson, A., & Yu, H. (1998). *Adolescents' worlds: Negotiating family, peers, and school.* New York: Teachers College Press.

Piaget, J. (1970). *The child's conception of movement and speed.* New York, NY: Basic Books.

Roschelle, J. & Jackiw, N. (2000). Technology design as educational research: Interweaving imagination, inquiry & impact. In A. Kelly & R. Lesh (Eds.), *Research design in mathematics & science education* (pp. 777–797). Mahwah, NJ: Lawrence Erlbaum Associates.

Roschelle, J. & Kaput, J. (1996). SimCalc MathWorlds for the mathematics of change. *Communications of the ACM, 39*(8), 97–99.

Roschelle, J., Kaput, J., & Stroup, W. (2000). SimCalc: Accelerating student engagement with the mathematics of change. In M. J. Jacobsen & R. B. Kozma (Eds.), *Learning the sciences of the 21st century: Research, design, and implementing advanced technology learning environments* (pp. 47–75). Hillsdale, NJ: Erlbaum.

Roschelle, J., Penuel, W. R., & Abrahamson, L. (2004). The networked classroom. *Educational Leadership, 61*(5), 4.

Roschelle, J., Tatar, D., Shechtman, N., Hegedus, S., Hopkins, B., Knudsen, J., et al. (2008). *Extending the SimCalc approach to grade 8 mathematics (SimCalc Technical Report 02).* Menlo Park, CA: SRI International.

Roschelle, J., Tatar, D., Shechtman, N., Hegedus, S., Hopkins, B., Knudsen, J., et al. (2007). *Can a technology-enhanced curriculum improve student learning of important mathematics? (SimCalc Technical Report 01).* Menlo Park, CA: SRI International.

Roschelle, J., Tatar, D., Shechtman, N., & Knudsen, J. (2008). The role of scaling up research in designing for and evaluating robustness. *Educational Studies in Mathematics, 68*(2), 149–170.

Ryan, A. & Pintrich, P. (1997). "Should I ask for help?" The role of motivation and attitudes in adolescents' help seeking in math class. *Journal of Educational Psychology, 89*, 329–341.

Skinner, E. & Belmont, M. (1993). Motivation in the classroom: Reciprocal effects of teacher behavior and student engagement across the school year. *Journal of Educational Psychology, 85*, 571–581.

Stroup, W. M., Ares, N. M., & Hurford, A. C. (2005). A Dialectic analysis of generativity: Issues of network-supported design in mathematics and science. *Mathematical Thinking and Learning, 7*(3), 181–206.

Stroup, W. M., Kaput, J., Ares, N., Wilensky, U., Hegedus, S. J., Roschelle, J., et al. (2002). *The nature and future of classroom connectivity: The dialectics of mathematics in the social space.* Paper presented at the Psychology and Mathematics Education North America conference, Athens, GA.

Tatar, D., Roschelle, J., Knudsen, J., Shechtman, N., Kaput, J., & Hopkins, B. (2008). Scaling up innovative technology-based mathematics. *Journal of the Learning Sciences, 17*(2), 248–286.

Treisman, U. & Fullilove, R. (1990). Mathematics achievement among African-American undergraduates at the University of California, Berkeley: An evaluation of the mathematics workshop program. *Journal of Negro Education, 59*(3), 463–478.

Turner, J., Thorpe, P., & Meyer, D. (1998). Students' reports of motivation and negative affect: A theoretical and empirical analysis. *Journal of Educational Psychology, 90*, 758–771.

Vahey, P., Roschelle, J., & Tatar, D. (2007). Using handheld technology to move between private and public interactions in the classroom. In M. van 't Hooft & K. Swan (Eds.), *Ubiquitous computing in education: Invisible technology, visible impact.* Hillsdale, NJ: Lawrence Erlbaum Associates.

Chapter 10
Toward a Theory of Personalized Learning Communities

Eric Hamilton and Martine Jago

Overview

We offer as axiomatic the notion that there are two worthy goals for curriculum or instructional design for learning environments, to simultaneously: (a) *customize* learning experiences to the individual, and (b) *connect* the individual to others in socially and intellectually meaningful ways. Learning environments whose affordances include both significant customization and meaningful interpersonal connection are referred to here as *personalized learning communities*, or PLCs. This chapter proposes a system of eleven design principles for PLC's (see Table 10.1), each of which emphasizes different ways to promote customized and connected learning experiences. Collectively, these principles should be understood as a system with important interactive effects and tantalizing possibilities for the design of high-performance PLC's.

The focus on customization and connectivity in PLCs contrasts sharply with the *one-size-fits-all* production-type education systems that accompanied and helped fuel the development of industrial societies (Weigel, James, & Gardner, 2009). Many students are naturally disposed to traditional classroom approaches and find the generally didactic pedagogies practiced in them to be productive venues that engage their effort, growth, and personal success. However, students who are not disposed to the one-size-fits-all approach often experience cycles of mutually reinforcing disengagement and withdrawal that may contribute to the rise to alienation, social failure, and poignant inequity (Skinner, Kindermann, & Furrer, 2009; Tarquin & Cook-Cottone, 2008). Further, even those who find relative success in one-size-fits-all settings are unlikely to have experienced the deeper and more effective learning suggested by research on highly customized, one-on-one, and learner-centered designs (Bloom, 1984; Bransford, Brown, Cocking, & Donovan, 2000).

E. Hamilton (✉) and M. Jago
Graduate School of Education and Psychology, Pepperdine University,
6100 Center Drive, Los Angeles, CA 90045, USA
e-mail: eric.hamilton@pepperdine.edu; martine.jago@pepperdine.edu

M.J. Jacobson and P. Reimann (eds.), *Designs for Learning Environments of the Future:*   263
International Perspectives from the Learning Sciences, DOI 10.1007/978-0-387-88279-6_10,
© Springer Science+Business Media, LLC 2010

Table 10.1 Eleven design principles for personalized learning communities

Modeling

    Emphasis on *models* systems thinking and ways to represent connections between ideas. The relationships or operations between ideas becomes as salient as ideas

Elicitation

    Emphadid on students expressing and representing the conceptual systems, intuitions and tacit understanding *they already possess.* "Draw out of" instead of "put into" the student

Consequentiality

    Emphasis on *feedback loops* in problem-solving, classroom, virtual world or other settings that are both meaningful to students and that are responsive to them

Adaptivity

    Emphasis on iterative revisions in feedback or consequence-rich settings. Assessment regards improvement and revision *processes* as important as knowledge *snapshots*

Sightlines

    Emphasis on creating powerful, diverse, and high-resolution fields of view for everyone in a classroom. Includes visualized representations of both cognition and content

Customization

    Emphasis on matcing high-feedback curriculum experience to individuals acheivement levels and learning styles. Includes emulating one-to-one *personalized tutoriala and mentoring* experience

Connectedness

    Emphasis on *socialization* in learning, including rich, multilayered connections between indivduals

Self-regulation

    Emphasis on ability to search for and apply new knowledge, manage one's participation in collaborative settings, tolerate ambiguity in unsolved problems, test ideas, reflect deeply on problems and frame intuitions

Hybrids

    Emphasis on diversity of learning modalities and fluid transitions between them, such as between individual reflection and group immersion, between virtual words and real context; interoperability of individuals–social–machine knowledge forms, and heterogeneous competencies

Generativity

    Emphasis on creativity and connections between ideas in problem-solving

Interactional bandwidth

    Emphasis on diverse means to express content and meaningful human interaction in the learning environment

Multiple research communities confirm an obvious observation: learners come into schools with strikingly different dispositions, and ways of knowing, learning, and socializing (Corno, 2008; Latz, Speirs Neumeister, Adams, & Pierce, 2009). If we can chart or design learning pathways that account for and successfully capita lize on – rather than stumble over – individual differences, this stretch of history may be remembered for breathtaking steps forward in fostering educational experiences for the majority of students that prepares them for the challenges of this century in socially equitable and personally meaningful ways. The purpose of the theory building to which this chapter aspires is progress toward a system of design principles for high-performance personalized learning communities.

The principles appearing in Table 10.1, and interactions between them, comprise core elements of an evolving theory of learning environment design. It is not meant to be comprehensive nor exclusive, but rather to line up with, help inform, and be informed by other theoretical perspectives. As a theory, it is intended to highlight an interwoven collection of human factors. Whereas the combination is eclectic ("sightlines" and "self-regulation" may be considered apples and oranges, for example), each is proposed to represent a powerful primitive that interacts with the others by being both a cause and effect of the other factors. This has potentially profound implications in that attending to each on the design side is likely to have multiple self-propagating or chain-reaction results across other system elements on the effects side. A set of 11 mutually interacting design principles implies $\sum (k) = (n^2 - n)/2$ or 55 pairwise connections. Each pairwise connection has important theoretical dimensions and variations, and the notion of self-propagating effects (i.e., three-way or more connections) expands this number of potential connections significantly.

The value of such a theory partly lies in suggesting a full landscape of mutually interactive human factors, as well as possibly obscure but meaningful connections between them. In this theory, because each principle gives meaning *to* the others, and each derives meaning *from* the others, the ensemble combinatorics – system designs that blend these interacting factors in novel ways – may create intriguing higher-order effects. Such effects are of course open to deeper specification, but the chapter's conjectural thrust is that they can be transformative and reach the goals of high-performance personalized learning communities.

The following sections outline each of the principles that we argue merit design emphases in future learning environments. A summary of these is a precursor to a discussion of how each can function as both cause and effect for the others in the form of a scenario illustrating the notion of an ensemble of mutually interacting design principles. In the chapter conclusion, we revisit the notion of higher-order effects promoting PLCs from such interactions.

Eleven Design Principles for Personalized Learning Communities

In their everyday lives, students continually participate in various complex dynamic systems (Lesh, 2006; Lesh, Yoon, & Zawojewski, 2007). Life rarely occurs or can be observed as a series of single variable causes of single variable effects. The ascendant education research and reform movements that promote systems thinking (e.g., National Academy of Engineering, 2005) at all levels of schooling include diverse strands that explicitly focus on *modeling*, which involves creating structured representations of systems for the purpose of exploring a domain of knowledge or interpreting complex systems (Hamilton, Lesh, & Lester, 2008).

The many flavors of modeling in contemporary education research collectively form a suite of approaches for rethinking and "remixing" curriculum for future learning environments, seeking to depart from the traditional and persistent tendency of schools to function primarily as didactic dispensers of declarative and procedural knowledge (Weigel et al., 2009). Across multiple definitions or interpretations, modeling emphasizes connected knowledge forms, adaptation of large ideas to new contexts, just-in-time learning, and complex reasoning in collaborative arrangements. Emphasis on modeling has a well-established lineage in the computer-supported collaborative learning community (e.g., Hmelo, Holton, & Kolodner, 2000; Kolodner et al., 2003; Lesh, Middleton, Caylor, & Gupta, 2008; Roschelle, Tatar, Shechtman, & Knudsen, 2008). In science education, various curriculum projects (e.g., Buckley et al., 2004) exemplify this trend with the development of replacement modules across multiple areas of the high school curriculum. Multiple new modeling oriented pedagogical frameworks have arisen from increased attention toward enabling learners to experience science curriculum in a manner more closely resembling both scientific practice and scientific phenomena (e.g., Clement and Rea-Remirez (2007)). Mathematics education researchers have similarly formulated multiple frameworks to feature modeling as central to the acquisition, use, and growth of mathematical ideas (English, Fox, & Watters, 2005; Swee Fong & Lee, 2009). One strand useful for this discussion has focused specifically on exposing and clarifying the conceptual models that youngsters possess, test and revise as part of group problem-solving settings. This strand, referred to as *model-eliciting activities* or MEAs (Lesh & Doerr, 2003), is the basis for efforts that advocate modeling as a foundation for future mathematics curricula (Lesh, Hamilton, & Kaput, 2007). The MEA approach involves the use of 30–50 min case study problems that middle school, high school, and college students solve in groups of three to five. Early MEA research efforts to expose student conceptual models by eliciting them was shown to have the unplanned result of producing high problem-solving performance from youngsters whose prior performance was uneven or weak (Lesh & Yoon, 2004). Among the design characteristics refined over 10 years of research (Lesh, Hoover, Hole, Kelly, & Post, 2000) was the constraint that scenarios represent meaningful contexts that would engage students in realistic problems for which testable models or solutions might be found. Now at the stage of scale-up funding from one of the US National Science Foundation's curriculum improvement programs (e.g., Diefes-Dex, 2007; Miller & Olds, 2007; Shuman & Besterfield-Sacre, 2007), applied MEA research highlights several additional design principles.

The first of these is *elicitation*, which is the key element to exposing conceptual models. The proposed framework rests heavily on the notion that because students engage in and form deep tacit insights about the complex systems they face in the world every day, the research-informed wisdom that teaching should match prior knowledge (Bransford et al., 2000; Clark & Mayer, 2003) can go farther. This principle suggests that teaching should elicit and leverage not only factual knowledge but also the systems thinking that youngsters already exercise intuitively, albeit in often hazy or unclear ways. Model elicitation as an instructional tool requires model *representation* by students that involves translating conceptual structures to representations. These representations are an expression of systems thinking, which once elicited can expose patchy and weak content structures that can then be refined, stabilized, and expanded (Hjalmarson, Cardella, & Adams, 2007). The focus of elicitation is relatively agnostic toward the philosophy of constructivism (Lesh & Doerr, 2003), stressing not just constructing conceptual structures but rather both revealing and revising existing ones as learners attempt to solve problems that are meaningful or consequential to them.

Meaningfulness or *consequentiality* is another element of the MEA research framework, and the third design principle in our PLC theory. Humans – school children included – need to experience feedback-rich contexts where they see intrinsically important consequences to their actions (Roth, 2007), immediately or soon after those actions, in sustained ways that allow them to revise or adapt their paths. Virtual worlds are examples of feedback-rich environments, as actions taken in a virtual world usually have an immediate consequence, whereby "when the system is poked, it pokes back" (R. Lesh, 2009, personal communication). Feedback to individual actions is at the heart of personalizing learning experience.

Feedback enables *adaptation*, the fourth PLC design principle. Designing for adaptation means creating conditions where students are encouraged to continually revise and improve the artifacts – such as papers and problem solutions – of their learning. We argue that adaptivity is the most powerful and natural force for learning students can bring to the classroom. Yet it is highly underleveraged and underappreciated in classrooms, where typically *snapshot* assessments of isolated individuals are employed that fail to convey how learners manage the *processes* of iteratively revising and improving performance, producing more sophisticated solutions to problems, and constructing more expansive knowledge sets.

As mentioned above, model-eliciting activities, or MEAs, focus on systems thinking. Research on the use of MEAs explores how youngsters express, test, and revise their models en route to building deeper understanding and more sophisticated problem-solving competencies. The MEA literature on expressing, testing, and refining models corresponds to the framework principles here of eliciting (expressing), consequentiality (testing) and adaptivity (revising) (Hamilton, 2007b). These principles also apply to other emerging learning environments.

For example, well-designed virtual worlds and the varied simulations or scenarios that can operate within them also nourish each of these three principles: they can *elicit* systems and complex thinking by engaging participants in varying, persistent scenarios. Virtual worlds have proven to simulate intrinsically motivating settings (Thomas & Brown, 2009). Actions taken in a virtual setting produce system condition changes resulting in responses that then elicit new actions. The sense of *consequentiality* or meaningful, rapid feedback loops is palpable, and even more vivid when other humans copresent are involved. Virtual worlds provide a tangible experience of social connectedness and agency, especially when compared to the unnatural configuration of being confined in chairs with minimal interaction with others in traditional classrooms (Thomas & Brown, 2009; Wagner, 2008). In individual and collaborative experiences in virtual simulations, there is a constant response to participant actions that means the underlying system conditions are in flux and thus elicit *adaptive* participant responses, a new round of consequences, and a new opportunity to adapt to altered conditions. Response latency in virtual world environments – the period between action and feedback in a digital media system – can be miniscule (measured often in seconds or even split seconds), especially relative to response latency in classroom settings (more typically measured in days or weeks, if ever, such as return of written assignments or tests). Yet research shows that minimal response latency and short feedback loops can be crucial for significant adaptive behavior, especially for children (Shute, 2008). Rapid and meaningful feedback loops invite attentional immersion and engagement, and can induce the flow experiences associated with optimal human performance (Csikszentmihalyi, 1996; Nakamura & Csikszentmihalyi, 2002).

The remaining PLC design principles discussed here begin with *sightlines*. An emphasis on sightlines implies designs that extend the ability of each person in a classroom to "see," whether content or cognition. We argue a severe limitation to promoting effective classroom learning is a lack of accurate sightlines that new technologies or other approaches are increasingly able to furnish. Teaching and learning in modern classrooms are shrouded in a sort of ubiquitous *guesswork*. Teachers draw hazy inferences about student thinking, and students do the same about teachers, as together they mediate the process of imparting and building knowledge. Many of the most important advances in learning environments can be summarized as enabling new sightlines into structured knowledge, human cognition, and human affect or emotion. For example, the underlying premise of model-eliciting-activities (MEAs) is to create scenarios allowing individuals to represent conceptual models, that is, to make them visible or to "see" these conceptual models. Another approach to making thought processes visible is the growing field of open-learner modeling, or OLM (Bull & Kay, 2005; Kay, 2000). OLM researchers seek to create ontology schematics that learners can examine to see depictions of their own thinking. Content sightlines give learners new ways to see and understand scientific or mathematical structure through visualizations and animations. In the Miriam Scenario discussed below, we give the example of teachers and students examining mathematics, and mathematics made more visible through the platform's sightlines.

Individualization is the next design principle that connects sightlines to greater individualization. The ability of a teacher to see each student's cognition more clearly provides the opportunity for tailoring or personalizing learning activities accordingly. This, in turn, helps foster effective teaching in one-to-one or tutorial experiences and is what led to Bloom's two-sigma conjecture of the comparative advantage of tutoring over classroom learning (Bloom, 1984). Learning environments leveraging new tools that allow more immediate and on-demand access to ways of seeing other's cognitions might be called "scaled individualization." In each case, the path to helping the student experience learning activities customized to his or her needs and competence level requires the ability of a teacher, peer, pedagogical agent, or indeed the student to *see*, in order to assess, the appropriate next step for learning.

The design principle of *connection* refers to the ability of a teacher or peer to understand and interact with cognitive models (of a student/peer), and to therefore act in ways informed by a more precise view of a student's thinking. This design principle also refers to increased meaningful connections within a learning community. Sightlines promote disclosure so that teachers can more readily observe student processing, which helps promote a greater connection between the teacher and the student. This, in turn, permits feedback specific to the student; that is, the learning environment becomes increasingly individualized as an artifact of greater connectivity. The logic chain continues: because tighter (less delayed) feedback loops facilitate effective learning, greater individualization should promote success in learning activities, and a concomitant deeper experience of community.

Self-regulation is a design principle that refers to skills that are emerging as increasingly important in contemporary learning (Azevedo, Guthrie, & Seibert, 2004). For example, students who have developed competencies to monitor and regulate their learning will know when to *ask* a teacher for help, when to *offer* help, when to *seek* help from other sources (e.g., pedagogical agents, digital objects that scaffold learning), and when to *function alone*. As curriculum models move away from trying to dispense *all* knowledge in a content area toward a focus on the big or centrally important ideas in a domain, students will need to develop the search, application, and technical fluency skills that help them acquire new knowledge for use in personally important or meaningful contexts. Such self-guided or self-regulated skills in learning are increasingly prerequisites for the smooth functioning of future environments that feature high-performance connectivity between students, and that permit greater individualization or tailoring to the user, as we attempt to illustrate in the Miriam Scenario below.

A premise of the *hybrids* design principle is that humans are organisms who instinctually seek diversity of experience. As biological or socio-cultural assertions go, this design principle lends itself to qualifiers, but many research communities, especially cognitive neuroscience, furnish significant theoretical justification for blending multiple modes of learning and socializing (e.g., Cacioppo, Norris, Decety, Monteleone, & Nusbaum, 2009; Frank, Doll, Oas-Terpstra, & Moreno, 2009). The hybrids design principle embraces diversity of experience as an essential element of successful learning that nurtures, for example, both basic skills and higher-order systems thinking.

Generativity is a design principle that encompasses an increasing emphasis on creativity in recent years in terms of research on building blocks of creative expression, human performance, adaptive expertise (Hatano & Inagaki, 2000), and case studies of pioneers in various fields (Adelson, 2003). There is a growing recognition that each student's creativity is not invariant but that conditions can be designed for nurturing and expanding its expression (Chuansheng et al., 2005; Mehlhorn, 2006). Appreciation of the cyber-enablements of creativity have led the US National Science Foundation to launch a completely new program of research investments in nurturing generative ability through information technology, through its CreativeIT Program (National Science Foundation, 2008). We use the term "generativity" to incorporate both creativity and the broader expression of original thoughts, and the connections and conceptual models that students form. This principle of future learning environment design is similar to the principles of elicitation (student expression), modeling (generative thought connects previously unconnected ideas), and hybrids (connecting the previously unconnected entails diversity of ideas).

The final design principle we propose is *interactional bandwidth*, which refers to the level of meaningful socialization and knowledge communication that is available in a classroom setting. As an example, the notion of bandwidth took hold in public consciousness with the early 110-baud rate modems connected to personal computers. The "second-generation" modem came out nearly three times faster, at 300 bits-per-second (bps) rates, and was hailed as "blazing," a description outdated almost as fast as it was uttered with the advent of the 1,200 bps modem. Such baud rates became referred to as a communication bandwidth for computing devices. We now have bandwidth on home desktop computers in the range of 10 megabits per second (mbs), and offices in the range of 100 mbs, with network backbones functioning in the gigabit orders of magnitude. This is one billion times higher bandwidth than the early machines. By analogy, the interactional bandwidth design principle in classroom learning environments can be framed in terms of a rhetorical question. What if the most high tech and interaction-rich classrooms of 2010 had an interactional bandwidth in the range of 1,200 bps? What would a classroom with an interactional bandwidth of 1 mbs look like? We propose that it is not that everything would go faster, which is one interpretation of the bandwidth metaphor. Rather, it is that *interactional* richness, including *cognitive density* will climb, dramatically (Hamilton, 2007a). It is in this transition from a 1,200 bps to a 1 mbs or higher system that the lofty goals of high-performance personalized learning communities can be attained.

Categories of Principles for Personalized Learning Communities

Each of the design principles for PLC, we argue, can be both a cause and an effect. That is, each can be a design factor or a direct result of other factors, and each can in some way be an emergent property of the system. Some of the principles might be more associated with learning *activities*. This is the case with the model-eliciting activities referenced earlier. Other principles might be learning *strategies*. Indeed, elicitation is a strategy that can be applied in modeling activities, as can adaptivity in the case of positioning learners in situations where a solution to a problem must continually be refined to accommodate new circumstances, or in virtual world scenarios with changing conditions that require continual adjustment. Another category of principle is that of a *dependency*, especially involving self-regulation and hybrid learning modes. In the Miriam Scenario that follows, learning success entails knowing when to ask for help, knowing when to seek help, deciding whether help would best come from an avatar, a peer, a teacher, or a digital library, and balancing the various interactions that such choices involve. Proficiency in an environment of that nature depends on the development of sophisticated self-regulatory competencies by students and teachers. The notion of a sightline and interactive bandwidth relates less to instructional strategies than to the *design features* of a learning environment. What affordances are designed into the environment to permit more accurate views of student cognition? For example, even a simple sightline affordance such as a personal response system (or clicker, i.e., a device that allows students in a class to select responses to questions asked by a teacher, with the responses aggregated and displayed to the teacher in real time), in turn, can foster a greater sense of community (through common voting and seeing results) and then rely on the reflective or metacognitive skills of the teacher to adjust a presentation that is more precisely calibrated to students.

The principles do not neatly fall into clear or mutually exclusive categories. In some environments, several principles might be closely associated; in others connections might be more tenuous. The next iteration of this theory may collapse multiple principles, or create "hubs" of principles or add principles, or change their granularity. One purpose of this chapter is to elicit analytic commentary to move this theory to its next iteration. Nevertheless, it is not necessary to create stable or mutually exclusive categories as these are intended to be iteratively revised and evolved.

Illustrating a Technology Ensemble Underlying a Personalized Learning Community

In the example that follows, we attempt to illustrate these design principles through a scenario describing a platform consisting of five different technologies (depicted in Fig. 10.1) that blend interdependent affordances and yield one instantiation of a personalized learning community. This platform is currently in development under support from the US Department of Education's Institute for Education Sciences (IES) (Hamilton & Harding, 2008). In this configuration, every student uses a tablet computer accepting pen or touch input. This is the first of four technologies blended into the overall system design. Achieving the two-sigma effects for personal tutoring proposed by Bloom

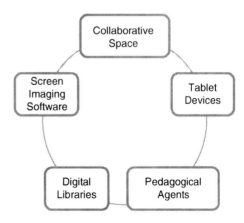

Fig. 10.1 Primary technologies blended into ALASKA platform

(1984) rely on the ability of a tutor to see how each individual student expresses her or his ideas. In a mathematics context, the tablet permits mathematical notations in a manner more fluid than a keyboard, and is thus more conducive to conveying mathematical thought. The second technology is a pedagogical agent or artificially intelligent program for each student. The agent can carry out simple dialogs and answer a range of domain-specific questions, in this case in the domain of precalculus. The third technology is a specialized library of applets and tools collected and developed by teachers. Whereas the implicit focus of a personalized learning community is on students, in this platform we intend for teachers to cocreate curriculum. Past research and common sense confirm that it is unrealistic to expect teachers to participate substantively in creating applets or other digital artifacts. This particular project, though, uses a fourth affordance, screen image video, in an effort to shortcut the expertise previously required to build high quality digital media.

The fifth technology in this ensemble is a communication system that permits the teacher to view both thumbnail and full-size images of student screens, send applets to them, and arrange peer tutoring between students independent of where they are seated. The collaborative network features allow students to see each other's workspace when given teacher's permission. The technology mix for the ALASKA (Agent and Library Augmented Shared Knowledge Areas) platform appears in Table 10.2. Whereas the following scenario is idealized, various combinations of the five technologies have been shown to promote learner engagement and success (e.g., Chen, Lattuca, & Hamilton, 2008). The scenario depicts not only the various principles, but also logic paths connecting the design principles. Tables 10.3 and 10.4, respectively, summarize several of the individual principles and interactions between them.

Table 10.2 Prominent categories of principles in current theory

| Principle | Category | | | |
	Learning activities	Learning strategies	Dependencies	Design feature
Modeling and systems thinking	✓	✓	✓	✓
Elicitation				✓
Consequentiality				✓
Adaptivity		✓	✓	✓
Sightlines				✓
Individualization	✓	✓	✓	✓
Connection	✓			✓
Self-regulation		✓	✓	✓
Hybrids				✓
Generativity	✓			
Bandwidth				✓

Table 10.3 Selected illustrations of principles

Connectedness. Miriam's rapport with her peers and the students exemplifies the multilayered connections that contribute to the success of an effective learning community. The multiple peer-tutoring relationships contribute to connectedness, including the sense of joint tasking with multiple structures for helping one another

Interactional bandwidth. The network system links students and teachers via the collaboration space. The bandwidth accommodates full screenshots of student work, retrieval of digital artifacts, and communication between teacher and students. Miriam provides an engaging learning environment which fosters the emergence of new performance competencies. The speed and depth of cognition is increased

Self-regulation. Students are much more in control of the technologies that mediate their experience, and make a steady flow of judgments about their own cognitive state, their ability to help others, their need for help, and managing their learning. Miriam's self-regulatory repertoire also expands, and her perception and management of the cognitive and instructional challenges changes significantly as the activity progresses

Elicitation. Miriam designs the exercise around drawing out of students their existing conceptual models on graphing and slope approximations to blend into finding an approximation of the exponential slope

Modeling. The use of the tablet over a collaborative space permits students to represent connections between mathematical ideas and mathematical processes directly to the teacher and to their peers

Sightline. Miriam is able to see all of the thumbnail images at once, or a few at a time, or focus in on one student's work. Students who are not seated adjacent to each other can still see each other's work when tutoring arrangements are made. The agents direct attention where it is most useful. The applets permit visualization of mathematical structures. The use of calculators highlights structural relationships between secant and tangent slopes

Hybrids. Students function in multiple modes, listening to a lecture, sketching their solutions, working in pairs, working independently. The avatar also functions in hybrid modes, passing on teacher comments or addressing the students directly

Customization. The various scaffolds, via the teacher, agents, peers and/or applets, each permit customization to the students

Consequentiality. This principle is realized through the rapid feedback loops that are enabled throughout the system. Their actions in the learning environment have immediate consequences in the form of meaningful feedback

Adaptivity. The premise of all of the feedback loops is to help guide students into improvement of their mathematical processing. Students adapt to the scaffolding guidance from the agent, peer tutors or applets as they progress through their problems. Miriam adapts to a new environment in which her role becomes fundamentally different

The Miriam Scenario

Miriam was excited. Barely 6 weeks into the precalculus course she was teaching, she felt a strong rapport with her students. Sure, she wished that the ability spread in her class was not so great, but she had already discovered with increasing frequency that the most extraordinary performances came from seemingly ordinary students who became highly engaged.

Table 10.4 Selected illustrations of interactions of principle

Sightlines–connectedness. Miriam can see thumbnails and recognize cognition. Sightlines connect her to the students who are aware that their workspace is not only visible but also available to her

Sightlines–interactional bandwidth. The network allows Miriam to have a global view of participants in the learning environment, facilitating insight into individual student processing or conceptual models

Customization–interactional bandwidth. The network permits rapid feedback loops to the individual, equivalent to personalized tutorials

Consequentiality–interactional bandwidth. The system permits rapid exchange of meaningful and personalized data packets, reducing cognitive downtime from students waiting for help and promoting flow in learning

Connectedness–interactional bandwidth. Peer tutoring becomes possible over the communication channels

Self-regulation–interactional bandwidth. Sue takes the initiative and signals to her avatar that she is prepared to accept help if it is available. The multilayered communication channels afford the opportunity for others to be surveyed discreetly

Self-regulation–hybrids. Instructional input comes via the instructor, avatar, and applets. The technological fluency and multitasking decision making in navigating these three is of a fundamentally different character than required in predigital instruction. For both students and teachers, fluid switching between diverse modalities is crucial to the learning process. A significant switch is that between immersion and reflection

Resources to Help

She also felt much more equipped for the class. She had worked with a group of teachers in developing a set of questions and answers to use in class, and had retrieved and tested a library of applets that were easy to use and helped explain topics in the curriculum. This was a sort of "pay in advance" where specific questions could be anticipated, and most of them answered a little more thoughtfully or with different illustrations than "on the fly" in class.

Today's Lesson

The lesson was a great topic. This session was one of the payoff days when putting a few ideas together would produce elegant mathematical results. The students had learned about slopes of secant lines being able to estimate the slopes of lines tangent to a curve. This would be a terrific introduction to the differential calculus they would take as seniors or in college. They had also learned about the curve of e^x, though they were not yet aware of its significance. And they had no idea of its amazing properties relative to its slope or the area under the curve – that they were equal to each other and to the function itself. The class discussion would be short and revolve around whether the curve was one that would lend itself to secant slope estimates. They used calculators to compute the slopes of the secant lines – the calculators let them compute increasingly precise tangent slope approximations using secant lines defined by two very close points. Miriam loved observing the students watch with puzzlement and pleasure as they discovered that the slope of the line tangent to e^x was e^x itself. Of course, she was not going to let on that anything unusual would take place. She led the discussion reviewing the underlying method of computing secant slopes to approximate tangent slopes and using their calculators to increase the precision of the estimate. She sent them the exercise applying this approach to $f(x)=e^x$ and watched them start. They needed to sketch the curve on their tablet computers and graphically depict the estimation process, then compute the estimates.

Some Students Got Off to a Quick Start

Her first step was to observe thumbnail views of a group of 20 students – she could peer into a subset of their screens with sufficient resolution to see that several of them were off to the races. She touched the "encourage/correct so far" icon on her response palette and then icons for the students. Though they were in different parts of the room, most heard warm, friendly remarks from their personal agents. Some simply received an encouraging gesture while a couple of agents stayed out of the way altogether. The agents had learned their students' preferences. They would later finish at different times, upon which their respective agent would send a notification to the teacher's agent, who posted a progress tally in the teacher's space.

Others Are Proceeding Well

Miriam could see the screens of another group of students – it was not a trivial exercise, and they were tentative in their work but seemed to have the right idea. Some were looking up a text explanation of rules of exponents, and in a couple of cases the agent was working with the students. Two of the agents asked their students how the estimate would change if the point of tangency was altered. The agents were ready both to watch their students develop modifications to answer the follow-up probes and to retrieve a few examples themselves. In these particular cases, the agent would suggest the students formulate a response before they experimented with the applets. Miriam was confident that this group of her charges was in good shape.

Some Are Stuck

She knew from the thumbnails of the workspaces that several students were unable to start the exercise, and indeed she saw some who seemed confused. Students routinely would type or jot any question that needed clarifying and send it to the teacher if she was not immediately available to help them. They could do so anonymously, not feeling embarrassed for asking a question "everyone else knows." Some of these questions simply needed a one or two word answer that she would either shoot back or simply say to the students across the room. Even when she was working with Jason (below) she was able to answer quick questions in this way that would have otherwise kept the students from proceeding.

Miriam's noticed that her screen displayed several similar questions from around the class about the number of significant digits as the secant points became closer. She realized she had not explained this clearly and must decide whether to break the flow of the class by reexplaining this topic, or whether to suggest an applet. She sent a message to the students with the similar questions. "Thanks for your question – I think that this applet might provide an answer. Take a look at it and let me know if it helps you get started. Your agent may suggest some other avenues but if this doesn't help let me know right away." A few minutes later, Miriam thumb nailed the screens of all these students and saw that they were all progressing. "Mike, Sarah, Tom, that explanation helped?" The agents certainly could have done the follow-up, but it seemed easier just for Miriam to ask. The three, located around the classroom, nodded without taking their eyes off the screen.

Some Do Not Start at All

Jason and Sue were a different story. They seemed lost. Sue had sent an alert that she did not really know where to begin, grateful for the anonymity of messaging. Jason didn't bother with a message, but he knew that his teacher could see from her station that he had not started. Miriam decided she would work directly with Jason after Sue's agent sent a discreet query to the agents of the fastest moving students to see if any would volunteer their "student" to help Sue answer some questions to get started. The agents brokered a quick connection and the two students were able to work on the problem together in Sue's workspace even though they weren't sitting together and would not have any other easy way to match up without the agents. Miriam was able to help Jason, and Sue received individualized help from another student although now, 6 weeks into the course, almost everyone seemed comfortable and trusting of their personal agents.

Reflection

Miriam tried to decide whether her job was harder or easier with this environment. Both, she determined. The days of running around the class figuring out who might need her help were over, as were the days of restating explanations she had given many times before, and guessing how many students were actually doing the mathematics at their desks. She was able to connect students where it made sense for one to help another, even if they were not sitting next to each other. But now that she saw more of what was going on in the class, she had to keep track of much more information and spend her time on the challenging work of understanding what her students were thinking. And the students were indeed thinking more. A number of the students who were stuck or lost would have figured out something else to do with their time while she picked one or two of them to help – so would the four or five who only needed a few minutes to do the exercise. It seemed that the students were spending a greater fraction of their class time engaged in real thinking and learning. There was a high performance expectation, and a high performance kind of resonance in the class. It was both easier and harder she decided, and certainly more complex; but far more rewarding. She felt challenged and knew that her students were functioning at a higher level throughout the class than they ever had before. Yes, more challenging and more rewarding.

Scenario Analysis

Tables 10.3 and 10.4, respectively, outline selected applications of the 11 design principles in Table 10.1 and the types of interactions between them that are at the crux of a PLC theory. This space-limited analysis touches on only a handful of the 55 dyadic connections between the design principles. A simple census, however, does not, in itself, convey the theoretical traction that might be possible from exploring bidirectional or higher-order effects from these principles on each other. The scenario entails – and we conjecture nurtures – self-regulatory skills in managing hybrid learning modes, or a kind of contextual fluidity. Students interact with intelligent avatars and transition to working with each other or to working alone. They listen to a short lecture. The avatars are hybrids of a different sort, sometimes speaking for themselves, sometimes passing along messages in the teacher's voice (Hamilton, 2005). In this scenario, improving the sightlines by allowing the teacher to see thumbnails and on-demand close-ups of any student's work enables more accuracy in the feedback loops (in other words, something actually happens when the student is working). New sightlines permit increased connections between both the teacher and the students, and the students with each other. The scenario suggests greater customization, and is replete with tailored and fast-feedback responses to the student. In addition, it encourages other self-regulatory skills such as help-seeking and help-offering behavior because of the greater connectivity that improves the interactional bandwidth enabled by peer tutoring. Each of these effects – the greater connection, self-regulation, hybridized learning modes and bandwidth – becomes a potential reverberating cause for new effects. We argue that such cascading cause–effect propagations and alternations between cause and effect is a promising avenue for understanding and exploiting the complex possible dynamics of new learning environments.

Whereas it is not currently possible to offer exact metrics for these design considerations individually, it is possible to illustrate them. For example, the scenario includes sightline enhancements outlined in Table 10.3. Studies reported by Chen

et al. (2008) and by Hamilton & Hurford (2007) test the conjecture that sightlines
such as those in the Miriam Scenario, by which a professor can observe and interact
with students through seeing what any student is writing in their mathematical
workspace, increase both learner engagement in the mathematics and the overall
level of mathematical discourse in the class. Statistically significant results on
learner engagement measured through experience sampling method (Barrett &
Barrett, 2001; Hsiang, 2006), along with interview data support the logic model
behind the use sightlines to enable rapid feedback (consequentiality), interpersonal
connection, and the nurturance of adaptive response. Research on the salutary effect
of any given principle (such as the investigations focusing on sightlines) on the
design of a learning community will necessarily, we believe, directly or indirectly
reference interactions with other principles.

Conclusion

A central conjecture of this chapter is that design principles, especially as they
entail learning technologies, can be combined in ways that are mutually augmenting and reinforcing. The nature of empirical support for an evolving theory of
future learning environments will necessarily vary for each principle and for each
way to combine the principles. One potential appeal of the proposed theory is that
the design principles can be tested and refined on a stepwise basis in ways that still
reflect on the whole system, and that help researchers and practitioners delve more
critically and meaningfully into the dimensions of personalized learning communities. Such an approach would analyze the effects of an intervention that emphasizes
a particular design principle. Studies that invoke this chapter's systems approach as
contributing to their respective theoretical frameworks could quite properly assess
causal links to common variables such as learning achievement. As an example,
peer tutoring emphasizes the design principle 7, of social connection in the learning
environment. The efficacy of peer tutoring for producing learning gains in a particular setting might be analyzed as the most salient variable, but the proposed
theory offers a landscape of related system factors, such as help-clarification
behavior, metacognition, and collaborative abilities. Analysis might reasonably
find tractable connections between these self-regulatory competencies (principle 8)
and competencies are intermingled with the sightline (principle 5), customization
(principle 6), and interactional bandwidth principles (principle 11), each of which
reinforces the underlying social connection. A study on peer tutoring and its inher-
ent reliance on social connection could thus provide entrée into a fuller system of
other principles. Observations of how individual principles affect the others and are
affected by them should produce new and finely grained logic models that connect
principles with each other and produce insight in exploiting the complex possible
dynamics of new learning environments.

The system of principles also can be used holistically, as an analytic grid, for full
platform interactive designs, such as considering how or why does a particular

classroom architecture or intervention seem effective in promoting personalization and community in learning. The analysis of the Miriam Scenario is an example of analyzing a platform from the vantage of the full platform.

Another more abstract path for studying mutually reinforcing design principles involves the development of metrics for the principles. For example, how can interactional bandwidth be indexed? What indicators can quantify socialization patterns? The development of metrics for each principle permits multivariate notions of change and, more broadly speaking, higher-order partial differential models of self-modifying, propagating, and dissipating system effects.

The language of design principles is only a scaffold for the next iteration of a quest to describe, understand, manage and optimize the dynamics of personalized learning communities. The 11 principles reflect a set of primitives. It is less important that they are at the same granularity or type than that they collectively contribute uniquely and meaningfully to a systems perspective. It is almost certain the number of design principles or primitives will fluctuate, and the definition of the principles will become more refined. If a theory of interacting design principles captures community interest, technology designs that blend multiple principles in novel or imaginative ways, and the first- and second-order effects of the interactions of these principles, may occupy a productive niche in future learning environment research and development.

References

Adelson, B. (2003). Issues in scientific creativity: insight, perseverance and personal technique - Profiles of the 2002 Franklin Institute Laureates. *Journal of The Franklin Institute, 340*(3), 163–189.

Azevedo, R., Guthrie, J. T., & Seibert, D. (2004). The role of self-regulated learning in fostering students'conceptual understanding of complex systems with hypermedia. *Journal of Educational Computing Research, 30*(1), 87–111.

Barrett, L. F. & Barrett, D. J. (2001). An introduction to computerized experience sampling in psychology. *Social Science Computer Review, 19*(2), 175–185.

Bloom, B. S. (1984). The 2 sigma problem: The search for methods of group instruction as effective as one-on-one tutoring. *Educational Researcher, 13*, 4–16.

Bransford, J. D., Brown, A. L., Cocking, R. R., & Donovan, S. (eds). (2000). *How people learn: Brain, mind, experience, and school (expanded edition)*. Washington, DC: National Academy Press.

Buckley, B. C., Gobert, J. D., Kindfield, A. C. H., Horwitz, P., Tinker, R. F., Gerlits, B., et al. (2004). Model-based teaching & learning with BioLogica: What do they learn? How do they learn? How do we know? *Journal of Science Education & Technology, 13*(1), 23–41.

Bull, S., & Kay, J. (2005, July 18-22, 2005). *A framework for designing and analysing open learner modelling*. Paper presented at the 12th International Conference on Artificial Intelligence in Education, Amsterdam, the Netherlands.

Cacioppo, J. T., Norris, C. J., Decety, J., Monteleone, G., & Nusbaum, H. (2009). In the eye of the beholder: Individual differences in perceived social isolation predict regional brain activation to social stimuli. *Journal of Cognitive Neuroscience, 21*(1), 83–92.

Chen, H. L., Lattuca, L. R., & Hamilton, E. R. (2008). Conceptualizing engagement: Contributions of faculty to student engagement in engineering. *Journal for Engineering Education, 97*(3), 339–353.

Chuansheng, C., Kasof, J., Himsel, A., Dmitaieva, J., Qi, D., & Gui, X. (2005). Effects of explicit instruction to be creative across domains and cultures. *Journal of Creative Behavior, 39*(2), 89–110.

Clark, R. C. & Mayer, R. E. (2003). *E-Learning and the science of instruction: proven guidelines for consumers and designers of multimedia learning.* San Francisco, CA: Jossey-Bass/Pfeiffer.

Clement, J. J. & Rea-Ramirez, M. A. (2007). Model based learning and instruction in science. *Science and Education, 16*(7–8), 647–652.

Corno, L. Y. N. (2008). On teaching adaptively. *Educational Psychologist, 43*(3), 161–173.

Csikszentmihalyi, M. (1996). *Creativity: Flow and the psychology of discovery and invention.* New York: Harper Collins.

Diefes-Dex. (2007). Collaborative research: Impact of model-eliciting activities on engineering teaching and learning: National Science Foundation Grant DUE-0717865 to Purdue University.

English, L. D., Fox, J. L., & Watters, J. J. (2005). Problem posing and solving with mathematical modeling. *Teaching Children Mathematics, 12*(3), 156–163.

Frank, M. J., Doll, B. B., Oas-Terpstra, J., & Moreno, F. (2009). Prefrontal and striatal dopaminergic genes predict individual differences in exploration and exploitation. *Nature Neuroscience, 12*(8), 1062–1068.

Hamilton, E. (2005). Affective composites: Autonomy and proxy in pedagogical agent networks. In J. Tao, J. Tan & R. E. Picard (Eds.), *Affective computing and intelligent interaction (ACII2005)* (Vol. 3784, pp. 898–906). Berlin: Springer Lecture Notes in Computer Science.

Hamilton, E. (2007a). Emerging metaphors and constructs from pedagogical agent networks. *Educational Technology (Special Issue, A. Baylor editor), 47*(1).

Hamilton, E. (2007b). What changes are occurring in the kind of problem-solving situations where mathematical thinking is needed beyond school? In R. Lesh, E. Hamilton & J. Kaput (Eds.), *Foundations for the future in mathematics education.* Mahweh, NJ: Lawrence Erlbaum Associates.

Hamilton, E., & Harding, N. (2008). *IES grant: Agent and Library Augmented Shared Knowledge Areas (ALASKA).* Institute for Education Sciences Award 305A080667.

Hamilton, E., & Hurford, A. (2007). Combining Collaborative Workspaces with Tablet Computing: Research in Learner Engagement and Conditions of Flow. Proceedings of the 37th ASEE/IEEE Frontiers in Education Conference, Milwaukee, WI, pages C3–C8.

Hamilton, E., Lesh, R., & Lester, F. (2008). Model-eliciting activities (MEAs) as a bridge between engineering education research and mathematics education research. *Advances in Engineering Education, 1*(2), 1–25.

Hatano, G., & Inagaki, K. (2000, April). *Practice makes a difference: Design principles for adaptive expertise.* Paper Presented at the Annual Meeting of the American Education Research Association, New Orleans, LO.

Hjalmarson, M. A., Cardella, M., & Adams, R. (2007). Uncertainty and iteration in design tasks for engineering students. In R. Lesh, E. Hamilton & J. Kaput (Eds.), *Foundations for the future in mathematics education.* Mahweh, NJ: Lawrence Erlbaum Associates.

Hmelo, C. E., Holton, D. L. & Kolodner, J. L. (2000). Designing to learn about complex systems. *Journal of the Learning Sciences, 9*(3), 247–298.

Hsiang, C. (2006). Digitization of the experience sampling method: transformation, implementation, and assessment. *Social Science Computer Review, 24*(1), 106–118.

Kay, J. A. (2000). *Accretion representation for scrutable student modelling.* Paper presented at the Proceedings of the 5th International Conference on Intelligent Tutoring Systems, Montreal, Canada.

Kolodner, J. L., Camp, J., Crismond, D., Fasse, B., Gray, J., Holbrook, J., et al. (2003). Problem-based learning meets case-based reasoning in the middle-school science classroom: putting learning by design(TM) into practice. *The Journal of the Learning Sciences, 12*(4), 495–547.

Latz, A. O., Speirs Neumeister, K. L., Adams, C. M., & Pierce, R. L. (2009). Peer coaching to improve classroom differentiation: Perspectives from project CLUE. *Roeper Review, 31*(1), 27–39.

Lesh, R. (2006). Modeling students modeling abilities: The teaching and learning of complex systems in education. *Journal of the Learning Sciences, 15*(1), 45–52.

Lesh, R., & Doerr, H. (Cartographer). (2003). *Beyond constructivism: A models & modeling perspective on mathematics teaching, learning, and problems solving.* Mahweh, NJ: Lawrence Erlbaum Associates.

Lesh, R., Hamilton, E., & Kaput, J. (2007). *Foundations for the future in mathematics education.* Mahweh, NJ: Lawrence Erlbaum Associates.

Lesh, R., Hoover, M., Hole, B., Kelly, A., & Post, T. (2000). Principles for developing thought revealing activities for students and teachers. In A. Kelly & R. Lesh (Eds.), *The handbook of research design in mathematics and science education.* Mahweh, NJ: Lawrence Erlbaum Associates.

Lesh, R., Middleton, J. A., Caylor, E., & Gupta, S. (2008). A science need: Designing tasks to engage students in modeling complex data. *Educational Studies in Mathematics, 68*(2), 113–130.

Lesh, R. & Yoon, C. (2004). Evolving communities of mind–In which development involves several interacting and simultaneous developing strands. *Mathematical Thinking & Learning, 6*(2), 205–226.

Lesh, R., Yoon, C., & Zawojewski, J. (2007). John Dewey revisited—Making mathematics practical versus making practice mathematical. In R. Lesh, E. Hamilton & J. Kaput (Eds.), *Foundations for the future in mathematics education.* Mahweh, NJ: Lawrence Erlbaum Associates.

Mehlhorn, J. (2006). Fostering group creativity. *Scientific American Mind, 17*(4), 78–79.

Miller, R., & Olds, M. (2007). Collaborative research: Impact of model-eliciting activities on engineering teaching and learning: National Science Foundation Grant DUE-0717862 to the Colorado School of Mines.

Nakamura, J. & Csikszentmihalyi, M. (2002). The concept of flow. In C. R. Snyder & S. J. Lopez (Eds.), *Handbook of positive psychology* (pp. 89–105). Oxford: Oxford University Press.

National Academy of Engineering. (2005). *The engineer of 2020: Visions of engineering in the new century.* Washington, DC: National Academy of Engineering.

National Science Foundation. (2008). *CreativeIT funding program - NSF 08572.* Retrieved July 1, 2009 from http://nsf.gov/pubs/2008/nsf08572/nsf08572.htm.

Roschelle, J., Tatar, D., Shechtman, N., & Knudsen, J. (2008). The role of scaling up research in designing for and evaluating robustness. *Educational Studies in Mathematics, 68*(2), 149–170.

Roth, W.-M. (2007). Mathematical modeling 'in the Wild': A case of hot cognition. In R. Lesh, E. Hamilton & J. Kaput (Eds.), *Foundations for the future in mathematics education.* Mahweh, NJ: Lawrence Erlbaum Associates.

Shuman, L., & Besterfield-Sacre, M. (2007). Collaborative research: Impact of model-eliciting activities on engineering teaching and learning: National Science Foundation Grant DUE-0717861 to the University of Pittsburgh.

Shute, V. J. (2008). Focus on formative feedback. *Review of Educational Research, 78*(1), 153–189.

Skinner, E. A., Kindermann, T. A., & Furrer, C. J. (2009). A motivational perspective on engagement and disaffection: Conceptualization and assessment of children's behavioral and emotional participation in academic activities in the classroom. *Educational & Psychological Measurement, 69*(3), 493–525.

Swee Fong, N. & Lee, K. (2009). The model method: Singapore children's tool for representing and solving algebraic word problems. *Journal for Research in Mathematics Education, 40*(3), 282–313.

Tarquin, K. & Cook-Cottone, C. (2008). Relationships among aspects of student alienation and self concept. *School Psychology Quarterly, 23*(1), 16–25.

Thomas, D. & Brown, J. S. (2009). Why virtual worlds can matter. *International Journal of Learning and Media, 1*(1), 37–49.

Wagner, C. (2008). Learning experience with virtual worlds. *Journal of Information Systems Education, 19*(3), 263–266.

Weigel, M., James, C., & Gardner, H. (2009). Learning: Peering backward and looking forward in the digital era. *International Journal of Learning and Media, 1*(1), 1–18.

Chapter 11
Afterword: Opportunities for Transformational Learning

Peter Reimann and Michael J. Jacobson

It would not surprise us if the most of the chapter authors in this book believed that their research contributed to principled insights into how to design inventions and innovations in learning environments with the potential to fundamentally enhance what it means to know and to learn, that is, to affect *transformational learning*. Indeed, most chapters represent research vignettes in which perspectives and examples of transformative changes in learning have taken place. However, even the largest of these projects have not been adopted wide scale by large state or national educational systems. The gap is stark between the potential for transformational learning, as illustrated in research such as reported in this volume, and the realities of most typical classroom environments in the countries reflected by the contributors of this volume. For example, the evidence from large-scale international studies into the state-of-the-art of teaching and learning with information technologies (e.g., Law, Pelgrum, & Plomp, 2008 for the case of science and mathematics education) suggests that large-scale changes in pedagogy are rare. Alas, teaching as we enter the second decade of the twenty-first century is by and large conducted as it was before the first computer made it into a classroom, and the assessments of learning are qualitatively not different from traditional paper-and-pencil testing of declarative knowledge acquisition rather than authentic assessments of conceptually deep understandings and complex skills.

However, we remain optimistic, as we suspect are the contributing authors, about the potential of research informed design perspectives to help seed perspectives that will lead to transformational learning. As a design community, we are starting to better understand ways to make learning technologies infrastructural (Roschelle et al., this volume) as well as making solid progress into what design principles might contribute toward the transformational (see Hamilton & Jago, this volume).

P. Reimann (✉) and M.J. Jacobson
Centre for Research on Computer-supported Learning and Cognition (CoCo),
The University of Sydney, Sydney, NSW 2006, Australia
e-mail: peter.reimann@sydney.edu.au

M.J. Jacobson and P. Reimann (eds.), *Designs for Learning Environments of the Future:
International Perspectives from the Learning Sciences*, DOI 10.1007/978-0-387-88279-6_11,
© Springer Science+Business Media, LLC 2010

Arguably, two main areas need to be aligned in order to foster transformational learning in the learning environments of developed countries: assessment methods and teaching practices. Many believe that assessment practices fundamentally drive other practices in education, with most current summative assessments primarily focusing on the acquisition of declarative knowledge and relatively low level procedural skills (Pellegrino, Chudowsky, & Glaser, 2001). From the perspective of the design of learning environments, a pivotal issue concerns the current practice whereby external summative assessments determine if particular approaches in learning environments were effective (with few opportunities for formative feedback), versus pedagogically innovative learning environments that integrate formative assessments for dynamic feedback about individual- and group-learning profiles. For the later approach to assessment, it is clearly necessary to keep high-stakes summative assessments separate from learning and teaching (Hickey, Suiker, Taasoobshirazi, Schafer, & Michael, 2006). In future learning environments, it will be important to find ways to use information about the performance of students that is generated online for formative assessment as currently this is not being taken into account (Horwitz et al., this volume; Mislevy, Steinberg, Almond, Haertel, & Penuel, 2003).

Regarding teaching practices, we believe that learning environments with rich representational and collaborative affordances in which integrated formative assessments are available have the potential to dramatically enhance pedagogical practices as teachers will then have access to a wide range of information about individual and collective aspects of learning in their classes. Of course, teachers will have to be prepared for new roles and new ways of teaching and learning in future learning environments. One way to approach this challenge is to regard teaching as a "clinical" profession (Crawford, Schlager, Penuel, & Toyama, 2008; Hinds, 2002), which, in turn, will require that teachers have access to the resources such as time and professional communities in order to develop and sustain a high level of adaptive professional expertise (Crawford & Brophy, 2006).

We are skeptical, though, that technology-specific educational effort alone will affect significant reforms of pedagogical practices in schools. Even with the compelling engagement of virtual and game-like worlds or the participatory nature of the Web 2.0 that provide rich opportunities for learning, but the lack of alignment with innovative pedagogical approaches, content, assessments, and societal goals for education, means that these *possibilities for learning may not be readily perceivable by critical stakeholders in the educational system and hence are likely to not be used.* Put another way, too often technology-based innovations for learning are solutions to problems that teachers currently do not have. Instead, it will be essential that innovative learning environments be designed in ways that take seriously the challenges teachers *currently* have, while also incorporating extensible features that will enable new future ways of learning and teaching.

Affecting transformational learning in future learning environments may possibly require "big" things to happen, such as what Dede (2008) refers to as a "seismic shift in epistemology." As an alternative, transformations of learning may result from cumulative "small" things, such as dynamics described in *How Hits Happen* (Farrell, 1998), where complexity perspectives are used to understand how the dynamics of popular music "hits" and other fads develop and propagate in markets and cultures. From this perspective, it may be that there will be nonlinear amplification of many *small* examples of transformational learning by students in a few classes that in turn stimulates the interests of teachers, parents, and even policy makers in other schools and school systems to try these new pedagogies and learning environments, and those successes stimulate further and wider-scale interest in these innovative design approaches for how learning and knowing might be as a cycle of positive feedback that propagates across an educational system. For example, an enabler might be the Web 2.0 that allows for information to be spread rapidly across any educational system.

We close by observing that regardless of what prevails – whether "big" policy mandated top-down infrastructural level changes or "small" bottom-up dynamics or, perhaps most likely, a "hybrid" of both top-down and bottom-up activities – as educational systems change and evolve, there is still a critical need for theory and research-informed designs for future learning environments. Just as medical or engineering research informs professional practices in those fields, so must professional practices in education be informed by research in multidisciplinary fields such as the learning sciences and more generally in education. It is our hope that the chapters in this volume contribute important perspectives to this ongoing dynamic of inventions and innovations in the environments of learning both for today and for the future.

References

Crawford, V. M. & Brophy, S. (2006). *Adaptive expertise: Methods, findings, and emerging issues.* Menlo Park, CA: SRI International.

Crawford, V. M., Schlager, M. S., Penuel, W. R., & Toyama, Y. (2008). Supporting the art of teaching in a data-rich, high-performance learning environment. In E. B. Mandinach & M. Honey (Eds.), *Data-driven school improvement* (pp. 109–129). New York: Teachers College Press.

Dede, C. (2008). A seismic shift in epistemology. *EDUCAUSE Review, 43*(May/June), 80 81.

Farrell, W. (1998). *How hits happen: Forecasting predictability in a chaotic marketplace.* New York, NY: HarperCollins Publishers.

Hickey, D. T., Suiker, S. T., Taasoobshirazi, G., Schafer, N. J., & Michael, M. A. (2006). Balacing varied assessment functions to attain systemic validity: Three is the magic number. *Studies in Educational Evaluation, 32*, 180–201.

Hinds, M. (2002). *Teaching as a clinical profession: A new challenge for education.* New York: Carnegie Corporation of New York.

Law, N., Pelgrum, W. J., & Plomp, T. (2008). *Pedagogy in ICT use ("Sites 2006").* Berlin: Springer.

Mislevy, R. J., Steinberg, L., Almond, R. G., Haertel, G. D., & Penuel, W. R. (2003). *Leverage points for improving educational assessment (PADI technical report 2).* Stanford, CA: SRI.

Pellegrino, J. W., Chudowsky, N., & Glaser, R. (eds). (2001). *Knowing what studens know: The science and design of educational assessment.* Washington, DC: Academic Press.

Index

A

Abstract, 3, 9, 24, 28, 120, 126, 127, 135, 151, 173, 174, 189, 193, 194, 240, 252, 256, 279
Affordances
  infrastructural, 238
  representational, 8–9
  technological, 7, 233
Agent-based modeling, 3, 17–56
Aggregation, 23, 207, 208
Allele, 62, 67, 69, 76, 78, 84, 85
Analysis, 5, 18, 25, 36–51, 53, 72, 78, 81, 85, 94, 98, 101, 115, 128, 147, 150–153, 155, 157, 162, 173–176, 178, 180–182, 184, 197–199, 211, 215, 218–220, 224–227, 242, 277–279
Animation. *See* Representation, animation
Annotations, 151, 152
Argumentation, 3, 149, 150, 153, 215, 240, 247, 249–251, 258
Artifact creation, 1, 92, 144–146, 148, 150, 153, 207, 213, 272
Artificial intelligence, 3, 119
Assessment. *See also* Evaluation
  embedded, 61, 63, 76, 80
  paper-and-pencil test, 283
Authenticity, 89, 93, 95, 104, 115, 147, 158, 218, 283
Authoring, 6, 30, 44, 82, 83, 91, 121, 132, 149, 150, 153, 170, 171, 173–175, 192, 207, 208, 215, 224, 227
Automap, 174–175, 178, 180

B

Beliefs, 100, 156, 200, 238
Biology, 55, 67, 81, 93, 95, 114, 116, 206, 214–216, 218, 221–223, 225
Blogs, 6, 149–151, 207

C

Calculus, 2, 22, 234, 241, 242, 274
Causal
  explanations, 189
  mechanisms, 22
  models, 55, 66
Cell, 62, 78, 169, 207, 219
Centrality, 14, 174, 177
Chemistry, 21, 24, 55, 91, 93
Chromosome, 62, 67, 69, 78, 84, 85
Cognitive
  interactivity, 211, 268, 270
  processes, 135, 143
  science, 19, 64, 125
  social processes, 149
  tools, 157
Coherence, 147, 151, 153, 157, 172, 177, 178
Collaboration, 5, 6, 10, 12, 83, 96, 107, 113, 115, 132, 143–184, 207–209, 212–215, 273
Collaborative
  inquiry, 90, 92, 93, 108, 229
  interactions, 10, 12, 133, 148, 158, 170
  learning, 90, 143–145, 154, 157, 184, 190, 266
Collaborative writing, 6, 147, 149–150, 173, 175, 178, 207
Community
  models, 6, 212–215, 218, 221, 224, 226–229, 266
  software, 214
Computer-based manipulative (CBM), 3, 61–85
Computer-supported collaborative learning (CSCL), 149, 184, 190
Concept degree centrality, 177
Concepts, 2, 7, 18, 36, 38, 52, 66, 83, 95, 114, 126, 134, 135, 144, 147, 148, 153, 157, 173–182, 190, 194, 210, 223, 227, 234, 235, 238, 242, 248, 253, 257–259

Conceptual change, 173
Constructionism, 55
Constructionist, 17–56
Constructivism, 210, 267
Content analysis, 25, 36–51, 78, 98, 115, 150, 153, 218, 219
Contextual interactions, 234
Critical thinking, 64, 144
Curriculum, 4, 6, 7, 17, 21, 24, 32, 61, 64, 65, 70, 73, 81–84, 89–108, 112, 113, 115, 118, 132, 143, 181, 195, 200, 205, 206, 209–216, 218–229, 234, 235, 239, 241–243, 247, 251, 257, 263, 265, 266, 269, 272, 274

D
Data
    collection, 67, 73, 97, 116, 130
    process, 7, 64, 70, 81
    quality, 73, 98, 130, 170
    visualizations, 43, 90, 106, 162, 228
Data mining, 8, 150, 169, 170
Declarative learning, 145, 173, 266, 283, 284
Deep structure
    conceptual, 135, 173–178, 181, 266, 267
    knowledge, 126, 133, 134, 156, 268
Design
    curriculum, 213, 227–228
    elements, 14
    learner centered, 1, 108, 123, 249, 256, 263
    principles, 7, 8, 18, 32, 250, 258, 263–272, 277–279, 283
    software, 6, 22, 30–34, 148, 235
    technological, 7, 233–259
    user centered, 12, 214
Design-based research (design experiments), 1, 4, 13, 90, 93–94, 105, 107, 214
Discourse, 237, 240, 249, 278
Discovery, 29, 63, 90, 133, 137, 210
Discussion, 5, 51–54, 67, 81, 90, 93, 105, 112–114, 121, 128, 130–133, 148, 152, 166, 169, 178–181, 199–201, 206, 242, 245, 247, 249, 251, 256–258, 265, 266, 274, 275
Documentarisation, 151
Documents-for-action (DofA), 150–153

E
Educational
    goals, 89
    reform, 21, 265, 284
Emergence, 205–208, 250, 273

Engineering, 3, 9, 17–56, 205, 256, 265, 285
Environments
    classroom, 2–4, 6, 7, 10–14, 90, 270, 283
    interactive learning, 4, 11, 64, 82, 192
    learning, 1–14, 18, 25, 52, 112, 114, 115, 123, 130, 133, 136, 150, 169, 190–192, 194, 199, 263–270, 273, 274, 277–279, 283–285
    virtual, 89–108, 111–116, 122, 124, 130, 132, 133, 167, 268
Equilibrium, 41
Ethnography, 249
Evaluation, 18, 107, 181, 189–201, 214, 215, 225. *See also* Assessment
Evidence-centered assessment design, 182
Evolution, 25, 33, 38, 39, 48, 89–108, 236
Experiment, 4, 10, 20, 30, 31, 33–35, 42, 43, 67, 78, 82, 84, 89–91, 93, 95, 98–102, 114, 115, 119, 123, 125–128, 130, 131, 134, 157, 193, 195–200, 214, 215, 240, 241, 247, 255, 275
Expert, 133, 155, 182, 210
Expertise, 9, 21, 158, 209, 210, 222, 227, 269, 272, 284
Explanation, 19, 23, 26, 36–38, 41–43, 49, 53, 65, 66, 98, 101, 130, 145, 170, 189, 192, 200, 245, 275, 276
Explorations, 19, 33, 34, 38–43, 64, 74, 96, 97, 171, 191, 244, 257

F
Fading, 8, 68, 115, 134, 135, 285
Fitness function, 206, 242
Force and motion, 21, 25
Frames of reference, 8, 144, 180

G
Gene, 3, 67, 69, 76, 84, 85
Genetics, 3, 4, 61–85
Genotype, 67, 69, 70, 79, 84, 85
GenScope, 3, 4, 9, 13, 61–64, 66, 73, 82
Glosser, 178–180
Graphs, 190, 193, 235, 242–247, 253, 255–257
Grounding, 22

H
High school, 24, 54, 61, 62, 206, 214, 215, 229, 234, 249, 266
History, 2, 11, 19, 90–92, 94, 116, 118, 137, 157, 177, 189, 193, 208, 264

Hyperlinks, 172
Hypermedia, 3
Hypertext, 5, 64

I

Ill-structured, 134, 138, 154, 160
Imagery, 8, 113, 150, 217, 233, 244, 272, 273
Immersion, 264, 268, 274
Indexing, 152, 208
Innovation, 1–14, 20, 144, 165, 181,
        205, 206, 209–211, 213, 214,
        239, 283–285
Inquiry
    activities, 6, 10
    skills, 64, 82, 96, 103, 112, 114
Instruction, 4, 9, 32, 38, 40, 44, 62, 63, 70, 74,
        80, 83, 90, 91, 93–95, 108, 130, 133,
        135, 155, 178, 189–192, 196, 199, 200,
        205, 206, 208, 209, 211, 239, 241, 263,
        266, 270, 273, 274
Instructional approaches, 222
Intelligent tutoring systems, 133, 182
Interactive learning environments. *See*
        Environments, interactive learning
International, 3, 14, 283
Internet, 92, 108, 113, 124, 131, 150, 178,
        206, 207, 248
Interviews, 18, 20, 25, 35–37, 41, 51, 52, 94,
        114, 122, 123, 130, 131, 166, 219, 221,
        224, 226–228, 247, 257, 278
Investigation, 18, 19, 62, 64, 70, 90, 91,
        95–98, 112, 133, 191, 211, 251, 278

K

Knowledge
    abstract conceptual, 9
    component, 55, 62, 66, 68, 69, 82, 98, 149,
        150, 155, 169, 192, 194, 209, 226,
        239–241, 257
    contextualized, 115–118, 125, 146
    deep structure (*see* Deep structure,
        knowledge)
    difficult, 6, 10, 11, 18, 19, 23, 24, 41,
        45, 52, 63, 70, 79–81, 83, 89, 95,
        104, 108, 125, 134–136, 152, 160,
        162, 166, 167, 201, 212, 219, 227,
        228, 237, 245, 254
    in-context, 64, 94, 152, 264
    interconnection, 207, 221
    metaconceptual (*see also* Scaffolding,
        metaconceptual)
    workers, 206

L

LAMS, 144
Learning
    activities, 4, 9, 11–13, 18, 63, 70, 90, 115,
        123, 126, 131, 133–135, 193, 212, 229,
        268–270, 272
    communities, 7, 8, 263–279
    discovery, 90, 133
    environments (*see* Environments, learning)
    processes, 149, 190
    science, 1, 3, 8, 10, 13, 24, 90, 94,
        107, 108, 112, 113, 118, 121, 174,
        190, 205, 206, 209, 211, 234, 237,
        240, 285
    tools, 13, 41
Linguistics, 256
Links, 48, 64, 82, 133, 169, 172, 174, 176,
        177, 180, 217, 223, 235, 273, 278

M

Map analysis, 174
MaterialSim, 3, 9, 11, 17–56
Mathematics, 2, 6, 7, 22, 25, 189–201,
        234–236, 238–247, 249, 250, 252,
        254, 256, 258, 259, 266, 268, 272,
        276, 278, 283
Memory, 146
Mental, 4, 244
Mental models, 4, 9, 53, 63, 65, 156, 174
Metacognition, 100, 278
Mirroring, 5, 147, 148, 154, 157, 158, 165,
        170, 173, 178, 181, 184
Misconceptions, 92, 114, 173, 247, 255
Modeling, 3, 8, 17–56, 65, 73, 120, 134, 182,
        184, 264–266, 268–270, 272, 273
Models
    agent-based, 17–56
    causal, 55, 66
    computer, 3, 8, 18, 22, 25, 27, 29, 30, 40,
        51, 62, 64, 134
    conceptual, 199, 266, 268, 269, 273, 274
    dynamic, 22, 25, 27, 35–38, 43, 50, 156
    mental, 4, 9, 53, 63, 65, 156, 174
    qualitative, 94, 215
    quantitative, 9, 94, 215
    scientific, 3, 52, 65
    synthetic, 5, 10, 12, 119–121, 125, 132
Molecular bonding, 24
Motion, 23, 95, 111, 121, 234, 235, 242, 243,
        245–247, 250, 252–256
Motivation, 11, 36, 94, 112–115, 132, 136,
        143, 147
Multimedia, 8, 64, 101, 113, 150, 211

Multimodal, 11
Multiple contexts, 104
Mutations, 62, 85

N
Narration, 244
NetLogo, 3, 9, 18, 30–33, 35, 42–44, 46, 48–50, 52, 56
Newsgroup, 148, 152
Newtonian mechanics, 23, 95
Nodes, 162, 180
Nonlinear, 285
Notes, 1, 11–13, 26, 50, 51, 67, 68, 74, 76, 78, 105, 107, 112, 113, 123, 137, 152, 153, 162, 177, 182, 225, 227, 237, 239, 241, 243–245, 247, 253, 257, 258
Novice, 22, 135

O
Organism, 3, 9, 62, 66, 67, 69, 70, 76, 78, 84, 269

P
Participation levels, 10–11
Pedagogical principles, 2
Pedagogy, 2, 6, 12, 13, 19, 56, 69, 115, 118–119, 125, 132, 145, 241, 263, 283, 285
Pedigree, 62, 70, 84, 85
Perception, 12, 99–101, 122, 130, 218, 253, 273
Phenotype, 62, 67, 69, 84, 85
Physical sciences, 21
Physics, 9, 21–25, 93, 134, 193
Physics education, 21–24
Prediction, 27, 65, 78, 79, 84, 98, 105, 196, 197, 243, 253
Problem-based, 145
Process model, 182, 184
Productive failure, 13, 134–136
Programming, 5, 9, 18–20, 32, 35, 56, 82, 92, 93, 146, 159, 181
Project-based science, 108
Protocols
    think-aloud, 64, 193

R
Raters, 128, 180
Reflection, 100, 119, 132, 147, 154, 178, 179, 181, 194, 209, 211, 213, 253, 257, 276–277
Reify, 66
Remote instrumentation, 148

Representation
    agent-based, 25, 27–30, 49, 52
    animation, 193, 235, 251
    bridging, 7, 233
    equational, 22, 23, 26–27
    multiple linked, 9, 247, 250, 251, 257
    and understanding, 66
    use in design, 2, 13
    use in science, 24
Representational growth, 26–30

S
Scaffolding
    cognitive, 210, 211
    supportive, 214
Science
    education, 18, 65, 89, 123, 124, 259, 266
    learning, 1, 3, 8, 13, 24, 90, 94, 107, 108, 112, 113, 118, 121, 174, 190, 205, 206, 209, 211, 234, 237, 240, 285
Scientific
    inquiry, 10, 18, 56, 89–108, 119, 123, 126
    investigations, 118
    models, 52, 65
    phenomena, 18, 20, 266
    reasoning, 119
    research, 24, 27, 30, 35–36, 191, 209, 211
Scientists, 5, 25, 27, 52, 65, 91, 94, 95, 116, 119
SimCalc, 2, 7, 11, 13, 190, 191, 233–245, 247–249, 251–259
Simulation, multi-agent, 24
Situated, 92, 96, 115–118, 189
Social construction, 210
Social Network Analysis, 162, 180
Subversion (SVN), 158–162, 166–169
Supportive, 4, 6, 7, 10, 18, 52, 66, 70–73, 76, 80–83, 89, 93, 94, 101, 102, 105, 107, 111, 113, 121, 122, 132, 136, 144, 146–150, 153, 155, 157, 158, 162, 165, 167, 168, 170–173, 178, 184, 190–194, 206, 207, 209, 210, 212, 214, 228, 229, 234, 236, 237, 239–244, 247, 251, 257–259, 266, 271, 278
Surface features, 126, 127
Symbol manipulation, 23
Symbols, 22, 235, 250

T
Teachers, 2, 6–8, 11, 12, 18, 27, 52, 61, 63–65, 70, 73, 74, 78–82, 89–92, 94, 95, 97, 99, 100, 104, 113, 116, 118, 119, 122–124, 127–130, 132, 166, 190, 193, 194, 196,

197, 199, 205, 206, 209–216, 218–221,
    223, 226–229, 233–245, 247–251,
    257–259, 268–270, 272, 274, 284, 285
Teacher training, 239, 257
Team learning, 144, 146, 155
Team skills, 5, 145–147, 153–157, 178–181
Team-training, 154
Teamwork, 146, 154, 155, 182
Technological, 7, 20, 22, 24, 52, 68–70, 82, 83,
    93, 113, 120, 181, 191, 215, 233–259
Technologies
    emerging, 209
    of learning, 2, 7, 9, 11, 233, 235, 237, 278,
    283
Technology, 1, 2, 5, 7, 8, 11–13, 20, 21, 30,
    63, 82, 83, 90, 91, 99, 101, 108, 121,
    144, 146, 153, 173, 184, 190, 191, 195,
    205–209, 214, 215, 221, 227, 229, 233,
    234, 236, 238–241, 244, 248, 256, 258,
    259, 268, 271–273, 279, 284
Text, 4, 5, 8, 11, 64, 69, 70, 82, 92, 93, 96,
    97, 101, 126, 147, 150–153, 159,
    173–175, 177, 178, 180–182, 193,
    207, 224, 243, 275
Thinking, 10, 45, 63, 64, 89, 132, 144, 190,
    191, 228, 245, 265–269, 272, 277
Tools. *See* Learning, tools
Trac, 5, 148, 158–160, 166–169, 171, 172,
    178, 182
Tracking, 158, 160, 252, 254
Transfer, 3, 5, 79, 115, 124–127, 131–136,
    156–157, 189, 190
Trialogic learning, 180

U
Understanding, 9, 13, 14, 18–24, 27, 29,
    32, 36, 38, 39, 49, 51, 52, 55, 63–66,
    72, 76, 82, 84, 94, 99–101, 114,
    118, 119, 124–127, 135, 136, 146,
    155, 177, 182, 189, 190, 201, 209–213,
    218, 219, 226, 242, 244, 245, 259,
    267, 277, 283

V
Verbal, 234
Video, 8, 35, 64, 70, 95, 150, 207, 208, 272
Video games, 104
Videotapes, 35
Virtual
    environments, *see* Environments,
        virtual
    reality (VR), 3, 8, 112
    worlds, 4, 5, 10–13, 90, 92, 93, 95, 107,
        111–137, 267, 268, 270
Visualization, 5, 8, 9, 11, 28, 30, 32,
    43, 55, 106, 112, 134, 143–184,
    228, 235, 268

W
Web 2.0, 6, 149, 205–229, 284, 285
Website, 36, 64, 73, 131, 244
Wiki, 5, 6, 144, 146–153, 158–163, 166–180,
    207–209, 215–219, 221–229
WikiNavMap, 5, 147, 171, 172
Wikipedia, 150, 153, 207

CPSIA information can be obtained at www.ICGtesting.com
Printed in the USA
LVOW030500120911

245854LV00007B/64/P